/HV8742.G72P741995/

Offenders, deviants or patients?
Second edition

D0024206

Offenders, Deviants or Patients? deals with a group of offenders that many find puzzling and worrying, even professionals who have daily contact with them – namely those who are seen as both 'mad' and 'bad'. Since the first edition of this book was published in 1980 there have been many changes in legal practices, treatment practices and public and professional attitudes towards the serious criminal offender who is deemed to be mentally abnormal; this second edition has been completely updated and revised to encompass those changes.

Herschel Prins explores the relationship between mental abnormality and criminal behaviour, the extent to which this relationship is used (or misused) in the criminal courts and the various facilities available for the treatment and/or incarceration of these offenders. Certain problematic forms of behaviour which are seen as particularly serious criminal offences are then examined, including sexual offending, violence and homicide, psychopathic disorder and fire-raising.

The all-important problem of assessment of risk in relation to those engaging in the foregoing behaviours is addressed in very practical fashion and there are training suggestions made for those working in this area.

Although a number of excellent texts on forensic psychiatry have appeared since the first edition of this work, there are still no competing texts aimed specifically at understanding the social context of offender-patients and offering a multi-disciplinary approach to this very important subject.

Offenders, Deviants or Patients? will be invaluable to all those who come into contact with serious offenders including psychiatrists and psychologists, social workers and probation officers, penal staff at all levels, lawyers, magistrates and the police.

Herschel Prins is a Professor at the Midlands Centre for Criminology and Criminal Justice at the University of Loughborough.

OAKTON COMMUNITY COLLEGE LIBRARY

HV6742 .G72 /41 AR2   C891

OFFENDERS, DEVIANTS, OR PATIENTS? LONDO

3 3211 00031 890 1

By the same author

Offenders, Deviants or Patients?
An introduction to the study of socio-forensic problems
Tavistock, 1980

Criminal Behaviour
An introduction to criminology and the penal system
Second edition
Tavistock, 1982

Dangerous Behaviour, the Law and Mental Disorder
Tavistock, 1986

Bizarre Behaviours
Boundaries of Psychiatric Disorder
Tavistock/Routledge, 1990

Fire-raising: Its Motivation and Management
Routledge, 1994

Offenders, deviants or patients?

Second edition

Herschel Prins

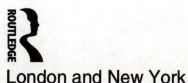

London and New York

OAKTON COMMUNITY COLLEGE
DES PLAINES CAMPUS
1600 EAST GOLF ROAD
DES PLAINES, IL 60016

First edition published 1980
by Tavistock
Second edition published 1995
by Routledge
11 New Fetter Lane, London EC4P 4EE

Simultaneously published in the USA and Canada
by Routledge
29 West 35th Street, New York, NY 10001

© 1980, 1995 Herschel Prins

Typeset in Times by LaserScript, Mitcham, Surrey
Printed and bound in Great Britain by
Mackays of Chatham PLC, Chatham, Kent

All rights reserved. No part of this book may be reprinted or
reproduced or utilised in any form or by any electronic,
mechanical, or other means, now known or hereafter
invented, including photocopying and recording, or in any
information storage and retrieval system, without permission in
writing from the publishers.

British Library Cataloguing in Publication Data
A catalogue record for this book is available from the British Library

Library of Congress Cataloging in Publication Data
A catalogue record for this book has been requested

ISBN 0–415–10220–0 (hbk)
ISBN 0–415–10221–9 (pbk)

This book is dedicated with affection and respect to my co-members and the staff of the Mental Health Review Tribunal for the Trent Region.

Contents

Illustrations

Foreword

One of the most perplexing features of human behaviour is the strong and enduring tendency towards deviance. It is no wonder that the early chapters of the Old Testament attempt to explain its origins, in a way that, it has to be said, cannot be regarded as the last words on the question. It is reasonably safe to conclude that the problems of human personality are beyond full comprehension and the eradication of non-conformity is an impossibility. In other words they present a continuing challenge to every society and to each generation.

Deviance and its control have, therefore, to be to be continually reviewed. At the heart of the problem are human nature itself, the structure of the society which defines the standards, and the pressures that cause the deviance. Central to any study, and a major problem, is the vast range of variation of personality itself. It is probably impossible to identify the true determinants of personality for the very concept is elusive, being at best an overall generalisation. Personality is many faceted, and as difficult to grasp as mercury.

Many branches of science seek to classify and categorise personality, and although great advances have been made, they cannot be said to have been particularly successful in practical terms. Indeed it has to be said that even the clearest understanding of the nature of personality would still leave unresolved many aspects of the social problem of the control of deviancy. The legitimacy of the control by society of its individual members is itself a social issue on which opinions are markedly different.

Perhaps the most significant aspect of these problems is the question of personal responsibility. At the deepest level it raises the question of free will and the extent to which the individual can be said to be in control of his or her actions and so properly held to be responsible for them. At the practical level there is need for a clear distinction, often expressed as 'mad or bad', on which responsibility can be determined and punishment and treatment decided.

In response to these uncertainties attempts have continually been made to build medical, psychological, psychiatric and legal models which seek, in very different ways, to regulate the problems that deviancy causes. Unhappily, but perhaps inevitably, each of these approaches tends to diverge from the others and many of them tend to display sharp internal inconsistencies. The legal approach, for example, appears to be firmly based on the concept of responsibility. It recognises this, for example, by taking into account immaturity, but tends to do so mechanistically by reference to artificial fixed age limits that ignore individual development. The law also seeks to take account of external pressures and so has to this end created the doctrine of external duress. The law in this way seeks to create a clear structure that can be applied by the courts. But the wide variety of personality and the different levels of maturity shown at any age present a challenge to courts that they find difficult to meet. Even if personality can be individually determined and assessed it is equally difficult to decide whether a person should be deemed responsible for actions in the context of the situation that was being faced. The question of self-control is crucial. There is rarely full agreement as to whether the standard to be applied should be subjective, giving full weight to the individual's nature, or objective, imposing external standards of what the artificial 'ordinary person' would have done. Assuming that two persons are subject to identical pressures towards wrongdoing, how is it possible to measure the effect on each of the crucial balance between the temptation and the resistance? How much allowance must be made for 'weakness of character', whatever that may mean?

The medical approach can with certainty explain a range of physical symptoms – damaged brain or defective senses – but when it attempts to explain individual reactions to situations – the kernel of psychology and the basis of psychiatry – then it fares little better than the law and certainty rapidly dissolves in the face of disputed assessments. The insights of psychology and the medical advances of psychiatry show advances towards greater understanding of the problems involved but do little to resolve the central question of responsibility.

It is against this background of uncertainty that the law seeks to help and control those who are so deviant as to require state intervention. Again, there is more confusion than clarity. If responsibility cannot be plainly determined, the decision as to whether there should be treatment or punishment is equally uncertain. It is small wonder that there is a feeling that many are punished, particularly by imprisonment, who should not be and others are given treatment without clear evidence that this will prove to be of benefit. It is only possible to conclude that the whole question of responsibility and the legitimacy of the reaction of the state to deviancy is full of uncertainties and problems.

Some fifteen years ago Herschel Prins wrote a book which approached these issues in a novel and challenging way. Instead of setting out the current state of knowledge in the various relevant branches of study – medicine, psychology, law and so on – in a short and inevitably over-simplified way, or of seeking to present a simplified outline of what is most fiendishly complicated, he chose another, more challenging approach. He used his wide reading in the many disciplines traditionally regarded as relevant and individual case studies of illustrative instances of deviance as a basis for his general speculations. He did not hesitate to raise the most fundamental questions, nor to use his grasp of the disciplines concerned and his knowledge of more mundane illustrations, gained from a wide and increasing practical experience, to show the difficulties and how they have been approached in practice.

The result was a most interesting book that could not fail to stimulate the reader to wider reading and to deeper thought than is usually encouraged by texts that are narrowly based merely in one or two of the relevant disciplines. He has now taken the trouble to revise his book, and present a thoroughly rewritten second edition.

The new edition is based on a very wide range of knowledge involving reference to current thinking and practice in medicine, psychiatry, psychology, legal and social work. It contains a great wealth of individual vignettes of actual cases and the consideration of the methods used to deal with the problems encountered in practice. It builds on his own now extensive practical knowledge of very many aspects of the subject. There is an underlying assumption that there has to be up-to-date and effective training so as to ensure that the current knowledge and experience is used to improve the work that the identification and control of deviancy requires.

This book can claim to offer an essential aspect of such training. It is a book that cannot fail to stimulate the reader. It is an up-to-date overview of the problems and practice that will inevitably enable the reader to develop his or her own thoughts and to bring into a clearer focus the many issues raised. It lies at the other extreme from the introductory primer, yet it covers a wide range of the essential material with clarity. No-one working in the field, or studying any of the many relevant professional skills, can fail to find the book of the greatest interest and have horizons widened by what is here presented.

Sir John Wood

Preface

In my view consumers of professional and technical literature are often unaware of the forces and influences that have shaped the careers, views and attitudes of the authors of the books they read. Such information can helpfully place the author's views in some kind of perspective and provide a more human face to an academic and professional presentation.

My family background influenced an early career choice of probation officer; my father and some of his close relatives had been engaged in work with the deprived and the deviant. From an early age I became actively acquainted with such problems; an acquaintance brought more sharply into focus when orphaned as a teenager. In my first appointment as a probation officer – at the far too tender age of twenty-two – I had responsibility for those offenders made subject of a psychiatric probation order with a requirement of residence at the local mental hospital. This experience confirmed an earlier interest in the links between delinquency and disturbed and disordered mental states. The foundations for such interest had been laid in my student days by the broad approach to psychopathology to which I had been introduced by the late Professor Halmos. This interest was to be developed further as a student probation officer through the criminology teaching of Hermann Mannheim and the forensic psychiatry teaching of Dr (later Professor) Trevor Gibbens. An opportunity to take further the links between psychiatry and criminology was afforded by two happy and stimulating years spent working with Peter Scott, whose death at an early age robbed forensic psychiatry and criminology of one of their most thoughtful teachers and practitioners. The approach I have taken in this book owes much to his influence.

In more recent years I have been much stimulated by the work and writings of Dr Murray Cox – consultant psychotherapist at Broadmoor and Honorary Fellow at the Shakespeare Institute, Birmingham University. His facility for heightening our understanding of disturbed and deviant conduct and to place it within the wider context of literature, myth and legend has been an invaluable source of enlightenment. It has been my privilege over the years to share the insights I have derived into disturbed and deviant individuals with an enormously varied range of colleagues, students and practitioners. Their perceptive and sometimes unanswerable questions have been a timely reminder of my ignorance and lack of perception. I owe an enormous debt to former colleagues (some close friends) from all stages of my career – in probation, psychiatric social work, central government, four universities and a number of national statutory and voluntary bodies. To have worked with such a wide range of professionals has been exciting, if onerous at times. For example, my former colleague, mentor and friend, the late Professor Max Hamilton at Leeds, to his great regret, never managed to develop in me any degree of statistical sophistication; he did, however, engender in me an acute awareness of the limitations of statistics in the social and human sciences!

To all of those who have helped my own learning and perception (and hopefully made me more aware of my 'blind-spots') I dedicate this book with affection and gratitude. Such dedication is made in the painful awareness that human affairs and problems are highly complex and the latter are frequently incapable of satisfactory resolution.

Acknowledgements

My warm thanks are due, once again, to Edwina Welham and her editorial and production colleagues at Routledge for their continued courtesy and assistance. Mrs Janet Kirkwood has, yet again, performed wonders on her word processor; my thanks to her, too, for her patience and efficiency. We have now produced six books together for Routledge in the past sixteen years in what I hope she will agree has been a mutually satisfying and harmonious relationship. My thanks are due to Dr Paul Bowden, Editor of the *Journal of Forensic Psychiatry*, for permission to reproduce in Chapter 3 some material contained in my paper 'The Diversion of the Mentally Disordered: Some Problems for the Criminal Justice System, Penology and Health Care' (Vol. 3(3), 1992) and for permission to reproduce some material used in Chapter 10 from my paper 'Literature as an Aid to Empathic Response: Hamlet Conditionally Discharged', which appeared in Vol. 3(1), 1992 of that journal. Some parts of Chapters 4, 8 and 9, which originally appeared in *Medicine, Science and the Law* (Vols 30(3), 1990; 31(1), 1991; and 31(4), 1991) are reproduced by kind permission of the British Academy of Forensic Sciences, who hold the copyright. My thanks are also due to John Wiley and Sons Ltd, the copyright holder, for permission to reproduce in Chapter 3 some material that appeared originally in Chapter 2 of C.R. Hollin and K. Howells (eds) *Clinical Approaches to the Mentally Disordered Offender* (1993). I am most grateful to my Tribunal colleague Professor Sir John Wood, CBE, for so kindly agreeing to write the Foreword. Finally, my warmest thanks once again to my wife, Norma, not only for reading the manuscript with her usual perceptive and critical eye, but also for sustaining me at times when I found myself sadly lacking in effort and inspiration.

Herschel Prins
Houghton-on-the-Hill, Leicestershire, 1994

Note on case examples

No attempt has been made to hide the identity of those persons whose cases have been in the public domain (for example, those who have been the subject of extensive media attention). In all other instances the cases derive from the author's long personal experience. Every effort has been made to disguise any identifying data so as to make the illustrations anonymous. On some occasions, 'composite' pictures have been drawn. Despite these necessary professional precautions, it is maintained that the examples provide authentic accounts of the problems they have been chosen to represent.

Part I

Legal and administrative frameworks

Chapter 1

Problem areas revisited

> Mr Podsnap settled that whatever he put behind him he put out of existence . . . Mr Podsnap had even acquired a peculiar flourish of his right arm in often clearing the world of its most difficult problems, by sweeping them behind him.
>
> (Dickens, *Our Mutual Friend*)

The first edition of *Offenders, Deviants or Patients?* was generally very well received and, somewhat to my pleasure (and surprise), there has continued to be a small but steady demand for it ever since. This despite significant changes in law, policies and practice since first publication and despite fresh insights derived from various studies and research findings. In Chapter 1 of the first edition I suggested that

> The rationale for this book has emerged as a result of a general interest developed over many years concerning the understanding and treatment of offenders. Recently, I have come to be particularly interested in the borderland area between mental disorder and criminal behaviour and in the relationships between the many disciplines and professionals that struggle to confront the problems inherent in these relationships. Thus, psychologists, sociologists, psychiatrists, lawyers, police scientists, social administrators, geneticists – to name but a few – have made contributions to this field.
>
> (Prins, 1980: 1)

This view is even more true today when we are witnessing an apparent increase in a variety of crimes, not least those involving force and seriously deviant behaviour of one kind or another. In recent years I have attempted to address the multi-disciplinary nature of the topic in a number of further contributions (see, for example Prins, 1986, 1991). The impetus for producing a revised and up-dated version of the work has already been alluded to briefly. Further impetus has come from the recognition that there is still need for a basic introductory but well-documented text in this field. When the first edition appeared there were no texts of any substance published in the UK that dealt with forensic-psychiatric topics. Although the first edition never set out or claimed to be an introduction to forensic psychiatry, in the absence of any other works by psychiatrists, it seems to have been used as an introductory text. Since then, a number of textbooks on forensic psychiatry have appeared, all offering (some in more detail than others) a highly professional discussion of some of the matters covered in my original and present texts. In 1981 Trick and Tennent produced a useful short introductory text. In 1984, Craft and Craft edited a substantial compilation of papers dealing specifically with mentally abnormal offenders. In 1988, Faulk produced a very useful text aimed more specifically (but not exclusively) at psychiatric trainees, and, in 1990, Bluglass and Bowden contributed to and edited the most comprehensive and magisterial text yet to have appeared in the field. More recently Gunn and Taylor (1993) have contributed to and edited a further major text in the field. The present work makes no attempt to compete with these volumes but, hopefully, may be seen as complementary to them; it is written by a non-medically qualified academic and practitioner.

The present text has needed to take into account a number of significant recent developments. For example, the Mental Health Act 1983, in its provisions for offender-patients, necessitated a number of changes in practice and procedure. The Government's proposals for Criminal Justice Reform (Home Office, 1990) were followed by the Criminal Justice Act 1991. This placed considerable emphasis upon the assessment of risk in relation to specific offences such as those of violence or of a sexual nature (Section 29(1) and (2)). Courts are now also required to seek psychiatric opinion before passing a custodial sentence in certain cases (Section 4). The Report of the Woolf and Tumin Inquiry (Home Office, 1991), the Report into *Complaints about Ashworth Hospital* (Department of Health, 1992) and the *Final Report of the Reed Committee* (Department of Health and Home Office, 1992) all allude to the need for close collaborative effort in what is increasingly being regarded as a multi-disciplinary field.

Since the first edition I have taught a variety of mental health and allied professionals involved in its subject matter. Much of the content of these workshops, seminars and lectures has been derived not only from the original version but also from feed-back and input from these participants. These have contributed increasingly to the content of this revised edition. I have also used much of the material in the present volume in my clinical criminology sequences on postgraduate masters' courses at Loughborough and Nottingham Trent Universities. I hope that the present volume will appeal therefore to a readership as diverse as that of the first. I have in mind the increasing numbers of 'law and order' professionals (sentencers, both full-time and 'lay'), the police, advocates, probation officers and prison and hostel staffs; to forensic-psychiatric clinicians (notably trainee clinical psychologists, psychiatrists, nurses and social workers); to civil servants in those departments of state most directly involved with the subjects discussed in the book (notably the Home Office, the Lord Chancellor's Department and the Department of Health); to those who sit on adjudicating bodies (such as the Parole Board and the Mental Health Review Tribunal); to workers in the voluntary sector; and to the teachers and mentors of all the above groups. Finally, I hope it will appeal to those members of the public who are often understandably perplexed and very anxious about the behaviour of those of their fellow citizens sometimes labelled as offenders, deviants or patients.

In this new edition I have taken the opportunity to review its structure and content. I hope that readers will find the topics now placed in a more logical sequence; this should make the text more coherent. The content has been revised substantially to take account of the changes referred to earlier. In the first edition I devoted a separate chapter to the problems of female offenders. It now seems preferable to deal with gender and related isses throughout the body of the text. I have dealt with the equally important issue of race in the same way. The decision not to feature these issues separately is not to be taken in any way as an indication of a failure on my part to recognise and appreciate their importance. I intend the opposite, to recognise their substance by placing them in a general context. It is also important to point out that there are now a number of excellent texts on gender and race issues; some of these are referred to at various places in the book. In similar fashion I have not (as in the first edition) devoted a separate chapter to the various forms of substance abuse (alcohol, other drugs, solvents, etc.) and crime. These aspects are also dealt with at various relevant places in the text. However, I have added a new chapter on 'Violence and homicide' because of increasing concerns about these topics.

A few words are also necessary about my choice of certain terminology. I gave a good deal of thought to a change of title. However, while dropping the somewhat cumbersome sub-title, the original title still seems to describe the various labels used for, and the fates suffered by, some of our fellow citizens. Some comments I made about them in the first edition are still, sadly, no less true today.

> They are, in the words of the late doctor Peter Scott, 'the unrewarding, degenerate, not nice offender(s)' (Scott 1975: 8). We shall see, at various places in this text, how the system shunts them in various directions, sometimes labelling them as offenders, sometimes as patients, sometimes as deviants. The labels frequently serve to offload real responsibility and are a convenient means of rationalizing our discomfort, ambivalence and non-involvement. These shunting exercises are, of course, compounded by our reluctance to face up to issues of treatment versus punishment. They also illustrate some of the dilemmas inherent in distinguishing between normality and abnormality, sickness and sin, care and control.
>
> (Prins, 1980: 2–3)

Readers may also notice that Chapter 4 is entitled 'Mental *disturbance* and criminality'. The choice of this word rather than 'disorder' or 'abnormality' has been made in order to encompass a wider range of mental states (some more or less permanent, others transient). My own use of the words accords with those used in a recent policy paper produced by the National Association for the Care and Resettlement of Offenders' Advisory Committee on Mental Health. In that paper mentally disturbed offenders were defined as follows:

Those offenders who may be acutely or chronically mentally ill; those with neuroses, behavioural and/or personality disorders; those with learning difficulties; some who, as a function of alcohol and/or substance abuse, have a mental health problem; and any who are suspected of falling into one or other of these two groups. It also includes those offenders where a degree of mental disturbance is recognised even though they may not be severe enough to bring it within the criteria laid down by the Mental Health Act, 1983. It also applies to those offenders who, even though they do not fall easily within the definition – for example some sex offenders and some abnormally aggressive offenders – may benefit from psychological treatments.

(NACRO, 1993: 4)

The individuals and their problems to be discussed in this book fall within this fairly catholic definition; the focus of the book is primarily clinical and psychopathological. However, where possible, opportunity has been taken to place this approach within a broader social and philosophical context. This chapter concludes with some case illustrations that hopefully will flesh out some of the broader concerns identified above.

FIVE CASE EXAMPLES

The problems presented by some of the individuals to be discussed in this book often appear in rather dramatic form – more particularly the notorious cases that excite the interest and attention of the media. The cases of individuals like Peter Sutcliffe, Denis Nilsen and the late Jeffrey Dahmer spring readily to mind and are the subject of comment in Chapter 2. However, there are many less dramatic and publicised cases where decisions as to the most appropriate form of disposal seem to be made almost serendipitously.

Example 1

'John' is in his fifties and comes from the West of England. Nearly two decades ago he was sent to a Special Hospital on a restriction order, having been diagnosed as suffering from psychopathic disorder. He had an extensive criminal record of sexual offences. The victims of his last (index) offence had been 'wooed' and 'groomed' by him for some time and were all young boys. After some years in hospital, where he had received a range of 'treatments' for his sexual deviancy, he was discharged into the community. He had been at liberty about four years when he was apprehended for further offences of a similar kind; but in these later offences he had used threats and force to secure compliance. Those responsible for supervising him (a psychiatrist and a social worker) thought he had been doing well. However, despite his favourable presentation to them he had been involved over many months in sexual misconduct. He was recalled from the community to hospital by the Home Secretary and also appeared in court charged with the new series of offences. He was again given a psychiatric disposal. Since that time he has remained in hospital; unsurprisingly he is a model patient but affords no optimism to those entrusted with his management that he has changed his basic sexual preferences. His psychopathic condition is regarded as 'untreatable' in psychiatric therapeutic terms. A crucial question must be – should he have been awarded a psychiatric disposal at his last court appearance, or would a prison sentence have been more appropriate?

Example 2

'Florence' is in her late sixties. She has had a severe alcohol problem for many years. When 'in drink' she becomes uncared for, noisy, abusive and frequently engages in minor 'public order' offences. Over the years she has been the subject of police cautions, short prison sentences, probation, periods in detoxification centres and short spells in hospitals. She 'floats' like some piece of flotsam upon the waters of the health care and penal systems. No-one wishes to 'own' her, and her condition is deteriorating slowly but steadily.

Example 3

'Paul' is in his early fifties. He has a long record of offences of indecent exposure ('flashing'). He admits readily that he has indulged in this behaviour on many more occasions than those for which he has been prosecuted and convicted. He has received a range of penal and health care disposals including numerous probation orders combined with psychiatric treatment. Despite the anxieties he feels at each court appearance and sentence he claims he is quite unable to break what has become a compulsion. Probation officers, psychiatrists and psychologists have all been involved in various forms of therapy for his problems – to no effect. Fortunately, he is the type of exposer whose behaviour, although highly distressing to his victims, has not progressed to more serious sexual deviance, such as rape.

Example 4

'Vincent' is a twenty-six-year-old Afro-Caribbean. He is considered by some psychiatrists to suffer from a form of schizophrenia that makes him highly suspicious of others and liable to engage in violence when he feels affronted or frustrated. He lives in an area where his fellow Afro-Caribbeans complain that they feel alienated and 'picked upon' more frequently by the police than their similar-aged white peers. It seems highly likely that his schizophrenic illness has been deemed to play a more significant role as a determinant of his behaviour than is justified by the facts. His behaviour and its origins pose important problems for the professions of psychiatry and law.

Example 5

'Pauline' is in her early forties and is serving a life sentence for her third conviction for arson with intent to endanger life. She has been preoccupied with fire since childhood, has engaged in making hoax calls to fire brigades and has become involved increasingly in more and more serious fire-raising behaviour. At various times she has been diagnosed as suffering from a personality disorder, from depression and from schizophrenia. No-one has considered that she easily fulfils the criteria for a conventional psychiatric diagnosis. She has spent time in both ordinary and secure (special) psychiatric hospitals. In such establishments she is both aggressive and disruptive; when in a state of tension she seeks to resolve it by lighting fires. The circumstances of the offence for which she received her current life sentence were that she thought her fellow residents in the after-care hostel were 'ganging up' on her. One evening, when they and the staff member on duty had gone to bed, she poured a quantity of paraffin over the furniture in the communal lounge and set fire to it by means of a fuse made from rags soaked in the same substance. She then left the premises. Fortunately, the smoke detector in the room alerted the residents. However, several of them suffered from temporary congestion of the lungs and needed brief hospital treatment. Over the years, many approaches have been tried with 'Pauline'. There had been signs that she was beginning to find more acceptable ways of expressing her resentful and angry feelings and coping with the difficulties these created. Despite this, the doctors who gave evidence at her trial were unanimous in their view that her condition was untreatable within the terms of the mental health legislation. The judge, in sentencing her to life imprisonment, commented on her actual and potential dangerousness. He indicated that she would not be released until those responsible for her management considered it safe to do so. As I shall show subsequently, such judgements about potential dangerousness are notoriously difficult to make.

These brief illustrations demonstrate some of the problems of drawing firm lines between normality and abnormality and 'madness' and 'badness'. In addition, they demonstrate the problems involved in selecting the most appropriate modes of management in the interests of both the offender-patient on the one hand, and the community on the other. They also illustrate the problems involved in having to distinguish those who merely have a nuisance value and those whose behaviour has a more malignant quality. All these and other issues are addressed in the following chapters. I begin my task by discussing the difficulties involved in determining responsibility (liability) for crime and the manner in which this may be eroded in a number of ways.

REFERENCES

Bluglass, R. and Bowden, P. (eds) (1990) *Principles and Practice of Forensic Psychiatry*, London: Churchill Livingstone.

Craft, M. and Craft, A. (eds) (1984) *Mentally Abnormal Offenders*, London: Baillière Tindall.

Department of Health (1992) *Report of the Committee of Inquiry into Complaints about Ashworth Hospital*, Vols 1 and 2 (Chairman, Sir Louis Blom-Cooper, QC), Cmnd 2028-I and -II, London: HMSO.

Department of Health and Home Office (1992) *Review of Health and Social Services for Mentally Disordered Offenders and Others Requiring Similar Services* (Chairman, Dr John Reed, CB), *Final Summary Report*, Cmnd 2088, London: HMSO.

Faulk, M. (1988) *Basic Forensic Psychiatry*, Oxford: Blackwell Scientific Publications.

Gunn, J. and Taylor, P.J. (1993) *Forensic Psychiatry: Clinical, Legal and Ethical Issues*, London: Butterworth-Heinemann.

Home Office (1990) *Crime, Justice and Protecting the Public: The Government's Proposals for Legislation*, Cmnd 905, London: HMSO.

—— (1991) *Prison Disturbances, April 1990: Report of an Inquiry by the Rt Hon. Lord Justice Woolf (Parts I and II) and His Honour Judge Stephen Tumin (Part II)*, Cmnd 1456, London: HMSO.

National Association for the Care and Resettlement of Offenders (NACRO) (1993) *Mental Health Advisory Committee: Policy Paper No. 1: Community Care and Mentally Disturbed Offenders*, London: NACRO.

Prins, H. (1980) *Offenders, Deviants or Patients?: An Introduction to The Study of Socio-Forensic Problems*, London: Tavistock.

—— (1986) *Dangerous Behaviour, the Law and Mental Disorder*, London: Tavistock.

—— (1991) 'Dangerous People or Dangerous Situations? – Some Further Thoughts', *Medicine, Science and the Law* 31, 25–37.

Scott, P.D. (1975) *Has Psychiatry Failed in the Treatment of Offenders?*, London: Institute for the Study and Treatment of Delinquency.

Trick, K.L. and Tennent, T.G. (1981) *Forensic Psychiatry: An Introductory Text*, London: Pitman.

FURTHER READING

General

Herbst, K. and Gunn, J. (eds) (1991) *The Mentally Disordered Offender*, London: Butterworth-Heinemann, in association with the Mental Health Foundation.

Race, culture and gender issues

Race and culture

Fernando, S. (1989) *Race and Culture in Psychiatry*, London: Routledge/Tavistock.

Institute of Race Relations (1991) *Deadly Silence: Black Deaths in Custody*, London: IRR.

Prins, H. (1990) *Bizarre Behaviours: Boundaries of Psychiatry*, London: Routledge/ Tavistock.

Gender

Allen, H. (1987) *Justice Unbalanced: Gender, Psychiatry and Judicial Decisions*, Milton Keynes: Open University Press.
Smart, C. (1989) *Feminism and the Power of Law*, London: Routledge.

Chapter 2

Responsibility (liability) for crime

Where there is a total defect of the understanding, there is no free act of the will.
(Sir Matthew Hale, *History of the Pleas of the Crown*, 1736,
quoted in Masters, 1993: 162)

[T]here is no free will in nature, and the concept of freedom of choice, the basis for
every moral edifice and all notions of conscience, is man-made and man-imposed.
(Masters, 1993: 162)

The matters to be discussed in this chapter are complex and I have, of necessity,
had to over-simplify some issues. In order to begin to understand them one
requires some acquaintance with the disciplines of ethics, law and psychiatry.
The complexity of the material is further compounded by the manner in which
certain terms are used, often synonymously, by a wide range of people. For this
reason, it will be necessary to comment on the meaning of words such as
responsibility, capacity, culpability and liability. For people are frequently like
Lewis Carroll's Humpty Dumpty, who, it will be remembered, said, 'in rather a
scornful tone', 'when I use a word . . . it means just what I choose it to mean –
neither more nor less' (*Through the Looking Glass*, Chapter 6).

The purpose of this chapter is to provide a map, analogous to those published
by the motoring organisations, which will outline the main contours of a complex
terrain and be deliberately devoid of finer detail. For the latter, the traveller must
turn to the more detailed charts provided by the Ordnance Survey or similar
organisations. I hope that the references to more substantial sources of information provided throughout the chapter will, in conjunction with the list of
Further Reading, serve to fill in these gaps.

The terrain to be surveyed in this outline map is divided into the following
areas. First, a brief consideration of some of the terms used in discussions of
responsibility for crime. Second, a comparatively short historical account of the
development of the concept of responsibility and allied matters. Third, a description of the manner in which the law[1] makes special provisions for what I have
chosen to call 'erosions' of responsibility. Fourth, a brief discussion of some

aspects of the relationship between mental disturbance and crime as a prelude to the more detailed discussion to be provided in Chapter 4.

SEMANTIC ISSUES

The layperson is likely to use terms such as responsibility or guilt in less precise fashion than would the lawyer or the student of jurisprudence. Thus, the former, if asked to define the word 'responsible', would probably come near to the dictionary definition: (1) 'liable to be called to account (to a person or for a thing)', (2) 'being *morally* accountable for one's actions; capable of rational conduct' (*Concise Oxford Dictionary*). The important point to be noted here is the emphasis I have added, because the law is not necessarily concerned with morally reprehensible conduct; for, as Finch has stated, 'clearly the spheres of law and morals do not necessarily coincide though legal and moral exhortations may coincide in certain cases' (1974: 4). In their discussion of the law relating to homosexuality and prostitution, the Wolfenden Committee made an important distinction between private and public morality. They considered that

> unless a deliberate attempt is made by Society, acting through the agency of the law, to equate the sphere of crime with that of sin, there must remain a realm of private morality and immorality which is, in brief and crude terms, not the law's business.
>
> (Home Office and Scottish Home Department, 1957: 24)

The layperson may also use the word 'irresponsible' to denote something more than legal lack of responsibility. For our purposes, 'irresponsible' means simply lack of legal responsibility and is not used in any lay, pejorative sense.

The word 'culpable' is found, not infrequently, in the literature on responsibility and related matters. For present purposes it is taken to mean blameworthiness in the criminal sense. However, if we do choose to use it in this way, we must acknowledge that a moral quality may creep into its usage. The word 'capacity' is also sometimes used as a synonym for legal competency. Thus, in legal terms, it would seem to denote a quality existing within an individual – for example, to form an intent to act in a certain way. The word liability is sometimes used as being synonymous with responsibility. The *Concise Oxford Dictionary* defines 'liable' as being 'legally bound, or under an obligation'. For my purposes, the term responsibility merely means liability to be dealt with by the criminal law and to be disposed of through the criminal justice system. As my friend and sometime colleague Professor Griew says, responsibility is a word

> so often bandied about; like an historical background it gives an air of learning to a discussion . . . it is a muddying word . . . liability is the better word as being less ambiguous.
>
> (1984: 60)

A final, but important point, needs to be made about the term 'liability'. As far as the law is concerned, liability can certainly go beyond responsibility in the sense of moral culpability. There are a number of offences, those of so-called 'strict liability' (sometimes called 'absolute liability'), for which individuals may be prosecuted and punished, even though they are unaware of the existence of facts which make their conduct a criminal offence. An example of this would be the case of a shopkeeper found to have purveyed contaminated meat or other foodstuffs even though he or she did not know they were contaminated. In recent years, the House of Lords (as supreme judicial review body) has indicated that there should be some restriction in the interpretation of offences of strict liability. A seminal case was that of *Sweet* v. *Parsley* (1969). This concerned a young woman who was originally convicted of being concerned in the management of premises (she being the tenant of a farmhouse in Oxfordshire which she sublet to various other tenants) in which the prosecution alleged cannabis had been smoked. Her conviction, after appeal, was eventually overturned as a result of a ruling in the House of Lords.

Components of legal blameworthiness

There are one or two additional terms that require clarification. An act does not make a person *legally* guilty unless his or her mind is also legally blameworthy (see also earlier comments on the difference between legal blameworthiness and moral turpitude). Lawyers denote this legal concept of guilt through the use of the Latin term *mens rea*. Simply put, this means having legally guilty intent or, more precisely, having the intention to commit an act that is wrong in the sense that it is legally forbidden. (See Hart, 1968, for full discussion.) We should note also that there must be an act or omission. Lawyers call this the *actus reus*. An omission is a failure to do something; a simple example would be failure to give precedence to persons on a pedestrian crossing. There are of course more complex and emotive situations in which a person may be charged with a failure to do something, for example an act which might amount in certain circumstances to serious negligence. Such a negligent act, if it caused the death of another, could lead to a charge of manslaughter. Normally such cases involve a degree of gross negligence in the sense of a reckless disregard of danger to the health and welfare of the victim.

BRIEF HISTORICAL CONTEXT

With certain exceptions (such as extreme youth or severe mental disturbance, as we shall see) men and women are held to be responsible (liable) for their acts and adjudged to be capable of exercising control over them. History reveals that the matter has not always been so entirely clear-cut. In early times it was customary for punishment to be imposed for the commission of a criminal act regardless of the mental state of the person concerned; indeed, in England and Wales, the common law gave considerable over-riding priority to the need to preserve law and order. The Old Testament provides instances mainly of severe forms of justice without mitigating features being much in evidence.

However, in certain cases, if the crime appeared to be unintentional, some mitigation of penalty was available, as, for example, through the provision of the cities of refuge for those who killed unintentionally. In addition, minors, 'imbeciles' and deaf mutes were often singled out for less harsh treatment (the phenomenon of *Shoteh* described in the Talmud). In the Roman era one can discern the beginning of an attempt to introduce some primitive idea of diminishment of responsibility, and in thirteenth-century England it seems to have been generally held that neither the child nor the madman should be held liable for crime. Henry de Bracton, author of one of the first major treatises on English law, stated that 'Furiosus non intelligit quod agit et anima et ratione caret, et non multumdistas a brutis' – 'an insane person is one who does not know what he is doing, is lacking in mind and reason and is not far from the brutes' (quoted in Walker, 1968: 33). Though benign to some degree, this appears to be a somewhat primitive statement equating mental illness with the behaviour of animals. Walker (1968) and Jacobs (1971) have drawn attention to an interesting error in another of Bracton's statements. It is worth alluding to briefly because it illustrates some of the problems involved in tracing the evolution of legal and other concepts. Bracton is alleged to have stated:

> and then there is what can be said about the child and the madman (*furiosus*), for the one is protected by his innocence of design and the other is excused by the misfortune of his *deed*.
>
> (quoted in Jacobs, 1971: 25; emphasis added)

It is not altogether clear from this text why the madman is not to be held responsible. Apparently Bracton took his text from a translation of the work of Modestinus. In its original form, this referred not to the misfortune of his deed ('infelicitas *facti*') but to the misfortune of his fate ('infelicitas *fati*'). This makes more sense, for in Roman law there appears to have been an assumption that an insane offender was punished sufficiently by his madness ('Satis furore ipso punitur').

Sometimes, complicated statements and concepts become lost or confused during translation. For example, it seems highly likely that much of the disagreement and controversy over some of Freud's views and findings have arisen because of the difficulties in finding suitable English interpretations of terms originally conceived and described in the German language. These particular difficulties have been usefully illustrated by the distinguished psychiatrist and philanthropist Bruno Bettelheim. He states that

> conversations with friends have disclosed that many, who, like myself, are native German-speakers, and emigrated to the United States in the middle of their lives, are quite dissatisfied with the way Freud's works have been

rendered in English. The number of inadequacies and downright errors in the translations is enormous

(Bettelheim, 1983: vii)

In the seventeenth century, the jurist Sir Edward Coke appeared to share the view of earlier authorities that the mad were punished sufficiently by their fate. In the same century, Sir Matthew Hale (in a treatise published in 1736, some sixty years after his death) tried to distinguish between the totally and the partially insane. In his view the latter would not be exempt from criminal responsibility (see Jacobs, 1971; Clarke, 1975). It seems fairly safe to assume that only very serious mental disorder ('raving lunacy') would have been recognised as giving exemption from serious crime – in particular, homicide. However, contrary to general belief, issues relating to insanity were gradually being raised more frequently in respect of crimes less serious than homicide. Eigen states that

the jurisprudence of insanity appears to have arisen not out of sensationalistic murders or grotesque personal assaults, but from what were rather more routine 'garden variety' crimes.

(1983: 426)

In addition, broader interpretations of what might constitute mental disorder were being admitted. For example, in the case of Arnold in 1724, the judge suggested that 'if a man be deprived of his reason, and consequently of his intention, he cannot be guilty' (quoted in Jacobs, 1971: 27). Similar views were expressed in the famous Leicestershire case of Laurence, fourth Earl of Ferrers, tried in 1760 by his peers for the murder of his steward, John Johnson. His history, trial and the climate of the times have been described in lively and quite scholarly fashion by a local author and solicitor, Arthur Crane (1990).

A subsequent case that brought the issue into sharper relief was that of Hadfield, who was tried for capital treason in 1800 for shooting at George III. Erskine, the counsel for Hadfield, obtained an acquittal on the basis of the defendant having sustained serious head injuries (sword wounds) during war service. These injuries had caused Hadfield to develop delusional ideas that impelled him to believe he had to sacrifice his life for the salvation of the world. Not wishing to be guilty of suicide and the obloquy that this would call down on his memory, he chose to commit his crime for the sole purpose of being executed for it. Hadfield's case is of interest for two reasons. First, it was *probably* the first time that brain damage (caused by injury) had been advanced as a relevant exculpatory factor. Second, Erskine, who was a brilliant advocate, was probably more easily able to secure Hadfield's acquittal at a time when public interest in, and sympathy towards, the 'mad' had been fostered by the long-standing and intermittent illness suffered by the King (a malady for which the diagnosis has always been disputed).

However, not all cases were brought to such a successful outcome for the defendant. A similar plea in the case of Bellingham (who in 1812 shot the Prime

Minister, Spencer Perceval) was unsuccessful, and he was condemned to death. Walker (1968) reports how a similar fate befell a contemporary of Bellingham's – an epileptic farmer named Bowler, who had killed a neighbour. However, it is the case of Daniel M'Naghten in 1843 that is of special interest, for it was the outcome of his case and the consideration of that outcome by the senior judiciary that resulted in the formulation of a legal test of insanity, a test still in force today, though rarely used. M'Naghten[2] was a Glaswegian wood-carver who seems to have suffered from what we would describe today as paranoid delusions. For example, amongst other delusions, he believed that the Tories were conspiring against him. As a result of these delusions, he attempted to kill the Prime Minister, Sir Robert Peel, but, not knowing what Peel looked like, he shot and killed Peel's Secretary, Edward Drummond, by mistake. At his trial, a number of eminent medical men testified to his unsoundness of mind and he was found not guilty by reason of insanity. It is worth noting here that although M'Naghten's mental disorder has never been put in doubt, it has also been suggested in more recent times that he *may* have belonged to an active political sect holding anti-Tory views. As a result of the verdict in M'Naghten's case the House of Lords decided to ask the judges to answer certain questions arising from it. Two of their answers have come to be known as the M'Naghten 'test' (sometimes described erroneously as the 'Rules'). The test states, in effect, that

> the jurors ought to be told in all cases that every man is to be presumed sane and to possess a sufficient degree of reason to be responsible for his crimes, until the contrary be proved to their satisfaction; and that to establish a defence on the ground of insanity, it must be clearly proved that, at the time of committing the act, the party accused was labouring under such a defect of reason, from disease of the mind, as not to know the nature and quality of his act he was doing; or if he did know it, that he did not know what he was doing was wrong.

> (quoted in Walker, 1968: 100)

In essence, there are two significant parts to the above statement. An accused has a defence, first, if they did not know the nature and quality of their act, or, second, if they did, they did not know that it was wrong. From the time they were first posited, the so-called 'rules' have understandably been the subject of criticism. In the first place, they were framed at a time when the disciplines of psychology and psychiatry were in an embryonic stage of development; a disproportionate degree of emphasis being placed upon the faculties of knowing, reasoning and understanding (cognitive processes) to the exclusion of emotional and volitional factors. (For a very useful discussion of some of these issues in Victorian times see Smith, 1981 and 1991.) Second, the 'rules' make use of such expressions as 'defect of reason', 'disease of the mind', 'nature and quality of his act'. These terms have caused numerous arguments concerning their precise legal definition and interpretation. Third, and perhaps more importantly, the criteria for 'M'Naghten madness' have been so tightly drawn that its use as a defence in cases of homicide has always been fraught with difficulty. Since the introduction of the Homicide Act of 1957, the introduction of the Mental Health Act 1959 and the total abolition of the death penalty in 1965, the insanity defence resulting in the 'special verdict' has been used in but a handful of cases each year.[3] Mackay reports that

> during the . . . period 1975 to 1989 there was a total of 52 successful insanity defences in England and Wales. The greatest number of special verdicts in any single year was six in 1975, 1976 and 1986 respectively, while the smallest number was a single insanity defence in 1982.
>
> (1991a: 16)

Although the insanity defence is open in cases other than homicide, it is comparatively rarely used. Out of Mackay's fifty-two cases, only about a third were for homicide. About 46 per cent were for other forms of serious assault. This is because until very recently (with the implementation of the Criminal Procedure (Insanity and Unfitness to Plead) Act 1991) a successful plea, even in the most minor cases, meant automatic detention in a mental hospital, sometimes for a long period of time (see Mackay 1983a, 1983b, 1991a and 1991b and later discussion).

In 1975, the Committee on Mentally Abnormal Offenders (Chairman the late Lord Butler of Saffron Walden) suggested a number of amendments to the M'Naghten provisions and called for the introduction of a new formulation of the special verdict, namely not guilty on evidence of severe mental disorder (illness or impairment) (Home Office and DHSS, 1975). The Committee proposed a definition of severe mental illness which would contain one or more of the following characteristics:

(a) Lasting impairment of intellectual functions shown by failure of memory, orientation, comprehension and learning capacity.
(b) Lasting alteration of mood of such degree as to give rise to delusional appraisal of the patient's situation, his past or his future, or that of others, or to lack of any appraisal.
(c) Delusional beliefs, persecutory, jealous or grandiose.
(d) Abnormal perceptions associated with delusional misinterpretation of events.
(e) Thinking so disordered as to prevent reasonable appraisal of the patient's situation or reasonable communication with others.

        Home Office and DHSS, 1975: para. 18.35 and Appendix 10)

To date, this particular recommendation of the Committee and, sad to say, many others, have not been acted upon. However, we shall see in Chapter 3 that some of their recommendations concerning court disposals have found their way into recent mental health legislation.

Reference has already been made to the Homicide Act 1957. The latter introduced the concept of diminished responsibility in cases of murder into

English law. (Its implementation in practice is the subject of later discussion.) To round off this short historical introduction, a few words are in order about the origins of this legislation. As just stated, the defence of diminished responsibility in cases of murder was new to English law, though it had been in force in Scotland for very many years. Its introduction followed the deliberations of the Royal Commission on Capital Punishment (1953). Jacobs states that

> The 1957 Act was essentially a compromise solution to the controversy over capital punishment. It appeased the retentionists by retaining as capital offences certain categories of murder by shooting and murder in the course of furtherance of theft; but the remainder, numerically more significant, carried a mandatory sentence of life imprisonment.
>
> (1971: 4)

Since the introduction of the Act the number of people convicted of man-slaughter by reason of diminished responsibility has been about seventy per year with an all-time low of forty-seven in 1990 (Home Office, 1992: 91). In the early days of legislation a substantial proportion of such people received hospital orders under the mental health legislation. Today, they are more likely to receive a prison sentence. Dell and Smith (1983) suggest that this shift has been due for the most part to changes in treatment recommendations made by the examining doctors (see also Dell, 1983; Griew, 1988; and later discussion).

This concludes my brief historical introduction. More recent elements will be picked up in the discussion of certain contemporary problems. But before I do so, I give brief consideration to what I can best describe as other possible 'erosions' of criminal liability.

'EROSIONS' OF LIABILITY (RESPONSIBILITY)

A word of explanation is necessary for my use of this phrase. To the best of my knowledge, it does not appear in any of the law textbooks and I have introduced it here with some hesitation merely for convenience. It is intended to serve as an 'umbrella' term for those situations, states of mind, being or attributes that may cause a man or woman to be held non-liable in law for their acts, or for their liability in law to be severely diminished in a variety of ways. The clearest illustration of this non-liability concerns children below a certain age.

Children

In English law, children below the age of ten cannot be found guilty of an offence. Children of this age and below are held to be *doli incapax* (not capable of crime). From the age of ten years and below fourteen years, they are also presumed to be incapable of committing an offence. However, this presumption may be rebutted by evidence that the child knew that what he or she was doing was wrong. For practical purposes, this means that a child between ten and fourteen can only be found guilty if the prosecution is able to prove that he or she committed the *actus reus* with *mens rea*. There are those who consider that with the *apparent* earlier age of maturity in children the age at which they can be held liable in law should be lowered.

Involuntary conduct and automatism

Before proceeding to examine the way in which the law takes account of certain abnormal mental states in determining the degree of liability that should be attached in law to an act or omission, we need to consider – albeit briefly – some aspects of involuntary conduct and the nature of the state known as automatism.

Involuntary conduct

Reference has already been made to the notion of intention. Implicit in this notion is an assumption that the act complained of should have been voluntary: that is, within the person's control. An act or omission to act is considered to be *involuntary* where it can be clearly shown to be beyond the control of the person. An often cited case is that of *Hill* v. *Baxter* (1958) in which it was alleged that the defendant had contravened the Road Traffic Act 1930 by driving dangerously. He pleaded that he had become unconscious and that he remembered nothing of the alleged accident. This plea was accepted by the magistrates on the grounds that severe loss of memory must have been caused by the sudden onset of illness which had overcome him. However, the Divisional Court (High Court) did not accept this, suggesting that he might just have fallen asleep. In expressing their view in this particular case, they did qualify it by stating that there might be some states of unconsciousness, or even clouded (interrupted) consciousness, such as those due to a stroke or an epileptic fit, which might exclude liability in similar cases. One of the judges hearing the appeal in this particular case suggested that similar exculpation from liability might have arisen if, for example, a man had been attacked by a swarm of bees and because of their action had lost directional control of the vehicle. Hart (1968) has made a useful two-fold distinction between those situations where the subject is conscious and where he or she is unconscious. I paraphrase it as follows:

1 *Conscious.*
   (a) Physical compulsion by another person.
   (b) Muscular control impaired by disease: for example in cases of chorea.
   (c) Reflex muscular contraction (for example, in the case of the hypothetical swarm of bees mentioned earlier).
2 *Unconscious.*
   (a) Natural sleep at normal time (see later discussion).
   (b) Drunken stupor. Hart cites the example of a woman in a drunken state 'overlaying' her child and thus killing it. (It could, of course, equally be a man.)

(c) Sleep brought on by fatigue (as, for example, in the case of the motorist cited above).
(d) Loss of consciousness involving collapse. Examples are to be found in certain conditions such as epilepsy or hypoglycaemic states.

It is fairly obvious that many of the above might lead to a successful plea for negation or serious reduction of criminal liability. Courts have to interpret such pleas according to individual circumstances, so that no general ruling can be found in the law reports or legal texts that will fit all cases. For example, if I fall asleep at the wheel of my car and cause an accident, am I to be considered to be exempted entirely from liability, or will the court suggest (as it did in the well-known case of *Kay* v. *Butterworth*, 1945) that I must have known that drowsiness was overcoming me and that, because of this, I should have stopped driving and thus averted an accident?

Automatism

Automatism is a phenomenon which may occur in situations where loss of consciousness is the cause of an *involuntary* (unintentional) act, which may in certain circumstances nevertheless be held to constitute a crime. For legal purposes, then, automatism means being in a state capable of action but not being conscious of that action. In certain cases it has been held that such a state can be offered as a defence because 'The act . . . is done by the muscles without any control by the mind, such as a spasm, a reflex action or a convulsion.' Hall Williams reminds us that 'The way the law has developed is to recognise two kinds of automatism; sane automatism and insane automatism' (1980: 279). If all the evidence in the case points towards mental abnormality, then the court has available a 'special verdict' (see earlier discussion) or, in the case of homicide, a verdict of diminished responsibility. But a blow on the head, a cerebral tumour (as in the case of *R.* v. *Charlson*, 1955) or sleepwalking (somnambulism) *may* be a justification for pleading sane automatism – in which case a complete acquittal may be possible. It is worth pointing out that the courts have, on the whole, been reluctant to accept pleas of automatism. This reluctance, as Maher *et al.* suggested, may stem

> from the fact that [the criminal courts] can ensure future control over an individual in order to prevent the repetition of possible dangerous behaviour . . . in only one of two ways; either by convicting him of a crime or by acquitting on the grounds of insanity (which leads to committal to a mental hospital). The courts have adopted two tactics to restrict the automatism defence to ensure control over categories of persons with conditions which can give rise to states of automatism.
>
> (1984: 95)

The first has already been referred to, namely to treat the case as one of insanity, with, until 1992, consequent indefinite hospitalisation (as in the cases of *Bratty*

v. *Attorney General for Northern Ireland*, 1963, *R.* v. *Kemp*, 1957, and more recently in the House of Lords decision in the case of *R.* v. *Sullivan*, 1984). In Sullivan's case, as in some others, the issue concerned the question as to what constituted a proper defence for an accused who had assaulted someone during the course of a seizure cause by psychomotor epilepsy. (The possibility that certain epileptic and similar conditions may be associated with violent behaviour will be examined in detail in Chapter 4.) The House of Lords, though obviously unhappy about attaching a label of 'insanity' to cases of epilepsy, held none the less that only a defence of insanity and not sane automatism was open to the accused. An important point arising from this judgment is that the idea of 'disease of the mind' (see earlier discussion) was to be given a very broad definition so that society 'would be protected against recurrence of dangerous conduct' (Maher *et al.* 1984: 96).

The second tactic adopted by the courts to restrict the automatism defence is to hold that being in a state of automatism is not a defence if the accused is in some way to blame or is at fault for getting into that condition: for example, through getting into a state of acute intoxication (see later discussion also). A review of some of the relevant case law reveals that it usually has been held that a person is responsible for the consequences of his decision either to do something (such as ingest drink or drugs) or not to stop some activity (for example, continuing to drive while beginning to feel overcome by the need to sleep). In a very comprehensive review of the topic, Mackay states that

> Automatism is a defence which continues to cause problems. The emergence of a plea based on 'unconscious voluntary action' . . . (Bratty v. Attorney General for Northern Ireland) . . . is with the exception of certain isolated cases, of comparatively recent origin and seems to reflect an increasing awareness by the courts of the practical need for a voluntary act before an accused can be convicted of a criminal offence.
>
> (1983b: 81)

For a comprehensive statement of the medical and legal aspects of various forms of automatism readers should consult Fenwick's (1990) excellent monograph. One obvious form of automatism is being in a somnambulistic state. Fenwick, in the monograph referred to above, provides an extended discussion of the relationship between somnambulism (sleep automatism) and criminal behaviour (pp. 12–18). In particular, he provides detailed guidance for those charged with having to try to establish a defence to a criminal charge on these grounds. He cites a number of important diagnostic factors, such as childhood and family history, disorientation on awakening, availability of evidence from witnesses to the event, amnesia for the event, trigger factors, lack of attempts to conceal the crime, the motiveless or out of character nature of the crime and, in cases of violent crime, the possibility of previous history of violence during a period of sleep automatism. From time to time, successful pleas in such cases are reported in the press. For example, a teenager who almost killed a friend during a nightmare was cleared of attempted murder by a Crown Court. It was alleged that, in the course of a nightmare, he stabbed a friend with a kitchen knife and beat him with a wooden club. A psychiatrist told the court that 'He committed this act during his sleep – during a night of terror.' The doctor told the court that he 'knew of eight or nine similar cases' (*Independent*, 9 March 1990: 5). In this case, the defendant obtained an acquittal. However, the law seems somewhat capricious in its interpretation and implementation, for in the case of *R*. v. *Burgess* the decision was somewhat different. Here it was held that a person (in this case a man called Burgess) who, while sleepwalking, acted violently without being consciously aware of what he was doing was suffering from a *disease of the mind* and not from non-insane automatism and so could be found not guilty of the offence by reason of insanity. At his trial, Burgess had admitted attacking a sleeping female friend by hitting her on the head with a bottle and grasping her round the throat. He said that he, too, had fallen asleep and was sleepwalking. Such apparently contradictory cases are not uncommon and the law is in obvious need of clarification. One recent improvement is that a finding of insanity does not now result in automatic detention in hospital.

ABNORMAL MENTAL STATES AND CRIME

Intoxication

Some of the clinical aspects of the relationship between alcohol, other substances of abuse, and criminality are dealt with in Chapter 4. I am concerned here solely with the legal implications of that relationship.

It is not uncommon in criminal cases, particularly those involving serious violence against persons or property, for a plea to be made by the accused that their liability should be diminished because of the effects of taking alcohol and/or other substances. In general, the law holds that being in a state of intoxication is no defence to crime; however, if the offence requires what lawyers call 'specific intent (such as that which would be required to fulfil the legal requirements for a finding of guilt on a charge of murder), the fact that the accused had been drinking might help to negate that intent and thus might provide a defence. Other examples of crimes requiring specific intent are theft, fraud and burglary (see, for example, the cases of *R*. v. *Burns*, 1973, and *R*. v. *Stephenson*, 1979). However, various legal decisions and interpretations on this matter appear to give evidence of some conflict of opinion. For example, in the case of *Bratty* already referred to, it was held that in crimes such as murder, where proof of a specific intent was required, the intent might be negated by drunkenness and the accused might thus be convicted of a lesser charge, for example manslaughter or even unlawful wounding.

However, the issue is not always quite so clear-cut. In the case of *R*. v. *Gittens* (1984) the appellant had been tried on counts of murder of his wife and the rape and murder of his fifteen-year-old step-daughter. An issue arose as to whether his admitted abnormality of mind which substantially impaired his 'mental responsibility' was caused by the drink or the drugs he had taken, as the prosecution contended, or whether it was due to *inherent* causes *coupled with the ingestion of drugs and drink*, as the defence contended. The jury had been directed to decide whether it was, on the one hand, the *drink and drugs* or, on the other, *the inherent causes* which were the main factors which caused him to act as he did. He was convicted of murder but appealed on the grounds that the jury had been misdirected in that the proper question for them was whether the abnormality arising from the inherent causes substantially impaired his responsibility for his actions. His appeal was upheld and his conviction for murder substituted by a Section 2 Homicide Act 1957 conviction for manslaughter. The former Lord Chief Justice, Lord Lane, giving judgment, said that it was improper in *any circumstances* to invite the jury to decide the question of diminished responsibility on the basis of 'what was the substantial cause of the defendant's behaviour'? The jury were to be directed, first, to disregard what they thought the effect on the defendant of the alcohol- and drug-induced mental abnormality was, since discussion of such abnormality was *not* within Section 2(1). They were *then* to go on to consider whether the combined effect of *other matters* which *did* fall within Section 2(1) amounted to such abnormality of mind as substantially impaired his mental responsibility within the meaning of substantial as set out in *R*. v. *Lloyd* (1967). This being so in this case, the jury, said Lord Lane, had been misdirected.[4]

In the case of *R*. v. *Lipman* (1970), the accused claimed successfully that he was under the influence of lysergic acid diethylamide (LSD) when he killed the girl he was sleeping with. Part of Lipman's defence consisted of the claim that as a result of his being in a drug-induced state he thought that he was being attacked by snakes; the immediate cause of his unlucky companion's death was asphyxia caused by having part of a sheet stuffed into her mouth. However, in the famous case of *R*. v. *Majewski* (1977) the House of Lords held that, in the case of an impulsive act such as an assault, intoxication of itself would not constitute a defence. It was alleged that Majewski had been a drug addict and that he also had a personality disorder. He had been drinking heavily on the day in question and had mixed alcohol with quantities of sodium nembutal and dexadrine. Having ingested what must have amounted to a highly lethal cocktail, Majewski became involved in a fracas in a pub in the course of which he assaulted the landlord and another customer. Having been removed from the premises, he returned, brandishing a piece of broken glass (Hall Williams, 1980). The case of Majewski tends to support the view that the law sees the ingestion of alcohol and other drugs as an aggravating rather than as a mitigating factor and that voluntary intoxication is no defence. However, if an accused could show that he or she was in a state of *involuntary* intoxication, he or she may have a defence, where, for example, the accused had been deliberately drugged or had had intoxicants poured into a non-intoxicating beverage without his or her knowledge. Such a form of defence in crimes requiring evidence of specific intent will not be likely to succeed if an accused takes alcohol against medical advice after using prescribed drugs or, for example, if he or she fails to take insulin for a diabetic condition. Mackay has drawn attention to the not infrequent contradictory interpretation of the law in such cases. He says, 'the tainting effect of intoxication has already gone too far and deserves to be fully reviewed by the courts at the earliest opportunity' (Mackay, 1980: 48).

Finally, Rix has introduced the proposal that we should make a distinction between intoxication and drunkenness. Such a clinical distinction would have interesting and potentially useful legal implications. He proposes that:

(1) the term 'alcohol intoxication' should refer to a state in which alcohol is present in the body; (2) its diagnosis should be based on toxicological evidence for the presence of alcohol in body fluids or tissues; and (3) the term 'drunkenness' should be used to describe behaviour displayed by people who have consumed, believe that they have consumed or want others to believe they have consumed, alcohol.

(Rix, 1989: 100)

Provocation

Section 3 of the Homicide Act 1957 provides for a manslaughter verdict on the grounds of provocation. It is not normally possible to 'run' defences under both Sections 2 and 3. This is because, as we shall see, Section 2 presupposes that a degree of mental derangement and abnormal behaviour will be established; in Section 3 a more 'normal' reaction might perhaps be presupposed. However, it is not hard to see that a person suffering from a degree of mental abnormality might be more easily provoked than the average person. Despite this, in cases where abnormality is not being pleaded, psychiatric evidence has been held to be inadmissible (as, for example, in the cases of R. v. Chard, 1971 and R. v. Turner, 1975). In the latter case, Lord Justice Lawton said:

trial by psychiatrists would be likely to take the place of trial by jury and magistrates . . . psychiatry has not yet become a satisfactory substitute for the common sense of juries and magistrates on matters within their experience of life.
(quoted in Hall Williams, 1980: 279)

However, in many cases, the dividing line between those behaviours that can be regarded as 'normal' and those that can be regarded as abnormal may not be quite as clear-cut as Lord Justice Lawton suggested. Some support for this contention is afforded in a study by Dell. She found that, 'in few cases, the jury had found the defendant guilty on the grounds both of diminished responsibility and of provocation' (Dell, 1984: 4)

In recent times, other complicated issues have arisen. From a legal point of view it has been understood for many years that the events leading to an act carried out under circumstances of alleged provocation must be recent. In the case of R. v. Ahulwalia (1990) it was held by the Court of Appeal that a judge's direction to a jury on a murder trial, defining 'provocation' as conduct causing a 'sudden loss of self control' was in accordance with well established law and could not be faulted. If that law was wrong, it was for Parliament to change it, not the courts.

(It should be noted that the appellant won her appeal against a murder conviction on other grounds.)

Much concern has been expressed recently about the apparent arbitrary fashion in which acts of provocation have been defined. Those worried about the rights of 'battered women' have been concerned that years of assaultive behaviour by husbands or partners that is patiently borne by their victims may not constitute a situation of provocation that culminates in legitimate retaliation or defence. The fact that it appears to have to be a result of a *sudden* and *recent* incident of violent behaviour seems to be quite arbitrary. One has much sympathy with this view, and the courts sometimes seem to reach conflicting decisions. For example, at Belfast Crown Court a woman succeeded in her plea of provocation in respect of a charge of murdering her husband. She had stabbed him to death after she had 'snapped' during a drunken row. The judge is stated to have told her: 'I am satisfied that what caused you to snap was not just one evening's ill treatment but the accumulation of six years' abuse (cf. the case of Ahluwalia above). He placed her on probation (*Independent*, 2 February 1993: 5). Another recent case concerned a 'devoted father who battered and strangled his unfaithful wife'. He was said to have 'snapped after years of humiliation at the hands of his wife'. The judge is said to have told him: 'I have never before encountered a more extreme case of *persistent* provocation [my emphasis] or degrading behaviour by a woman towards a man . . . you were goaded beyond anyone's breaking point' (*Independent*, 6 April 1993: 3). Clearly some clarification of the law is required if we are not to witness these and a number of other apparently conflicting judgments.

Unfitness to plead (being 'under disability')

We saw earlier how the provisions and implementation of the 'special verdict' arise in cases where it has been shown that a defendant was seen to be very seriously mentally disordered at the time of *committing the offence*. We now have to consider the situation if an accused is said to be suffering from mental disorder at the time of the *trial*. By tradition, and in accordance with English justice, a court has to be satisfied that accused persons can, first, understand the charges against them, second, exercise their right to challenge a juror, third, follow the evidence against them and, fourth, instruct counsel in their defence. If the accused is considered to be unable to put the foregoing into effect, he or she has customarily been held to be 'unfit to plead' or, to use the term now favoured, to be 'under disability in relation to the trial' ('under disability' for short). (Cases of deaf-mutism may also occur rarely. Very occasionally a person may also be deemed to be 'mute of malice'. I am not considering such cases here.)

The issue of unfitness to plead is raised fairly infrequently; mainly because a person has to be very seriously disabled psychiatrically in order to satisfy the relevant criteria. I have, however, come across a few examples in my own work. The first concerned a man who was suffering from such serious psychotic delusions that in the course of them he killed his wife. He was still severely psychiatrically deluded at the time of his trial and subsequently. The second case concerned a young man who was found to be so impaired in intelligence and understanding that he, too, was found unfit to plead. A third case concerned a man who, while in the grip of severe psychotic delusions, attacked a near relative. Mackay found some 302 'disability' cases for the fourteen-year period 1976–89 (269 males and 33 females). From about 1982 onwards the numbers showed a gradual decline – with eleven cases only in the final year surveyed (Mackay, 1991a: 2–3).

Until fairly recently the only disposal available on a finding of 'disability' was committal to a psychiatric hospital. This might be for a considerable period of time and the *facts* of the case might never be determined. It is possible (and in some cases even probable) that someone found to be under disability might well have had a defence to the charges if they had been put to the test in court. As long ago as 1975 the Butler Committee was unhappy about the arrangements in force (Home Office and DHSS, 1975). In recent years a momentum for change has been growing. As a result of parliamentary and other pressures the law has now been changed, allowing not only more flexible disposals but the facts of the case to be determined speedily. The main provisions of the Criminal Procedure (Insanity and Unfitness to Plead) Act 1991, which came into force on 1 January 1992, are contained in Section 3. They may be summarised as follows:

1 Where a person is found not guilty by reason of insanity or found to be under disability (unfit to plead) a Crown or Appeal Court will no longer be bound to order detention in hospital under a restriction order within the terms of the Mental Health Act 1983 (Sections 37/41), *except in murder cases*.
2 The following disposals are now available:
   (a) an order for admission to hospital (an 'admission order') with the option of an added restriction order;
   (b) a Guardianship Order under Section 37 of the Mental Health Act;
   (c) an order for supervision and treatment. In effect this will be much like a probation order with a requirement for medical treatment under Section 3 of the Powers of the Criminal Courts Act 1973 – as amended by Sections 8 and 9 and Schedule 1 of the Criminal Justice Act 1991. Supervision will be effected by either the probation or social services and the order will be for two years. The accused will also be required to be under the care of a registered medical practitioner. However, in the event of non-compliance by the accused there are no penal sanctions for a return to court or revocation of the order.
   (d) An order for absolute discharge.

Other provisions

Other provisions of interest include the requirement for medical evidence to be given by two registered medical practitioners, at least one of whom must be approved under Section 12 of the Mental Health Act 1983. It may come as a surprise to some readers that the old legislation did not carry such a requirement for the court to consider psychiatric or other medical evidence. No doubt this was a 'throw-back' to the days when laypeople were called in cases of an insanity or similar defence to give evidence as to the accused person's state of mind. The new legislation also provides – in cases of unfitness to plead – for a speedy jury trial of the facts and a requirement for a finding based upon them.

These new provisions go a long way to meet the criticisms of the old legislation (see Prins, 1992). It will be interesting to see what effect they have on the numbers of persons pleading insanity or unfitness to plead in future. As already noted, the inflexibility of the previous legislation led to the provisions being rarely used. A prospective long-term study being undertaken by my colleague Professor R.D. Mackay of De Montfort University, Leicester, may well provide some interesting information on the matter.

Diminished responsibility

The term 'diminished responsibility' is used here in the special technical sense of the Homicide Act 1957. Section 2 of the Act states that

> Where a person kills or is party to the killing of another, he shall not be convicted of murder if he was suffering from such abnormality of mind (whether arising from a condition of arrested or retarded development of mind or any inherent causes or induced by disease or injury) as substantially impaired his mental responsibility for his acts or omissions in doing or being party to the killing.

It will be seen that the Section permits the recognition of a degree of partial responsibility (liability). A plea of diminished responsibility may be raised by the accused, and, if contested, will be decided by a jury 'on the balance of probabilities'. This test is somewhat less strict than the 'beyond all reasonable doubt' burden of proof required in most criminal trials. As already noted, the number of cases in which diminished responsibility has been pleaded and the number of hospital disposals in these cases have been diminishing in recent years (Dell, 1983; Dell and Smith, 1983). In a later contribution Dell suggested three main reasons for this change in sentencing practice. I paraphrase her remarks as follows:

1 Increasing difficulty in obtaining places for these particular offenders in the Special Hospitals. This difficulty has been closely associated with an increase in the reluctance of psychiatric staff to consider as treatable those suffering from psychopathic disorder.

2 A reluctance on the part of psychiatrists to recommend placement in an ordinary psychiatric hospital. It is suggested that, because of the factors outlined above, judges have no alternative but to send those considered to be psychopathic to prison.

3 For those suffering from other and more treatable conditions – such as depressive illness – Dell's research suggests that the decision to award custodial as distinct from hospital disposals is likely to have been due to retributive sentencing on the part of the judiciary (Dell, 1984: 14–24).

In addition to these problems of disposal, the wording of the Act itself has caused serious difficulties; some of these will be the subject of comment in the case illustrations to be considered shortly. As Samuels has pointed out, 'the notion of impaired responsibility, substantially impaired responsibility, is difficult to grasp. Can there be degrees of responsibility?' (Samuels, 1975: 198). Since an important decision in the case of *R.* v. *Byrne* (1960), the issue of responsibility has clearly been one for the jury to decide. However, it is not an uncommon experience for psychiatrists to be asked whether or not *they* consider responsibility to be impaired. In many instances they have been prepared to answer such questions in an attempt to help the judiciary resolve difficult questions in sentencing, but the question is not, however, psychiatric, but fundamentally one of law and morality. Moreover, it appears from a recent decision (*R.* v. *Vernege*, 1982) that a jury is not bound to accept the psychiatric evidence that responsibility is substantially diminished, even if there is unanimous psychiatric opinion to that effect; as we shall see later, this was certainly the case in *R.* v. *Sutcliffe* (1981) (see also Prins, 1983; Hall Williams, 1980; Spencer, 1984).

Returning to our discussion of semantics, we may ask ourselves: what interpretation should be given to the term 'abnormality of mind'? Two aspects of this question may be discerned. First, whether or not an abnormality of mind existed, and, second, whether it affected the defendant's 'mental responsibility' for his or her actions. The late John Hamilton, an experienced forensic psychiatrist and one-time Medical Director of Broadmoor Special Hospital, gave support to the view of Samuels (1975) and others when he asked: 'What on earth does [mental responsibility] mean?' (1981: 434); and, as already suggested, are psychiatrists necessarily the most appropriate persons to give such opinions? Kahn, a general psychiatrist, once posed the dilemma for psychiatrists in these matters very well:

In deviation from the normal, particularly where behaviour is concerned, there may not necessarily be a medical contribution at all. The treatment may be purely legal or social action. The aim is to bring the behaviour into conformity . . . the psychiatrist comes into the study of some human problems only by invitation, and this invitation may not be wholehearted. It is as if the psychiatrist is expected to claim authority in every problem of living, only to have that claim challenged even while his help is being sought.

(1971: 230)

Thus, even before specific matters of motivation and its interpretation are raised and challenged under our adversarial system of justice, there seems to be, as Kahn suggests, a fundamental ambivalence to be overcome. Aspects of this ambivalence are well attested to in a seminal paper by Kenny. He begins his contribution with an incisive discussion of the case of Hinckley, who attempted to assassinate President Reagan. He makes some trenchant observations about the role of expert witnesses, particularly psychiatrists:

> The law should be reformed by changing statutes which force expert witnesses to testify beyond their science, by taking the provision of expert evidence out of the adversarial context, and by removing from the courts the decisions whether a nascent discipline is or it not a science.
>
> (Kenny, 1984: 291)

Brief reference has already been made to the notion of an 'abnormality of mind'. In the case of Byrne – a sexual psychopath already referred to – Lord Parker, then Lord Chief Justice, described abnormality of mind and its legal implications in the following terms:

> Inability to exercise will-power to control physical acts, provided that it is due to abnormality of mind from one of the causes specified [i.e. in the Homicide Act] is sufficient to entitle the accused to the benefit of the [defence]; difficulty in controlling his physical acts depending on the degree of difficulty may be. *It is for the jury to decide on the whole of the evidence* whether such inability or difficulty has, not as a matter of scientific certainty, *but on the balance of probabilities* been established, and in the case of difficulty is so great as to amount in their view to *substantial* impairment of the accused's mental responsibility for his acts.'
>
> (*R*. v. *Byrne*, 1960; emphasis added)

Four further points emerge from this statement. First, such a definition reinforces the much wider interpretation of mental disorder than that within the narrow confines of the M'Naghten 'rules' referred to earlier. Second, it seems to acknowledge that will-power can be impaired, introducing to some extent the American concept of 'irresistible impulse' – a concept not popular hitherto with English jurists. Third, we can draw the inference that the judiciary could permit the view that the mind can be answerable for behaviour. Fourth, the question of *substantial* impairment was also a matter for the jury to decide, but *how* it arose and its *causes* were questions for the doctors. As to the meaning of 'substantial', it has been held subsequently that '"substantial" does not mean total . . . the mental responsibility need not be totally impaired, destroyed altogether. At the other end of the scale, substantial does not mean trivial or minimal' (*R*. v. *Lloyd*, 1967). In order to illustrate further some of the problems that have been already alluded to, I now use the cases of Sutcliffe, Nilsen, Telling and, more recently, Dahmer.

Example 1: Peter Sutcliffe

The case of Peter Sutcliffe attracted such notoriety that some of the key issues concerning the diminishment or otherwise of his 'mental responsibility for his acts' have tended to be overshadowed by the horrendous nature of his crimes and the furore surrounding the circumstances of his detection and eventual arrest (see, for example, Prins, 1983; Burn, 1984). However, Sutcliffe's case, together with those of Dennis Nilsen, Michael Telling and Jeffrey Dahmer, highlights, in compelling fashion, many of the issues I have sought to address in the last few pages of this chapter. A court will frequently accept a plea of diminished responsibility on the basis of agreed and uncontested psychiatric evidence: that is, the psychiatrists for the prosecution and for the defence are all agreed on the diagnosis.[5] It will be recalled that the issue of diminished responsibility is raised by the defence and that its proof rests on a *balance of probabilities*. And, as already indicated, if such a plea is accepted by the judge (in a non-contested case) or by a jury (after a trial of the issue) a person who would otherwise have been liable to conviction for murder will be convicted of manslaughter with a wide range of options available as to sentence.

As is now well known, the trial judge in Sutcliffe's case – Mr Justice Boreham – refused (as was his right) to accept the agreed views of both prosecution and defence and decided to put the issue of Sutcliffe's mental responsibility for his acts to a jury. It is important to ask why this very experienced judge embarked upon this particular course of action when four highly experienced senior psychiatrists were all agreed on Sutcliffe's disordered mental state.

There are a number of possibilities. First, although a plea of Section 2 diminished responsibility is only available in a murder case, the judge may have been very conscious of the fact that the public might have considered it to be a somewhat contradictory and idiosyncratic state of affairs that allowed Sutcliffe to plead *guilty* to the *attempted murder* of seven women and *not guilty* to the murder of thirteen (when the fact that he had actually *committed* the murders was not being disputed – merely his criminal responsibility for so doing). To the general public (but not of course to the legally informed) it might have seemed somewhat disturbing that such pleas were acceptable when, presumably, only good fortune saved the lives of seven of his victims. Hence, the judge might well have considered that 'public interest' demanded that the issues involved be made absolutely clear.

Second, the judge would no doubt have been very conscious of the public's more general concern about the case and the notoriety attaching to it. It might have seemed to him to have been doing both the case and the public less than full justice to have disposed of it without a full public inquiry into the defendant's alleged motivation and mental state.

Third, the judge, having read the papers relative to the case beforehand, might well have wondered at the apparent discrepancies between what

Sutcliffe was alleged to have told the police in the course of their prolonged interviews with him, what he was alleged to have confided to the prison officers and what he told the psychiatrists who examined him. (See Spencer, 1984: 106–113 for a full discussion of some of these issues.)

Fourth, the judge would no doubt have considered the possibility of putting the case to a jury in the knowledge that, following a finding of guilty to *murder*, he could not only pass a life sentence, but could also add *a recommendation as to what the minimum sentence should be*, by virtue of Section 1(2) of the Murder (Abolition of Death Penalty) Act 1965. This possibility would not be available to him in a finding of Section 2 manslaughter. A sentence of imprisonment would also keep control over his eventual release within the penal system, even if he were subsequently transferred to hospital while serving his sentence.

For all these reasons, the judge's decision seems very understandable, though the final outcome of indefinite detention in hospital or prison could have been predicted.

According to media accounts of the trial we had the somewhat unusual (some would say undignified) spectacle of all the psychiatric witnesses being cross-examined by the prosecution – including their own – when only a few hours before all parties in the case had been agreed on the course of action that should be taken. The manner in which the psychiatric evidence was received and commented upon in the media (notably the press) during the trial revealed very clearly the ambivalence of society towards the intervention of psychiatry in matters of criminal behaviour that I referred to earlier. This ambivalence is of course compounded by the fact that our adversarial system of justice does not lend itself comfortably to the discussion and deliberation of complex and finely drawn issues of intent and motivation. Psychiatrists, in their day-to-day practice, are accustomed to dealing with grey areas of motivation and far less with the black and white issues of fact demanded by the constraints of our system of criminal law. Some people have suggested that the psychiatrists could have made a better showing in court. They were certainly subjected to a good deal of criticism, if not ridicule. On going over the various press accounts of the case, much of this appears to have been ill-founded, given the constraints already referred to and the fact that reporting can be highly selective. It is quite likely that some of the statements imputed to the psychiatric witnesses, like 'he had diagnosed schizophrenia in a quarter of an hour', were made within the context of more detailed statements and further qualified in some way. (See Prins, 1983, and in particular the notes referred to therein for reference to the press accounts.)

Although I shall be considering the relationship between mental disorder and criminality in Chapter 4, it is appropriate at this point to make brief comment about the relationship between some forms of schizophrenia and crime, since a type of schizophrenic illness was the diagnosis the psychiatrists gave to Sutcliffe's condition.

We can say that the relationship between schizophrenia and crime in general is very slight and not often *causally* associated. However, the *particular* diagnosis given for Sutcliffe's disorder was *paranoid* schizophrenia. This disorder is characterised to a large extent (but not exclusively) by delusions. There are a number of well-documented cases concerning persons who have committed homicide and other serious offences whilst under the influence of these, the most well known probably being the case of Daniel M'Naghten already referred to.

The most important point to remember about the paranoid disorders (and their variants) is that individuals are likely to appear quite sane and intelligent in all other aspects of their lives. It is only when the actual subject matter of their delusional belief is touched upon that their symptoms may emerge with unexpected and frightening impact. It is not altogether surprising, therefore, that Sutcliffe was able to cover his tracks, because one can be highly paranoid yet also be highly evasive and cunning. And as already indicated, the individual's delusional system may be so well excapsulated that it may not emerge until and unless the matters upon which the system has fastened are explored in a detailed and systematic examination by a skilled psychiatric assessor. It is therefore not to be wondered at that the police and prison officers obtained one impression of Sutcliffe and the psychiatrists another; much depends upon the questions one asks and the manner and skill with which one asks them.

At the time of his trial other diagnoses of Sutcliffe's disorder seem to have been ruled out. We know that he is alleged to have suffered a head injury at some point. In some instances, if head injuries are serious enough to result in brain damage, they can produce delusional symptoms (as in the case of Hadfield referred to earlier). Neither does a diagnosis of psychopathic disorder appear to have been entertained. Given his past history, background and apparent long-standing paranoid ideation, such a diagnosis would seem unlikely. An unequivocal diagnosis of paranoid schizophrenia does not seem to be without its difficulties either, given Sutcliffe's conflicting statements and his apparent capacity for acting with insight in order to avoid detection. Spencer suggests that

> In his *apparent* simulation of insanity, his alleged and God-inspired delusions and the sadistic undertones of his killings, Sutcliffe falls exactly halfway between the murderers John George Haigh and Neville Health.
>
> (1984: 112–13); emphasis added)

Spencer also suggests that a better defence for Sutcliffe might have been that he suffered

> from a clear-cut abnormality of mind of a strangely paranoid type. Starting in 1969 with an unexplained attack on a prostitute and enhanced in 1979 by trivial humiliation, it developed into a bizarre, homicidal hatred of women, particularly prostitutes or alleged prostitutes. It continued with a strongly

sadistic overtone and possibly – perhaps probably – as the result of a low-grade schizophrenic process. Whether or not the basis was schizophrenic, there was surely substantially more than minimal or trivial diminishment of responsibility?

(1984: 113)

The rest of the story is well known. The jury, with its 10–2 majority verdict, found Sutcliffe guilty of murder. It is important to emphasise that in doing so they did not necessarily reject the argument that Sutcliffe was suffering from a form of paranoid schizophrenia, only that it did *not constitute an abnormality of mind of sufficient degree to substantially impair his mental responsibility for his acts*. He was sentenced to life imprisonment and Mr Justice Boreham made a recommendation that he serve a minimum of thirty years. Almost exactly a year later – on 25 May 1982 – he was refused leave to appeal. However, subsequent events seem to have vindicated the views of the psychiatrists. Sutcliffe's mental condition deteriorated steadily in prison, where not only did his delusions become much more severe, but he was also the victim of a serious assault by a fellow prisoner. Despite the increasing severity of his symptoms, his vulnerability to attack and the difficulty his management posed for the prison medical authorities, it was not until the end of March 1984 that the Home Secretary signed the necessary documents under the Mental Health Act to give effect to Sutcliffe's transfer to a high security hospital. Such a transfer order had been supported by the statutorily required psychiatric evidence of two very experienced doctors as long ago as 1982 (*Guardian*, 28 March 1984). No doubt the Home Secretary of the day considered that the public had by now had its pound of flesh and such a move – although three years too late – was now unlikely to be politically embarrassing.

The outcome of the Sutcliffe case demonstrates very clearly the unsatisfactory nature of the diminished responsibility defence. It supports the arguments of those who wish to see the abolition of the mandatory life sentence for murder, a move that at the time of writing was being given further consideration by the Home Secretary (subsequently rejected). It also demonstrates the establishment's somewhat cautious approach and apparent lack of courage in effecting humane disposals unless they are thought to be politically expedient.

Example 2: Dennis Nilsen

In 1983 very similar problems were to emerge in the almost equally notorious case of Dennis Nilsen. Nilsen admitted to killing fifteen young men and dissecting, boiling and burning their bodies in order to dispose of them. He was sentenced to life imprisonment, the judge adding a minimum recommendation that he serve twenty-five years. The jury had convicted him of murder by a majority verdict of 10–2 on all but one of the counts against him.

In the latter case they reached a unanimous verdict. In arguing for a manslaughter verdict Nilsen's counsel had tried to convince the jury that 'anybody guilty of such horrific acts must be out of his mind' (*The Times*, 5 November 1983). In Nilsen's case, unlike Sutcliffe's, there had been no unanimous prior agreement by the psychiatrists, nor was Nilsen's alleged mental disorder as floridly psychotic or akin to the layperson's notion of madness as was Sutcliffe's. Nilsen was said to be suffering from a severe personality disorder; he was also said to have suffered because of abnormal sexual development. The psychiatrists disagreed not only as to the nature of the diagnosis in his case, but also as to whether it constituted an abnormality of mind within the meaning of the Homicide Act. However, no-one reading the press accounts of Nilsen's life history, his crimes and his attitudes towards his victims could fail to agree that his behaviour was decidedly abnormal by any standards (*The Times*, 5 November 1983; *Guardian*, 5 November 1983). (For a sensitive lay attempt to explore Nilsen's motivation and background, see Masters, 1985.)

One of the key issues that emerges from Nilsen's case is similar to that which emerged in Sutcliffe's – namely the difficulty in fitting the inherently imprecise concepts used in psychiatry into the confining strait-jacket of the present law. However, there is an important difference between the two cases. Sutcliffe's disorder was one that might be improved by treatment, even if not completely cured. The most florid and intrusive features of his delusions could be treated and abated by medication to some extent. In Nilsen's case, his personality disorder, even it if had constituted an abnormality of mind, was considered to be largely untreatable so that a penal as opposed to a hospital disposal may seem only marginally less helpful. As I shall show in Chapter 5, some personality disorders *are* capable of minimal improvement – given the right approach and environment. It could be argued, at least hypothetically, that under prevailing conditions of prison overcrowding and lack of resources the penal disposal in Nilsen's case might not be particularly helpful.

Example 3: Michael Telling

On 29 June 1984 Michael Telling was jailed for life for the manslaughter of his second wife, Monika. Following a nine-day trial, he had been found guilty of manslaughter, but not of murder, by a *unanimous* jury verdict. It is of interest to note that the jury only took two and a half hours to reach their verdict. It was alleged that Telling had not really matured from the days when he was an extremely disturbed boy and that he had demonstrated a continuing marked lack of ability to control his impulses and emotions. (This description of lack of impulse control has aspects in common with those in the case of *R*. v. *Byrne* quoted earlier.)

The facts in Telling's case are, to some extent, only minimally less bizarre than those in Sutcliffe's and Nilsen's. Admittedly he had only committed one murder, but the circumstances of that single killing seem not only gruesome, but highly pathological. According to the press reports (*Guardian*, 30 June 1984), Telling shot his wife after she had allegedly taunted him beyond endurance with details concerning her sexual exploits with members of both sexes. After killing her, he moved her body around the house for a week or so, calling in occasionally to kiss and talk to the corpse as it lay on a camp-bed. He then placed the body in a half-built sauna in the house. Five months later he decided to take the body to Devon. Having tried unsuccessfully to bury it (the ground being too hard for digging because of the prolonged summer drought), he dumped it in some bracken overlooking the river Exe. He cut off the head and took it with him. It was subsequently found in the boot of his car. In Telling's case, two psychiatrists testified that Telling's responsibility was diminished and one testified against that view. It is difficult to tell whether the jury was more influenced by the opinions of the two psychiatrists who viewed him as suffering from a disorder that would diminish his responsibility, or whether it was his bizarre activities following the killing which led them to the view that he 'must have been mad' to have behaved in that fashion. Samuels has some very apt words on this latter point:

> If a defendant just kills his victim for what appears to be a very ordinary motive such as greed or jealousy, diminished responsibility stands little chance of being established, but if the defendant has a history of mental trouble, goes in for perverted sexual practices with the victim before and after death, *mutilates the body, cuts it up* [or] sends it through the post . . . then the more horrible the killing the more likely diminished responsibility will be established, because *the further removed from normal behaviour the behaviour of the defendant, the more he appears to be mentally ill*, or so the submission runs.
>
> (1975: 199–200; emphasis added)

Example 4: Jeffrey Dahmer

Although Jeffrey Dahmer committed his numerous murders in the USA and was dealt with by the American criminal justice system, his case has certain points in common with that of Dennis Nilsen. One of these was the attempt by his defence counsel to satisfy the court that his responsibility for his crimes was diminished by an abnormality of mind. In Dahmer's case a defence of insanity had to be entered, because in the USA there is no exact equivalent of our Homicide Act. However, the relevant state statute contains reference to a lack of 'substantial capacity to appreciate the wrongfulness of his conduct or conform his conduct to the requirements of the law' (Masters, 1993: 227).

Dahmer's long career of killing ended by chance (as had Sutcliffe's) when he was apprehended on another matter by two Milwaukee police patrolmen.

On going to his apartment they were confronted by a gruesome collection of polaroid pictures of dead males, severed heads and partially dismembered torsos. Later, the police were to discover more tangible evidence – a refrigerator containing a severed head, a freezer containing two more heads and a human torso. Two skulls and a complete skeleton were found in a filing cabinet, as was a large plastic drum containing three further torsos in various stages of decomposition. Following his arrest, and for the ensuing two weeks, Dahmer confessed 'that he had killed sixteen men in Milwaukee over a period of four years' (Masters, 1993: 4).

To the outside world, Dahmer was a quiet, inoffensive factory worker. It is of interest to note that he had been the subject of investigation at one stage for unwelcome acts of indecency with males in a 'bath house'. However, the proprietors are said not to have wished for the matter to be taken further on account of the adverse publicity it might have occasioned. It is also of concern to note that on another occasion he had been convicted of a sexual assault, and that while awaiting sentence he had committed his fifth murder. With hindsight, it would seem that he had already given indications of his sinister preoccupation with deviant sexuality and with death. From his history it emerges that he had an overpowering need to possess and control his victims – to the point of collecting and storing their remains after death. Some would see this as a variant of necrophilia.

As in Nilsen's case, Dahmer's advocate sought to convince the court that a person who indulged in such compulsive behaviour must be mad rather than merely bad, that he could in fact 'retain a perfectly clear idea of what is right and good and still be compelled to do what is wrong and bad' (Masters, 1993: 88). An impressive array of psychiatric witnesses gave evidence (seven gave evidence, eight had examined him). Much play was made of his long-standing sexual problems, prolonged alcohol abuse and difficulties in making social relationships with both males and females. Despite the expert evidence, his plea failed. The jury retired on Friday, 14 February 1992 and returned earlier than anticipated, with their verdicts (majority verdicts of 10–2 on five of the counts) on Saturday 15 February. He was sentenced to life imprisonment with no eligibility for parole before seventy years. He was subsequently killed in prison.

From the foregoing four accounts it is not difficult to see the problems involved in reconciling the disciplines of law and psychiatry. There are, of course, other and somewhat less notorious cases that have posed the same dilemmas and questions. I shall refer to some of these inconsistencies in my concluding observations, but, before doing so, brief reference is made to the offence of infanticide and to the pleading of mental states in mitigation.

Infanticide

Apart from the Homicide Act, the law makes *specific* provision for the erosion of responsibility in cases of killing in one other way. This is through the Infanticide

Act 1938. This enactment (which amended an earlier Act of 1922, which in turn had revised much earlier legislation) was introduced in order to relieve women from the death sentence for murder who, under certain specific circumstances, had caused the death of their children. The judges felt a great deal of reluctance about having to pass a death sentence in such cases (Bluglass, 1990). In the context of this chapter, its creation is of interest in that it gave statutory recognition to a *specific state of mind* in a woman who caused, by any wilful act or omission, the death of her child *under the age of twelve months* when the balance of her mind was disturbed by reason of her not having fully recovered from the *effect of giving birth to a child, or by reason of the effect of lactation consequent upon that birth*. The Act was passed at a time when more emphasis was placed upon what were thought to be the adverse effects of childbirth upon a woman's *mental state* than would perhaps be considered relevant today.

When one examines those cases currently prosecuted (an average of six per year for the period 1980–90; Home Office, 1992: 121) there are nearly always significant factors operating in addition to psychiatric disorder following the birth. For example, adverse social conditions or a severely stressful and complex personal situation that would more likely than not enable the case to be dealt with under the provisions of the Homicide Act. A recently reported case illustrates the points well:

A woman killed her four-year-old daughter shortly after the latter witnessed her mother killing her seventeen-month-old baby brother by strangulation. In this case the prosecution accepted pleas of diminished responsibility and the woman was discharged on condition that she receive hospital treatment. Defending counsel said that the woman had experienced a slow build-up of pressure and had suffered a depressive disorder from the birth of her son. In theory, had she killed this child within the first twelve months of his life instead of at seventeen months, she could have been charged with infanticide as well perhaps as being charged with the murder of the four year old.

(*Guardian*, 27 November 1984: 5)

This case highlights the somewhat outmoded and arbitrary nature of the infanticide defence. The Butler Committee proposed that the offence itself could be subsumed under the defence of diminished responsibility and this seems sound (Home Office and DHSS, 1975: paras 19–26), but the Criminal Law Revision Committee favoured its retention (1980: paras 100–104: 114: 1). It seems to me that the fewer unnecessary 'special defences' there are the better.

Pleading mental state in mitigation of penalty

In the previous pages I have considered the various ways in which a person's mental state may be proffered as a specific defence in criminal proceedings. In other less specific situations it is of course always open to a court to receive psychiatric and/or other medical evidence that may be taken into account in mitigation of penalty. Courts do not seek psychiatric advice in a large number of cases. Research shows that overall they do so in about 5 per cent of cases, though naturally the decision to ask for or proffer reports will depend heavily upon the type of offence and the circumstances of the individual defendant (see Craft, 1984; Gibbens *et al.*, 1977; Mackay, 1986; Prins, 1980; Soothill *et al.*, 1983; Sparks, 1966). When a clear recommendation is made by a psychiatrist for a medical disposal, courts tend to follow this advice in almost all cases, though of course they are not obliged to do so. Requests for psychiatric reports will come from a variety of sources: from the bench itself, from advocates, from probation officers and other social workers and occasionally from the police or Crown Prosecution Service. The manner in which these reports may be obtained is discussed in the next chapter.

CONCLUSION

In this somewhat discursive chapter I have tried to illustrate a number of situations and cases in which those accused of crime (and, in particular, serious crime) may proffer a disturbed or abnormal mental state in exculpation of liability to be dealt with as an ordinary offender, that is, as absolving them wholly or partly from criminal liability. These measures may be summarised briefly. First, there is the specific defence of insanity, which, if successful, will result in the 'special verdict' of not guilty by reason of insanity. Second, there is the defence of being unfit to plead (being under disability in relation to the trial). Third, there is the plea of diminished responsibility in homicide cases only. Fourth, there is the special case of infanticide. Fifth, there is the more general opportunity to plead mental disorder or disturbance in mitigation of penalty.

In attempting to deal with a complex topic, I have had to take a number of short cuts and to give insufficiently detailed attention to some important legal, ethical, philosophical and psychiatric concepts. The law is complicated not only because it has evolved slowly over time in relation to a wide range of cases, but also because concepts of mind, of disease and of culpability have not evolved in a natural and uniform sequence. For example, developments in medicine, psychology and psychiatry have affected the way in which personal responsibility for behaviour has to be viewed today compared with a hundred and fifty years ago. In addition, public attitudes to those who practise the art and science of medicine, particularly psychiatry, affect the climate of opinion in which these practitioners, judges and lawyers play out their roles within the arena of the court.

To some, the law appears to be unnecessarily complicated. For example, proposals to adopt the French concept of *demence* (as in the Code Napoléon) find favour with some critics (for example, Fitzgerald, 1981). The adoption of this concept would provide quite simply that where an accused was suffering from *demence* he or she could be deemed to be not capable of crime and exculpated from all liability. (This would apply in particular to cases now dealt with under the M'Naghten ruling and those found to be 'under disability'.) The Butler

Committee made a not wholly dissimilar proposal in relation to diminished responsibility (Home Office and DHSS, 1975). They suggested that if the mandatory life sentence for murder was to be abolished, the defence of diminished responsibility (with all the complexities and contradictions and ambiguities illustrated in the Sutcliffe, Nilsen, Telling and Dahmer cases) would be obsolete; the judge could then exercise the widest possible discretion in sentencing. Failing abolition, the Committee recommended a rewording of Section 2 of the Homicide Act. This would be to the effect that if the defendant was found to have a mental disorder (as defined by the [then] Mental Health Act 1959) that was such as to be an extenuating circumstance, then the charge could be reduced to manslaughter. However, the Criminal Law Revision Committee (1980) and Bluglass (1980) have pointed out that offences currently dealt with as cases of diminished responsibility would be excluded unless a wider interpretation of mental illness (undefined in the Mental Health Act) was to be allowed.

Dell has put the case for change very powerfully:

> if the mandatory life sentence for murder was abolished, there would be an end to the stretching and manoeuvres which have now to be undertaken in order to give homicides suitable, instead of unsuitable, sentences. Not only the defendant, but judges, doctors and lawyers would benefit from the change.

> (1984: 60)

Zeegers has highlighted some of the more positive elements in notions of diminished responsibility.

> Our far from perfect society, with imperfect laws, imperfect courts, imperfect ways of handling drop-outs, imperfect social care, imperfect people and imperfect knowledge of the human mind, should be very careful and reserved in its verdict. Applying penal law means an appeal to us all, to acknowledge *our* responsibility. A healthy society ought to accept responsibility, and ought to show concern towards its members, especially to those who prove to be not mentally able to cope.

> (1981: 444)

It seems to me that some of the reforms suggested in this chapter would go some way towards establishing that sense of community, responsibility and humaneness that Zeegers evokes in the above passage.

With this important message in mind we can now proceed to Chapter 3, in which I provide an account of the main disposals available to the courts for those adjudged to be mentally disturbed in a variety of ways and the methods through which these disposals are implemented. It is important to emphasise here the need to view the information presented in this book *as a whole*. The material has been divided in somewhat arbitrary fashion in an attempt to achieve clarity of presentation.

NOTES

1   Unless stated to the contrary, the law is that in force in England and Wales.
2   The spelling of his name has varied considerably over the years. I have used that favoured currently. (For a fascinating account of his case, see West and Walk, 1977.)
3   There are two, virtually obsolete, exceptions to the abolition of the death penalty: theoretically it would still be possible to face it for 'Piracy with violence' or 'high treason'. Until the Criminal Damage Act 1971, arson in the Royal Dockyards was also punishable with the death penalty.
4   I am grateful to my daughter – Miss Helen E. Prins, LLB, Solicitor – for drawing this case to my attention.
5   Acceptance by the courts of pleas of diminished responsibility on *agreed* psychiatric evidence has only occurred since 1962. Between 1957 and 1962 (following the decision in *R*. v. *Matheson* in 1958) the issue had to be put to a jury in all cases (Bartholomew, 1983).

REFERENCES

Cases cited

Bratty v. *Attorney General for Northern Ireland* [1963] AC 386.
Hill v. *Baxter* [1958] 1 QB 277.
Kay v. *Butterworth* [1945] 173 LT 191.
R. v. *Ahulwalia* [1992] *Independent* Law Report, 4 August: 7.
R. v. *Burgess* [1991] *Independent* Law Report, 27 March: 9.
R. v. *Burns* [1973] 58 Cr. App. R. 364.
R. v. *Byrne* [1960] 2 QB 396–455.
R. v. *Chard* [1971] 56 Cr. App. R. 268.
R. v. *Charlson* [1955] 1 All ER 859.
R. v. *Gittens* [1984] *Law Society Gazette*, 5 September.
R. v. *Kemp* [1957] 1 QB 399.
R. v. *Lipman* [1970] 1 QB 152.
R. v. *Lloyd* [1967] 1 QB 175–181.
R. v. *Majewski* [1977] AC 443.
R. v. *Matheson* [1958] 42 Cr. App. R. 154 1 WLR 474.
R. v. *Quick* [1973] QB 910 and 3 WLR 26.
R. v. *Robertson* [1968] 3 All ER 557.
R. v. *Stephenson* [1979] 3 WLR 193.
R. v. *Sullivan* [1984] 3 WLR 123.
R. v. *Sutcliffe* (*The Times* and *Guardian*, May 1981).
R. v. *Turner* [1975] 2 WLR 56.
R. v. *Vernege* [1982] *Crim. Law Rev.* December 598–600.
Sweet v. *Parsley* [1969] 1 All ER 347.

Text references

Bartholomew, A.A. (1983) *R*. v. *Sutcliffe*, 'Letter', *Medicine, Science and the Law* 23: 222–223.
Bettelheim, B. (1983) *Freud and Man's Soul*, London: Chatto and Windus.
Bluglass, R. (1980) *Psychiatry, the Law and the Offender – Present Dilemmas and Future Prospects*, Seventh Dennis Carroll Memorial Lecture, Croydon: Institute for the Study and Treatment of Delinquency.

Bluglass, R. (1990) 'Infanticide and Filicide', in R. Bluglass and P. Bowden (eds), *Principles and Practice of Forensic Psychiatry*, London: Churchill Livingstone.

Burn, G. (1984) *'Somebody's Husband, Somebody's Son' The Story of Peter Sutcliffe*, London: Heinemann.

Clarke, M.J. (1975) 'The Impact of Social Science on Conceptions of Responsibility', *British Journal of Law and Society* 2: 32–44.

Craft, M. (1984) 'Psychiatric Reports for the Courts', in M. and A. Craft (eds), *Mentally Abnormal Offenders*, London: Baillière Tindall.

Crane, A. (1990) *The Kirkland Papers: 1753–1869. The Ferrers Murder and the Lives and Times of a Medical Family in Ashby-de-la-Zouch*, Ashby-de-la-Zouch, Leics: Crane Press.

Criminal Law Revision Committee (1980) *Offences Against the Person*, Cmnd 7844, London: HMSO.

Dell, S. (1983) 'The Detention of Diminished Responsibility Homicide Offenders', *British Journal of Criminology* 23: 50–60.

—— (1984) *Murder into Manslaughter: The Diminished Responsibility Defence in Practice*, Maudsley Monograph No. 27, Oxford: Oxford University Press.

Dell, S. and Smith, A. (1983) 'Changes in the Sentencing of Diminished Responsibility Homicides', *British Journal of Psychiatry* 142: 20–34.

Eigen, J.P. (1983) 'Historical Developments in Psychiatric Forensic Evidence: The British Experience', *International Journal of Law and Psychiatry* 6: 423–429.

Fenwick, P. (1990) *Automatism, Medicine and the Law*, Psychological Medicine Monograph Supplement 17, Cambridge: Cambridge University Press.

Finch, J. (1974) *Introduction to Legal Theory* (second edn), London: Sweet and Maxwell.

Fitzgerald, E. (1981) 'Is the System Fair to the Likes of Peter Sutcliffe?' *Guardian*, 25 May: 11.

Gibbens, T.C.N., Soothill, K.L. and Pope, P.J. (1977) *Medical Remands in the Criminal Court*, Institute of Psychiatry, Maudsley Monograph No. 25, Oxford: Oxford University Press.

Griew, E. (1984) 'Let's Implement Butler on Mental Disorder and Crime', in R. Rideout and B. Jowell (eds), *Current Legal Problems*, London: Sweet and Maxwell for University College London.

—— (1988) 'The Future of Diminished Responsibility', *Criminal Law Review* February: 75–87.

Hall Williams, J.E. (1980) 'Legal Views of Psychiatric Evidence', *Medicine, Science and the Law* 20: 276–282.

Hamilton, J. (1981) 'Diminished Responsibility', *British Journal of Psychiatry* 138: 434–436.

Hart, H.L.A. (1968) *Punishment and Responsibility: Essays in the Philosophy of Law*, Oxford: Clarendon Press.

Home Office (1992) *Criminal Statistics, England and Wales, 1990*, Cmnd 1935, London: HMSO.

Home Office and Department of Health and Social Security (1975) *Report of the Committee on Mentally Abnormal Offenders* (The Butler Committee), Cmnd 6244, London: HMSO.

Home Office and Scottish Home Department (1957) *Report of the Committee on Homosexual Offences and Prostitution* (The Wolfenden Committee), Cmnd 247, London: HMSO.

Jacobs, F.G. (1971) *Criminal Responsibility*, London: Weidenfeld and Nicolson.

Kahn, J.H. (1971) 'Uses and Abuses of Child Psychiatry: Problems of Diagnosis and Treatment of Psychiatric Disorder', *British Journal of Medical Psychology* 44: 291–302.

Kenny, A. (1984) 'The Psychiatric Expert in Court', *Psychological Medicine* 14: 291–302.

Mackay, R.D. (1980) 'The Taint of Intoxication', *International Journal of Law and Psychiatry* 13: 37–48.

—— (1983a) 'Fact and Fiction about the Insanity Defence', *Criminal Law Review* April: 247–255.

—— (1983b) 'The Automatism Defence – What Price Rejection?' *Northern Ireland Law Quarterly* 34: 81–105.

—— (1986) *The Role of Psychiatric Court Reports in the Crown Court Trial Process*, Leicester: Leicester Polytechnic Law School Monographs.

—— (1991a) *The Operation of the Criminal Procedure Insanity Act 1964: An Empirical Study of Unfitness to Plead and the Insanity Defence*, Leicester: Leicester Polytechnic Law School Monographs.

—— (1991b) 'The Decline of Disability in Relation to the Trial', *Criminal Law Review* February 87–97.

Maher, G., Pearson, J. and Frier, B.M. (1984) 'Diabetes Mellitus and Criminal Responsibility', *Medicine, Science and the Law* 24: 95–101.

Masters, B. (1985) *Killing for Company*, London: Jonathan Cape.

—— (1993) *The Shrine of Jeffrey Dahmer*, London: Hodder and Stoughton.

Prins, H. (1980) *Offenders, Deviants or Patients?: An Introduction to the Study of Socio-Forensic Problems*, London: Tavistock.

—— (1983) 'Diminished Responsibility and the Sutcliffe Case: Legal, Psychiatric and Social Aspects', *Medicine, Science and the Law* 23: 17–24.

—— (1992) 'Epilepsy and Criminal Law: A Supplementary Comment', *Medicine, Science and the Law* 32: 255–256.

Rix, J.B. (1989) '"Alcohol Intoxication" or "Drunkenness": Is There a Difference?', *Medicine, Science and the Law* 29: 100–106.

Royal Commission on Capital Punishment (1953), *Report* Cmnd 8932, London: HMSO.

Samuels, A. (1975) 'Mental Illness and Criminal Liability', *Medicine, Science and the Law* 15: 198–204.

Smith, R. (1981) *Trial by Medicine: Insanity and Responsibility in Victorian Trials*, Edinburgh: Edinburgh University Press.

—— (1991) 'Legal Frameworks for Psychiatry', in G.E. Berrios and H. Freeman (eds), *150 Years of British Psychiatry 1841–1991*, London: Gaskell.

Soothill, K.L., Adserballe, J., Bernheim, T., Dasananjali, T.W., Harding, T., Thomas, T., Reinhold, F. and Ghali, H. (1983) 'Psychiatric Reports Requested by Courts in Six Countries', *Medicine, Science and the Law* 23: 231–241.

Sparks, R.F. (1966) 'The Decision to Remand for Mental Examination', *British Journal of Criminology* 6: 6–26.

Spencer, S. (1984) 'Homicide, Mental Abnormality and Offence', in M. and A. Craft (eds), *Mentally Abnormal Offenders*, London: Baillière Tindall.

Walker, N. (1968) *Crime and Insanity in England (Vol. I)*, Edinburgh: Edinburgh University Press.

West, D.J. and Walk, A. (1977) *Daniel Macnaughton: His Trial and the Aftermath*, Ashford: Gaskell Books for Royal College of Psychiatrists.

Zeegers, M. (1981) 'Diminished Responsibility – A Logical, Workable and Essential Concept', *International Journal of Law and Psychiatry* 4: 433–444.

FURTHER READING

Note: Items marked with an asterisk are focussed rather more on American problems and attitudes but they also contain material relevant to UK practice.

Books

Sentencing – general

Ashworth, A. (1983) *Sentencing and Penal Policy*, London: Weidenfeld and Nicolson.
Thomas, D.A. (1973) *Principles of Sentencing*, London: Heinemann.
—— (1982) *Current Sentencing Practice*, London: Sweet and Maxwell.
Walker, N. (1980) *Punishment, Danger and Stigma: The Morality of Criminal Justice*, Oxford: Basil Blackwell.

Relationship between psychiatry and the law

*Beran, N.J. and Toomey, B.D. (eds) (1977) *Mentally Ill Offenders and the Criminal Justice System: Issues in Forensic Services*, London: Praeger.
*Bromberg, W. (1979) *The Uses of Psychiatry in the Law: A Clinical View of Forensic Psychiatry*, London: Quorum Books.
*Fersch, E.A. (1980) *Psychology and Psychiatry in Courts and Corrections: Controversy and Change*, New York: John Wiley.
*Fingarette, M. and Hasse, A.F. (1979) *Mental Disabilities and Criminal Responsibility*, London: University of California Press.
Flew, A. (1973) *Crime or Disease?* London: Macmillan.
*Guttmacher, M. (1968) *The Role of Psychiatry in Law*, Springfield, Ill.: Charles C. Thomas.
*Jeffery, C.R. (1977) *Criminal Responsibility and Mental Disease*, Springfield, Ill.: Charles C. Thomas.
Moore, M.S. (1984) *Law and Psychiatry: Rethinking the Relationship*, Cambridge: Cambridge University Press.
Morris, N. (1982) *Madness and the Criminal Law*, London: University of Chicago Press.
—— (1983) 'Mental Illness and the Criminal Law', in P. Bean (ed.), *Mental Illness: Changes and Trends*, Chichester: John Wiley.
*Slovenko, R. (1973) *Psychiatry and Law*, Boston: Little Brown and Co.
Stone, A.A. (1984) *Law, Psychiatry and Morality: Essays and Analysis*, Washington, DC: American Psychiatric Press.

Forensic psychiatry

Craft, M. and Craft, A. (eds) (1984) *Mentally Abnormal Offenders*, London: Ballière Tindall.
*Halleck, S.L. (1967) *Psychiatry and the Dilemmas of Crime*, New York: Harper and Row.
*Halleck, S.L. and Bromberg, W. (1968) *Psychiatric Aspects of Criminology*, Springfield, Ill.: Charles C. Thomas.
Macdonald, J.H. (1969) *Psychiatry and the Criminal* (second edn), Springfield, Ill.: Charles C. Thomas.
*Sadoff, R.L. (1975) *Forensic Psychiatry: A Practical Guide for Lawyers and Psychiatrists*, Springfield, Ill.: Charles C. Thomas.
Trick, K.L.K. and Tennent, T.G. (1981) *Forensic Psychiatry: An Introductory Text*, London: Pitman Medical.
Whitty, C.W.M. and Zangwil, O. (1977) *Amnesia: Clinical, Psychological and Medico-Legal Aspects* (second edn), London: Butterworth.

Forensic psychology

Green, R.K. and Schaefer, A.B. (1984) *Forensic Psychology: A Primer for Mental Health Professionals*, Springfield, Ill.: Charles C. Thomas.
Havard, L.R.C. (1981) *Forensic Psychology*, London: Batsford.
Lloyd-Bostock, S.M.A. (ed.) (1981) *Psychology in Legal Contexts: Applications and Limitations*, London: Macmillan.
Wright, F., Bahn, C. and Reiber, R.W. (1980) *Forensic Psychology and Psychiatry* (Vol. 347 of the Annals of the Academy), New York: New York Academy of Sciences.

Articles

Bingley, W. (1991) 'Law and the Mentally Disordered', *Current Opinion in Psychiatry* 4: 869–871.
Briscoe, O.V. (1975) 'Assessment of Intent – An Approach to the Preparation of Court Reports', *British Journal of Psychiatry* 127: 461–465.
Chiswick, D. (1978) 'Insanity in Bar of Trial in Scotland: A State Hospital Study', *British Journal of Psychiatry* 132: 598–601.
Eagle, M. (1983) 'Responsibility, Unconscious Motivation and Social Order', *International Journal of Law and Psychiatry* 6: 263–291.
Griew, E. (1984) 'Another Nail in M'Naghten's Coffin', *New Law Journal* 134: 935–936.
McLean, A.M. and Marland, V.A. (1978) 'The Brennan Case: Medico-Legal Insanity?', *Medicine, Science and the Law* 18: 124–127.
Moore, M. (1979) 'Responsibility for Unconsciously Motivated Action', *International Journal of Law and Psychiatry* 2: 323–347.
—— (1983) 'The Relevance of Philosophy to Law and Psychiatry', *International Journal of Law and Psychiatry* 6: 177–192.
Morse, S.J. (1979) 'Diminished Capacity: A Moral and Legal Conundrum', *International Journal of Law and Psychiatry* 2: 271–298.
Smith, R. (1980) 'Scientific Thought and the Boundary of Insanity and Criminal Responsibility', *Psychological Medicine* 10: 15–23.
Wootton, B. (1980) 'Psychiatry, Ethics and the Criminal Law', *British Journal of Psychiatry* 136: 525–532.

Chapter 3

Systems of disposal

I must Create a System or be enslaved by another Man's.
(Blake, 'Jerusalem')

Our little systems have their day;
They have their day and cease to be.
(Tennyson, 'In Memoriam')

The aim of this chapter is to provide an outline account of the main methods for dealing with mentally disturbed offenders. To achieve this I have divided it into three sections. The first is devoted to a short historical background against which current management practices may be viewed, and provides some information on the numbers involved. The second consists of an account of the methods by which the mentally disturbed and disordered may be diverted from the criminal justice system – a practice becoming increasingly important. The third outlines the main health care and penal disposals available to the courts including short descriptions of the available facilities.

HISTORICAL CONTEXT AND POPULATION

Historical context

The history of the treatment of mentally disturbed individuals who offend is closely bound up with the history of more general provision for the care of the mentally disordered. Such care and control appears to have a cyclical pattern – a kind of 'flavour of the month' quality, often demonstrated more by passionate (and sometimes irrational) conviction than by objective appraisal of need. Cynical observers might consider that such patterns have much in common with a tendency to reinvent the wheel. The phenomenon has been most ably and humorously described in a number of contributions by Allderidge (1979, 1985) and others. For example, Parker has suggested that 'From early times the mentally disordered in England seem to have been afforded some protection, in principle at least, from the customary consequences of wrongdoing' (1980: 461; and see also Chapter 2 of this volume). In a later contribution, she states:

> The practice of confining some of the insane stretches back more than 600 years in England. The type of detained patient has varied, always including those considered to be dangerous. . . . The forms of security employed have changed little over the period; perimeter security, internal locks and bars and individual restraint by both physical and chemical means have been in continuous use to a greater or lesser degree in various guises up to the present day.
>
> (Parker, 1985: 15)

A similar haphazard and sometimes irrational approach can be seen in the deployment of community care services, bedevilled as they have been (and still are) by underfunding and lack of co-ordination. Despite current and sophisticated calls for remedy, as, for example, in the Final Summary Report of the Reed Committee (Department of Health and Home Office, 1992), it appears to be the case that funding is still in short supply; and current National Health Service and local government changes continue to be used as an excuse for obfuscation and inactivity. For mentally disturbed offenders are 'the people nobody owns' (Prins, 1993).

History teaches us that to be both 'mad' and 'bad' places those so designated at the bottom of the social priority pecking order. There is another unfortunate consequence of this phenomenon – namely that those who work with them may sometimes feel alienated and contaminated, and to be as exposed to adverse public opinion as their patients or clients.

This is not the place to provide a detailed historical account of the relevant legislation, but a few observations may help to provide a context for what is to follow. From as early as the beginning of the eighteenth century, provision existed for those who were considered to be mad and dangerous; it was not until the nineteenth century that special measures were introduced for the *public* as opposed to the *private* care and treatment of the mentally disordered. Such provisions were almost entirely custodial in nature and services for criminal lunatics, as they were then called, developed separately and in piecemeal fashion. They developed largely as a result of notorious cases such as those of Hadfield and M'Naghten referred to in Chapter 2. In the early twentieth century the trend to provide more specific legislation continued, as, for example, in the Mental Deficiency Act of 1913. This enabled courts to deal more effectively with mentally defective (handicapped) people who committed crimes by removing them from the penal system and placing them in hospital care. Minor refinements to the 1913 legislation were made in the 1920s, and the Criminal Justice Act of 1948 made it possible for psychiatric treatment to be made a formal requirement of a probation order for the first time. The Homicide Act 1957 and the Mental Health Acts of 1959 and 1983 made a wider range of disposals available for mentally disturbed offenders.

I conclude these brief contextual remarks with a short summary of certain trends that appear, in recent times, to have been influential in the treatment (and sometimes non-treatment) of the mentally disturbed in general and the mentally disturbed offender in particular.

1 There were growing demands for the run-down of the older mental hospitals. Hindsight indicates that such demands were perhaps premature and based upon predictions about the size of future psychiatric populations and psychiatric needs that were not altogether to be fulfilled (Tooth and Brooke, 1961). This was coupled with a certain degree of over-optimism concerning the long-term benefits of anti-psychotic medication.

2 There was a lack of emotional, professional and financial investment in community provision for a seriously disadvantaged and often unattractive group of people, the 'hard to like' or 'not nice' patients described by Scott (1975). This has been amply demonstrated in more recent times by the reluctance on the part of many professionals to accept responsibility for their management (see also Gostin, 1985; Parker, 1985).

3 Challenges were made to some powerfully held assumptions about the nature and causes of mental disorders. These challenges were led not infrequently by psychiatrists themselves, as, for example, in the work of Laing and Esterson (1970) and Szasz (1974).

4 An increasing concern was felt about psychiatric patients' rights and there was a concentration upon civil liberties issues – as represented in the 1983 Mental Health Act. Such concern was laudable, but had certain iatrogenic consequences, not the least of these being the possible practice of defensive psychiatry and an accompanying denial of patients' rights to treatment. A further consequence of this trend is said to have been the increasing number of mentally disordered people in penal establishments (see below).

5 A justified growing concern was felt about the degree to which black and other ethnic minority groups appear to be over-represented in penal and psychiatric populations and about the numbers of their untimely deaths (see, for example, Littlewood and Lipsedge, 1989; Institute of Race Relations, 1991).

6 There was a reduction in the primacy of medicine in the treatment of the mentally disordered. This is evidenced by the medical profession's own acknowledgement that a team approach may be preferable in the treatment of mental disorder. However, it has also been accompanied by a jostling for improved positions and status on the part of nurses, psychologists and social workers, especially in the field of forensic psychiatry. The nursing profession in particular has from time to time been a powerful force in decisions as to acceptance or non-acceptance of patients. As we shall see later, its influence has also been particularly powerful in the day-to-day management of the Special Hospitals.

Such changes in medical practice and orientation also have important implications for the future of the prison health care services. For example, Her Majesty's Chief Inspector of Prisons, in a recent report into conditions at HM Prison Brixton, recommended as follows:

It would be of considerable assistance if the prison hospital, wholly or in part (including part for an intensive care ward), could be up-graded and staffed to a standard so that it could be designated as a psychiatric hospital within the meaning of the Mental Health Act.

(Home Office, 1991a: para. 4.54).

The Chief Inspector and his colleagues also went on to state that

Not only has the Prison Medical Service a duty of care to its patients, but also such care clearly falls within the need to look after prisoners with humanity even if this includes making up for the (hopefully temporary) failings of the NHS. The cost of this extra service should be borne by the health authorities responsible for the patients' care. *Arrangements should be made to charge the district authorities, on a case by case basis, the full cost of the service.* This might well prove to be the most effective way of improving NHS services.

(para. 4.54; emphasis added)

The present unsatisfactory state of affairs has been well summed up by Chiswick, who states that

Unfortunately, but not surprisingly, the courts and their associated institutions provide a clumsy and inappropriate vehicle for the delivery of health care . . . [this group of offenders and alleged offenders] is likely to contain people who are disadvantaged by social, medical and psychiatric morbidity. They have complex treatment requirements which are unlikely to be met through the deliberations of the criminal justice system.

(1990: 755–756)

I shall return to the importance of this statement when I consider diversion. But, before doing so, it is necessary in concluding this account to comment upon the size of the population involved.

Mentally disturbed offenders in the prison population

Estimates of the prevalence of psychiatric and psychological disorders in remand and sentenced penal populations vary enormously, depending upon the populations studied and the variations in methodology. In the UK, Gunn and colleagues (Gunn *et al.*, 1978, 1991a and 1991b) have made substantial contributions to the topic; and Grounds (1991a, 1991b and 1991c) has expressed strong but persuasive views about the incarceration of the psychopathic. It would appear, from a variety of studies, that about one-third of the prison population requires some kind of psychiatric intervention and that in remand populations this number increases. (For a summary see Bowden, 1978; Prins, 1991a; Grounds, 1992; NACRO, 1993.) In their most recent study, Gunn *et al.* (1991a and 1991b) examined a series of *sentenced* prisoners in England and Wales. They contended, by extrapolation from their sample, that the sentenced population includes over 700 men with psychosis, and around 1,100 would warrant transfer to hospital for psychiatric treatment. Provision of secure treatment facilities, particularly long-term medium secure units, needs to be improved. Services for people with personality, sexual and substance abuse disorders should be developed in both prisons and the health service.

(1991a: 338)

There is still a shortfall of about 1,500 places in semi-secure or secure non-Special Hospital provision (Department of Health and Home Office, 1992: 48). Gunn *et al.* advocate a complementary development of health care *and* penal provision for offenders with personality and similar disorders (see also Swinton, 1991). When a more detailed breakdown of their results taken from the *actual* sample is examined, some interesting facts emerge. Of the 652 men involved, 0.8 per cent had organic disorders, 2 per cent psychosis, 6 per cent neurosis, 10 per cent personality disorder and 23 per cent substance misuse. Three per cent of the total were judged to require transfer to hospital for psychiatric treatment, 5 per cent required treatment in a therapeutic community setting and a further 10 per cent required additional psychiatric assessment or treatment within the prison. The numbers give cause for considerable concern and merely serve to flesh out the anecdotal evidence of unsuitable detention and of suicidal behaviour in prison as shown graphically in the reports by Tumim (Home Office, 1990) and by Woolf and Tumim (Home Office, 1991c).

Given that all surveys tend to show a significant degree of psychiatric morbidity in penal populations one must ask whether the presence of such morbidity *necessarily* indicates a need for transfer to hospital – informally or formally. If the answer to such a question is no, then this poses further consideration of the future of the Prison Health Care Service. The Home Office policy statement *Custody, Care and Justice* (1991b) recognises that prison is not the best place for people suffering from mental disturbance; but it also seems to recognise the inevitability that such persons will come into custody from time to time, for the report goes on to state that 'where it is *unavoidable* that those requiring in-patient treatment are committed to prison, then they should be transferred to suitable health service facilities as soon as possible' (p. 101; emphasis added). This seems to contrast with the wish expressed by Judge Tumim that prisons themselves should offer an appropriate redesignated hospital environment in which compulsory treatment might be used under the provision of the Mental Health Act 1983. More recently, the *Review of Health and Social Services for Mentally Disordered Offenders and Others Requiring Similar Services* places considerable emphasis in its recommendations on the need for the Prison Health Care Service to undertake early assessment of those prisoners thought to be suffering from mental disorder (Home Office and Department of Health, 1991: Recommendation 6.5). A note of caution should be sounded. If prison hospitals were to be designated as hospitals within the meaning of the Mental Health Act 1983, it might mean that unless rigorous safeguards were applied, they could become the dumping grounds of the 'not nice' patients the NHS appears to be so reluctant to take. Great care would be needed to avoid such an evasion of responsibility.

A final word of caution is necessary in concluding this part of the discussion. This concerns the tendency to accept too readily that those mentally disturbed offenders detained in prison are there because if they were not they would be in hospital. For many years, the view put forward by Penrose (1939) that there was an inverse relationship between prison and mental hospital populations has held considerable sway. In 1939, he published his famous study which became known in criminological circles as 'Penrose's Law', namely that as prison populations rose mental hospital populations declined and vice versa.

Bowden, in a recent critical study of this so-called 'law', states that

> The suggestion appears to have been that there was a relatively stable mass of individuals who were in one form of environment, asylums, rather than another, prison. The two were used interchangeably. The benefit of the asylum was its effect on reducing crime.
>
> (1993: 81)

Careful examination of remand and sentenced penal populations reveals that such a state of affairs is not as clear-cut as Penrose and later writers have suggested. Moreover, Penrose's so-called 'law' provided support for those who favoured the now somewhat discredited transcarceration hypothesis (see, for example, Scull, 1984). Further support for such criticism comes from Fowles, who made a meticulous study of prison and mental hospital populations over a twenty-five-year period. He suggests that

> The mental hospitals have been run down but the full-blooded closure pro-gramme is still in its relatively early stages and its effects will not be felt for some time to come. Those remaining in the mental hospitals are unlikely to be of the age and sex normally associated with crime [Moreover,] it is not possible to obtain comparable age distributions for prison populations and hospital residents.

Fowles goes on to suggest a further complicating factor, namely

> That former patients who are discharged from long-stay mental hospitals may be defined officially as living in the community but that may only mean that they are in the wards of a privately owned nursing home. The 'community' is any hospital/home not owned by the NHS.
>
> (1993: 71–72)

Such criticisms of a hypothesis that may have been all too readily accepted in the past merely indicate that the relationship between criminality and mental disturbance (to be examined fully in the next chapter) is a much more complex matter than some people have supposed (see also Walker, 1977). Simplistic thinking of the kind briefly alluded to above has important implications for the provision of services and the best use of resources needed to maintain them.

DIVERSION: KEEPING THE MENTALLY DISTURBED INDIVIDUAL OUT OF THE CRIMINAL JUSTICE SYSTEM

Even if we adopt a somewhat cautious approach to the estimates of the numbers of mentally disturbed persons held in penal establishments at various stages of their careers and accept the caveats entered by Fowles and Bowden, we are still forced to acknowledge that a sizeable proportion of them should not be there. Moreover, we are also forced to conclude that not only should they not be *in prison* but that perhaps they *should not have entered the criminal justice system in the first place*. In Chapter 2 I showed how one form of diversion from the criminal justice system operates through a finding of 'unfitness to plead' (being under disability). In recent years, there has been a growing concern about the problem. As long ago as 1975 the Butler Committee recommended that mentally disturbed offenders should be dealt with other than through the courts:

> Where any apparent offender is clearly in urgent need of psychiatric treatment and there is no risk to members of the public the question should always be asked whether any useful public purpose would be served by prosecution . . . these remarks apply in cases of homicide or attempted homicide or grave bodily harm as in less serious cases.
>
> (Home Office and DHSS, 1975: 266)

Some fifteen years later the Home Office, in its now well-known circular No. 66/90 (Home Office, MNP/90/1/55/8), reiterated this view. Paragraph 2 of the circular states:

> It is government policy that, wherever possible, mentally disordered persons should receive care and treatment from the health and social services. Where there is sufficient evidence, in accordance with the principles of the Code for Crown Prosecutors, to show that a mentally disordered person has committed an offence, careful consideration should be given to whether prosecution is required by the public interest.

The circular provides very detailed advice to all those agencies likely to be involved in dealing with mentally disturbed offenders (for example, the police, crown prosecution service, probation, social services, courts, health authorities, prison health care service).[1]

Concern about the most appropriate course of action to be taken in respect of mentally disordered offenders is, of course, not new. Two examples from history will suffice to make my point.

Example 1

This concerns the case of a young man named Hwaetred, as recounted by St Guthlac (AD 674–714), who lived in so-called Dark Ages rural England.

> A young man named Hwaetred became afflicted with an evil spirit. So terrible was [his] madness that he tore his own limbs and attacked others with his teeth. When men tried to restrain him, he snatched up a double-bladed axe and killed three men. After four years of madness and with emaciated body he was taken by his parents to several sacred shrines. But he received no help. One day, when his parents were wishing more for his death than for his life, they heard of a hermit [Guthlac] on the Isle of Crowland. They took their possessed son, with limbs bound, to the hermit.
> (Felix, *Life of St Guthlac*, quoted in Roth and Kroll, 1986: 100)

The modern recounters of this ancient tale make some interesting and highly pertinent comments. First, they indicate that the young man's condition was seen as an illness; his deviance was *not* minor, for he killed three men. However, there is no talk of revenge or attribution of criminality or of guilt. As they say, it would have been quite simple to have hunted him down and killed him, but, instead, attempts were made to restrain and control him within his own community. His parents, desperate as many of the parents of the psychotically ill are today, seek yet further remedy in the guise of a wise man (a latter-day psychiatrist perhaps?) in the hope that a cure may be effected. One would not wish to make too much of the vignette but it does encapsulate some of the issues raised in Roth and Kroll's account and one wonders how a truly multi-disciplinary case conference today would answer the question: 'What would you have done with this young man?'

Example 2

Some twelve hundred years later, an incident showing the other side of the coin is recorded in the *Lancet* of 14 April 1883 (pp. 648–649).

Malice or Madness?

> What is justly described as a 'shocking scene in a prison' has just occurred at Dartmoor. An exceptionally 'bad' young man, who was sentenced to seven years' penal servitude in August, 1879, he having been no less than nine times previously convicted and flogged, was being examined in prison on Tuesday last on a charge of a violent assault on a warder, whom it seems he nearly killed with a spade when his violence was such that with great difficulty several warders put him in irons. The story is sickening in its

brutality. What, however, must most powerfully strike the medical reader is that the narrative very closely resembles one of the old stories of a struggle with a madman in the days before the humane system of non-restraint was introduced into the asylums of this country. The question we are actuated to ask – and it is one which ought to be pressed strongly on the consideration of the Home Office – is whether this young man is not mad? He was convicted nine times before he reached the age of eighteen. More-over his rage is manifestly that of mania, rather than a sane being. . . . Looking at the treatment – wholly unworthy of a civilised country – which Thomas Jones is undergoing in a dark cell at Dartmoor, it would be well if the enquiry necessary to reassure the public mind that a madman is not being punished when he ought to be placed under treatment could be instituted at once . . . it cannot be permitted that prison authorities should reproduce the horrors of the Spanish inquisition in one of Queen Victoria's gaols, and withal mistake a lunatic for a felon.

(Rollin, 1993: 575)[2]

The dictionary defines 'divert' as 'to turn aside or to deflect' and 'diversion' as 'deflecting, deviation, diverting of attention, manoeuvre to secure this, feint' (*Concise Oxford English Dictionary*). That part of the definition calling attention to diverting of attention and feinting probably reflects a great deal of what goes on among the professionals involved in the exercise of their diversionary func-tions! A selection of cases from a variety of agencies concerned with criminal justice, penology, health care and social services submitted to the present writer as convener of a seminar on diversion certainly seemed to reflect this tendency.

The exercise of discretion concerning prosecution has a long if somewhat obscure history. Hetherington (1989) traces its origins to the reign of Henry VIII. However, it was not until the latter part of the nineteenth century that the office of Director of Public Prosecutions was introduced (see also Wood, 1988). Currently, the decision to prosecute rests with the Crown Prosecution Service, which is guided by a *Code for Crown Prosecutors* within which the prosecutor has to have regard for the need for prosecution in 'the public interest'. A number of factors govern this latter consideration, such as likely penalty, staleness (that is, the offence was committed so long ago that its prosecution would be of questionable merit), youth, old age and infirmity, complainant's attitude, and *mental illness or stress*. On this last aspect the *Code* states:

Whenever the crown prosecutor is provided with a medical report to the effect that an accused or a person under investigation is suffering from some form of . . . psychiatric illness . . . and the strain of criminal proceedings may lead to a considerable worsening of his condition, such a report should receive anxious consideration. This is a difficult field because in some instances the accused may have become mentally disturbed or depressed by the mere fact that his misconduct has been discovered and the crown prosecutor may be dubious about a prognosis that criminal proceedings will adversely affect his condition to a significant extent. Where, however, the crown prosecutor is satisfied that the probable effect upon the defendant's mental health outweighs the interests of justice in that particular case, he should not hesitate to discontinue proceedings. An independent medical examination may be sought, but should generally be reserved for cases of such gravity as plainly require prosecution but for clear evidence that such a course would be likely to result in a permanent worsening of the accused's condition.

(Crown Prosecution Service, n.d.: 4)

A number of questions arise from this statement.

1 How much is known about the variations in practice that may occur in making decisions either not to prosecute, or to discontinue prosecution once it is under way within the terms of the general power to withdraw or offer no evidence through Section 23 of the Prosecution of Offences Act 1985? Grounds indicates that 'There is a large gap in research knowledge of this area. Little is known about what happens to mentally disordered offenders *who do not enter criminal proceedings* and these gaps need to be filled if a complete picture is to be obtained'. He goes on to suggest that 'Such research might also indicate whether more mentally disordered offenders could or should be diverted away from criminal proceedings' (Grounds, 1991b: 40; emphasis added). However, a recent report on an experimental diversion scheme in Scotland would seem to indicate positive outcomes in some cases. The majority of the cases diverted for treatment by the procurators-fiscal (similar in most respects to crown prosecutors in England and Wales) were first offenders, were older than non-diverted offenders and, interestingly, half were female. The author concluded that

The procurator-fiscal is successful in selecting suitable cases in that he can identify people with significant psychological problems. The people who are referred generally have not received help . . . through the normal channels of health care and it is therefore appropriate that the procurator-fiscal's department should act as a conduit through which they can obtain assistance.

(Cooke, 1991: 790)

The aim seems laudable enough, but one wonders whether it might not be better to improve services and resources for such people *before* diversionary activity becomes necessary (see also Chiswick, 1990). Similarly successful outcomes have recently been reported upon by James and Hamilton (1991) in their review of a selection of cases diverted from the criminal justice system in a London Magistrates' Court. (An interesting example of a scheme in the USA is to be found in Palermo *et al.*, 1991.) Most studies indicate that failure to identify appropriate resources and to match them to need is frequently due to problems of communication within the system, a point made very cogently in recent contributions by Joseph (1992) and Joseph and Potter (1993).

A formal diversionary measure was that originally contained in Section 136 of the Mental Health Act 1959 and re-enacted with the same section number in the

Act of 1983. This provides a constable with power to remove to a place of safety a person found in a place to which the public have access who appears to be suffering from mental disorder, and who is in immediate need for care or control. If the constable thinks it necessary to remove that person in his or her own interests or for the protection of others he or she may do so. The person may be detained for a maximum of seventy-two hours for the purposes of being examined by authorised mental health professionals. Such examination may or may not lead to admission to hospital either informally or under the compulsory powers of the Act. The Section has certain merits, but it also has some accompanying disadvantages. All too often a police station is used as a place of safety and police stations are not the best places for detaining the madly distressed. The police are not always certain of their powers, but research seems to indicate that they are competent at recognising florid psychosis when they see it. There are often delays in the arrival of the relevant professionals (approved doctor and social worker) and communication between all parties is not always good. Guidelines for effective and sympathetic action have been set out by the Mental Health Act Commission and adopted by the Government (Department of Health and Welsh Office, 1990: Chapter 10). However, research suggests that countrywide implementation is patchy; in one year, 1989–90, just over a thousand such removals by the police took place – the lowest figure for six years (Department of Health, 1992a: 13). (See also Rogers and Faulkner, 1987 and Bean *et al.*, 1991, for detailed accounts of practice in this country and Teplin and Pruett, 1992, for an account of similar procedures in the USA).

2 How much notice should be taken of an accused's view of his or her right to prosecution? Would some mentally disordered offenders *prefer* to be prosecuted in the normal way?

This if of vital importance. As we saw in Chapter 2 until the introduction of the Criminal Procedure (Insanity and Unfitness to Plead) Act 1991 a successful defence of insanity or unfitness to plead would involve immediate hospitalisation – sometimes with a restriction order being added. In addition, there was a comparatively rare chance of the *facts* of the case being speedily examined and determined. Furthermore, hospitalisation under the Mental Health Act 1983 may in any event result in a much longer period of incarceration than if the defendant had been dealt with by way of imprisonment.

3 Given the current state of psychiatric services (and in particular *general* psychiatric services), is it certain that a psychiatric disposal will necessarily offer the best solution? This applies with considerable force to the personality disordered and (in legal terms) to the psychopathic offender. As already noted, hospitals and psychiatrists seem increasingly reluctant to accept such persons. The proposals put before the Butler Committee (Home Office and DHSS, 1975) by the late Dr Peter Scott for the designation of special units for such people within the prison system could perhaps be re-examined. (One is mindful of the useful approach being taken towards such offenders at establishments like Grendon Underwood.) A clearer emphasis on the potential for inducing change

in this group of admittedly highly problematic people might raise prison staff morale and offset some of the more debilitating effects induced by a climate still too much pervaded by notions of mere 'humane containment'.

4 Once offenders are in prison, particularly on remand, are prison staff given enough help to spot those who may be suffering from mental disorder? For example, the depressed prisoner may be difficult to pick out in an already overcrowded penal establishment; moreover, depression is an illness often unrecognised by the unwary; some prisoners may conceal the fact that they have a serious mental health problem, as, for example, in the case of the highly encapsulated delusional system of the morbidly jealous or psychotically deluded individual (see Chapter 4). In a recent survey of the psychiatric profiles of difficult/disruptive prisoners, Coid (1991) found a small number of inmates whose psychotic delusions appeared quite unknown to the prison staff. If Judge Tumim's proposals were given serious consideration, could not prison hospitals deal with cases of transient mental illness without recourse to transfer? With a few exceptions, mentally ill individuals are not ill all of the time. The closer alignment of the Prison Health Care Service to the NHS and a re-examination of the possibility of special units for the psychopathic might together help to revive the rehabilitative ethos in the prison system.

5 An important jurisprudential question needs consideration. To what extent should offenders, even though mentally ill, be held responsible for their actions? We might exclude the floridly psychotic at the time of the offence and perhaps some of the seriously mentally impaired. How far down the line of what Foucault once termed the 'psychiatrization of delinquency' should we go? Such a practice tends to make the prison system the dumping ground for 'badness', and it continues to negate rehabilitative measures within it. The *disadvantages* of non-prosecution have also been alluded to by forensic psychiatrists. For example, Smith and Donovan suggest that

> Excusing offending may not always be in the patient's interests. The formal legal process can be a valuable exercise in reality testing. The patient [in this instance they are writing about offences committed by psychiatric inpatients] can measure his or her own perceptions of his or her own behaviour against those of society. This can be a useful preparation for life outside hospital. The knowledge that prosecution is routine rather than exceptional, may deter further assaults and help aggressive patients to accept responsibility for their behaviour. Sometimes encouraging such patients to accept responsibility can be clinically beneficial and help to instil a sense of justice in other patients on the ward.
>
> (1990: 380; see also Carson, 1992)

Smith and Donovan also state that non-prosecution

> can reinforce the patient's belief that he or she need not control his or her behaviour. It may also leave staff feeling unsupported and there may be similar consequences if the court imposes a minimal penalty.
>
> (1990: 381)

Such concerns are echoed outside the UK. In a recent paper on the issue of determining criminal responsibility in France, Lloyd and Bénézech state:

> The main problem . . . was how to determine the exact amount of free will each individual had at the time of the criminal offence. It was relatively easy to assess the absence of criminal responsibility in cases of severe mental disorder or handicap; intermediate mental states, however, presented considerable difficulties in assessment, as did the measuring of constraints on the free will of normal men and women.
>
> (Lloyd and Bénézech, 1991: 282)

6 In deciding upon diversion or discontinuance, how much consideration should be given to the views of the victims? This is a delicate and difficult matter with considerable ethical implications.

7 Can we identify more clearly those aspects of law and practice that tend to militate against the effective use of diversion? There is anecdotal evidence to suggest that agencies tended to disclaim responsibility (notably financial) for the individual. The sad saga of the patchy development of secure accommodation attests to the importance of trying to ensure that funds are 'ring-fenced' (Department of Health and Home Office, 1992). At the individual (case) level, would not the notion of funds travelling with the offender-patient offset a great deal of 'buck-passing'? At a more personal level, professionals are often reluctant to see a problem from the other person's point of view. This is not necessarily deliberate obfuscation or intransigence on their part, but is a product of differences in role perceptions amongst professionals trained in different ways. Far more needs to be done to address relationship problems of this kind and forensic-psychiatric or criminology centres could play a significant role in this. In the midst of inter-professional squabbles the offender-patient suffers and the more inadequate of them continue to play their 'stage army' parts in the criminal justice and health care arenas.[3] The homeless (see NACRO, 1992; Scott, 1993) and those from ethnic minority groups, particularly the Afro-Caribbean population, fare particularly badly in this respect. The mentally handicapped are another sad illustration – a truly vulnerable group whom nobody really wishes to own. They may find themselves with increasing frequency back within the criminal justice system – a phenomenon that the Mental Deficiency Act 1913 was designed expressly to prevent.

It is apparent that we still have a long way to go in establishing effective systems of diversion. Its practice may be summarised crudely in the following five stages:[4]

- *Stage 1* Informal diversion by the police.
- *Stage 2* Formal implementation of Section 136 of the Mental Health Act 1983.
- *Stage 3* Referral for psychiatric examination before court hearing and discontinuance of prosecution at any stage.

- *Stage 4* Disposal through the mental health services at court or after sentence.
- *Stage 5* Disposal through these services at a later stage in sentence (for example, transfer from prison to hospital).

OTHER HEALTH CARE DISPOSALS

In order to keep the material in this section within reasonable bounds, I provide merely an outline account of facilities. Readers wishing to obtain more detailed information will find it in the works cited and in the works listed for Further Reading at the end of the chapter. (Only brief references are made to practice in other European countries and in America and Canada. Those wishing to seek information on practices there will find the *International Journal of Offender Therapy and Comparative Criminology* and the *International Journal of Law and Psychiatry* particularly useful.)

I have confined my description, almost exclusively, to provisions for adult offenders. As I draft this chapter, however, the call for heavier penalties for a small number of persistent young offenders, some of whom may be quite disturbed, grows daily more clamorous. (Any student of social history knows that such calls are age-old.) The fact that some two hundred thousand people signed a petition to ensure that the Home Secretary 'imprisoned' for life the two young killers of James Bulger is an indication of how punitive attitudes can be. A few words are in order, therefore, concerning provisions for that very small number of children and young persons under sixteen held in a variety of institutions who have committed homicide and other grave crimes.

A person convicted of murder who was less than eighteen at the time the offence was committed will be ordered to be detained 'during Her Majesty's Pleasure' (Section 53(1), Children and Young Person's Act 1933). To all intents and purposes this is similar to a life sentence, except that the offender may be detained 'in such place and under such conditions as the Secretary of State may direct'. The places chosen for such detention will vary according to the age and mental condition of the offender and his or her circumstances, all of which may change over time. Thus, the youthful offender may start his or her sentence in a local authority residential establishment (such as a community home with education) or a Youth Treatment Centre controlled by the Department of Health, such as St Charles in Essex and Glenthorne in Birmingham. These centres cater for some very highly disturbed young persons. The youthful offender may also be detained in a Special Hospital, Young Offenders' Institution or, if detained for long enough, he or she may be transferred to an adult prison. Persons who are under *seventeen* and convicted of crimes other than murder, for which a sentence of life imprisonment may be passed on an adult, may be sentenced to detention for life under Section 53(2) of the Children and Young Persons' Act 1933 (as amended by the Criminal Justice Act 1961). Such a sentence has virtually the same effect as one of detention during Her Majesty's Pleasure.

The oversight of the care and control of children and young persons subject to the sentences just outlined rests jointly with the Home Office and with the Department of Health. The latter is the central government department having overall responsibility for the care and control given by local authorities and others to all children and young persons.

The conditions under which 'Section 53 offenders' are detained and the provisions for their care have been examined recently by Boswell in an empirical study of twenty-five such detainees. Her report revealed a number of serious deficiencies. These included: lack of adequate help in assisting these young people to understand the reasons for their behaviour; disruption in their education, caused by their being moved from child care to penal provision as they grew older; and a lack of adequate training in social skills. She also found a disturbing degree of child physical and sexual abuse in their backgrounds (Boswell, 1991). Sadly, such care has been found wanting on several occasions in other institutional settings in recent times, as for example in Leicestershire (see the inquiry by Andrew Kirkwood, QC, into child care and management [Leicestershire County Council, 1993], and Judge Tumim's inquiries into suicides in prison establishments[5]). The problem seems to be a perennial one (Prins, 1991b). Children and young persons discharged into the community from such sentences will generally be supervised by the probation service working in close co-operation with local authority social services departments.

The material that follows is divided into three sub-sections. The first is concerned with 'enquiries into mental state and allied matters'; the second deals with 'hospital provision'; and the third covers 'penal provision'. In order to attempt a degree of clarity the sub-sections have been further divided into sub-divisions.

Enquiries into mental state and allied matters

In Chapter 2 reference was made to the state of mind of those accused of offences such as homicide and other grave crimes. I now consider, briefly, the procedures available for causing inquiry to be made into the mental state of such persons. In the cases of those charged with murder, reports are prepared *automatically* by the Prison Health Care Service. The practice seems to have arisen mainly because of the importance attached in the past to the need to secure detailed psychiatric evidence in cases where the death penalty could still be imposed and because of the seriousness with which all accusations of murder were (and still are) treated. The extent to which the probation service provides pre- and post-sentence information is now governed by the Criminal Justice Act 1991 (Section 3(5)) and the practice is laid down in the guide *National Standards for the Supervision of Offenders in the Community* (Home Office *et al.*, 1992). Other reports into the accused's mental and physical state may be prepared at the instigation of the Director of Public Prosecutions (DPP) or by the accused's legal advisers. In almost all cases of alleged murder the reports will be prepared in custody; however, in recent years, and in certain exceptional cases, an accused has been allowed bail with a condition that he or she remain in a psychiatric hospital in order for reports to be prepared. In murder and some other cases, where the accused's mental condition gives rise to doubts as to diagnosis or the case is problematic in other ways, the psychiatric investigations should also include very thorough physical, neurological and haematological investigations.

Statutory authority for obtaining reports

In cases other than murder, where, as I have indicated, reports are obtained automatically, the courts may remand a convicted offender for the specific purpose of obtaining reports. Sections 4(1) and 4(3) of the Criminal Justice Act 1991 require courts to obtain and consider medical reports on an offender who is, or appears to be, mentally disordered before passing a custodial sentence (other than in cases where the penalty is fixed by law, that is, murder). Courts are also required to consider any information that relates to the offender's mental condition and the likely effect of a custodial sentence on it or any treatment that may be available for it. When courts are considering cases where there is a significant risk of danger to others (as in cases of violence or serious sex offending) 'pre-sentence information in the form of psychiatric reports will normally be relevant' (Ashworth et al., 1992: 65).[6]

Remands to hospital

Section 35(1) of the Mental Health Act 1983 empowers courts to order the remand of an accused person to hospital for the preparation of a report into his or her mental condition. This provides an alternative to remanding an accused in custody in situations in which it would not be practicable to obtain the report if he or she were remanded on bail (for example, if an accused decided to breach a bail requirement that he or she reside in hospital for examination, the hospital would be unable to prevent that person from leaving; the remand to hospital under Section 35 gives the hospital power to detain the accused). This power to remand to hospital applies to any person awaiting trial by the Crown Court for any offence punishable with imprisonment, or any person who has been convicted but not yet sentenced (but excludes persons charged with murder). The power may be exercised only if an appropriately authorised medical practitioner (see below) reports orally or in writing that there is reason to believe that the accused is suffering from mental illness, psychopathic disorder, severe mental impairment or mental impairment. In the first instance, a remand may be for up to twenty-eight days; after this initial period the accused may be remanded for periods of up to twenty-eight days for a maximum of twelve weeks. It should be noted that the criteria for remands to hospital are more limited than those which obtain for remands on bail. In the case of remands to hospital the court must be satisfied that the accused is suffering from one of the four forms of mental disorder just described and for which a hospital order may be made (see below). In the period 1989–90 some 283 such admissions took place (Department of Health, 1992a: 13).

Remands for treatment

Section 36 of the Mental Health Act 1983 empowers the Crown Court to remand an accused person to hospital for treatment (other than a person charged with an offence the sentence for which is fixed by law). The court must be satisfied on the written or oral evidence of *two* authorised medical practitioners that the accused is suffering from *mental illness or severe mental impairment* of a nature or degree which makes it appropriate for him or her to be detained in hospital for medical treatment. In the first instance, the remands may be for up to twenty-eight-days. The remand may be renewed at twenty-eight day intervals for a period of up to twelve weeks. The court is also empowered to terminate the remand for treatment at any time, for example in the event of the accused recovering or in the event of the court hearing that no effective treatment is possible. In the period 1989–90 thirty-eight such admissions occurred (Department of Health 1992a: 13).

Interim hospital orders

In addition to their powers under Sections 37 and 41 of the Mental Health Act 1983 (see below) courts are empowered under Section 38 of the Act to make an interim hospital order. As with the preceding provisions, the court has to be satisfied on duly approved medical evidence that this is the most appropriate course of action and that an accused is suffering from one of the four categories of mental disorder defined in the Act. The provision is likely to be of use in those cases where the court and the hospital wish to make some evaluation of an accused's likely response to treatment without irrevocable commitment on either side. An interim hospital order may be made in the first instance for a period of up to twelve weeks; it may be renewed for periods of up to twenty-eight days to a maximum total period of six months. The court may also terminate an interim hospital order after considering the written or oral evidence of the Responsible Medical Officer (RMO) at the hospital, or if it makes a full hospital order (see below), or if it decides to deal with the offender in some alternative fashion. Sixty-nine such admissions occurred in the period 1989–90 (Department of Health, 1992a: 13).

Hospital orders

Section 37 of the Mental Health Act 1983 enables courts to make hospital or guardianship orders.[7] In order to do so the court must be satisfied that:

(a) having regard to all the circumstances, including the nature of the offence, antecedents of the offender and the unsuitability of other methods of disposal, a hospital order is the most suitable method of dealing with the case.
(b) the accused has been *convicted of* an offence punishable with imprisonment (other than murder). In the Magistrates' Court an order may be made without proceeding to conviction provided that the court is satisfied that the defendant committed the act or made the omission charged, and that the person is suffering from mental illness or severe mental impairment.
(c) that the offender is suffering from mental illness, psychopathic disorder, mental impairment or severe mental impairment of a nature or degree so *that it is appropriate for the offender to be detained in hospital for medical treatment*, and in the case of mental impairment or psychopathic disorder that the medical treatment *is likely to alleviate or prevent a deterioration in the patient's condition*. This is based on statements by two doctors, at least one of whom is approved for the purpose by a local health authority under the provisions of Section 12(2) of the Act. It should be stressed that the condition *must* be one that merits compulsory detention in hospital and is not one that could be treated by other means, for example by a requirement for mental treatment under a probation order.

It should be noted that the 1983 Act now requires, in cases of mental impairment and psychopathic disorder, an indication that treatment will alleviate or prevent a deterioration in the condition. Before making such an order the court must also be satisfied that arrangements have been made for the offender's admission to hospital.

A hospital order lasts initially for six months, is renewable for a further six months and is then renewable at annual intervals. An offender-patient may be discharged by the RMO at any time. The patient or his or her nearest relative may also make an application for discharge from the order to a Mental Health Review Tribunal (MHRT) in the period between the expiration of six months and the expiration of twelve months beginning with the date of the order; and in any *subsequent* period of twelve months. Under Section 117 of the Act, after-care must now be provided by the health authority in conjunction with the local authority social services department for those who cease to be compulsorily detained under Section 37 and who leave hospital.

In 1991, the courts in England and Wales made about 700 hospital orders. For the period 1981–91 the average figure was about the same (Home Office, 1993a: Table 12).

Restriction orders

Section 41 of the Mental Health Act 1983 enables a Crown Court (but *not* a Magistrates' Court) to make a restriction order. The criteria for making such an order are as follows:

1 That following conviction it appears to the court, having regard to
  (a) the nature of the offence,
  (b) the offenders' antecedents and
  (c) the risk of his or her committing further offences if discharged,
  that a restriction order is necessary *for the protection of the public from serious harm.*
2 That at least one of the medical practitioners authorised under Section 12(2) of the Act whose written evidence is before the court has also given that evidence orally.

The criterion I have italicised was not in the 1959 Mental Health Act and was inserted in the new legislation to ensure that only those offender-patients who were considered likely to constitute a serious risk of harm to the public would be subjected to the serious restrictions on liberty that follow the making of such an order. Until very recently, serious harm to the public had not been further defined. However, in the cases of *R.* v. *Courtney* (1987) and *R.* v. *Birch* (1989), it has been made clear that the risk of serious harm must be to the public *at large* and is not intended to apply when the harm (as, for example, homicide) had been directed in highly circumscribed circumstances to a *specific individual* such as a spouse. There has been a recent increase in the number of restricted patients detained in psychiatric hospitals. For example: 'On 31 December 1991, the number of restricted patients detained in psychiatric hospitals rose to 2,143. This figure was 9 per cent higher than in 1990 and some 27 per cent higher than the 1985 low of 1,692' (Home Office, 1993a: 2).

A restriction order may be made either for a specific period or without limit of time (the latter being the most frequently adopted). The effects of a restriction order are as follows:

1 The offender-patient cannot be given leave of absence from the hospital, be transferred elsewhere, or be discharged by the RMO without the consent of the Home Secretary.
2 The Home Secretary may remove the restrictions if he considers they are no longer required to protect the public from serious harm. Should the order remain in force without the restriction clause, it has the same effect as an order made under Section 37 of the Mental Health Act 1983.
3 The Home Secretary may at any time discharge the offender-patient absolutely or subject to conditions. In considering those restricted cases (a) which are considered to be particularly problematic, (b) which are considered to need special care in assessment, and (c) where there may be thought to be a fear of possible future risk to the public, the Home Secretary will seek the advice of his Advisory Board on Restricted Patients (known formerly as the 'Aarvold' Board). This body was set up following the recommendation of a committee chaired by the late Sir Carl Aarvold. It had examined the circumstances in which an offender-patient (Graham Young) had come to re-offend shortly after his discharge into the community from Broadmoor (Home Office and

DHSS, 1973; see also Chapter 9, this volume). The Advisory Board is quite independent of the Mental Health Review Tribunal and its main concern is with proffering advice to the Home Secretary about the likely risk to the public of releasing the more problematic restricted offender-patient back into the community. It should be stressed that the Advisory Board does not deal with every restricted case, but only with those 'cases needing special care in assessment' (Home Office and DHSS, 1973: 9). (See Egglestone, 1990 for a useful history of the Board and its functions.)

Under Section 73 of the Mental Health Act 1983 a Mental Health Review Tribunal may exercise its own powers concerning restricted patients in the following fashion:

1 The Tribunal *must* order the patient's *absolute* discharge if it is satisifed that:

(a) the offender-patient is not now suffering from one of the forms of mental disorder specified in the Act which makes it appropriate for him or her to be detained in hospital for medical treatment; *or*

(b) it is not necessary for the health and safety of the offender-patient or for the protection of other persons that he or she should receive such treatment; *and*

(c) it is not appropriate for the offender-patient to remain liable to be recalled to hospital for further treatment.

However, in the important case of *R.* v. *K* (1990) it was held that a Tribunal which was satisfied that a restricted patient was not suffering from a mental or psycho-pathic disorder was nevertheless entitled to order the conditional discharge of the patient and was not, as had hitherto been held to be the case, obliged to order his or her absolute discharge. On the face of it this decision does not appear to be in accord with what the architects of the 1983 Act had in mind, since Sections 72 and 73 taken together appear to make it mandatory upon the Tribunal to discharge the patient absolutely in the absence of mental disorder. The court appeared to have in mind the possibility of a need for a residual power to recall in the event of relapse at some future date. The court held that Section 73 gave the Tribunal power to impose a conditional discharge and retain such control over patients not then suffering from mental disorder or not to a degree requiring continued detention in hospital. The court considered this to be an important discretionary power and not one to be set aside lightly in the absence of words to the contrary.

2 A conditionally discharged offender-patient may be recalled to hospital by the Home Secretary at any time during the duration of the restriction order. It has also been held by the Court of Appeal (*R.* v. *Secretary of State for the Home Department ex parte K*, 1990) that the Home Secretary does not have to rely on medical evidence in order to recall to hospital a restricted patient, even if medical opinion was of the view that the patient was not suffering from mental disorder. This wide discretion is held to lie entirely in the hands of the Home Secretary and the public interest will, if necessary, take precedence. An order for conditional discharge may contain a range of requirements held to be conducive to the

welfare of the offender-patient and, more importantly, for the protection of the public. Examples of such requirements might be that the offender-patient should live at a specified place, should not contact certain individuals and should be under the supervision of a probation officer or social worker and a psychiatrist. These professionals are required to make reports to the Home Secretary at regular intervals, not only concerning the offender-patient's general progress, but more specifically on any matters giving rise to immediate concern (see Chapter 9). Under the 1959 Act Tribunals could only *advise* the Home Secretary on the discharge of restricted patients. As can be seen they now have the power themselves to order the patient's discharge. In order to exercise their stronger powers, Tribunals (which consist of legal, psychiatric and lay members) must be chaired by a senior legal practitioner approved by the Lord Chancellor such as a Circuit Judge or person of equivalent status.

Transfer of prisoners found to be mentally disordered

Sections 47–52 of the Mental Health Act 1983 enable the Home Secretary to transfer sentenced or unconvicted prisoners from prison to hospital if they are found to be suffering from mental disorder as defined in the Act (as in the case of Peter Sutcliffe described in Chapter 2). Under the provisions of Section 47 an order in respect of a sentenced prisoner *may* be made without restrictions, but it will be much more likely to be made with restrictions under the provisions of Section 49. In the period 1989–90 a total of 152 prisoners were transferred (Department of Health, 1992a: 13). If the Home Secretary is notified by the RMO or an MHRT that such a person no longer needs treatment for mental disorder, he has two possibilities open to him:

1 If the offender-patient has become eligible for parole or has earned statutory remission, he can order his or her discharge.
2 Alternatively he can order that the patient be remitted to prison to serve the remainder of his or her sentence. (For illustrations of the effects of such transfers upon sentenced prisoners, see Grounds, 1990 and 1991.)

'Psychiatric probation orders'

Any court has the power to make a probation order with a requirement that an offender receive psychiatric treatment by a qualified practitioner as an in-patient or an out-patient. The Powers of Criminal Courts Act 1973 – as amended by the Criminal Justice Act 1991, Schedule 1(5) permits this form of treatment provided:

1 the offender consents to the making of the order (note that a probation order under the 1991 Act is now a sentence of the court);
2 a hospital, or other establishment, will receive him or her and is willing to provide treatment;

3   the court has before it the oral or written evidence of one doctor (approved under Section 12(2) of the Mental Health Act 1983) indicating that the offender's condition requires, and may be susceptible to, treatment (but is not such as to warrant his or her detention in pursuance of a hospital order). Such an order may be made for a period of up to three years.

As far as the hospital or other institution is concerned, the offender-patient has informal status and there is no power to detain him or her compulsorily (as there is under the provisions of the Mental Health Act). Should the offender-patient leave, the probation officer may of course take action for breach of requirement of the probation order. However, it is not open to the court to sanction proceedings for a breach of the order if the offender-patient merely refuses a physical form of treatment, such as ECT or drugs. 'Psychiatric Probation Orders' (as they are usually called) are of use in cases of milder forms of illness and where it is thought there is no indication of potential serious harm to the offender and/or the public. Such limited research (for example, Grunhut, 1963; Lewis, 1980) as has been carried out on their use suggests that they work best in circumstances where there is good co-operation between the doctor and the probation officer. In 1991, there were 903 psychiatric probation orders in force – 784 for non-residential treatment and 119 for residential. The number of orders made with a requirement for residential treatment has declined in recent years (Home Office, 1993b: Table 2.2).

The arrangements for the disposal of mentally disordered offenders are set out diagramatically in Figure 3.1 and summarised in the Appendix to this chapter.

Hospital provision: secure and semi-secure accommodation

A number of mentally disordered and disturbed offenders will be detained in ordinary psychiatric hospitals. Those who have committed grave crimes and are considered to be an immediate danger to the public will, as we shall see shortly, be detained in a Special Hospital. In the latter stages of their rehabilitation these patients may well be transferred to a local psychiatric hospital or secure unit as part of a phased return to the community. As noted in Chapter 1, some psychiatric hospitals have become increasingly reluctant in recent years to accept the more difficult or disruptive offender-patients. (It is important to point out that, overall, the numbers of patients compulsorily detained in psychiatric hospitals, compared with the total populations of such institutions, is very small – about 7 per cent: 'During 1989–90, admissions of mentally disordered offenders made up 9% of all formal admissions . . . most of these were under Section 37 of the Mental Health Act, 1983' [Department of Health, 1992a: 4]). Such reluctance has resulted not only in an accumulation of such patients in the Special Hospitals, but also in a consequent delay in implementing their return to the community. These delays and 'clogging up' were a major preoccupation of the Glancy (DHSS, 1974) and Butler Committees. In their interim report the latter urged that priority be given to the establishment of interim secure measures and secure units (Home

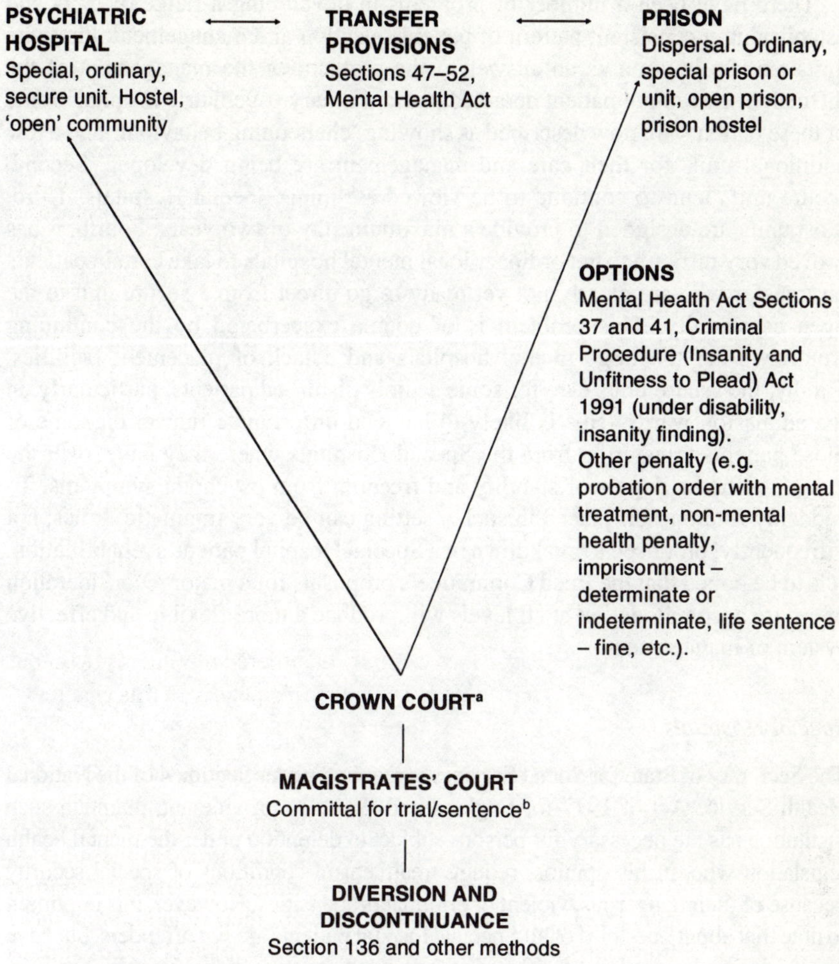

PSYCHIATRIC HOSPITAL
Special, ordinary, secure unit. Hostel, 'open' community

←→

TRANSFER PROVISIONS
Sections 47–52, Mental Health Act

←→

PRISON
Dispersal. Ordinary, special prison or unit, open prison, prison hostel

OPTIONS
Mental Health Act Sections 37 and 41, Criminal Procedure (Insanity and Unfitness to Plead) Act 1991 (under disability, insanity finding).
Other penalty (e.g. probation order with mental treatment, non-mental health penalty, imprisonment – determinate or indeterminate, life sentence – fine, etc.).

CROWN COURT[a]

MAGISTRATES' COURT
Committal for trial/sentence[b]

DIVERSION AND DISCONTINUANCE
Section 136 and other methods

Notes: [a] The powers available to the Crown Court are also exercisable on appeal by the Court of Appeal.
        [b] Magistrates may also commit to the Crown Court with a view to a hospital order being made *with restrictions*.

Figure 3.1 Disposal of mentally disordered and disturbed offenders through the mental health, criminal justice and penal systems

Office and DHSS, 1974; see also Gostin, 1985). In the event, earmarked funds for their establishment were used for other purposes and in some areas, as noted earlier, there is still a shortfall of semi-secure places (Brindle, 1990; Department of Health and Home Office, 1992).

There have been a number of problems in developing a range of units and establishing a consistent pattern of patient selection and management. First, the units tend to be seen as an answer to the problem of the management of the difficult or disruptive patient detained in the ordinary psychiatric hospital. Some of these patients are now described as showing 'challenging behaviour' and a few additional units for their care and management are being developed. Second, secure units tend to continue to be viewed as 'mini-'Special Hospitals. Third, most units are designed to provide a maximum stay of two years. Fourth, it has proved very difficult to get ordinary local mental hospitals to take certain patients on transfer who are clearly not yet ready to go direct from a secure unit to the open community. This problem is of course exacerbated by the continuing 'run-down' of the large mental hospitals and a lack of placement facilities. Finally, the secure units care for some acutely disturbed patients, particularly on the admission wards. This is likely to have an unfortunate impact on some of those patients transferred from the Special Hospitals where they have, over the years, reached a degree of stability and freedom from psychotic symptoms. To suddenly find oneself placed in such a setting can be very traumatic. It has, not infrequently, produced a breakdown in a Special Hospital patient's rehabilitation. It is to be hoped that the Reed Committee's proposals for a major reconsideration of secure accommodation at all levels will produce a more flexible and effective system of management.

Special Hospitals

The Secretary of State for Social Services is required under Section 4 of the National Health Service Act of 1977 for England and Wales to provide and maintain such institutions as are necessary for persons subject to detention under the mental health legislation who, in his opinion, require treatment in conditions of special security because of their dangerous, violent or criminal propensities. However, it is important to note that about one-third of all Special Hospital patients are *not* offenders, but have been admitted because of their difficult or disruptive behaviour in ordinary psychiatric or mental handicap hospitals. There are three (formerly four) Special Hospitals in England (Broadmoor, Rampton and Ashworth – formerly Moss Side and Park Lane) but none in Wales or Northern Ireland. The State Hospital at Carstairs in Scotland is the equivalent of a Special Hospital in England and the Central Hospital at Dundrum in Dublin performs some of the functions of an English Special Hospital. The English Special Hospitals were formerly administered directly by the Department of Health. Following various inquiries and reports into their management, it was decided to bring them into line with other National Health Service hospitals and there is now a special health authority for all of them (the Special Hospitals Service Authority, SHSA). Because Northern Ireland has no Special Hospital, it sends a few of its more dangerous offender-patients to Carstairs or, more rarely, to Ashworth. (For fuller accounts of the English Special Hospital system, see Hamilton, 1985 and 1990; Department of Health, 1992b.)

Broadmoor (Berkshire). This is the oldest of the Special Hospitals, having been established in 1863; it currently has a population of about 400 patients. Once beset by severe overcrowding, some relief was afforded by the building of Park Lane (now part of Ashworth) Hospital. However, the provision for female patients remains less than satisfactory. It takes mostly mentally ill and psychopathic patients. Its management has been the subject of extensive recent reviews, most notably by the Health Advisory Service (whose recent report was highly critical of some practices within the Hospital) and the subject of three separate inquiries into the sudden death of patients. The Health Advisory Service Report stated that 'An unfortunate air of uniformity and consistency reinforces the atmosphere of an institution, albeit tempered by changes in furnishing' (National Health Advisory Service and DHSS Social Services Inspectorate, 1988: 3).

Rampton (North Nottinghamshire). This hospital (established in 1914), like Broadmoor, has also suffered from overcrowding and isolation in the past. Unfortunately it has also suffered from allegations of ill-treatment of patients; in 1980 it was the subject of a highly critical review in which it was described as 'a backwater . . . the main currents of thought about the care of mental patients have passed it by' (DHSS, 1980: iii). Rampton is now much less overcrowded, containing some 400 patients, mainly, but not exclusively, mentally impaired and psychopathic. In recent years it has been revitalised as a result of an energetic review board and the appointment of younger and more forward-looking staff in all disciplines and at all levels. Certainly it is no longer the 'backwater' of a decade ago.

Ashworth Complex (Maghull, Liverpool). This complex consists of the former Moss Side (established 1933) and Park Lane (established 1974) Hospitals. At one time Moss Side took mainly mentally impaired patients but following integration with Park Lane it takes all three categories, though there is some degree of specialisation. Park Lane is the newest of the Special Hospitals, taking mainly the mentally ill and the psychopathic. The total population of the hospitals is about 600 patients.

The English Special Hospitals have at various times come in for a good deal of justified criticism, but even their severest critics have acknowledged that these institutions have to undertake a tremendously difficult task in attempting to combine containment, clinical treatment and rehabilitation in a climate of opinion that, as has already been suggested, does not give high priority to the care of the 'mad and the bad'. Perhaps one of the most devastating indictments of them has been the publication of the extensive investigation of complaints about Ashworth Hospital (Department of Health, 1992b). The catalogue of mismanagement and incompetence at all levels that this inquiry revealed demonstrates all the weaknesses inherent in closed institutions. Such weaknesses are demonstrated all the more clearly by the fact that abuses at Ashworth were

occurring during the period in which members of the Mental Health Act Commission (established under the 1983 Mental Health Act) were visiting regularly.
I impute no disrespect to some of my former Commission colleagues, but it has
always seemed a little odd to me that the four members of the inquiry team were
all members of the Commission.

In a recent paper Coid has suggested that very little attention has been paid
more generally to the quality of life of detained patients:

> The quality of life of detained patients has not received adequate attention
> despite the responsibilities placed on hospital staff and the special problems
> faced by these patients. . . . It is important for future research to overcome
> difficulties in developing objective measurements and set the appropriate
> standards of quality of life that detained patients should expect.

(1993: 611)

Despite this criticism, a good deal of research has been carried out into the
characteristics and needs of Special Hospital patients, not only by the former
Special Hospitals Research Unit, but also by a variety of psychiatric professionals working within the hospitals (see, for example, Bailey and
MacCulloch, 1992). Though the climate has to be one of containment and the
security of the public given paramount importance, much therapy is being carried
out by nursing, psychiatric, psychology, social work, occupational and other
staff. The Hospitals now have stronger links with various academic departments
of psychiatry, psychology and criminology and are recognised as training centres
for all psychiatric professionals working in forensic settings. Hopefully, the new
administrative arrangements that have been set in train to establish closer links
with National Health Service care will foster the changes and development still
required. (For an up-to-date review of the history and current state of the Special
Hospitals, see Bartlett, 1993.)

A recent report (Department of Health and Home Office, 1994) has recommended a scaling down of the present Special Hospitals and the consequent
accommodation of patients in smaller units. Other recommendations include the
fostering of academic and research activities and the eventual achievement of
trust status for the remaining Special Hospitals and for the new units. The
Government has indicated its intention to outline the extent to which it will
accept these recommendations by January 1995.

Maximum secure accommodation in Scotland and Eire

Scotland

The State Hospital at Carstairs (established in 1944) in Lanarkshire has its
functions defined by Section 90 of the Mental Health (Scotland) Act of 1984:
'The Secretary of State shall provide such hospitals as appear to him to be
necessary for persons subject to detention . . . who require treatment under

conditions of special security' (quoted in Hamilton, 1990: 1371). Currently it houses over 200 patients, the majority suffering from psychotic illness. As already indicated, it very occasionally receives patients from Northern Ireland.

Eire

The Central Hospital at Dundrum in Dublin has a predominantly male population of some 100 offender-patients, about half of whom are said to be suffering from psychosis (mainly schizophrenic illness). A large number of admissions appear to come from prison transfers. Smith, writing rather pessimistically (but perhaps also realistically), says: 'There are treatment triumphs, but there are many failures, suggesting that remission of illness is not encouraged by security hospitalisation' (1990: 1353).

Penal provisions

Prison psychiatric services

Acts of 1774 and 1779 required prisons to appoint a physician and an organised full-time medical service began with the establishment of the Prison Commission in 1877 (Bluglass, 1990; Gunn, 1985). Such appointments were the forerunners of a range of other professional appointments which were subsequently to swell the ranks of prison staffs, such as chaplains, psychologists, specialist nursing officers, probation officers, education personnel and works and occupations staff.

The history of the Prison Medical Service (now renamed Prison Health Care Service) reveals that there were a number of early attempts to describe and classify mentally disordered offenders received into prison. Perhaps the most significant of all of these was a report which appeared by East and de Hubert (1939) which paved the way for the foundation of Grendon Underwood Psychiatric Prison in 1962 (see below). It should also be noted that the Prison Health Care Service has general oversight of the total care of both prisoners and staff and also a concern with environmental health matters (Smith, 1984). Psychiatric assessment and management is only one aspect of the work. There have been a number of suggestions for the closer integration of the Prison Health Care Service and National Health Service and on balance this would seem to be a desirable outcome. (See the evidence of the Royal College of Psychiatrists to the May Committee on the Prison Service: Home Office et al., 1979). However, in a comprehensive study of prison medical services the House of Commons Select Committee, reporting in 1986, concluded that this was too simple a solution and that some specialist services would also be required. The current trend is for the Prison Health Care Service to 'buy in' specialist and other facilities (House of Commons, 1986; Prins, 1992).

As noted earlier, there are still numbers of mentally disordered offenders who should be in hospital and an even greater number who, whilst not fulfilling the strict criteria for transfer under the mental health legislation, would benefit from psychiatric management. Prisons are certainly not the best places for managing mental disorder, the more so because notions of treatment seem to have been abandoned for 'positive custody' since the late 1970s (Home Office *et al.*, 1979).

Be this as it may, the prison service has designated certain prisons and units as places where prisoners may be offered psychiatric help and management. The most notable of these is Grendon Underwood Psychiatric Prison in Buckinghamshire. It was established under medical governorship in 1962 and aimed to be a therapeutically oriented institution for those offenders who showed mental disorder or whose offences suggested a degree of psychiatric morbidity (Faulk, 1990). Inmates are not sent there directly by the courts; the High Court has made it clear that courts are not empowered to make such directions or requests. Prisoners are selected by the Prison Health Care Service in conjunction with Grendon staff.

Since Grendon opened, much has been written about its success or otherwise. If one takes mere reconviction rates as a yardstick, then Grendon probably does no better than any other penal establishment. However, if one looks at social adjustment, or rather lack of personal *maladjustment*, then Grendon does seem to do rather better than other prisons. More importantly, Grendon can offer useful pointers to the management of prisoners in a more effective and humane way, much as Barlinnie did in the Scottish prison service (Whatmore, 1990). Currently, a non-medical governor is in charge of Grendon and the main therapeutic thrust is upon offering psychiatric help to other penal institutions and towards working with more rigorously selected inmates, notably suitable psychopaths and sex offenders (Faulk, 1990). More recently, a wing for the treatment of acutely psychiatrically ill inmates has been established. The latter are sent to Grendon because of their acute mental disturbance and in the knowledge that in some cases formal transfers under the Mental Health Act 1983 take a considerable time to put into effect (see Selby, 1991).

Other therapeutic work is being carried out at Parkhurst Prison Hospital and the prison's C Wing. The prison hospital, housed in a separate building, accommodates some ninety inmates, the majority of whom are there for psychiatric assessment and treatment. There is a good inmate/nurse ratio, including the welcome development of the presence of female staff. The hospital provides a specialist psychiatric service to the three other large prisons on the Isle of Wight and Kingston Prison, Portsmouth (a small specialist prison for mainly domestic life-sentence prisoners). It also offers an assessment and treatment facility for inmates referred from other parts of the prison system and guidance on the long-term management of chronically mentally disordered prisoners who do not fall within the categories of the Mental Health Act 1983, or for whom it has proved impossible to find an NHS bed. C Wing aims to manage some twenty-five inmates with long sentences who have proved difficult and disruptive in other prisons and whose behaviour indicates long-standing psychological difficulties. It seems to bear some comparison with the special unit at Barlinnie (Cooper, 1990; Evershed, 1991). There are special units in other prisons, for example at Wormwood Scrubs, Wakefield and the Young Offenders' Institution at Feltham. Finally, as already indicated, if an inmate fulfils the strict criteria of the Mental Health Act for compulsory admission to hospital, the Home Secretary may, on medical evidence, authorise a transfer to hospital either before or after sentence.

Release on parole and life licence

From time to time, offenders serving long determinate sentences or life imprisonment may suffer from a degree of mental disturbance that requires a continuing degree of oversight and management in the community. Such cases call for very close collaboration and co-operation between psychiatric and social work professionals. The arrangements for parole and life licence are contained in the Criminal Justice Acts of 1967, 1972 and 1991.

The 1991 Act introduces two new schemes for the early release of determinate sentence prisoners. The first is *the Automatic Conditional Release Scheme* (ACR). All prisoners serving less than four years will fall within this scheme. Such prisoners will be released automatically mid-sentence. There is compulsory supervision from the date of release up to three-quarters of the way through the sentence. The Act provides that some sex offenders may be made subject to supervision up to the end of their sentence at the discretion of the sentencing judge. In such cases it may well be that the offender's mental condition will be an important factor for consideration.

The second is *the Discretionary Parole Scheme*. The discretionary element in the earlier parole scheme is retained for prisoners serving sentences of four years and over. They will become eligible for release on parole mid-sentence, but will be released automatically two-thirds of the way through (as under the previous scheme) if parole is not granted. Parole Board members will visit and interview the prisoner. The Parole Board will be responsible for the final decision on suitability for release for prisoners serving less than seven years and it will have to state reasons for its decisions. For prisoners serving more than seven years the Home Secretary will retain final responsibility as to release but will be advised by the Board. All prisoners released under this scheme will be under supervision, and as with the Automatic Conditional Release Scheme, some sex offenders will be supervised up to the end of their sentence.

Section 34 of the 1991 Act also introduces *Discretionary Lifer Panels*. These panels consider cases of prisoners serving discretionary sentences of life imprisonment (that is, for offences other than murder) who have passed their tariff stage (that is, the period deemed to be necessary for purposes of deterrence and retribution). In such cases, the prisoner has the right to appear before the panel, to be represented, and to see all the papers relevant to his or her release. In respect of other life sentence cases, the arrangements remain much as they were under the previous legislation. All life-sentence panels will normally be chaired by a member of the judiciary and the panel must also include a psychiatrist and preferably a probation service representative and a criminologist. Some of the problems involved in the decision-making process in discretionary parole and life-sentence cases are addressed in Chapter 9.

Supervision in the community

A parolee or life licensee will be supervised by a member of the probation service (and occasionally a psychiatrist) and a conditionally discharged restricted offender-patient may be supervised in the community by a probation officer or a local authority social worker and a psychiatrist. The probation service derives its authority for this supervision from the Probation Rules. The authority for local authority social workers to carry out the supervision of conditionally discharged offender-patients is contained in health service legislation concerned with the general duties of local authorities to provide care and after-care for psychiatric patients, as now further clarified in Section 117 of the Mental Health Act 1983. Between five and six hundred such cases may be under active supervision in the community in any year. Of these, about one-third are supervised by the probation service. Release may be conditional upon compliance with certain requirements, such as living in a specified place, under certain conditions, or refraining from certain employments or from contacting named individuals. The Aarvold Committee considered that the choice of supervisor should normally depend upon those who knew best the offender-patient, his or her history and social background. The Committee also considered that where there was

> no clear-cut indication, or where it is especially important to ensure that supervision and support will be thorough, the responsible medical officer . . . might approach both the Principal Probation Officer and the Director of Social Services . . . asking them to consult and consider how supervision could best be handled.
>
> (Home Office and DHSS, 1973: 17)

Support for these views was echoed by the Butler Committee. They considered that

> supervision should be undertaken by the person who can bring most to the case in the way of knowledge, expertise and resources in the particular circumstances of the case. The arrangements may need to take particular account of the needs of public safety.
>
> (Home Office and DHSS, 1975: 124)

It has been my experience that local authority social workers are rather less enthusiastic about taking on these cases than are probation officers. I believe this to be partly because local authority social workers are less familiar with work with adult offenders and the control element that is often required (see also Chapter 9). They also have to give priority to a more diverse range of statutory duties (particularly concerning child care) than do members of the probation service. However, there are now much better-defined obligations laid upon those local authority social workers who will act as 'Approved Social Workers' under the Mental Health Act 1983, and their roles have also been more clearly set out. It may well be that they will now begin to feel less reluctant to embrace work with this admittedly small but very challenging group of clients.

It is essential that there is open and constructive liaison with the psychiatrist concerned with the case. Clear procedures for such liaison should be established, set out and acknowledged. To achieve this the Home Office and the Department of Health and Social Security issued, in 1987, three overlapping sets of guidelines for social supervisors, psychiatrists and discharging hospitals (Home Office and DHSS, 1987a, 1987b, 1987c).

Not infrequently decisions may have to be made at a time of crisis. For example, an offender-patient's behaviour may have deteriorated to the extent that recall to hospital may need to be considered. In each area where restricted cases are being carried, the worker with the day-to-day responsibility for managing the case (which is best shared with a colleague) should have direct access to the psychiatrist involved in treating the offender-patient, and to his or her own senior management. The latter not only enhances accountability, but also provides a moral and practical support for the worker. A perceived lack of such support has been one of the most common complaints made to me during workshops devoted to this client patient group. In cases of emergency, Home Office officials are available for consultation – if necessary after normal office hours (see Baxter, 1991). The names and telephone numbers of these officials should be made known to the workers responsible for the day-to-day supervision of the case as a matter of routine. In situations other than those requiring recourse to *immediate* advice, the officer supervising the case should make a report to the Home Office (with copies to the local psychiatric consultant responsible for the case and, if appropriate, to the hospital RMO). Cases in which such advice might be sought would include those where there appears to be an actual or potential risk to the public, where contact with the offender-patient has been lost, where there has been a substantial breach of the conditions of discharge, where the offender-patient's behaviour suggests a need for recall for further in-patient treatment, or where the offender-patient has been charged with or convicted of a further offence.

If the offender-patient is recalled by order of the Home Secretary, the latter is obliged under Section 75 of the Mental Health Act 1983 to refer his or her case to a Mental Health Review Tribunal within one month of his or her recall. In deciding whether or not to issue a warrant for recall the Home Secretary will treat every case on its merits. If an offender-patient has been hospitalised in the past for very serious violence or for homicide, comparatively minor irregularities of conduct or failure to co-operate with the terms of the conditional discharge *might* well be sufficient to merit the consideration of recall.

Similar issues arise of course in relation to prisoners released on life licence or on parole. If all goes well, the conditions of a life licence, such as the requirements to live in a specific place, to report to the probation officer, to receive visits or not to take specific employments, may be cancelled – but usually not before some four or five years have elapsed. The life licence itself remains in force for life. In the case of conditionally discharged restricted patients the requirements for supervision, or the order for conditional discharge itself may be lifted by the Home Secretary or by a Mental Health Review Tribunal.

Currently there are some five to six hundred life-sentence prisoners being actively supervised by the probation service. It will have become obvious from what has already been said about the supervision of restricted cases that this is a very difficult area of work. As with the supervision of restricted offender-patients, the probation officer will have a dual concern for the welfare of the licensee and the protection of the public; in some instances the latter may well have to take precedence over the former. The supervision of life licensees and similar cases requires skills and commitment of a very high order. There are some who consider that the supervision of such cases should only be undertaken by very experienced probation officers or those of senior officer status (see, for example, Floud and Young, 1981: 142). The Home Office and the probation service take the supervision of such cases very seriously indeed (see, for example, Home Office *et al.*, 1992: Chapter 8).

CONCLUSION

In this chapter I have attempted to achieve the following objectives: (1) to provide a short historical context against which to view current practices concerning the treatment of mentally disturbed offenders; (2) to outline methods of diversion from the criminal justice system; (3) to describe the main health care and penal disposals; and (4) to provide a background against which to set the more clinical considerations to be addressed in Part II. It should be apparent that we still have a long way to go to achieve a more effective and humane system of management. The long-term closure plans for our older mental hospitals with little by way of replacement in terms of adequate community provision do not augur well for the future of a group doubly disadvantaged by being labelled as both mad and bad. Present confusions in health service and local authority organisation and funding merely serve to compound these difficulties.

APPENDIX A: SUMMARY OF THE DISPOSAL OF MENTALLY DISORDERED AND DISTURBED OFFENDERS THROUGH THE CRIMINAL JUSTICE, PENAL AND HEALTH CARE SYSTEMS

The provisions of the Mental Health Act 1983, the Criminal Procedure (Insanity and Unfitness to Plead) Act 1991 and the Powers of Criminal Courts Act 1973, as amended by the Criminal Justice Act 1991 (Schedule 1(5)), enable the courts to investigate and deal with a wide range of behaviour from the more mildly disturbed to the seriously mentally abnormal.

The provisions are summarised as follows:

(A) Hospital, guardianship and other orders

1 Section 37(1) of the Mental Health Act 1983 enables courts to make hospital orders or guardianship orders in the event of:
   (a) conviction for an offence (but in certain cases in the Magistrates' Courts without proceeding to conviction);
   (b) two doctors (at least one of whom is approved by a local health authority for the purpose under Section 12(2) of the Act) stating that the offender is suffering from mental illness, psychopathic disorder, mental impairment or severe mental impairment of a nature or degree which makes it appropriate for him/her to be detained in hospital for medical treatment; and, in the case of psychopathic disorder or mental impairment, that such treatment is likely to alleviate or prevent a deterioration of his/her condition;
   (c) a hospital being willing to accept the person or, in the case of guardianship, the local authority being willing to receive the person, provided he or she is over sixteen;
   (d) the circumstances being such that a hospital order is the most suitable method of dealing with the case.

2 Courts may also make orders for remand for treatment and may make interim hospital orders:
   (a) Section 36 enables the Crown Court to remand an accused to hospital for treatment if he or she is suffering from mental illness or severe mental impairment. The person may be detained for up to twenty-eight days – renewable for periods of twenty-eight days up to a maximum of twelve weeks.
   (b) Section 38 enables a court to make an interim hospital order in the case of a person convicted of an offence punishable by imprisonment (other than murder). The court must be satisfied that the person is suffering from mental disorder as defined in the Act. Period of detention: up to a maximum of six months in all.

3 In order for the evidence to be obtained for medical reports the following provisions may be used:
   (a) the person may be remanded in custody for three weeks (renewable) for the appropriate reports to be prepared;
   (b) remand on bail for periods of four weeks at a time. Reports may be prepared in this way on an in-patient or an out-patient basis;
   (c) remand to hospital under Section 35 of the Mental Health Act 1983. (Court must be of the belief that the person concerned is suffering from mental disorder as defined in the Act.) This provision (brought into effect in October 1984) gives courts a stronger option than a remand or bail with a requirement for medical examination. Problems often arise in obtaining the preliminary medical opinion *before* such a remand can be made. The period of detention under this section is up to twenty-eight days, renew-

able for twenty-eight days at a time to a maximum of twelve weeks in order for this examination and assessment to be made.

4 A person already in custody (either undergoing sentence or awaiting trial), whose mental state becomes such as to require compulsory detention in a hospital, may be transferred under the provision of Sections 47–49 of the Mental Health Act 1983.

(B) Probation and mental treatment

Section 3 of the Powers of the Criminal Courts Act 1973 as amended by the Criminal Justice Act 1991 (Schedule 1(5)) permits treatment if:

1 the offender-patient consents;
2 a hospital (or other establishment) will receive him or her, and is willing to provide treatment;
3 the oral or written evidence of one doctor (approved under Section 12(2) of the Mental Health Act) indicates that the offender's condition requires, and may be susceptible to, treatment, but is not such as to warrant his or her detention in pursuance of a hospital order.

(C) Other disposals

1 A defence of insanity may be raised before a Crown Court and if accepted by the jury will lead to a 'special verdict' of 'not guilty by reason of insanity'. The court, under recent legislation, now has the option of: admitting the person to hospital, with or without an order restricting discharge; an absolute discharge; a supervision and treatment order. (On a successful plea in a murder case the court must impose a restriction order.)
2 A finding of unfitness to plead (now known as being 'under disability in relation to the trial'). This has the same effect if accepted as in (1) above.
3 A defence of diminished responsibility under the Homicide Act 1957 may be raised (but only in murder cases); if accepted it leads to a conviction for manslaughter, leaving the court free to make any order it wishes.
4 No action in respect of the mental disorder (that is, the court makes a non-psychiatric disposal).

NOTES

1 Since the publication of the circular, interest in various forms of diversion has gathered momentum. The National Association for the Care and Resettlement of Offenders (NACRO) is currently pioneering a number of research projects on the working of diversion schemes in various parts of the country. It is estimated that there are now (in 1994) over one hundred such experimental schemes. Another voluntary body, MIND (the National Association for Mental Health), has provided an interesting account of a scheme in North Humberside (1993), and the Mental Health Foundation, with the financial sponsorship of the Home Office and the support of the Department of Health and Lord

Chancellor's Department, has been holding a series of conferences on diversion, amongst other topics, in each regional health authority in England and Wales.

2   Cases such as these illustrate the importance of a historical perspective on contemporary problems. Such a perspective may help us to take a more balanced and less impulsive view and alert us to the dangers of reinventing the wheel referred to in the text. Those wishing to gain such a perspective from a study of original rather than secondary sources could profitably consult Bynum *et al.* (1985a, 1985b and 1988).

3   The sad fate of many of these individuals and the possible remedies for their better care have been well set out in a lecture given by Lord Justice Mustill (1991).

4   These are not discrete stages and there may well be overlap. I have set them out in this fashion in an attempt to clarify the picture.

5   Judge Tumin's report indicates that 'in the period 1981 to the end of September, 1990, there were 56 incidents of self-inflicted death involving those under the age of 21. The average was 18.58 years. Of the 52 cases in which inquests have been held there were 37 verdicts of suicide' (Home Office 1980: 22, para. 3.34). Research conducted on prison populations indicates there is a 'four-fold increase in suicide rates amongst prisoners compared to the general population' (McClure, 1987, quoted in Johnson *et al.*, 1993: 137). Johnson *et al.* also make the point that, 'in contrast with the general population, forensic patients are more likely to commit suicide using a violent method and are more likely to have a suicide verdict recorded by the coroner'. For further information concerning comparative suicide rates in various 'custodial' institutions, see Haycock (1993).

6   As noted in Chapter 2 courts remand only rarely for psychiatric reports. However, as already indicated, murder cases will always be investigated, as most likely will be certain other crimes such as arson and some sexual offences (see later discussion). In addition, any oddness on the part of the accused whilst held in custody or during appearance in court may prompt a remand for psychiatric opinion. In recent years prison doctors have prepared 6,000–7,000 reports on prisoners annually (Home Office, 1993a). There are no comparable figures easily available for reports obtained on bail. Probation officers can play a highly significant part not only in acting as primary screeners, but also in providing very valuable background information to both the court and the examining psychiatrist should a report be requested. The Butler Committee wished to see an extention of this screening role (Home Office and DHSS, 1975: 2.46). (For reviews of current practices in obtaining reports and of the relevant literature, see references in Chapter 2.)

7   In practice, few orders for guardianship are made by the courts. Their use under the civil powers of the Act is also comparatively infrequent. In a recent study, Grant reports that 'the majority of cases were made under the Civil Section (Section 7) (114 of the 123 new cases between April, 1986 and March 1987)' (1992: 321). See also Wattis *et al.* (1990).

REFERENCES

Cases cited

R. v. *Birch* [1989] Court of Appeal, *Independent* Law Reports, 12 May: 14.
R. v. *Courtney* [1987] Court of Appeal, *Crim. Law Rev.*, February 1988: 130.
R. v. *Merseyside Mental Health Review Tribunal ex parte K* [1990] 1 All ER 694, CA.
R. v. *Secretary of State for the Home Department ex parte K* [1990] 1 All ER 703.

Text references

Allderidge, P. (1979) 'Hospitals, Madhouses and Asylums: Cycles in the Care of the Insane', *British Journal of Psychiatry* 134: 321–324.
—— (1985) 'Bedlam: Fact or Phantasy', in W.F. Bynum, R. Porter and M. Shepherd (eds), *The Anatomy of Madness: Essays in the History of Psychiatry. Vol. 2: Institutions and Society*, London: Tavistock.
Ashworth, A., Cavadino, P., Gibson, B., Harding, J., Rutherford, A., Seago, P. and Whyte, L. (1992) *Introduction to the Criminal Justice Act, 1991*, Winchester: Waterside Press.
Bailey, J. and MacCulloch, M. (1992) 'Patterns of Reconviction in Patients Discharged Directly to the Community from a Special Hospital: Implications for After-Care', *The Journal of Forensic Psychiatry* 3: 445–461.
Bartlett, A. (1993) 'Rhetoric and Reality: What Do We Know about the English Special Hospitals?' *International Journal of Law and Psychiatry* 16: 27–51.
Baxter, R. (1991) 'The Mentally Disordered Offender in Hospital: The Role of the Home Office', in K. Herbst and J. Gunn (eds), *The Mentally Disordered Offender*, London: Butterworth-Heinemann in association with the Mental Health Foundation.
Bean, P., Bingley, W., Bynoe, I., Faulkner, A., Rassaby, E. and Rogers, A. (1991) *Out of Harm's Way*, London: MIND.
Bluglass, R. (1990) 'Prison Medical Services', in R. Bluglass and P. Bowden (eds), *Principles and Practice of Forensic Psychiatry*, London: Churchill Livingstone.
Boswell, G. (1991) *Waiting for Change: Section 53 Offenders: An Exploration of Experiences and Needs*, Norwich: Social Work Development Unit, University of East Anglia (for the Prince's Trust).
Bowden, P. (1978) 'Men Remanded into Custody for Medical Reports: The Selection for Treatment', *British Journal of Psychiatry* 32: 320–331.
—— (1993) 'New Directions for Service Provision', in W. Watson and A. Grounds (eds), *The Mentally Disordered Offender in an Era of Community Care*, Cambridge: Cambridge University Press.
Brindle, D. (1990) '800 Inmates Wrongly Kept in Special Hospitals', *Guardian*, 19 September.
Bynum, W.F., Porter, R. and Shepherd, M. (eds) (1985a) *The Anatomy of Madness: Essays in the History of Psychiatry. Vol. 1: People and Ideas*, London: Tavistock.
—— (eds) (1985b) *The Anatomy of Madness: Essays in the History of Psychiatry. Vol. 2: Institutions and Society*, London: Tavistock.
—— (eds) (1988) *The Anatomy of Madness: Essays in the History of Psychiatry. Vol. 3: The Asylum and Its Psychiatry*, London: Tavistock.
Carson, D. (1992) 'Holding the Patient to Account at the Gate-Keeping Stage', *Criminal Behaviour and Mental Health* 2: 224–233.
Chiswick, D. (1990) 'Applied Criminology', *Current Opinion in Psychiatry* 3: 754–757.
Coid, J. (1991) 'Psychiatric Profiles of Difficult/Disruptive Prisoners', in K. Bottomley and W. Hay (eds), *Special Units for Difficult Prisoners*, Hull: Centre for Criminology and Criminal Justice, University of Hull.
—— (1993) 'Quality of Life for Patients Detained in Hospital', *British Journal of Psychiatry* 162: 611–620.
Cooke, D.J. (1991) 'Treatment as an Alternative to Prosecution: Offenders Diverted for Treatment', *British Journal of Psychiatry* 158: 785–791.
Cooper, D. (1990) 'Parkhurst Prison: C Wing', in R. Bluglass and P. Bowden (eds), *Principles and Practice of Forensic Psychiatry*, London: Churchill Livingstone.
Crown Prosecution Service (n.d.) *Code for Crown Prosecutors*, London: CPS.
Department of Health (1992a) *Statistical Bulletin* 2(7).
—— (1992b) *Report of the Committee of Inquiry into Complaints about Ashworth*

Hospital, Vols 1 and 2 (Chairman, Sir Louis Blom-Cooper, QC), Cmnd 2028-I and -II, London: HMSO.

Department of Health and Home Office (1992) *Review of Health and Social Services for Mentally Disordered Offenders and Others Requiring Similar Services* (Chairman, Dr John Reed, CB), *Final Summary Report*, Cmnd 2088, London: HMSO.

—— (1994) *Report of the Working Group on High Security and Related Psychiatric Provision* (Chairman, Dr John Reed, CB), London: Department of Health and Home Office.

Department of Health and Social Security (DHSS) (1974) *Revised Report of the Working Party on Security in NHS Psychiatric Hospitals* (Glancy Report), London: DHSS.

—— (1980) *Report of the Review of Rampton Hospital*, (Boynton Report), Cmnd 8073, London: HMSO.

Department of Health and Welsh Office (1990) *Mental Health Act 1983: Code of Practice*, London: HMSO.

East, W.N. and de Hubert, W.H.B. (1939) *Psychological Treatment of Crime*, London: HMSO.

Egglestone, F. (1990) 'The Advisory Board on Restricted Patients', in R. Bluglass and P. Bowden (eds), *Principles and Practice of Forensic Psychiatry*, London: Churchill Livingstone.

Evershed, S. (1991) 'Special Unit, C Wing, HM Prison Parkhurst', in K. Herbst and J. Gunn (eds), *The Mentally Disordered Offender*, London: Butterworth-Heinemann in association with the Mental Health Foundation.

Faulk, M. (1990) 'Her Majesty's Prison Grendon', in R. Bluglass and P. Bowden (eds), *Principles and Practice of Forensic Psychiatry*, London: Churchill Livingstone.

Floud, J. and Young, W. (1981) *Dangerousness and Criminal Justice*, London: Heinemann.

Fowles, A.J. (1993) 'The Mentally Disordered Offender in the Era of Community Care', in W. Watson and A. Grounds (eds), *The Mentally Disordered Offender in an Era of Community Care*, Cambridge: Cambridge University Press.

Gostin, L. (ed.) (1985) *Secure Provision: A Review of Special Services for the Mentally Ill and Mentally Handicapped in England and Wales*, London: Tavistock.

Grant, W. (1992) 'Guardianship Orders: A Review of Their Use under the 1983 Mental Health Act', *Medicine, Science and the Law* 32: 319–324.

Grounds, A.T. (1990) 'Transfers of Sentenced Prisoners to Hospital', *Criminal Law Review* June: 544–551.

—— (1991a) 'The Transfer of Sentenced Prisoners to Hospital 1960–1963: A Study in One Special Hospital', *British Journal of Criminology* 31: 54–71.

—— (1991b) 'The Mentally Disordered in Prison', *Prison Service Journal* 81: 29–40.

—— (1991c) 'The Mentally Disordered Offender in the Criminal Process: Some Research and Policy Questions', in K. Herbst and J. Gunn (eds), *The Mentally Disordered Offender*, London: Butterworth-Heinemann in association with the Mental Health Foundation.

—— (1992) Lecture based upon an unpublished report presented to the Forensic Psychiatry Section meeting of the Royal College of Psychiatrists, York, 15 February.

Grunhut, M. (1963) *Probation and Mental Treatment*, London: Tavistock.

Gunn, J. (1985) 'Psychiatry and the Prison Medical Service', in L. Gostin (ed.), *Secure Provision: A Review of Special Services for the Mentally Ill and Mentally Handicapped in England and Wales*, London: Tavistock.

Gunn, J., Robertson, G., Dell, S. and Way, C. (1978) *Psychiatric Aspects of Imprisonment*, London: Academic Press.

Gunn, J., Maden, A. and Swinton, M. (1991a) 'Treatment Needs of Prisoners with Psychiatric Disorders', *British Medical Journal* 303: 338–341.

—— (1991b) *Mentally Disordered Prisoners*, London: Home Office.

Hamilton, J.R. (1985) 'The Special Hospitals', in L. Gostin, (ed.), *Secure Provision: A*

Review of Special Services for the Mentally Ill and Mentally Handicapped in England and Wales, London: Tavistock.

—— (1990) 'Special Hospitals and the State Hospital', in R. Bluglass and P. Bowden (eds), *Principles and Practice of Forensic Psychiatry*, London: Churchill Livingstone.

Haycock, J. (1993) 'Comparative Suicide Rates in Different Types of Involuntary Confinement', *Medicine, Science and the Law* 33: 128–136.

Hetherington, T. (1989) *Prosecution in the Public Interest*, London: Waterlow.

Home Office (1990) *Report of a Review into Suicide and Self-Harm in Prison Service Establishments in England and Wales* (Report by Judge Stephen Tumin to Home Secretary) Cmnd 1383, London: HMSO.

—— (1991a) *HM Prison Brixton: Report by HM Chief Inspector of Prisons*, London: HMSO.

—— (1991b) *Custody, Care and Justice: The Way Ahead for the Prison Service in England and Wales*, London: HMSO.

—— (1991c) *Prison Disturbances, April 1990: Report of an Inquiry by the Rt Hon. Lord Justice Woolf (Pts I and II) and His Honour Judge Stephen Tumim (Pt II)* Cmnd 1456, London: HMSO.

—— (1993a) 'Statistics of Mentally Disordered Offenders', in *Home Office Research and Statistics Department Statistical Bulletin: Issue 02/93*, February 17: 4, London: HMSO.

—— (1993b) *Probation Statistics for England and Wales* February. London: Home Office.

Home Office and Department of Health (1991) *Review of Health and Social Services for Mentally Disordered Offenders and Others Requiring Similar Services: Reports of the Community Advisory Group and of the Prison Advisory Group*, London: Home Office and Department of Health.

Home Office and Department of Health and Social Security (DHSS) (1973) *Report on the Review of Procedures for the Discharge and Supervision of Psychiatric Patients Subject to Special Restrictions* (Aarvold Report), Cmnd 5191, London: HMSO.

—— (1974) *Interim Report of the Committee on Mentally Abnormal Offenders* (The Butler Committee), Cmnd 5698, London: HMSO.

—— (1975) *Report of the Committee on Mentally Abnormal Offenders* (The Butler Committee), Cmnd 6244, London: HMSO.

—— (1987a) *Mental Health Act, 1983: Supervision and After-Care of Conditionally Discharged Restricted Patients: Notes for the Guidance of Social Supervisors*, London: Home Office and DHSS.

—— (1987b) *Mental Health Act, 1983: Supervision and After-Care of Conditionally Discharged Restricted Patients: Notes for the Guidance of Supervising Psychiatrists*, London: Home Office and DHSS.

—— (1987c) *Mental Health Act, 1983: Supervision and After-Care of Conditionally Discharged Restricted Patients: Notes for the Guidance of Hospitals Preparing for the Conditional Discharge of Restricted Patients*, London: Home Office and DHSS.

Home Office and Secretary of State for Scotland and for Northern Ireland (1979) *Report of the Committee of Inquiry into the UK Prison Services* (Chairman, Sir John May), Cmnd 7673, London: HMSO.

Home Office, Department of Health and Welsh Office (1992) *National Standards for the Supervision of Offenders in the Community*, London: Home Office.

House of Commons (1986) *Third Report from the Social Services Committee, Session, 1985–1986*, London: HMSO.

Institute of Race Relations (1991) *Deadly Silence: Black Deaths in Custody*, London: IRR.

James, D.V. and Hamilton, L.W. (1991) 'The Clerkenwell Scheme – Assessing Efficacy and Cost of a Psychiatric Liaison Service to a Magistrates' Court', *British Medical Journal* 303: 282–285.

Johnson, C., Smith, J., Crowe, C. Donovan, M. (1993) 'Suicide among Forensic Patients', *Medicine, Science and the Law* 33: 137–144.

Joseph, P. (1992) *Psychiatric Assessment at the Magistrates' Court*, London: Home Office and Department of Health.

Joseph, P. and Potter, M. (1993) 'Diversion from Custody' – 'I: Psychiatric Assessment at the Magistrates' Court' and 'II: Effect on Hospital and Prison Resources', *British Journal of Psychiatry* 162: 325–330 and 330–334.

Laing, R.D. and Esterson, A. (1970) *Sanity, Madness and the Family: Families of Schizophrenics*, Harmondsworth: Penguin.

Leicestershire County Council (1993) *The Leicestershire Inquiry, 1992: Report of an Inquiry into Aspects of the Management of Children's Homes in Leicestershire between 1973 and 1986* (Chairman, Andrew Kirkwood, QC), Leicester: Leicestershire County Council.

Lewis, P. (1980) *Psychiatric Probation Orders: Roles and Expectations of Probation Officers and Psychiatrists*, Cambridge: Cambridge Institute of Criminology.

Littlewood, R. and Lipsedge, M. (1989) *Aliens and Alienists: Ethnic Minorities and Psychiatry* (second edn), London: Unwin Hyman.

Lloyd, M.G. and Bénézech, M. (1991) 'Criminal Responsibility in the French Judicial System', *Journal of Forensic Psychiatry* 2: 281–294.

McClure, G.M.G. (1987) 'Suicide in England and Wales 1975–84', *British Journal of Psychiatry* 150: 309–314.

MIND (1993) North Humberside Association for Mental Health, Hull, (information pack).

Mustill, M. (1991) 'The Mentally Disordered Offender: A Call for Thought', lecture delivered at King's Fund Centre, London, 2 May.

National Association for the Care and Resettlement of Offenders (NACRO) (1992) *Revolving Doors: Report of the Telethon Inquiry into the Relationship between Mental Health and Criminal Justice*, London: NACRO.

—— (1993) *Mental Health Advisory Committee: Policy Paper No. 1: Community Care and Mentally Disturbed Offenders*, London: NACRO.

National Health Advisory Service and Department of Health and Social Security (DHSS) Social Services Inspectorate (1988) *Reports on Services Provided by Broadmoor Hospital* (HAS/SSI/88/8h/1), London: Department of Health.

Palermo, G.B., Smith, M.B. and Liska, F.J. (1991) 'Jails versus Mental Hospitals: The Milwaukee Approach to a Social Dilemma', *International Journal of Offender Therapy and Comparative Criminology* 35: 205–216.

Parker, E. (1980) 'Mentally Disordered Offenders and Their Protection from Punitive Sanction, *International Journal of Law and Psychiatry* 3: 461–469.

—— (1985) 'The Development of Secure Provision', in L. Gostin (ed.), *Secure Provision: A Review of Special Services for the Mentally Ill and Mentally Handicapped in England and Wales*, London: Tavistock.

Penrose, L. (1939) 'Mental Disease and Crime: Outline for a Study of European Statistics', *British Journal of Medical Psychology* 18: 1–15.

Prins, H. (1991a) 'Mental Abnormality and Criminality: An Uncertain Relationship', *Medicine, Science and the Law* 30: 247–258.

—— (1991b) 'Editorial: The Avoidance of Scandal – A Perennial Problem', *Medicine, Science and the Law* 31: 277–279.

—— (1992) 'The Diversion of the Mentally Disordered: Some Problems for Criminal Justice, Penology and Health Care', *Journal of Forensic Psychiatric* 3: 431–443.

—— (1993) 'The People Nobody Owns', in W. Watson and A. Grounds (eds), *The Mentally Disordered Offender in an Era of Community Care*, Cambridge: Cambridge University Press.

Rogers, A. and Faulkner, A. (1987) *A Place of Safety*, London: MIND.

Rollin, H. (1993) 'A Hundred Years Ago: Malice or Madness?', *British Journal of Psychiatry* 162: 575.

Roth, M. and Kroll J. (1986) *The Reality of Mental Illness*, Cambridge: Cambridge University Press.

Scott, J. (1993) 'Homelessness and Mental Illness', *British Journal of Psychiatry* 162: 314–324.

Scott, P.D. (1975) *Has Psychiatry Failed in the Treatment of the Offender?*, London: Institute for the Study and Treatment of Delinquency.

Scull, A. (1984) *Decarceration: Community Treatment and the Deviant: A Radical View* (second edn), Cambridge: Polity Press.

Selby, M. (1991) 'HMP Grendon: The Care of Acute Psychiatric Patients: A Pragmatic Solution', in K. Herbst and J. Gunn (eds), *The Mentally Disordered Offender*, London: Butterworth-Heinemann in association with the Mental Health Foundation.

Smith, C. (1990) 'The Central Mental Hospital, Dundrum, Dublin', in R. Bluglass and P. Bowden (eds), *Principles and Practice of Forensic Psychiatry*, London: Churchill Livingstone.

Smith, J. and Donovan, M. (1990) 'The Prosecution of Psychiatric Inpatients', *Journal of Forensic Psychiatry* 1: 379–383.

Smith, R. (1984) *Prison Health Care*, London: British Medical Association.

Swinton, M. (1991) 'Prisons, Hospitals and the Mentally Abnormal Offender', *Current Opinion in Psychiatry* 4: 661–664.

Szasz, T. (1974) *The Myth of Mental Illness*, New York: Harper and Row.

Teplin, L.A. and Pruett, N.S. (1992) 'Police as Streetcorner Psychiatrist: Managing the Mentally Ill', *International Journal of Law and Psychiatry* 15: 139–156.

Tooth, G.C. and Brooke, E.M. (1961) 'Trends in the Mental Hospital Population and their Effect on Future Planning', *Lancet* 1: 710.

Walker, N.D. (1977) *Behaviour and Misbehaviour: Explanations and Non-Explanations*, Oxford: Blackwell.

Wattis, J., Grant, W., Trayner, J. and Harris, S. (1990) 'Use of Guardianship under the 1983 Mental Health Act', *Medicine, Science and the Law* 30: 313–316.

Whatmore, P. (1990) 'The Special Unit at Barlinnie Prison, Glasgow', in R. Bluglass and P. Bowden (eds), *Principles and Practice of Forensic Psychiatry*, London: Churchill Livingstone.

Wood, J. (1988) 'Relations with the Police and the Public and with Overseas Police and Judicial Authorities', in J.E. Hall Williams (ed.), *The Role of the Prosecutor: Report of the International Criminal Justice Seminar Held at the London School of Economics and Political Science, January 1987*, Aldershot: Avebury.

FURTHER READING

Historical aspects

Berrios, G.E. and Freeman, H. (eds) (1991) *150 Years of British Psychiatry, 1841–1991*, London: Gaskell.

Crammer, J. (1990) *Asylum History: Buckinghamshire County Pauper Lunatic Asylum – St John's*, London: Gaskell.

Foucault, M. (1985) *Madness and Civilisation: A History of Insanity in the Age of Reason*, London: Tavistock.

Porter, R. (1987) *A Social History of Madness: Stories of the Insane*, London: Weidenfeld and Nicolson.

Scull, A. (ed.) (1981) *Madhouses, Mad-Doctors and the Madman: The Social History of Psychiatry in the Victorian Era*, London: Athlone Press.

Legislative matters: general

Gunn, J. (1979) 'The Law and the Mentally Abnormal Offender in England and Wales', *International Journal of Law and Psychiatry*, 2: 199–214.

Hoggett, B. (1990) *Mental Health Law* (third edn), London: Sweet and Maxwell.

Jones, R. (1994) *Mental Health Act Manual* (fourth edn), London: Sweet and Maxwell.

Mental Health Act Commission (1985 and onwards) *Biennial Reports*, London: HMSO.

Verdun-Jones, S. (1989) 'Sentencing the Partly Mad and the Partly Bad: The Case of the Hospital Order in England and Wales', *International Journal of Law and Psychiatry* 12: 1–17.

Mental Health Review Tribunals

Gostin, L. and Fennell, P. (1992) *Mental Health: Tribunal Procedure* (second edn), London: Longman.

Peay, J. (1989) *Tribunals on Trial: A Study of Decision Making Under the Mental Health Act 1983*, Oxford: Clarendon Press.

Wood, J. (1993a) 'Reform of the Mental Health Act 1983: An Effective Tribunal System', *British Journal of Psychiatry* 162: 14–22.

Wood, J. (1993b) 'Future Directions for Mental Health Law', in W. Watson and A. Grounds (eds), *The Mentally Disordered Offender in an Era of Community Care*, Cambridge: Cambridge University Press.

Institutions

Berry, M.J. (1985) *Secure Units: A Bibliography*, Special Hospitals Research Report No. 18, London: DHSS.

Boyle, J. (1984) *The Pain of Confinement: Prison Diaries*, Edinburgh, Canongate.

Gostin, L. (1986) *Institutions Observed: Towards a New Concept of Secure Provision in Mental Health*, London: King Edward's Hospital Fund.

Jones, K. and Fowles, A.J. (1984) *Ideas on Institutions: Analysis of the Literature on Long-Term Care and Custody*, London: Routledge and Kegan Paul.

Millham, S., Bullock, R., Hosie, K. and Little M. (1988) *The Characteristics of Young People in Youth Treatment Centres*, Bristol: Dartington Social Research Unit, University of Bristol.

Stewart, G. and Tutt, N. (1987) *Children in Custody*, Avebury: Gower.

Community aspects

Coker, J.B. and Martin, J. (1985) *Licensed to Live*, Oxford: Blackwell.

Graham, A. and Thomson, I. (1990) 'Guardianship – A Part of Caring', *Community Care*, 8 February: 22–23.

Home Office, NACRO and The Mental Health Foundation (1994) *The NACRO Diversion Initiative for Mentally Disturbed Offenders: An Account and an Evaluation*, London: Home Office.

Mental Health Foundation (1994) *Report of the Mental Health Foundation into Community Care for People with Severe Mental Illness* (Chairman Sir William Utting, CB), London: MHF.

Murray, D.J. (1989) *Review of Research on Re-Offending of Mentally Disordered Offenders*, Research and Planning Unit, Paper 55, London: Home Office.

Norris, M. (1984) *Integration of Special Hospital Patients into the Community*, Aldershot: Gower.

Prins, H. (1993) 'Service Provision and Facilities for the Mentally Disordered Offender', in C.R. Hollin and K. Howells (eds), *Clinical Approaches to the Mentally Disordered Offender*, Chichester: John Wiley.

Part II

Clinical considerations

Chapter 4

Mental disturbance and criminality

> How sad and bad and mad it was . . .
> (Browning, 'Confessions')

I made reference in previous chapters to certain forms of mental disturbance and their possible relationship to criminal conduct. Such reference was in very general terms; in this chapter, I consider aspects of mental disturbance and its relationship to criminality in more detail.

The term 'mental disturbance' is used here, as in previous chapters, to include mental disorder as defined in the Mental Health Act 1983 in England and Wales. This includes mental illness (which in the Act is not further defined), mental impairment, severe mental impairment, psychopathic disorder and any other disorder or disability of mind. The use of the term 'mental disturbance' also enables us to consider a wide range of other disorders and abnormalities, some of which would not satisfy the criteria for compulsory hospitalisation under the Mental Health Act. Admittedly, 'mental disturbance' is a somewhat vague term and, as we have seen, it has certainly led to difficulties for the courts in trying to determine what constitutes such an abnormality within the meaning of the Homicide Act 1957. The term is used here merely to encompass a range of disordered mental states, but its imperfections are recognised. As we shall see, it is in many ways easier to define mental illnesses, especially those with clear-cut aetiology; it is less easy to define with any degree of acceptable precision such conditions as mental handicap (learning difficulty), particularly in its milder presentations, and conditions such as personality (psychopathic) disorder. What we do know with some certainty, however, is that mental disturbance is likely to be present at all levels of society, including political and other leaders. Sometimes this may have frightening consequences (see, for example, Freeman, 1991).

'MOVING THE GOALPOSTS'

At the outset we are faced with the difficult task of trying to establish any clear causal connections, or even associations, between mental disturbance and criminality. This is because we are trying to make connections between very different phenomena, and these phenomena are the subject of much debate concerning both substance and definition. It is as though the 'goalposts' for the game are constantly being shifted. Let us take mental disturbance first. There are those who seek to suggest that some forms of mental disturbance do not even exist. A major proponent of this view is that redoubtable critic of psychiatry and psychiatrists – Professor Szasz – himself a psychoanalytic psychiatrist. In one of his more recent books (Szasz, 1987) he summarises most of what he has said on this topic over several decades, namely that persons are often diagnosed as mentally ill on the grounds that they have problems in living and that these problems affront society, therefore psychiatry is used to remove them from public view and conscience. This is a very bald and somewhat over-simplified view of Szasz's work. He has recently written a powerful answer to some of his critics (see Szasz, 1993). His arguments have an attractive seductiveness but they also contain elements of rhetoric which have been criticised cogently, by other psychiatrists and by non-psychiatrists (for example Mindham *et al.* 1992; Roth and Kroll, 1986; Sedgwick, 1982).

In the 1960s there existed a popular view that much mental illness had its origins in 'conspiracies' and 'mixed messages' within families (see, for example, Laing and Esterson, 1964). At the other end of the 'spectrum' we have the more biological-psychiatric view, as set out, for example, in some of the standard textbooks of psychiatry such as that of Slater and Roth (1969) and others. Professor Gunn puts the position into perspective very well, when he states

> somewhere in the confusion there is a biological reality of mental disorder . . . this reality is a complex mixture of diverse conditions, some organic, some functional, some inherited, some learned, some acquired, some curable, others unremitting.
>
> (1977a: 317)

This complex picture is also compounded by the fact that the prevalence and presentation of mental disorders appear to change over time. Hard facts concerning the epidemiology and substance of mental disorders, even for periods as recent as the nineteenth century, are not easy to come by. Some researchers (such as Hare, 1983; Scull, 1984) have concluded, albeit tentatively, that the schizophrenic illnesses as we know them today possibly did not exist on any large scale in earlier times. However, anecdotal and some clinical evidence would indicate that this assertion needs to be viewed with some caution (see Bark, 1985; Prins, 1987; Gunn, 1993; Eastman, 1993).

It is also worthwhile mentioning that in earlier times there may well have been individuals presenting with psychiatric symptoms in whom, these days, we would recognise a physical or organic origin (see later discussion and Klawans 1990a, 1990b, 1991). In the middle ages, for example, malnutrition produced pellagric states with their psychological and psychiatric consequences. The use of bad flour probably produced ergot poisoning which in turn could produce signs and symptoms of psychiatric illness. It has been suggested that episodes of the 'dancing mania' seen in mediaeval Italy and other countries were due to such a cause (Camporesi, 1989). Lead was commonly used in making cooking utensils and for water pipes; this could produce lead poisoning which in turn produced confused and disturbed behaviour.

Occupations also have their hazards. Few people can recall why Lewis Carroll described the 'Hatter' at the tea party as 'mad'; he did so because people who worked in the hat-making industry might be exposed to mercury, and mercurial poisoning can produce signs and symptoms of so-called mental illness. It has been suggested that Isaac Newton's well-known episodes of withdrawal from public life and activity may have been due not to depressive illness, as had been thought hitherto, but to the effects of the mercuric substances with which he experimented (Klawans, 1990b). It is of some interest to note that we are currently concerned about the effects of lead emissions, particularly on children's behaviour; and there are those who believe that poor-quality diet (particularly if it includes large quantities of 'junk' foods and additives) can produce hyper-active and anti-social behaviour in some children. However firm evidence of this, both in the USA and in Britain, is not available.

When we come to consider criminal behaviour we are faced with problems similar to those outlined above. At its simplest, crime is merely that form of behaviour defined as illegal and punishable by the criminal law. At various times in our history, acts judged as criminal have been redefined, or even removed from the statute books – as, for example, in the case of attempted suicide and adult male consenting homosexual acts committed in private. *New* offences are also created, particularly in times of war or civil commotion. Moreover, our increas-ingly complex technological society has necessitated the introduction of a wide range of laws and regulations governing many aspects of our conduct. Since much criminal behaviour is somewhat arbitrarily defined, and there are argu-ments about the existence and definition of mental abnormalities (disturbance), it is hardly surprising that we experience difficulty in trying to establish con-nections between these two somewhat ill-defined and complex behaviours. In view of this, it is even less surprising that we find difficulties in estimating the numbers of mentally disordered offenders in penal and other populations (see Chapter 3 and useful surveys by Wessely and Taylor, 1991, and Hodgins, 1993). Whatever the difficulties may be, there are a number of occasions when mental disturbances seem to be closely associated with criminal conduct and some aspects of this connection are now considered in more detail.

AN OUTLINE CLASSIFICATION

Mental disorders have been classified in a variety of ways. The two most commonly used classification systems – particularly for research purposes – are the *Diagnostic and Statistical Manual of Mental Disorders* published by the American Psychiatric Association (in its fourth revised version: APA, 1994) and *The ICD-10 Classification of Mental and Behavioural Disorders* published by the World Health Organisation (1992). These substantial volumes cover every aspect of diagnosis and classification and should be referred to by those who wish to pursue this topic in detail. Table 4.1 provides a much simplified classification followed by some explanatory comment.

Table 4.1 Outline classification of mental disorders

The functional psychoses	the affective disorders schizophrenic illnesses
The neuroses (psychoneuroses, neurotic reactions)	mild depression anxiety states hysteria (hysterical reactions) obsessional states
Mental disorder as a result of infection, disease, metabolic and similar disturbances, trauma	(including the epilepsies)[a]
Mental disorder due to the ageing process	(for example, the dementias)
Abnormalities of personality and sexual disorders [b]	
Substance abuse (alcohol, other drugs, solvents, etc.) [c]	
Mental impairment (learning disabilities); also known as mental handicap, retardation [d]	(including chromosomal abnormalities)

Notes: [a] The inclusion of the epilepsies needs of a word of explanation. Strictly speaking, the epilepsies are not mental disorders as such but are *neurological* disturbances (disorders). They are included here because they sometimes produce psychological and psychiatric disturbances.
   [b] Personality disorder (psychopathic disorder) is considered in its own right in Chapter 5. Sexual disorders are considered in Chapter 8 because they may present as sexual *deviation* in the form of offending.
   [c] For reasons of space a separate chapter has not been devoted to this problem but reference made to it where relevant in other chapters.
   [d] This condition has been known throughout history by many different names. Fortunately, some of the older and more pejorative terms such as feeble-mindedness, idiocy, deficiency, amentia, are now no longer used.

The somewhat arbitrary nature of the above classification will become obvious when we consider some of the conditions in a little more detail. It is also very important to recognise that many of these disorders will overlap, that their prevalence may appear to change over time and be influenced by social norms. This is of great importance at the present time because of justified concerns about possible misdiagnoses of mental disturbances in certain ethnic minority groups such as Afro-Caribbeans. The classification is merely offered to provide some structure for the following comments. (Readers who wish to pursue the topic in more depth should consult APA, 1994, WHO, 1992, and any of the standard textbooks of psychiatry referred to at the end of this chapter.)

THE FUNCTIONAL PSYCHOSES

This term is commonly used to described a group of severe mental disorders for which, as yet, the evidence of underlying organic brain disturbance has not been demonstrated. However, it seems likely that in time, it may be possible to prove a neuro-biochemical cause for some of these disorders. The two illnesses subsumed under this heading are (1) the *affective disorders* (*manic-depressive illness*) and (2) the *schizophrenic illnesses*. I consider first the affective disorders. In doing so, I must emphasise that *only the barest outline* is provided of this and the following disorders. Specialist texts should be consulted for detail concerning their aetiology and management.

Affective disorders

The underlying characteristic of an affective disorder is a basic disturbance of mood. In cases of *mild* depressive disorder (see later), the disturbance of mood may be sufficiently slight for it to be almost unnoticeable to those quite close to the person. In *severe* depressive disorder, the mood disturbance is much more pronounced; a useful *aide-mémoire* is that the main characteristics are those of 'loss' (of energy, of libido [sexual drive], weight, appetite, interest in oneself and one's environment). Such features may be so pronounced that the person concerned may be quite unable to perform normal daily routines and functions. Accompanying characteristics may include varying degrees of tension, severe feelings of guilt, lack of concentration, disturbances in sleep patterns and pre-occupation with what the sufferer believes to be disturbed bodily functions (such as bowel or bladder movements). Some forms of depressive disorder are also characterised by agitation, restlessness and irritability. In very severe states of depression (true *melancholia*), the person may be so retarded that suicidal action will generally be precluded. However, as recovery takes place, such thoughts may become prominent and the person may put them into action. It is, therefore, of the utmost importance that such persons and their families be counselled as to the dangers of seeking premature discharge from hospital.

At the other end of the spectrum is the condition known as mania or hypomania. This is the very opposite of depressive illness. Here, activities are grossly speeded up, grandiose ideas are developed and the person becomes uncontrollably excitable, over-active, socially disinhibited and totally lacking in insight. Attempts by others to interfere with what the sufferer believes to be his or her lawful activities may result in serious injury to themselves. The total lack of insight normally demands admission to hospital under compulsion, where, given treatment, the condition can be remedied. It is important to note that one of the remedies currently in use – lithium carbonate – requires careful and regular monitoring since this powerful drug can harmfully affect liver and other functions.

There is no clear consensus as to the classification and aetiology of affective disorders. Some hold the view that two types may be discerned – *endogenous* (that is, where no clear precipitating factors can be seen) and *exogenous* (or reactive); in the latter, some stressful life event is said to have precipitated the illness. When states of depression alternate with episodes of manic illness the term *manic-depressive psychosis* is sometimes used. Some authorities refer to the depressive phase of this particular illness as 'bi-polar' depression, using the term 'unipolar' depression for those cases in which manic illness is not present. The classifications are important from a treatment point of view; generally speaking, endogenous depression (if it is intractable) responds best to moderate applications of ECT (electro-convulsive therapy) and exogenous depression responds better to moderate medication coupled with psychotherapy of some kind. Naturally there are cases in which the treatment indications are not as clear-cut as I have suggested.

Severe affective disorder and crime

Occasionally, we find cases in which a person charged with a grave offence such as homicide is found to have been suffering from a severe depressive disorder at the time of the offence. West, in his study of cases of *Murder Followed by Suicide*, suggested that sufferers from psychotic depression may

> become so convinced of the helplessness of their misery that death becomes a happy escape. Sometimes, before committing suicide, they first kill their children and other members of the family. . . . Under the delusion of a future without hope and the inevitability of catastrophe overtaking their nearest and dearest as well as themselves, they desire to kill in order to spare their loved ones suffering.
>
> (1965: 6)

Schipkowensky has also stressed the extent to which the 'patient feels his personality is without value (delusion of inferiority). His life is without sense, it is only [one of] everlasting suffering', and he feels that he 'deserves to be punished for his imaginary crimes' (1969: 64–65).

I recall the case of a young man under my supervision. He was in his early twenties. He became so convinced that the world was a terrible place in which to live that he attempted to kill his mother, his sister and then himself. Only swift medical intervention saved all their lives. Following a court appearance, he was made the subject of hospital care; he responded well to treatment and made a good recovery.

Trying to estimate the extent and duration of a depressive illness and its relevance to serious offences such as homicide is very difficult. Gunn *et al.* put the position very clearly:

> it is very difficult to establish *unless several helpful informants are available* whether a depressed murderer is depressed because he has been imprisoned for life, depressed because of the conditions in which he has been imprisoned,

depressed by the enormity of his crime, or whether he committed murder because he was depressed in the first place.

(1978: 35; emphasis added)

This comment by Gunn and his colleagues about the value of informants is very significant for social workers and others because they often have an important part to play in ensuring that a *comprehensive* social history of the offender-patient is obtained. Such a role has, to some extent, been eroded by recent criminal justice legislation (for example, the Criminal Justice Act 1991) with its heavy emphasis on the assessment of current, as opposed to past, behaviour. Often, it is only when this vital information has been gathered that one can see the individual against the background of his or her social milieu, and the stresses that may have arisen within it. Moreover, glimpses of his or her life-style against this social background may provide important diagnostic and prognostic clues – a matter to which I shall return in Chapter 9. Finally, in this brief discussion of depression and crime, a statement by Higgins is significant:

Depression may result in serious violence, tension and pre-occupation build-ing up over a protracted period and an assault committed in a state of grave psychological turmoil. The act itself might then act as a catharsis, the indivi-dual not afterwards appearing depressed nor complaining of depression *and the diagnosis then being missed.*

(1990: 348; emphasis added)

Manic and hypomanic disorder

I have already alluded to some of the main features of this disorder. From time to time, persons suffering from varying degrees of manic disorder will come to the attention of the courts because of their outrageous, insightless and therefore potentially dangerous behaviour. The following is a fairly typical case. It con-cerned a car salesman in his twenties. He initially impressed his employer as a bright, energetic and enthusiastic worker. However, it was not long before his ideas and activities took a grandiose and highly unrealistic turn. For example, he sent dramatic and exaggerated letters daily to a wide range of motor manu-facturers. His behaviour began to deteriorate rapidly, he lost weight through not eating (he 'never had time') and he rarely slept. One night, in a fit of temper directed towards his 'unsympathetic' employer, he returned to the car show-rooms, smashed the windows and did extensive damage to several very expen-sive cars. He appeared in court, was remanded for psychiatric reports, and eventually hospitalised under the Mental Health Act.

The attributes of this type of offender-patient are worth re-emphasising since such individuals justify the 'illness' label very clearly. They think themselves omnipotent and become convinced that their wildest ideas are, in fact, very practical. Because memory is unimpaired, they are capable of giving rationalised arguments and explanations to support their actions. It is important to stress that such persons are very difficult to treat without compulsion since they resist the idea that there is anything wrong with them. However, though lacking insight, they can appear deceptively lucid and rational. As already noted, they can be not only hostile, but also physically aggressive to those they think are obstructing them in their plans and activities (see also Higgins, 1990).

Schizophrenic illnesses

At one time, it was customary to speak of schizophrenia in the singular; to some extent this is still the case, but increasingly the recognition that there are a variety of 'illnesses' within this term has led to the use of the word in the plural or the use of the descriptive term the *schizophrenias*.

Controversy exists concerning aetiology and classification. At the present time, it can be stated that although environmental and social factors may play a significant part in the onset and duration of such illnesses, there are certainly likely to be neuro-biochemical factors which may determine the onset of the illness in the first instance.

The most important single characteristic feature of schizophrenic illness is the disintegration and, in some cases, apparent gradual destruction of the personality. The term schizophrenia does not, as many laypeople think, mean being in 'two minds' (a tendency fed by the media), nor does it mean 'split personality' as in *Dr Jekyll and Mr Hyde* – characteristically sane one minute, mad the next. In the schizophrenic illnesses we are dealing with what can best be regarded as a splintering of the mind – the personality shatters and disintegrates into a mass of poorly operating components rather than a neat division into two parts. In particular, there is likely to be a degree of incongruity between thoughts and emotions.

The main signs and symptoms of the illness fall under the following broad headings, though they will not necessarily be present in every case. As we shall see, some of them are of considerable importance from a forensic point of view.

1 *Disorders of thinking*. Delusions are common; for example, a person may believe that his or her thoughts are being stolen by others.
2 *Disorders of emotion*. These may range from excessive anxiety and perplexity, and a flattening of mood (sometimes interrupted by severe outbursts of rage), on the one hand, to complete incongruity of effect, on the other: for example, giggling at something sad.
3 *Disorders of volition*. The key characteristic here is likely to be apathy and a consequent withdrawal from social intercourse. The individual may behave in a very negative fashion – a condition known technically as *negativism*.
4 *Psycho-motor symptoms*. Periods of complete lack of emotion or a stuporose state may be interspersed with outbursts of unpredictable violence.
5 *Hallucinations*. In the schizophrenias, these are mostly of an auditory nature. They may consist of voices which tell the individual to do certain things, or alternatively the person may state that his or her thoughts can be heard or

controlled by others. Occasionally, the person may believe that people are interfering with them: for example, if this supposed interference is sexual, it may result in an unprovoked assault on an innocent stranger.

Over the years psychiatrists (with varying degrees of agreement) have tended to classify the schizophrenic illnesses in the following, somewhat over-simplified, fashion, which I list below for the sake of clarity. (In actual practice, the divisions are more complicated and not so clear-cut.)

1 *Simple schizophrenia.* In these cases, the onset appears to be fairly gradual, occurs in early adult life and is so insidious that the initial signs and symptoms may not be recognised by those near to the sufferer. Social behaviour is impoverished and the emotions appear to be 'blunted' or shallow. The course of the illness and its lengthy duration may gradually 'wear away' the personality, involving a schizophrenic 'process' of steady deterioration.

2 *Hebephrenic schizophrenia* (from the Greek: 'youthful'). The onset, which occurs most frequently in late teenage or early adult life, is often quite dramatic and accompanied by delusions and hallucinations. The person may deteriorate fairly rapidly and require urgent treatment.

3 *Catatonic schizophrenia.* This condition is seen much more rarely today than in the past; this is due in part to the early use of certain drugs that seem helpful in this condition. The key characteristics are withdrawal from social intercourse accompanied by muteness, the latter sometimes interspersed with occasional episodes of unprovoked violence. In some cases the limbs may be rigid and board-like. In others, they take on a curious characteristic known as flexibilitas cerea (waxy flexibility) in which the limbs are placed and left in the most contorted positions almost indefinitely. Attempts to return them to normal merely result in the patient returning them to their original position. The violent outbursts shown by such patients are fortunately rare; these, and the violence exhibited in cases of acute hypomania, probably account for the small number of incidents of serious violence committed by psychiatric patients.

4 *Paranoid schizophrenia and paranoid states.* In these cases the keynotes are irrational over-suspiciousness and ideas of self-reference. Such persons may be convinced that people are continually talking about them, for example accusing them of sexual indiscretions or persecuting in other ways. Such irrational ideas are highly impervious to rational explanation and discussion.

It is important to stress once again that the above outlines have been greatly over-simplified. For example, no reference has been made to those illnesses on the 'borderland' of schizophrenia such as the schizo-affective disorders, where, as the term implies, the sufferer may show signs and symptoms of both a schizophrenic and an affective (depressive) nature. It is also important to remember that some of the signs and symptoms of the schizophrenic illnesses can be present in other disorders, including certain organic conditions and alcohol- or other drug-induced psychoses.

Schizophrenic illness and crime

Although the schizophrenias are generally regarded as the most seriously disabling of the psychiatric disorders and patients suffering from them represent the
largest proportion of hospital in-patients, there is disagreement as to the extent to
which the illnesses contribute to criminality. A great deal of this disagreement
arises because of differences in the populations studied and the sampling techniques used. However, in relation to *certain* offences the schizophrenic illnesses
seem to play a significant role. For example, studies by Taylor and Gunn (1984)
and Taylor (1985) of remand prisoners in London suggest that the risk of violence
among men with schizophrenia is high. They found, for example, a 'substantially
higher prevalence of schizophrenia among men convicted of homicide . . . and
arson . . . than would be expected in the general population of Greater London'
(Taylor and Gunn, 1984: 194; see also Taylor, 1993). However, when non-penal
populations are examined the results appear to be somewhat different. For
example, Mackay and Wight conducted a small postal survey of members of an
association for sufferers from schizophrenia and their families. They wished to
find what proportion of schizophrenics had ever found themselves in contact with
the police and/or the criminal process and what forms of criminal/anti-social
behaviour brought this contact about. From an admittedly small number of
replies (about 8 per cent of the relevant membership) from relatives and schizophrenics themselves, the results revealed that 'such behaviour is for the most part
trivial, and that in a high proportion of cases the sufferers are not prosecuted but
. . . removed . . . to a hospital by the police or a social worker' (Mackay and
Wight, 1984: 192; see also Chapter 3 of this volume). Similar results appear to
have been found in a large-scale follow-up study of over five hundred schizophrenic patients discharged from Swedish hospitals in 1971 (Lindqvist and
Allebeck, 1990).

Despite these apparent conflicts it is important that the possibility of some
relationship between schizophrenic illnesses and crime is not overlooked. In a
recent review of the topic Taylor states with some prescience that 'Most violence
by most psychotic people should be predictable, and preventable through treatment, given the resource. Both material provision and skilled sensitive supervision or peer group support must be included in a resource allocation' (1993: 83;
see also my discussion in Chapter 9). A similar conclusion has been reached in
another comprehensive review of the topic by Tidmarsh (1990). In a number of
cases the offending occurs during the prodromal (onset) state of the illness and
not when it presents in florid form.

The following examples help to illustrate the foregoing remarks.

Serious violence In Chapter 2 I showed how some forms of schizophrenic
illness may be associated with criminal violence, as, for example, in the case of
Peter Sutcliffe. Some years ago, a man called John Ley – a former Australian
senior law officer – was convicted of conspiring to murder a man he deludedly

believed to have seduced his wife. Ley was sentenced to death but after sentence was found to be suffering from a paranoid illness. He was sent to Broadmoor, where he subsequently died. In more recent times, Ian Ball was ordered to be detained in a Special Hospital as a result of his elaborate and skilful (yet highly delusional) plan to kidnap Princess Anne. And of course, there have been numerous cases in the USA of murderous attacks on public personages by individuals allegedly suffering from a variety of schizophrenic illnesses. It is very important to stress again that people suffering from this type of disorder may begin to demonstrate 'oddnesses' of behaviour *for some time before the disorder emerges in an acute or very obvious form*. Sensitive intervention at such a stage may, in some cases, help to prevent a tragedy.

It is also most important to emphasise (as we noted in the case of Peter Sutcliffe in Chapter 2) that a seriously paranoid person is highly likely to appear perfectly 'sane' and in command of him- or herself in all other respects. The illness is usually so well encapsulated (contained) that an unwary or unskilled observer may be very easily misled. It is only when the matters which the delusional system has fastened upon are broached that the severity of the disorder is revealed. Morbid or delusional jealousy is a case in point. Such persons, usually men, often develop a fixed and unshakeable belief that their spouse or partner is being unfaithful to them. What *may* have begun, perhaps, as a belief in a minor transgression, rooted in reality, develops into florid and persistent irrationality. The victim will be followed and confronted with accusations of sexual infidelity. The person suffering from the disorder will often go to the most extraordinary lengths to substantiate and rationalise his beliefs: for example, he will examine the spouse or partner's underclothing for signs of seminal staining in order to prove that intercourse has taken place with another partner. Her possessions and correspondence may be constantly searched for evidence of illicit 'love letters'. Sometimes the innocent partner may become so terrified and cowed by the accusations that she may falsely confess to the behaviour. Such confession may only serve to aggravate the delusional beliefs of the disordered partner even further and, as a result, the object of the delusions may be violently assaulted or even killed.

The irrational nature of this disorder has been well described in mythology and the world's great literature. There are examples in *The Decameron* and in the work of Tolstoy. There is probably no more graphic illustration of its irrationality and its imperviousness to treatment than in Shakespeare's *Othello*.

But jealous souls will not be answered so;
They are not ever jealous for the cause,
But jealous for they are jealous; 'tis a monster
Begot upon itself, born on itself.
                              (Act III, Scene iv)

And the condition is further depicted by Shakespeare in *The Winter's Tale*, where the irrationally jealous Leontes says:

were my wife's liver
Infected, as her life, she would not live
the running of one glass.
                              (Act I, Scene ii)

So graphically does Shakespeare depict the condition that it has sometimes been described eponymously as the 'Othello Syndrome'. (For a brief further description see Prins, 1990: Chapter 2, and for a fuller account see Enoch and Trethowan, 1991: 3). It is, of course, important to place this disorder within a wider social and cultural context of envy and jealousy. This has been done very effectively in a number of papers by Mullen (see, for example, Mullen, 1993).

The management of delusional jealousy is extremely difficult, as no wholly effective cure has been found for it. The most florid symptoms may abate with the use of medication; psychotherapy has been tried but with limited success. In view of the almost intractable nature of the disorder and its not infrequent disastrous outcome, the best advice to the partner or spouse, if she survived the attack, may be to remove herself from the vicinity and change her identity. When the time comes for the assailant to be discharged into the community under supervision (most likely after many years of incarceration), it may be possible to insert into the order for discharge a requirement that he does not go near or contact the partner. Infringement of such a requirement or an early warning of its likelihood could lead to immediate recall if danger seemed to threaten (see also Chapters 3 and 9).

More minor offences   As we have seen, those suffering from schizophrenic illnesses sometimes commit minor offences. What forms do these take? In some cases, where the illness is of insidious onset, there is often an accompanying decline in social competence; in which case the sufferer may well succumb to temptations (sometimes prompted by others) that they might well have resisted had they been in good mental health. Those suffering from so-called 'simple schizophrenia' may demonstrate a steady diminution of social functioning accompanied by a withdrawal from society. Such sufferers may come to the attention of the criminal justice system through offences such as begging, breach of the peace (insulting words and behaviour) or vandalism (wilful damage). They often form part of the so-called 'stage-army' described by Rollin (1969), shunted between hospital, prison and community and referred to in Chapter 3 above.

The bizarre crime   Occasionally, a crime is committed which shocks the community because of its bizarre ferocity or depravity. Such offenders often demonstrate senseless and quite appalling cruelty. The perpetrators show lack of feeling which seems quite incomprehensible to most of us. In such cases, it is *sometimes* found that a schizophrenic illness of insidious onset has occurred, but, as indicated earlier, its presence may have been tragically overlooked. Occasionally, a case of sadistic sexual murder appears to fall into this category; however, more frequently, such crimes will be committed by the severely personality disordered (psychopathic) individual, to be described in the next chapter.

Summary   Although, as I have indicated, the incidence of the schizophrenic illnesses in relation to crime is apparently very low, it may be of considerable importance in *particular* cases; it is for this reason that I have sought to emphasise some of these. For those who may have professional involvement with the person concerned (for example, probation officers and other social workers, penal institution and residential staffs, the police, general practitioners and personnel officers), it is as well to be aware of the significance of even slight changes in behaviour, but also more importantly, to be aware of *a-typical* behaviour. These may give clues (along with other evidence) to the possibilities of an underlying schizophrenic illness; intervention at an early stage may, as already suggested, help to avert a tragedy (see, for example, Gunn and Taylor, 1993: Chapter 8).

The neuroses/psychoneuroses/neurotic reactions and crime

The terms 'neuroses' and 'psychoneuroses' (which for the most part are used synonymously), when used correctly, describe a wide range of conditions which are characterised by certain fairly specific mental and physical signs and symptoms. They usually have as their origin the existence of some mental conflict of which the sufferer may frequently be quite unaware. Many neurotic conditions are severely disabling (particularly the obsessive/compulsive states). As with the classification of mental disturbance more generally, there is no absolute consensus about the classification of the neuroses, but the following will suffice for our purposes:

1   mild depression;
2   anxiety states;
3   hysterical states;
4   obsessive/compulsive states.

In this chapter I concentrate upon mild depression, anxiety and hysterical states; and even this concentration will need to be somewhat superficial. Those wishing to obtain a comprehensive account of these disorders should consult Sims (1988). It is as well to remember that the classification given about is not discrete, that is, the conditions and their symptoms frequently overlap. We also need to remember a distinction between (a) common neurotic traits (seen in most of us); (b) more serious neurotic traits or reactions; and (c) fully developed neurotic illnesses.

Mild depression

Instance of mild depression may not always be recognised immediately. This is because the behaviour of the individual concerned may depart only slightly from the norm; however, many of the signs and symptoms of serious (psychotic) depression referred to earlier may be present but in less severe form. A useful forensic example was that of the married woman of sixty, of impeccable previous character, who, for no apparent reason (she had plenty of money with her), stole a tin of beans from a supermarket. The offence seemed quite out of character and when she appeared in court she was remanded for psychiatric investigation. This subsequently showed that she had suffered from mild depression (which was accompanied by confusion) for a considerable time. She was placed on probation with a requirement for treatment as an out-patient. In a small-scale study, made over thirty years ago, Woddis (1957) cites several cases in which stealing occurred against a background of depressive illness. Most of his examples were of middle-aged or late middle-aged women, but he also cites the unusual case of a young man of twenty-one charged with persistent stealing of motor cars. He had a history of recurrent mild depressive attacks which seemed to be clearly associated in time with his car thefts. Abreactive treatment using the drug pentothal revealed that his offences had started at the time his father had been burned to death in a lorry accident. The young man had intense feelings of guilt that he had not reached his father in time to rescue him. When these matters were brought more clearly into consciousness and clarified, the stealing stopped. As already noted, some cases of shoplifting may be associated with mild depressive disorder which is accompanied by a degree of confusion and absent-mindedness. These phenomena have been usefully explored in papers by Gudjonsson (1987, 1990), Mortimer (1991a, 1991b), Reason and Lucas (1984) and Harper (1994). From time to time, I have come across cases of young men and women who have claimed that they embarked upon a series of crime because they felt 'low' or 'fed up' – as though the offending would supply a 'buzz' or a 'lift' for their low spirits. Occasionally, their past and recent histories have revealed a number of depressive elements but it would have been difficult to have applied the clinical label 'neurotically depressed' to many of them. These examples illustrate the need for very careful history-taking so that the relevance of depressive factors may be assessed as accurately as possible – a point stressed by all the authors cited.

Anxiety states and crime

True anxiety states are characterised by a morbid or pervasive fear or dread. They may occur as a single symptom or in conjunction with other psychiatric disturbances – such as depressive illness. Often, such anxiety can be seen to be associated with some specific environmental situation or stress (as in the recently labelled Post-Traumatic Stress Syndrome). In other cases it is said to be 'free-floating' – a nameless and non-specific dread. Symptoms can include palpitations, giddiness, nausea, irregular respiration, feelings of suffocation, excessive sweating, dry mouth and loss of appetite. Anxiety states in their 'pure' form do not often account for criminality, but morbidly anxious individuals may feel so driven by their anxieties that they may commit an impulsive offence. Such offences also seem to occur in individuals where the anxiety is accompanied by, or associated with, an obsessive and perfectionist personality. One such young man made a serious and unprovoked attack upon an innocent passer-by in the street. As he put it, 'I just exploded. I don't know why; the tension I had been feeling recently became unbearable.' Subsequent psychotherapy over a long period revealed a very vulnerable personality accompanied by a lack of self-esteem and a compulsive need to work in order to keep unnamed anxieties at bay. Later, as psychotherapy continued, it became apparent that many of his problems were associated with his relationship with his father, which bordered upon hatred. The innocent bystander just *happened* to look like his father and, therefore, the assault was in many respects no mere accident.

Finally, I should emphasise that anxiety has been discussed here in a very specific and narrow sense. I am not referring to situations where an offender or alleged offender is apparently almost pathologically anxious in the context of his or her present predicament (for example, facing a court hearing or being detained in prison). Gunn's comments quoted earlier in relation to severe depression are equally relevant in this context.

Hysterical and associated states and crime

The clinical condition of hysteria has a long history and can be defined loosely as the existence of mental or physical symptoms for the sake of some advantage (for example, compensation or attention of some kind), although the sufferer is not completely aware of the motive. Enoch has stated that 'there has been much argument about the value of the term "hysteria" and some authors have suggested discarding it altogether, although no substitute has found universal acceptance' (1990: 805). As with schizophrenia, the term is often used quite incorrectly by laypersons. It is not to be equated with 'having hysterics' or acting histrionically (highly dramatically), though both these characteristics may be demonstrated by hysterics in certain situations. It also needs to be distinguished from hysterical personality. Hysterical symptoms can be classified in a somewhat over-simplified fashion as follows:

1 Those associated with the senses, for example deafness or blindness.
2 Those associated with motor symptoms, for example paralysis, spasms or tremors (somatisation disorder/Briquet's Syndrome).
3 Those where mental symptoms present, such as memory loss (which may sometimes be associated with a fugue or wandering state), pseudo-dementia, Ganser Syndrome (see later), stupor, hysterical phobias. These may also present as anxiety and depressive states in which the person may react in difficult or unpleasant situations with symptoms of these latter disturbances of mind. The key-notes in all these disorders are symptoms of *conversion or dissociation*. Conversion symptoms may occur, for example, in hysterical states in the form of fits which may be superficially similar to those produced

in epilepsy due to organic causes (see later). Dissociation arises when the individual has a conflict which produces anxiety, but the latter is overcome by some manifestation of physical or mental illness which submerges the real anxiety. Because of the processes at work, one not infrequently notices in hysterical individuals that the emotions which should accompany events or memories of them are often inappropriate; thus, an account of an incident given by an hysteric, which one would expect to produce sadness, may be given with a bland smile on the face. Such a phenomenon is frequently described as 'la belle indifférence' (sublime (beautiful) indifference).

From a forensic point of view, it will be obvious that a number of these conditions are of considerable importance – of these, hysterical amnesia, fugues and the Ganser Syndrome are the most significant and are now considered in more detail. Amnesias due to *organic* disorders or disease are dealt with in the section concerned with these states, but, again, there are obvious areas of overlap.

In some instances, it is difficult, if not impossible, to distinguish a genuine hysterical illness from simulation of malingering. The following are useful pointers to possible differences:

1 In malingering, the motivation is more or less at a conscious level. The symptoms are usually of sudden onset and have some connection with a situation the malingerer is keen to avoid (see also Enoch, 1990).
2 The malingerer's symptoms are usually over-acted and exaggerated, as was the case with Haigh, the so-called 'acid bath murderer', who feigned insanity to avoid conviction and sentence for murder (for details, see Prins, 1990: Chapter 5). It is possible for even highly professional and skilled workers to be misled occasionally; some chronic mental hospital patients or clinic attenders can become quite adept at picking up and simulating a range of psychiatric signs and symptoms.
3 The signs may be present only when the malingerer is being observed. This is very important from a forensic-psychiatric point of view, as a true picture of the supposed malingerer may emerge only after fairly lengthy and close observation on remand.
4 Symptoms may be sometimes made to order. For example, if the examiner of the suspected malingerer suggests that a certain symptom of illness being feigned is absent in the individual's presentation, the malingerer will sometimes try to produce it.
5 When feigning illness, many of the usual signs and symptoms associated with the real illness may be missing.

There are two other conditions allied to malingering that must be mentioned as they are also of forensic-psychiatric interest. The first is *pseudo-dementia* and the second is the *Ganser Syndrome*.

Pseudo-dementia, as the name implies, is closely akin to malingering or simulation of insanity. An individual of normal intelligence may say, for example, that 4 + 4 = 9, or will incorrectly give or strangely twist the most simple facts. In these cases, the examiner will usually have the impression that the person knows the right answers. However, differential diagnosis is sometimes very difficult, because pseudo-dementia may co-exist alongside a genuine organic defect or illness. The Ganser Syndrome is, in many ways, very like pseudo-dementia and takes its name from the physician S.J.M. Ganser who first described the condition in a lecture given in 1897 – calling it 'A Peculiar Hysterical State'. Ganser stated that:

> The most obvious sign they present consists of their inability to answer correctly the simplest questions which are asked of them, even though by many of their answers they indicate that they have grasped, in a large part, the sense of the question, and in their answers they betray at once a baffling ignorance and a surprising lack of knowledge which they most assuredly once possessed, or still possess.
>
> (translated in Schorer, 1965: 123)

As with pseudo-dementia, it is sometimes very difficult in practice to distinguish a true Ganser state from behaviour caused by an organic disorder. (For more detailed discussion, see Prins, 1990: Chapter 2; Enoch, 1990.)

Another phenomenon that should be mentioned here is so-called 'hysterical amnesia'. From time to time, offenders may claim an amnesic episode for their crime or the events leading up to it. A classic example was that of Gunther Podola, tried and convicted in 1959 for killing a police officer (*R*. v. *Podola* [1959] 3 All ER 418). There appears to be a consensus that the difference between a genuine and feigned amnesia attack is more likely to be one of degree than of kind. Both conditions may co-exist in the same person and be serving a common purpose, namely loss of memory for an alleged crime. Power (1977) suggests that the following pointers may help to elicit whether an amnesia is genuine:

1 An amnesic episode of sudden onset and ending may be suggestive of a feigned loss of memory.
2 The crime itself may give clues. Motiveless crime may be committed in an impulsive fashion, without any premeditation or attempt to conceal it; it may be committed with unnecessary violence and in the presence of witnesses.
3 Careful comparisons of the accounts given by the police and by the defendant may provide helpful evidence of inconsistencies.
4 Have there been past amnesic episodes? If so, the current episode *may* be more likely to be a genuine one (see also Taylor and Kopelman, 1984).

Before passing on to 'organic' factors it is important to mention two hysterical-type phenomena that have assumed an increasing degree of importance in recent years. The first concerns the controversial phenomenon of so-called 'multiple personality disorder'. The most up-to-date and generally accepted diagnostic criteria are: (1) the existence within the person of two or more distinct personalities, each with its own relatively enduring pattern of perceiving, relating to and thinking about the environment and self; and (2) at least two of these personalities or personality states taking full control of the person's behaviour. The presentation is likely to be characterised by the co-existence of relatively consistent, but alternate, separate, sometimes very numerous, identities with recurring episodes of distortion of memory and frank amnesia. Recent studies suggest that such disorders may not be as rare as was once thought to be the case, but an alternative view is that the medical attention such persons receive merely serves to facilitate the expression of the symptomatology and adds to its proliferation. The debate continues. (For further discussion, see Prins, 1990: Chapter 2; Merskey, 1992; Lasky, 1982.)

The second concerns the phenomena known as Munchausen's Syndrome and Munchausen's Syndrome by Proxy. In the first form of the disorder the person complains of, and receives extensive treatments for, various somatic complaints, travelling from one hospital to the next (sometimes they are called 'hospital hoboes' or 'hospital addicts'). The term Munchausen Syndrome is considered by many to be a misnomer. First, because the famous eighteenth-century nobleman from whom the name of the condition derives may have been a great fabricator and wanderer, but he was *not* addicted to hospitals. Second, the term is considered to be too narrow for what is believed to be a wide range of personality disorders. In a subsidiary condition, Munchausen's Syndrome by Proxy, a mother or significant other may inflict a variety of injuries upon a child, requiring hospital treatment. In such cases, there appears to be a thread of attention-seeking behaviour and the derivation of vicarious satisfaction from the attention given to the child. The condition received a great deal of publicity in recent times because it was one of the diagnoses ascribed to Beverley Allit, the hospital child killer. (See Prins, 1990: Chapter 2, for detailed references to these conditions.)

Mental disorder as a result of 'organic' and allied conditions

For the sake of simplicity I propose to consider all of the above under the broad, but somewhat unscientific, rubric of 'organic' disorders. The reason for paying them a fair amount of attention is because professionals without a medical training are often, understandably, somewhat ill-informed about the physical (organic) disorders that may play an important part in a person's behaviour or misbehaviour. This applies particularly to those in social work and the counselling professions, where an understanding of behaviour is frequently based on the over-emphasis of psychological, social and emotional influences. The importance of what might be called 'brain behaviour' in determining responsibility for crime, in an age in which we now have sophisticated devices for measuring such activity, has been well described recently in an important paper by Fenwick (1993), and more recently by Buchanan (1994).

Infections

These include meningitis, encephalitis and a number of viral infections. It is not uncommon for marked changes in behaviour to occur after an infective illness such as encephalitis; in particular these changes may sometimes be accompanied by the development of aggressive and anti-social tendencies.

Huntington's Chorea/disease

This is a comparatively rare, directly transmitted, hereditary condition. The onset of the illness (which is terminal) is most likely to occur in the middle years of life and is characterised by a progressive deterioration of physical, mental and emotional functioning, including the choreiform movements characteristic of the disease. Sufferers from the condition may sometimes behave unpredictably and become anti-social, though such instances are not common. Because of the clear hereditary transmission of the disease and its terminal nature, relatives need much counselling and support. Sufferers and their families can be helpfully referred to a branch of Combat – the organisation catering for Huntington's sufferers and their families.

General paralysis of the insane (GPI)

This disorder develops as a result of a primary syphilitic infection and attacks the central nervous system (CNS). Symptoms may appear many years after the original infective incident. The individual may suddenly indulge in un-characteristic acts of impropriety and some of these may be of a delinquent nature. Any 'outrageous' behaviour on the part of a person of previous good character in a setting lacking discernible social and familial stresses should alert one to the *possibility* of the disorder being present. These days GPI is seen rarely (at the turn of the century it was widespread); this is due largely to earlier diagnosis and the use of antibiotic drugs.

Alcoholic poisoning and crime

The prolonged and regular ingestion of alcohol may bring about serious brain damage with consequent behaviour change. This in turn may lead to disinhibited and anti-social conduct. Both chronic alcoholism and alcoholic psychosis are characterised by memory impairment. Such impairment often results in the person attempting to fill in gaps in their accounts of events by use of their imagination – a phenomenon known technically as 'confabulation'. Alcohol acts as a cerebral depressant (though people often mistakenly regard it as an effective euphoriant). It may be taken to disinhibit one's behaviour in order to commit a crime. In a recent monograph, Fenwick (1990) has shown how important it is to understand the effects of alcohol on people who may already be suffering from a degree of brain dysfunction. (For more general treatments of the relationship between alcohol, other drugs and crime, see Collins, 1982; Gunn and Taylor, 1993; Chapter 11; Hore, 1990; Evans, 1990; Gordon, 1990.)

Other toxic substances

Earlier in this chapter reference was made to the effects of such substances as lead, contaminated flour, etc. on behaviour. In addition, chemicals used in industrial processes may affect behaviour and produce states of confusion and/or aggression. Such effects on behaviour, though rare, are worth looking out for since their importance may be overlooked by the unwary.

Metabolic, endocrine and other disturbances and crime

Hypoglycaemia (low blood sugar) may occur in certain predisposed individuals who have gone without food for a prolonged period. Judgement may become impaired, they may show extreme irritability coupled with a degree of confusion; and in such a state they may come into confrontation with the criminal justice system. The preceding comments apply with equal force to those with untreated or unrecognised diabetes. In such cases, prompt action may be necessary before coma and/or death intervene(s). Those with untreated excess thyroid levels (thyrotoxicosis) may become irritable, aggressive and occasionally anti-social. In recent years, considerable interest has been focused upon the relevance of the menstrual cycle to criminality, particularly violent criminality. Dalton (1982) has suggested that the true Pre-Menstrual Syndrome (PMS) is a condition marked by progesterone deficiency, which starts from ovulation and reaches its climax some seven days before menstruation. It is held to be associated with a number of symptoms, including irritability, migraine, depression and erratic behaviour. Dalton has suggested that, in addition to these symptoms, seriously assaultive behaviour may sometimes occur. She has been involved in cases in which such behaviour has been held to constitute an 'abnormality of mind' within the meaning of the Homicide Act 1957. However, such defences do not appear to have become widespread (D'Orban, 1983).

Brain trauma, tumour, brain disease and crime

It is important to emphasise that, from time to time, cases of brain trauma or tumour are missed – sometimes with tragic consequences. An injury to the brain (however caused) is more than likely to produce a degree of concussion which may sometimes be prolonged. Such injuries may give rise to mental retardation (learning disability) or to forms of epilepsy (see later discussion). Such persons may also be amnesic, but such amnesia will differ from the amnesia described earlier. Following recovery of consciousness, there may be noisy delirium – a condition *not* observed in hysterical or malingered amnesia. Organically amnesic

persons may sometimes appear to be normal initially and only gradually, following careful examination, does it emerge that they have been behaving 'automatically' (see Fenwick, 1990). In contrast, in cases of hysterical amnesia,
memory may return spontaneously within twenty-four hours or so. Organically
amnesic persons are likely to want to do their best to remember events and may
appear to be annoyed by their defective memory; in contrast, hysterical amnesics
may show a complete inability to recall any events before a specific time. In
addition, hysterically amnesic persons, unlike organically amnesic individuals,
may have perfect command of their speech and be well in control of their other
faculties (see also Lasky, 1982: esp. Chapter 8).

A case reported in a provincial newspaper illustrates some of the tragic
forensic consequences of brain damage. This concerned a former miner, aged
thirty-six, whose personality changed after suffering severe head injuries in a pit
accident. Following essential brain surgery, he suffered hallucinations and
became aggressive towards his family. During one of these episodes he threw
burning coals around the living room, setting fire to the house. He was charged
with arson, convicted, and made the subject of a probation order with a requirement that he take medical treatment (*Leicester Mercury*, 29 September 1984: 11).

Occasionally, the dementing processes of advancing or old age may be associated with behaviour that is not only out of character, but that also may be highly
impulsive, disinhibited and aggressive. Any such behaviour occurring 'out of the
blue' in mid-life, that seems odd, out of character and carried out (perhaps
repeatedly) in the presence of witnesses, should alert us to the possibility of a
dementing process or to the presence of a malignancy of some kind. Tests are
now available which enable even quite small tumours to be diagnosed. In addition, psychologists have a range of personality and other tests that can determine
with a good degree of accuracy the presence and extent of a dementing or similar
process. (For more detailed consideration of the disorders referred to above see
Sellars *et al.* 1993; Gunn and Taylor, 1993; Chapter 7; Tancredi and Volkow,
1988; Miller, 1992.)

Epilepsies, associated disorders and crime

The epilepsies in their various presentations are not, strictly speaking, psychiatric
illnesses, but neurological disorders manifested primarily by an excessive or
abnormal discharge of electrical activity in the brain. Many thousands of people
will have an epileptic attack of one kind or another at some stage in their lives;
even for those who have major attacks, it is usually possible to lead a perfectly
normal life with the aid of medication.

There are many forms of epilepsy and these have been described in detail by
Fenton (1984) and Toone (1990). Some forms of epilepsy may be caused by head
injury or brain damage, others are of unknown origin (idiopathic). There are
several types of epileptic phenomena: *grand mal* (a major convulsion); *petit mal*
(often so minor as to be non-discernible to the onlooker); *temporal lobe epilepsy*

(sometimes characterised by sudden, unexpected alterations of mood and behaviour – and of particular forensic interest); *Jacksonian epilepsy* (a localised cerebral convulsion following traumatic brain damage); partial seizures; and more generalised convulsive seizures.

Fenwick, in a number of papers, has described in some detail the relationship between epileptic seizures and diminishment of responsibility for crime (see, for example, Fenwick, 1993). Gunn has carried out a number of important surveys into the relationship between epilepsy and crime more generally (particularly crimes of violence) (see Gunn, 1977b and 1978, for detailed accounts). He found that more epileptic males were taken into custody than would be expected by chance – a ratio of some 7–8:1,000. This is much higher than the proportion of epileptics found in the general population. About one-third of Gunn's cases were found to be suffering from temporal lobe epilepsy and temporal lobe cases were found to have a higher previous conviction rate. However, it was the group suffering from idiopathic epilepsy who had received disproportionately more convictions for violence than any other group.

Gunn cautions us not to place too much emphasis on the relationship between epilepsy and crime. In doing so, he makes three important points. First, the epilepsy itself may generate social and psychological problems, which in turn may lead to anti-social reactions. Second, harmful social factors, such as over-crowding, parental neglect and allied problems, may lead to a higher than average degree of both epilepsy and anti-social behaviour. Third, environmental factors such as those just described may lead to behavioural disturbances that not only result in brushes with the law, but may also aggravate accident and illness proneness. Such disturbances in themselves may produce an excess prevalence of epileptic phenomena.

Although, as Delgado-Escueta *et al.* (1981) have stated in a very influential paper, there is no strong proof of a general relationship between epilepsy and crime (particularly violent crime), it may well be important in the individual case. For this reason, expert assessment is very important, as is careful community monitoring. This is particularly the case if the person is on medication. Not only does this need to be taken regularly, but horrendous results may occur if such medication is taken with alcohol (even in small amounts) or with illicit drugs. It is also important to recognise that repetitive fits over prolonged periods may result in further brain damage.

A somewhat controversial case illustrates some of the problems described above. A young woman of nineteen, of previous good character and employed as a nanny, killed a twenty-month-old baby in her charge. She was said to be suffering from a form of epilepsy 'that could be triggered by her surroundings'. She was convicted of manslaughter on the grounds of diminished responsibility and placed on probation for three years with a requirement for in-patient treatment. The child's parents were very unhappy with the decision, stating that 'the judge just smiled nicely at her . . . a child killer will be on the streets in three months . . . justice has not been done' (*Independent*, 24 June 1987: 2). (For a more detailed account of this case, see

Hindler, 1989.) Gunn (1978) has described an interesting case of a man convicted and sentenced to life imprisonment for killing his wife. He probably did so during an epileptic attack or its immediate aftermath.

There is a further collection of signs and symptoms akin to epileptic phenomena, usually described as Episodic Dyscontrol Syndrome. It has been suggested that there may be a very small group of people who, in the absence of demonstrable epilepsy, brain damage or psychotic illness, may show explosively violent behaviour without any clearly discernible stimuli. Their life histories show an early onset of violent tendencies in a setting of chaotic domestic and social lives. The family may include other members who have also shown anti-social behaviour. The histories of men and women who demonstrate Episodic Dyscontrol Syndrome have much in common with some of the aggressively psychopathically disordered to be described in the next chapter. Fenton suggests that within the group of people suffering from Episodic Dyscontrol Syndrome, there may be a small number of

> emotionally inhibited people, who habitually exercise tight control over their aggressive feelings. . . . However, if exposed to prolonged and intolerable provocation, especially from a person with whom they have a close emotional involvement, they may react with explosive aggressive behaviour, for which they have great remorse afterwards.

(1984: 201)

(See also Lucas (1994) for an extensive critical review.)

Mental impairment (learning disability), chromosomal abnormalities and crime

Mental impairment

As indicated earlier, various descriptive terms have been used for what we now term learning disabilities. It is important to stress that laypeople sometimes confuse mental *illness* with mental *impairment* (the term I shall use henceforth); the two conditions are entirely separate but they can co-exist in some individuals.

In general and over-simplified terms, it can be said that the mentally *ill* person starts life with normal intelligence, but for a variety of reasons (as described earlier in this chapter) may become ill and deviate from the so-called 'norm'. The mentally *impaired* person never had the endowment of normal intelligence, or lost it in infancy or in early life. The point is demonstrated very clearly in the use of the older descriptive terms for the condition, 'amentia', or 'oligophrenia', both of which mean lack or absence of mind. It must be stressed that mental impairment is a relative concept. It used to be assumed, quite incorrectly, that the degree of impairment could be assessed purely in terms of intellectual capacity as measured on IQ tests. Though these may be of some importance, it is imperative to have regard for the social functioning of the individual, in particular family and social supports or lack of them.

Causal factors

There are a very large number of known possible causes for mental impairment. Some of the most important are listed below:

1 Infection in the parent, notably rubella (German measles) contracted in early pregnancy.
2 Disease in infancy or early childhood, for example meningitis or encephalitis (as already discussed).
3 Brain damage to the infant before, during or after birth. This may occur as a result of prematurity, or as a result of anoxia (lack of oxygen) due to various causes. Brain damage after birth may occur as a result of child abuse ('battering') or neglect by parents or others.
4 Chromosomal abnormalities, of which the best known is Down's Syndrome (once known as Mongolism) – see later discussion.
5 Other 'inborn' causes, for example, the disorder known as phenylketonuria – a condition in which some children are unable to cope with the phenyalaline content of normal diets; failure to observe a correct dietary programme will result in severe mental impairment.
6 Exacerbation of an existing mild mental impairment (from whatever cause) by lack of social and intellectual stimulation, poor nutrition and poor ante-and post-natal care.
7 Exposure to certain illicit drugs in pregnancy (such as LSD); or exposure to certain therapeutic drugs and vaccines used in infancy.
8 Exposure to radiation.

Mental impairment and crime

Cases of mild or moderate mental impairment are the most likely to come to the attention of the criminal justice system. In any event, as Day points out, 'The contribution of the mentally handicapped to the criminal statistics is small.' He goes on to suggest that

> Although the prevalence of offending in the mentally handicapped appears to have remained unchanged over the years, some increase is to be anticipated in the coming years as implementation of Care in the Community policies expose more mentally handicapped people to greater temptations and opportunities for offending and the 'hidden offences' which occur regularly in institutions become more visible.
>
> (Day, 1993: 116; see also Day, 1990; Reid, 1990; Langton *et al.*, 1993)

The following is a summary of the ways in which the mentally impaired are likely to come to the attention of the criminal justice system:

1 The degree of impairment may be severe enough to prevent the individual from understanding that his or her act was legally wrong. In such cases, issues of criminal responsibility will arise (see Chapter 2).

2 The moderately mentally impaired individual may be more easily caught in a criminal act.

3 Such offenders may be very easily used by others in delinquent escapades and find themselves acting as accomplices – sometimes unwittingly, sometimes not.

4 An individual's mental impairment may be associated with an organic disorder that may make him or her particularly unpredictable, aggressive and impulsive.

5 A number of mentally impaired offenders have problems in making understood their often harmless intentions. Thus, a friendly overture by them may be misinterpreted by an uninformed or unsympathetic recipient as an attempted assault. The initial overture may be rebuffed therefore. This may lead to surprise and anger on the part of the mentally impaired individual and he or she may then retaliate with aggression.

6 A moderately mentally impaired individual may be provoked quite readily into an uncharacteristic act of violence.

7 The attitude to legitimate expressions of sexuality of some of the mentally impaired may be naive, primitive, unrestrained and lacking in social skills. Such deficits may account for the high proportion of sexual offences which appear to be found in the backgrounds of detained mentally impaired patients in special and other hospitals.

8 Mentally impaired persons may be especially vulnerable to changes in their social environment that would not have the same impact upon their more well-endowed peers. A moderately mentally impaired person may manage perfectly well as long as he or she has the support of parents or other relatives. Should this be disrupted by death, or for any other reasons, such persons may then indulge in delinquent acts as a means of trying to relieve the stresses of their situation.

The following short case extracts demonstrate the vulnerability of the mentally impaired to changes in circumstances and other pressures.

Example 1

In this case a man aged twenty-six was charged with causing grievous bodily harm to a young woman by hitting her over the head with an iron bar. She was entirely unknown to him, and though he denied the offence vehemently, he was convicted by the Crown Court on the clearest possible evidence. As a child he had suffered brain damage, which had resulted in a mild degree of mental impairment, accompanied by the kind of impulsive, aggressive and unpredictable behaviour referred to in (4) above. He had been before the courts on a number of occasions and had eventually been sent to a mental handicap hospital. He was discharged some years later to the care of his mother. Subsequent to his discharge, he committed the offence described above and was placed on probation. His response was poor. He was impulsive and erratic, and regressed to very childish behaviour when under stress. The family background was quite disturbed: the parents had divorced when the offender was quite small; a brother suffered from a disabling form of epilepsy; and other members of the family showed decidedly eccentric life-styles. Shortly after the probation period expired the man committed a particularly vicious and unprovoked assault on a small girl and was sentenced to a long term of imprisonment.

Example 2

This case illustrates the problems identified under (6) above. For many years, a mildly mentally impaired man in his forties had worked well under friendly but firm supervision. His work situation changed, with the result that his new employers felt he was being lazy and they did not have much sympathy for his disabilities. In addition, his new work-mates teased and picked on him. One day, one of them taunted him about his lack of ability with the opposite sex. Goaded beyond endurance, the defendant stabbed his tormentor with a pitch-fork in his chest, causing quite serious internal injuries. When the case came before the Crown Court, evidence was given as to his mental condition, his social situation and the manner in which he had been provoked. The court made a hospital order under the Mental Health Act.

Other kinds of vulnerability

From the foregoing it will be seen that the mentally impaired person may be especially vulnerable to pressures from others. When this takes the form of alleged pressure to confess to crimes they may not have committed, the situation can become very serious indeed. Unfortunately, there have been a number of cases in which impressionable and suggestible individuals (some of them form-ally assessed as mentally impaired) have been the victims of miscarriages of justice. For example, three young men were alleged to have been responsible for the murder of Maxwell Confait. All three were deemed to be especially vul-nerable because of varying degrees of handicap. The same applied to the late Stephen Kisko. In the latter case the Court of Appeal ruled that 'special care needs to be taken in cases where the defendant suffers from a "significant degree of mental handicap" if the only evidence against him is his confession' (Kellam, 1993: 361). Kellam goes on to make the important point that 'There seems no reason to think that the Court meant to limit [handicap] to lack of intellectual capacity alone' (p. 362). The Police and Criminal Evidence Act 1984 introduces

certain safeguards in respect of police interrogations, most notably the availability of an 'appropriate adult' when vulnerable persons are being interviewed.
(Vulnerability would include both the mentally ill and the mentally impaired, and
those thought for other reasons to be especially suggestible. For an international
survey of cases, see Beaumont, 1986.) Despite the introduction of these safeguards, there are still inadequacies in the system, notably lack of adequate formal
training for interrogators and for 'appropriate adults'. However, some progress is
being made and psychologists have made significant contributions to this area of
work (see, for example, Gudjonsson, 1992; Shepherd, 1993). The problems
involved in placing reliance upon evidence from mentally disordered witnesses
was, as Dell (1993) suggests, crucial to the work of inquiries such as that into
complaints about Ashworth Hospital (Department of Health, 1992). As Dell
indicates, 'The report gives a comprehensive review of the issues involved in
interviewing mentally disordered people of various types, and in assessing the
reliability of their evidence' (Dell, 1993: 5).

Chromosomal abnormalities and crime

In the early 1960s, a considerable degree of interest was aroused by the finding
that a number of men detained in special hospitals and prisons carried an extra Y
chromosome (XYY).[1] Such men were often found to be taller than average, came
from essentially *non-delinquent backgrounds* and occasionally had records of
violence. Subsequent research has proved inconclusive concerning the prevalence of such abnormalities not only in penal and similar populations but also
in the the community at large. Although the leads offered have potential for
further and interesting development, there appears to be no firm evidence to
suggest a strong causal link between specific genetic defects or abnormalities and
crime, particularly violent crime. In a review of a number of studies in this area,
Day concludes 'that the personal variable of tallness, intelligence and educational
grade and the social variables of parental and family background bore a closer
relation to the possibility of conviction that genotypic abnormalities' (1993:
113). (*Disorders of personality* are considered in Chapter 5. *Sexually deviant
behaviours* are considered in Chapter 8.)

A CONCLUDING CAUTIONARY NOTE

This chapter inevitably has had to encompass in brief form a wide range of
complex material. Because of this, it would be all too easy for the reader to
conclude that we are on sure ground in describing and delineating mental disturbances and disorders. The truth is that there are still vast grey areas in this field and
much more work is needed before we can be at all certain as to aetiology and the
best methods of treatment. Despite this, much valuable work has been, and is
being done, notably in the field of brain biochemistry and its associated disciplines. Trying to equate mental disturbances with criminal behaviour is therefore

quite hazardous, especially when we recall that crime itself is not a static phenomenon. It is also important to remember that both gender and race play a very important part in any study of the relationship between mental disturbance and crime. We are still unsure as to why certain ethnic minority groups (notably Afro-Caribbeans) are over-represented in penal and psychiatric populations, though some possibilities have been explored recently (see SHSA, 1993). Women, when they offend, tend to receive proportionately more psychiatric disposals than men. Fewer women are assessed as psychopathic than men; they are more likely to be described as hysterics. Is this because such diagnoses are clinically correct or because a male-dominated society and criminal justice system tends to label women in this way? Some workers (for example, Allen, 1987) suggest that the apparent discrepancies in sentencing are less than obvious. Allen's central thesis is that such divergencies cannot be explained entirely by differences in the mental make-up of male and female offenders and that such divergencies occur regardless of their psychiatric symptomatology. She makes the often forgotten point that the 'importance of the current imbalance lies not so much in the excess of psychiatry in relation to female offenders as its deficiency in relation to males' (Allen, 1987: xii). (See also Worrall, 1990; Smart, 1989.) It is hoped that the material in this chapter will encourage readers to explore further for themselves; it is a vast, complex but exciting arena and one of its great attractions is its multi-disciplinary nature. Some of the behaviours only touched upon in this chapter are now given more detailed treatment in those that follow.

NOTE

1 A brief word of explanation concerning normal chromsome distribution may be helpful. Normal human cells contain forty-six chromosomes; these are arranged in twenty-three pairs of different shapes and sizes. They may be seen and classified under high-power microscopy once they have been suitably prepared for examination. Different chromosomes contain different genes. One pair of chromosomes called X and Y determine sex. In the female these consist of a matched pair, XX, and in the male an unmatched pair, XY. This normal patterning may sometimes become altered (translocated) in a variety of ways, resulting in an extra X or extra Y chromosome or some other variant.

REFERENCES

Allen, H. (1987) *Justice Unbalanced: Gender, Psychiatry and Judicial Decisions*, Milton Keynes: Open University Press.
American Psychiatric Association (APA) (1994) *Diagnostic and Statistical Manual of Mental Disorders*, DSM IV, Washington, DC: APA.
Bark, N.M. (1985) 'Did Shakespeare Know Schizophrenia? The Case of Poor Mad Tom in King Lear', *British Journal of Psychiatry* 146: 436–438.
Beaumont, M. (1986) 'Confessions and the Mentally Ill', *Law Society Gazette* 3 September: 2573–2574.
Buchanan, A. (1994) 'Brain, Mind and Behaviour Revisited', *Journal of Forensic Psychiatry* 5: 232–236.

Camporesi, P. (1989) *Bread of Dreams: Food and Fantasy in Early Modern Europe*, Cambridge: Polity Press.

Collins, J.M. (ed.) (1982) *Drinking and Crime: Perspectives on the Relationships between Alcohol Consumption and Criminal Behaviour*, London: Routledge.

Dalton, K. (1982) 'Legal Implications of PMS', *World Medicine* 17: 93–94.

Day, K. (1990) 'Mental Retardation: Clinical Aspects and Management', in R. Bluglass and P. Bowden (eds), *Principles and Practice of Forensic Psychiatry*, London: Churchill Livingstone.

—— (1993) 'Crime and Mental Retardation', in K. Howells and C.R. Hollin (eds), *Clinical Approaches to the Mentally Disordered Offender*, Chichester: Wiley.

Delgado-Escueta, A.V., Mattson, R.H. and King, L. (1981) 'The Nature of Aggression during Epileptic Seizures', *New England Journal of Medicine* 305: 711–716.

Dell, S. (1993) 'When Special Means Sinister', *Journal of Forensic Psychiatry* 4: 5–8.

Department of Health (1992) *Report of the Committee of Inquiry into Complaints about Ashworth Hospital*, Vols 1 and 2 (Chairman, Sir Louis Blom-Cooper, QC), Cmnd 2028-I and II, London: HMSO.

D'Orban, P.T. (1983) 'Medico-Legal Aspects of the Pre-Menstrual Syndrome', *British Journal of Hospital Medicine* 30: 404–409.

Eastman, N.L.G. (1993) 'Forensic Psychiatric Services in Britain: A Current Review', *International Journal of Law and Psychiatry* 16: 1–26.

Enoch, D. (1990) 'Hysteria, Malingering, Pseudologia Fantastica, Ganser Syndrome, Prison Psychosis and Munchausen's Syndrome', in R. Bluglass and P. Bowden (eds), *Principles and Practice of Forensic Psychiatry*, London: Churchill Livingstone.

Enoch, D. and Trethowan, W.H. (1991) *Uncommon Psychiatric Syndromes* (third edn), London: Butterworth-Heinmann.

Evans, M. (1990) 'Unsocial and Criminal Activities and Alcohol', in R. Bluglass and P. Bowden (eds), *Principles and Practice of Forensic Psychiatry*, London: Churchill Livingstone.

Fenton, G. (1984) 'Epilepsy, Mental Abnormality and Criminal Behaviour', in M. Craft and A. Craft (eds,) *Mentally Abnormal Offenders*, London: Baillière Tindall.

Fenwick, P. (1990) *Automatism, Medicine and the Law* (Psychological Medicine Monograph, Supplement No. 17), Cambridge: Cambridge University Press.

—— (1993) 'Brain, Mind and Behaviour; Some Medico-Legal Aspects', *British Journal of Psychiatry* 163: 565–573.

Freeman, H. (1991) 'The Human Brain and Political Behaviour', *British Journal of Psychiatry* 159: 19–32.

Gordon, A. (1990) 'Drugs and Criminal Behaviour', in R. Bluglass and P. Bowden (eds), *Principles and Practice of Forensic Psychiatry*, London: Churchill Livingstone.

Gudjonsson, G. (1987) 'The Significance of Depression in the Mechanism of Compulsive Shoplifting', *Medicine, Science and the Law* 27: 171–176.

—— (1990) 'Psychological and Psychiatric Aspects of Shoplifting', *Medicine, Science and the Law* 30: 45–51.

—— (1992) *The Psychology of Interrogations, Confessions and Testimony*, Chichester: Wiley.

Gunn, J. (1977a) 'Criminal Behaviour and Mental Disorders', *British Journal of Psychiatry* 130: 317–329.

—— (1977b) *Epileptics in Prison*, London: Academic Press.

—— (1978) 'Epileptic Homicide: A Case Report', *British Journal of Psychiatry* 132: 510–513.

—— (1993) 'Epidemiology and Forensic Psychiatry', *Criminal Behaviour and Mental Health* 3: 180–193.

Gunn, J. and Taylor, P.J. (eds) (1993) *Forensic Psychiatry: Clinical Legal and Ethical Issues*, London: Butterworth-Heinmann.

Gunn, J., Robertson, G., Dell, S. and Way, C. (1978) *Psychiatric Aspects of Imprisonment*, London: Academic Press.

Hare, E. (1983) 'Was Insanity on the Increase?', *British Journal of Psychiatry* 142: 439–455.

Harper, D.J. (1994) 'Absent-Mindedness and Shoplifting – A Case Study', *Medicine, Science and the Law* 34: 74–77.

Higgins, J. (1990) 'Affective Disorders', in R. Bluglass and P. Bowden (eds), *Principles and Practice of Forensic Psychiatry*, London: Churchill Livingstone.

Hindler, C.G. (1989) 'Epilepsy and Violence', *British Journal of Psychiatry* 155: 246–249.

Hodgins, S. (1993) 'The Criminality of Mentally Disordered Persons', in S. Hodgins (ed.), *Mental Disorder and Crime*, London: Sage.

Hore, B. (1990) 'Alcohol and Crime', in R. Bluglass and P. Bowden (eds), *Principles and Practice of Forensic Psychiatry*, London: Churchill Livingstone.

Kellam, A.M.P. (1993) 'False Confessions: A Note on the McKenzie Judgement', *Psychiatric Bulletin* 17: 361–362.

Klawans, H.L. (1990a) *Toscanini's Fumble and Other Tales of Clinical Neurology*, London: Bodley Head.

—— (1990b) *Newton's Madness and Further Tales of Clinical Neurology*, London: Bodley Head.

—— (1991) *Trials of an Expert Witness: Tales of Clinical Neurology and the Law*, London: Bodley Head.

Laing, R.D. and Esterson, A. (1964) *Sanity, Madness and the Family*, London: Tavistock.

Langton, J., Krishnan, V., Cumella, S., Clarke, D. and Corbett, J. (1993) 'Detentions in a Mental Handicap Hospital: A Ten-Year Retrospective Survey', *Journal of Forensic Psychiatry* 4: 81–95.

Lasky, R. (1982) *Evaluating Criminal Responsibility in Multiple Personality and Related Dissociative Disorders*, Springfield, Ill.: Charles C. Thomas.

Lindqvist, P. and Allebeck, P. (1990) 'Schizophrenia and Crime: A Longitudinal Follow-Up of 644 Schizophrenics in Stockholm', *British Journal of Psychiatry* 157: 345–350.

Lucas, P. (1994) 'Episodic Dyscontrol: A Look Back at Anger', *Journal of Forensic Psychiatry* 5: 371–407.

Mackay, R.D. and Wight, R.E. (1984) 'Schizophrenia and Anti-Social (Criminal) Behaviour – Some Responses from Sufferers and Relatives', *Medicine, Science and the Law* 24: 192–198.

Merskey, H. (1992) 'The Manufacture of Personalities: The Production of Multiple Personality Disorder', *British Journal of Psychiatry* 160: 327–340.

Miller, L. (1992) 'Neuropsychology, Personality and Substance Abuse in a Head Injury Case: Clinical and Forensic Issues', *International Journal of Law and Psychiatry* 15: 303–316.

Mindham, R.H.S., Scadding, J.G. and Cawley, R.H. (1992) 'Diagnoses Are Not Diseases', *British Journal of Psychiatry* 161: 686–691.

Mortimer, A. (1991a) 'Alleged Shoplifters and Psychiatric Out-Patients: Drugs, Absent-Mindedness and Mental State Compared', *Medicine, Science and the Law* 31: 119–122.

—— (1991b) 'Making Sense of Shoplifting – A New Classification', *Medicine, Science and the Law* 31: 123–126.

Mullen, P. (1993) 'The Crime of Passion and the Changing Cultural Construction of Jealousy', *Criminal Behaviour and Mental Health* 3: 1–11.

Power, D.J. (1977) 'Memory, Identification and Crime', *Medicine, Science and the Law* 17: 132–139.

Prins, H. (1987) 'Understanding and Managing Insanity: Some Glimpses into Historical Fact and Fiction', *British Journal of Social Work* 17: 91–98.

—— (1990) *Bizarre Behaviours: Boundaries of Psychiatric Disorder*, London: Tavistock/Routledge.

Reason, J. and Lucas, C. (1984) 'Absent-Mindedness in Shops – Its Incidence, Correlates and Consequences', *British Journal of Clinical Psychology 23*: 121–131.

Reid, A. (1990) 'Mental Retardation and Crime', in R. Bluglass and P. Bowden (eds), *Principles and Practice of Forensic Psychiatry*, London: Churchill Livingstone.

Rollin, H. (1969) *The Mentally Abnormal Offender and the Law*, Oxford: Pergamon.

Roth, M. and Kroll, J. (1986) *The Reality of Mental Illness*, Cambridge: Cambridge University Press.

Schorer, C.E. (1965) 'The Ganser Syndrome', *British Journal of Criminology 5*: 120–131.

Scull, A. (1984) 'Was Insanity on the Increase? A Response to Edward Hare', *British Journal of Psychiatry* 144: 432–436.

Sedgwick, P. (1982) *Psycho-Politics*, London: Pluto Press.

Sellars, C., Hollin, C.R., and Howells, K. (1993) 'Mental Illness, Neurological and Organic Disorder and Criminal Behaviour', in K. Howells and C.R. Hollin (eds), *Clinical Approaches to the Mentally Disordered Offender*, Chichester, Wiley.

Shepherd, E. (ed.) (1993) *Aspects of Police Interviewing* (Division of Legal and Criminological Psychology, Monograph No.18), Leicester: British Psychological Society.

Shipkowensky, N. (1969) 'Cyclophrenia and Murder', in A.V.S. de Rueck and R. Porter (eds), *The Mentally Abnormal Offender*, London: J. and A. Churchill.

Sims, A. (1988) *Symptoms in the Mind: An Introduction to Descriptive Psychopathology*, London: Baillière Tindall.

Slater, E. and Roth, M. (1969) *Clinical Psychiatry* (third edn), London: Baillière Tindall and Cassell.

Smart, C. (1989) *Feminism and the Power of Law*, London: Routledge.

Special Hospitals Service Authority (SHSA) (1993) *Report of the Committee of Inquiry into the Death in Broadmoor Hospital of Orville Blackwood and a Review of the Deaths of Two Other Afro-Caribbean Patients: 'Big, Black and Dangerous?'* (Chairman, Professor Herschel Prins), London: SHSA.

Szasz, T. (1987) *Insanity: The Idea and Its Consequences*, New York: Wiley.

—— (1993) 'Curing, Coercing and Claims-Making – a Reply to Critics', *British Journal of Psychiatry* 162: 797–800.

Tancredi, L. and Volkow, N. (1988) 'Neural Substrates of Violent Behaviour: Implications for Law and Public Policy', *International Journal of Law and Psychiatry* 162: 797–800.

Taylor, P.J. (1985) 'Motives for Offending among Violent and Psychotic Men', *British Journal of Psychiatry* 147: 491–498.

—— (1993) 'Schizophrenia and Crime: Distinctive Patterns in Association', in S. Hodgins (ed.), *Mental Disorder and Crime*, London: Sage.

Taylor, P.J. and Gunn, J. (1984) 'Violence and Psychosis – I: Risk of Violence among Psychotic Men', *British Medical Journal* 288: 1945–1949.

Taylor, P.J. and Kopelman, M.D. (1984) 'Amnesia for Criminal Offences', *Psychological Medicine* 14: 581–588.

Tidmarsh, D. (1990) 'Schizophrenia', in R. Bluglass and P. Bowden (eds), *Principles and Practice of Forensic Psychiatry*, London: Churchill Livingstone.

Toone, B. (1990) 'Organically Determined Mental Illness', in R. Bluglass and P. Bowden (eds), *Principles and Practice of Forensic Psychiatry*, London: Churchill Livingstone.

Wessely, S. and Taylor, P.J. (1991) 'Madness and Crime: Criminology versus Psychiatry', *Criminal Behaviour and Mental Health* 1: 193–228.

West, D.J. (1965) *Murder Followed by Suicide*, London: Macmillan.

Woddis, G. (1957) 'Depression and Crime', *British Journal of Delinquency* VIII: 85–94.

World Health Organisation (WHO) (1992) *The ICD-10 Classification of Mental and*

Behavioural Disorders: Clinical Descriptions and Diagnostic Guidelines, Geneva: WHO.

Worrall, A. (1990) *Offending Women: Female Law-Breakers and the Criminal Justice System*, London: Routledge.

FURTHER READING

Readers wishing to explore general aspects of psychiatry in more detail can usefully consult:

Gelder, M., Gath, D. and Mayou (1983) *Oxford Textbook of Psychiatry*, Oxford: Oxford University Press.

Organic aspects of mental disturbance are covered comprehensively in:

Lishman, A. (1987) *Organic Psychiatry: The Psychological Consequences of Cerebral Disorder* (second edn), Oxford: Blackwell.

Psychological aspects of crime have recently been usefully explored by:

Blackburn, R. (1993) *The Psychology of Criminal Conduct: Theory, Research and Practice*, Chichester: Wiley.

Some aspects of the impact of changes in the care of the long-term mentally ill and the implications for offending can be found in:

Leff, J. (ed.) (1993) *The TAPS Project: Evaluating Community Placement of Long-Stay Psychiatric Patients* (especially the section by Dayson), *British Journal of Psychiatry* Supplement 19, Vol. 162.

A useful summary of trends in substance abuse and crime may be found in *Criminal Justice Matters* Vol. 12, Summer 1993, published by the Institute for the Study and Treatment of Delinquency, King's College, London.

The most comprehensive epidemiological survey of the relationship between crimes of violence and the mentally abnormal is that carried out by Häfner and Böker:

Häfner, H. and Böker, W. (1982) *Crimes of Violence by Mentally Abnormal Offenders: A Psychiatric and Epidemiological Study in the Federal German Republic*, Cambridge: Cambridge University Press.

The International Academy of Law and Mental Health publishes regular *Bulletins* containing extensive bibliographical material dealing with many of the matters discussed in this chapter.

Chapter 5

Psychopathic disorder: a useful label?

And thus I clothe my naked villainy . . .
And seem a saint when most I play the devil.
                    (*Richard III*, Act I, Scene iii)

In its present state of development the concept of psychopathy is fuzzy at the edges
and in need of refinement.

(Roth, 1990: 449)

In this chapter I trace briefly the historical development of the concept of
psychopathic disorder against the background of more general observations on
personality. Causal, or supposed causal, factors are then described, a simple
classification is suggested and some of the key characteristics of the disorder are
outlined as a prelude to comments on management.

PERSONALITY

Within the constraints of this chapter it would be impossible to write at length
about personality; however, a few words are necessary in order to provide a
context for what follows. Not only are there difficulties in defining personality
with any degree of accuracy, but it is a word used in common parlance to cover
a variety of attributes. Trethowan and Sims suggest that

Personality may be either considered subjectively, i.e. in terms of what the
[person] believes and describes about himself as an individual, or objectively
in terms of what an observer notices about his more consistent patterns of
behaviour. . . . Personality will include such things as mood state, attitudes
and opinions and all these must be measured against how people comport
them- selves in their social environments. If we describe a person as having a
'normal' personality, we use the word in a statistical sense indicating that
various personality traits are present to a broadly normal extent, neither to

gross excess nor extreme deficiency. Abnormal personality is, therefore, a variation upon an accepted, yet broadly conceived, range of personality.

(1983: 225)

There are a very large number of personality variations which may constitute 'disorders' if they stray far enough from this spectrum of normality. Some examples of personality variations are the paranoid, schizoid, explosive, hysterical, obsessive, depressive and affectionless. A useful classification is provided by Tyrer (1990). Schneider (1958) regarded personality disorder not as an illness in the conventional medical sense, but as a variation of personality which could only be defined in relation to the average man or woman – the man or woman on the 'Clapham omnibus' so beloved of lawyers.

The modern concept of personality disorder seems to represent two interlocking notions. The first suggests that it is present when *any* abnormality of personality causes problems *either* to the person himself or herself *or* to others. The second, and the one with which we are more specifically concerned in this chapter, carries a more pejorative connotation; it implies unacceptable, anti-social behaviour coupled with a notion of dislike for the person showing such behaviour and a rejection of them (see also Rutter, 1987). As we shall see, the word 'psychopath' is sometimes used for this purpose. Such usage has led to many difficulties for lawyers, sentencers, psychiatrists and other health care and criminal justice professionals.

One way of regarding psychopathic disorder is to view it as lying at the far end of a spectrum of behaviour disorders (see Figure 5.1). The danger in doing this is that we may make precipitate moral judgements about such behaviour without giving enough consideration to its possible aetiology.

In summary, we may say that the personality disorders (of which psychopathy is but one) consist of a group of disorders in which the basic personality appears to be noticeably abnormal, either in the balance of its components and their quality and expression, or in its total aspect.

1	2	3	4
Minor behaviour (personality disorder)[a]	More serious pesonality disorders, unusual and affectionless personalities	'Pseudo-psychopathy' (due to established brain damage, temporal lobe disease, infections, etc. (e.g. encephalitis)	'Essential psychopathy'[b]

Notes: [a] In this figure I have used the terms 'personality disorder' and 'behaviour disorder' synonymously. Some authorities prefer to reserve the term 'behaviour disorder' for use in childhood conditions only.

[b] Sometimes described as 'true' or 'nuclear' psychopathy.

Figure 5.1 Simple classification of personality and psychopathic disorders

PSYCHOPATHIC DISORDER: CONTEXTUAL BACKGROUND

Those readers wishing to gain a ~~detailed~~ understanding of the historical and contextual background to personality disorders in general, and psychopathic disorder in particular, should consult Berrios (1993) and Coid (1993). The following is a simplified account of a complex history. Pinel (1806), the French psychiatrist, is usually given the credit for the description of the characteristics we currently regard as psychopathic. However, if one looks at his work, it appears that he probably included a number of cases that we would not today regard as falling within the classification of psychopathic disorder. In 1835 the English psychiatrist and anthropologist Prichard formulated the well-known concept of moral insanity. He described it as a

madness, consisting of a morbid perversion of the natural feelings, affections, inclinations, temper, habits, moral dispositions and natural impulses, without any remarkable disorder or defect of the intellect or knowing or reasoning faculties, and particularly without any insane illusion or hallucination.

(quoted in Coid, 1993: 116)

It is important to place Prichard's oft-quoted remarks in context. To Prichard, the term 'moral' meant emotional and psychological and was not intended to denote the opposite of immoral as used in modern parlance. In the 1880s Koch (1891) formulated the concept of constitutional psychopathy, one much in line with the then current thinking and interest in hereditary factors in the causation of criminality. At the beginning of the twentieth century we see the use of the terms 'moral defective' and 'moral imbecile'. These found expression in the English Mental Deficiency Act of 1913. In the 1930s interest developed in neurological factors and their relationship to anti-social behaviour as evidenced in the various claims made for the relevance of encephalitis, epilepsy and chorea. Subsequently, interest turned to psychoanalytic interpretations of the genesis of psychopathic disorder followed by a development of interest in more socially based explanations, as evidenced by the increasing popularity of the term 'sociopath' in the USA. Interest in the concept in the UK was reawakened by the introduction of the term into the Mental Health Act, 1959 (following the recommendations of the Percy Commission [Home Office and Ministry of Health, 1957]), and its restatement (with a more circumspect view about limitations as to its management) in the 1983 Act.

Currently, the usefulness of the concept has been debated by a working group chaired by Dr John Reed. The Group was set up by the Department of Health and the Home Office in September 1992 to review the treatment options for persons with personality (psychopathic) disorders, their appropriate location and arrangements for their treatment. In addition, and more specifically, the Working Group was charged with considering any changes in legal provisions. (It is of interest to note that the Butler Committee had, *inter alia*, been charged with a similar task in 1975 [Home Office and DHSS, 1975], and there had been a joint DHSS and Home Office Consultation Document on the topic in 1986 [DHSS and Home

Office, 1986]). The Group was also asked to advise on future directions for research into long-term management and follow-up.

The report of the Working Group has now been published. They concluded that considerably more research was needed into the nature of psychopathic disorder, its classification and management. In addition they recommended dropping the term 'psychopathic disorder' and substituting for it the term 'personality disorder'; the latter term would not be further defined. (Department of Health and Home Office, 1994.)

In summary, it is possible to trace three important themes in the development of the concept. The first, as Coid suggests, was the concept of abnormal personality as defined by social maladjustment, which was developed in France and further developed powerfully in the UK, leading to the current legal definition of psychopathic disorder. The second was a concept of mental degeneracy, also originating in France. Persons so afflicted were considered to have 'fragile' personalities. The third was the German notion of defining abnormal psychopathic personality types (after Schneider, 1958). Currently the debate over classification seems to centre on whether psychopathic disorder should be defined according to the abnormal behaviour or to abnormal personality; a debate entered into by authorities such as Blackburn (1993). In brief, we may say that over the years approaches to the personality disorders, including psychopathic disorder, have been characterised by the *traditional psychiatric* approach; the postulation of some *basic psychological deficiency*; the *social deviance* or *social incompetence* approach; the *psychoanalytic and the psychodynamic* approaches; and, in more recent years, *neuro-psycho-physiological* approaches (see Prins, 1988, for further comment).

The historical development of the term 'psychopathic disorder' is summarised in Figure 5.2.

Clinical versus legal

From a clinical point of view, the term 'psychopathic disorder' does not currently find favour; indeed, neither of the two standard classificatory works of

Manie sans délire ─────────→ moral insanity ─────────→ moral imbecility

(defectiveness) ─────────→ (constitutional) psychopathic inferiority

─────────→ 'neurotic character' ─────────→ psychopathy and sociopathy

─────────→ anti-social personality disorder ─────────→ dissocial personality.

Note: It is important to stress that these descriptive terms and the theorising from which they derive come in the main from studies of incarcerated and criminal psychopaths. As Widom and Newman (1985) have pointed out, we also need more detailed studies of the prevalence of psychopathic disorder in non-institutionalised populations.

Figure 5.2 Development of term 'psychopathic disorder'

psychiatry, the DSM IV (APA, 1994), nor the ICD-10 (WHO, 1992) uses it. The former uses the term 'Anti-social Personality Disorder' and the latter, 'Dissocial Personality Disorder' (see Tyrer, 1989). It is perhaps important to realise that whatever term one uses, such usage is likely to be influenced by current social notions of decency and responsibility (Treves-Brown, 1977). These in turn influence clinical judgement and definition (Chiswick, 1992).

As we saw in Chapter 4, the relationship, in general, between mental disorder and criminality is at best equivocal and the subject of continuing controversy. Notions of what constitutes mental disorder change over time and crimes 'come and go' on the statute books. It is, therefore, hardly surprising that there has been much debate and not a little acrimony. In a recent work, Bavidge has suggested that philosophers who wish to discuss 'issues of responsibility and the law'

[take on] the thankless task of stalking the boundaries between law, psychiatry and philosophy, which like most border territories are matters of wars and disputes, of danger and confusion.

(Bavidge, 1989: 11)

He might equally well have been writing about anyone wishing to explore the problems inherent in tackling the concept of psychopathic disorder. From a practitioner's point of view, Coid has stated helpfully that although 'there is still little agreement on the nature of the conditions encompassed by the term . . . it is a concept that remains at the core of clinical practice in forensic psychiatry' (Coid, 1989: 750). Over the years, contributions to the debate about the disorder have come from within and without the profession of psychiatry; few disciplines have been held to lack relevance to such discussion. Acute observations have come from social scientists and lawyers who have raised important philosophical and jurisprudential issues. Many years ago, Barbara Wootton pointed out the dangers of the circular arguments that bedevil our understanding of the condition: 'the circular process by which mental abnormality is inferred from anti-social behaviour while anti-social behaviour is explained by mental abnormality' (1959: 250). Despite continuing concerns about the viability of the concept, mental health and penal professionals are asked to assess, and sometimes to try to manage, such people. For these reasons, it is probably not unrealistic to suggest that the personality disorders in general, and psychopathic disorder in particular, are the 'Achilles' heel' of psychiatry. Tyrer has rather wittily suggested that 'the diagnosis of personality disorder is similar to an income tax form; it is unpleasant and unwanted, but cannot be avoided in psychiatric practice' (1989: 240). Others have gone much further in their condemnation of the concept as currently framed, suggesting that it is no less than a moral judgement pretending to be a diagnosis (for example, Blackburn, 1988, 1993; Lewis and Appleby, 1988).

Dissatisfaction with the use of the term had been expressed in a DHSS report entitled *A Review of the Mental Health Act, 1959* (DHSS *et al.*, 1976). The report suggested the substitution of the term 'severe personality disorder'. The authors defined this as such a persistent abnormality of mind as would seriously affect an individual's life and adjustment to society and which was so severe as to render them a serious risk to themselves or to others. The Mental Health Act 1959 had defined psychopathic disorder as a

persistent disorder or disability of mind (whether or not including subnormality of intelligence) which results in abnormally aggressive or seriously irresponsible conduct on the part of the patient and requires or is susceptible to medical treatment.

It should be noted that the 1959 Act retained the association with defect or intelligence and the definition included as a criterion susceptibility to medical treatment. (Medical treatment in this context included various forms of treatment under medical *supervision*.) The Mental Health Act of 1983, Section 1(2), retained the classification of psychopathic disorder in the following terms:

psychopathic disorder means a persistent disorder or disability of mind (whether or not including significant impairment of intelligence) which results in abnormally aggressive or seriously irresponsible conduct on the part of the person concerned.

Because strong feelings had been expressed that the compulsory detention of those suffering from psychopathic disorder should be dependent upon a reasonable prospect of response to treatment, the diagnostic criteria in the definition were separated from the susceptibility to treatment clauses. These are contained in Sections 3, 37 and 47 of the Act. These made compulsory admission for treatment available only if it can be stated that medical treatment is likely to alleviate or prevent a deterioration in the individual's condition. This was an important proviso because it recognised the difficulties involved in treating psychopaths, but kept the door open for therapeutic optimism (see also later discussion). It also serves to emphasise the fact that the term psychopathic disorder should be used sparingly and not as a 'dustbin' label for those clients or patients who are merely difficult, unco-operative or unlikeable (see the discussion under management below).

Over forty years ago the psychiatrist Eliot Slater suggested that 'if we were to drop the term altogether, we should be obliged to invent an equivalent or to overlook a whole series of clinically very important phenomena' (1948: 277). Some empirical work carried out by some colleagues and I fairly recently would suggest that Slater's view is still valid (Tennent *et al.*, 1990: 44).

CAUSAL FACTORS

The search for postulated causes has as long a history as the concept itself. As we shall see, these have included genetic and hereditary predisposition, cortical disturbance and immaturity and familial and environmental influences. Coid (1989, 1992) has recently emphasised the need for continuing research into environmental and constitutional aspects. He also indicates a valuable caution in espousing the notion of psychopathic disorder as a single entity. He suggests that

> The sheer complexity and range of psychopathology in psychopathic disorder has previously led to the suggestion that these individuals could be considered to suffer from a series of conditions that would best be subsumed under a broad generic term 'psychopathic disorders' rather than a single entity (Coid, 1989). This would have two immediate advantages. Firstly, it demarcates a poorly defined area that requires further empirical research and where future developments are unlikely to come from a purely trait-based concept of the relevant psychopathology. Secondly, it aligns these syndromes to the legal concept 'psychopathic disorder' within the Mental Health Act 1983.
>
> (Coid, 1993: 156)

This latter observation seems to me to be important in relation to current controversies over the treatability of detained patients alleged to be suffering from psychopathic disorder. Cogent proposals for the introduction of change have been made by Grounds (1987), Dell and Robertson (1988) and Robertson (1992).

Recently, the High Court has challenged the treatability provisions of the 1983 Act. In a decision against the finding of the Canons Park Mental Health Review Tribunal, the Divisional Court held that the Tribunal had acted unlawfully in refusing to release a twenty-eight-year-old woman detained under Section 3 of the Act and diagnosed as suffering from psychopathic disorder within the meaning of the Act. The court held that, under the Act, detention of psychopaths was lawful only when they were treatable (the patient had, it was alleged, refused to participate in group therapy), and the Tribunal had clearly found that treatment in hospital would neither alleviate nor prevent a deterioration of her condition. Lord Justice Mann, giving judgment (with which Mr Justice Sedley concurred), stated that 'Parliament has enacted that an untreatable psychopath, howsoever dangerous, cannot be detained, however deep' the reservations (*Andrews* v. *Canons Park Mental Health Review Tribunal*, 26–8 January 1994). Such a ruling has important implications for the detention of those detained as suffering from psychopathic disorder and the criteria upon which such detention is based more generally; not surprisingly, the Mental Health Review Tribunal appealed against the decision of the Divisional Court. That appeal was upheld by the High Court in a decision handed down on 16 February 1994 (RCJ Case No. 93/1099/D).

As indicated, the aetiology of psychopathic disorder is obscure and subject more to emotively held beliefs than upon proven aetiological facts. The literature is vast and readers who wish to pursue the subject in more depth are advised to consult the References and Further Reading cited at the end of this chapter.

As with many other disorders and deviations the 'nature' v. 'nurture' debate has raged for many years in relation to psychopathy. Evidence has been adduced from twin, neurological, chromosomal and other studies to suggest the importance of innate factors (Coid, 1989; Weller, 1986). Equally convincing evidence has been provided by the environmentalists who suggest that family background and social milieu are all-important, particularly in relation to the psychopath's singular incapacity for 'role-taking' (Gough, 1956). This theory of role-taking deficiency finds some support from the work of Blackburn (1984), who suggests that seriously psychopathically disordered individuals (such as those seen in Special Hospitals and prisons) tend to view others as being malevolently disposed towards them (see also Finlay-Jones, 1991). Other psychologists, for example Hare and his colleagues (Hare, 1978; Hare and Schalling, 1978; Hare *et al.*, 1991), have made substantial contributions to the study of psychopathic disorder. Hare and his colleagues have undertaken a major task in summarising and bringing together research findings from the fields of abnormal psychology, neuro-and psycho-physiology, learning theory and theories of socialisation. Much of the evidence obtained under experimental (laboratory) conditions seems to be in accord with the day-to-day experience of clinicians and others in this field. The following appraisal attempts to summarise some of the most important findings as reported by Hare and his colleagues and due acknowledgement is made to these authors.

Studies of the cerebral cortex

I referred in Chapter 4 to the importance of certain 'organic' factors in the aetiology of violent behaviour. These factors are very relevant in attempting to understand the behaviour of the psychopath, particularly those judged to be seriously aggressive (see Weller, 1986). Studies using the EEG (Electro-Encephalogram) have tended to show that the slow wave activity found in the brain rhythms of some aggressive psychopaths bears some degree of resemblance to the EEG tracings found in children. These findings (which I have over-simplified) have led to a hypothesis of *cortical immaturity*. The theory may also explain why the behaviour of some aggressive psychopaths seems to become less violent with advancing years because, as with children, the brain matures.

Two further conclusions derived from work in this field may also be noted here. First, psychopathy may be associated with a defect or malfunction of certain brain mechanisms concerned with emotional activity and the regulation of behaviour. Second, it has been suggested that psychopathy may be related to a lowered state of cortical excitability and to the attenuation of sensory input, particularly input that would, in ordinary circumstances, have disturbing consequences. This may partially explain the apparent callous and cold indifference to the pain and suffering of others which is demonstrated by some seriously psychopathically disordered individuals.

The importance of the autonomic nervous system

Clinical and other experience has always tended to show the psychopath's general *apparent lack of anxiety, guilt and emotional tension*. In recent years, experiments carried out under laboratory conditions have tended to give confirmation to these clinical impressions. For example, it has been shown that during periods of relative quiescence psychopathic subjects tend to be *hypoactive* on several indices of autonomic activity, including resting level of skin conductance and cardiac activity. This activity can be measured comparatively easily by galvanometric and similar devices. However, it is worth noting here that some of these findings have been criticised. For example, Feldman (1977) has suggested that too many conclusions have been based solely upon laboratory tests and that too few comparative studies have been undertaken of 'control' populations derived from non-penal or non-specialist hospital sources. Also, it should be pointed out that lack of anxiety, guilt and emotional tension are not characteristics peculiar to the psychopathically disordered. Rather they seem to show this lack in *more extreme form* than the general population.

Psychopathic disorder and the concept of arousal

There is some laboratory evidence to suggest that psychopathy is related to cortical *under-arousal*. Because of this, the psychopath (particularly the seriously aggressive) may seek stimulation with arousing or exciting qualities. It is certainly true that even so-called 'normal' offenders, when asked about their motivation for offences, often report that they derived a 'high' or that they did it 'for kicks'. McCord states that 'most psychopaths do not seek security as a goal in itself; rather they crave constant change, whirlwind variety, and new stimuli' (1982: 28). McCord suggests that Ian Brady and Myra Hindley illustrate the 'psychopath's craving for excitement'. He says that they 'explained their actions as simply ways to attain new levels of excitement, a new "consciousness" and a temporary escape from boredom' (p. 28).

This need for excitement – the achievement of a 'high' – has been described more recently, and very graphically, in Wambaugh's (1989) book about Colin Pitchfork. Pitchfork was convicted of the rape and murder of two teenage girls in Leicestershire during the period 1983–6. In interviews with the police, he allegedly stated that he obtained a 'high' when he exposed himself to women (he had previous convictions for indecent exposure prior to his two major offences) and that he also obtained a 'high' from the knowledge that his victims or likely victims were virginal. He also described an additional aspect of his excitement, namely obtaining sex outside marriage. As with others assessed as psychopathic, he demonstrated a great degree of charm; for example, he was able to get his wife to forgive him for a number of instances of admitted unfaithfulness. Rieber and Green also give great prominence to this phenomenon of thrill-seeking. They 'describe the psychopath as performing a Mephisto Waltz on the tightrope of danger' (quoted by Vetter, 1990: 82).

This craving for excitement commented upon by McCord and others may render the psychopath unaware or inattentive to many of the more subtle cues required for the maintenance of socially acceptable behaviour and for adequate socialisation. Mawson and Mawson (1977) suggest that psychopaths show a greater degree of variability in autonomic functioning than non-psychopaths. The authors theorise that a biochemical disturbance may manifest itself in abnormal oscillations in neuro-transmitter functioning. They also make the further very interesting suggestion that future research might elucidate possible links in disturbances in neuro-transmitter functioning in such diverse conditions as schizophrenias, Parkinson's Disease and hyperactivity in children. In respect of the latter, the work of Rapoport (1989) on obsessive compulsive disorder is of interest, as is the work of Newson (1992) on pathological avoidance syndrome (see also Dolan, 1984).

Psychopathy and learning

It is also possible to conclude, albeit tentatively, that psychopaths do not develop conditioned fear responses readily. Because of this, they find it difficult to learn responses that are motivated by fear and reinforced by fear reduction. There is also experimental evidence to suggest (again confirmed in clinical practice) that psychopaths are less influenced than are normal persons by their capacity to make connections between past events and the consequences of their present behaviour.

CLASSIFICATION

In Figure 5.1 I provided a classification of psychopathic personality disorder. Some further comment on the figure can be conveniently provided at this point. The terms 'pseudo-psychopathy' and 'essential psychopathy' require some explanation. In the first place they are very closely linked. The term 'pseudo-psychopathy' is meant to denote an 'as if' situation. That is, the disorder has the appearance of 'essential psychopathy', but is one in which it seems possible to ascribe some reasonably clear cause. As already indicated in Chapter 4, there is some evidence to suggest a fairly clear link between the development of seriously anti-social behaviour (particularly that associated with serious aggression) and exposure to infections of various kinds. Illnesses such as encephalitis or meningitis can be particularly important. The same considerations apply to brain damage. Supporting evidence for such links can be found, for example, in cases where psycho-surgery has been used inappropriately in the treatment of certain cases of neurosis. Such treatment may produce side effects which can consist of bouts of aggression and highly anti-social conduct. The classification I have suggested in column 2 would have assigned to it the swindlers, cheats, etc. (the affectionless personalities) who act without remorse. It might also include those ruthless businessmen and women and politicians who trample on others to fight their way to the top. The category would also include those whom Henderson (1939) described as 'predominantly creative psychopaths'. According to Henderson, these would embrace such personalities as Lawrence of Arabia, but this seems to be stretching the concept of psychopathic disorder somewhat too far and to render it near meaningless. Gunn and Robertson (1976) have indicated that those individuals I would consign to column 2 could best be given a diagnostic category of 'neurosis (anti-social) behaviour'.

It should be noted here that psychiatrists seem to differ quite widely in the extent to which they agree upon the particular diagnostic signs that go to make up the diagnosis of psychopath. Davies and Feldman (1981), in a study of thirty-four psychiatric specialists, found that although only two did not regard psychopathy as a clinical entity, there was considerable disagreement about the precise importance of each diagnostic sign (see also Tennent *et al.*, 1993; Cope, 1993).

It is also of interest to recall the point made in Chapter 4 that those labelled as psychopaths are almost invariably male. Far fewer females carry the psychopathic label. In a carefully executed piece of research, Guze (1976) found an unexpected association between psychopathy and hysteria. He suggested that were this finding to be confirmed by further research it would help to account for the apparent striking sex differences in the two disorders. Such research would have interesting parameters. For example, what are the respective parts played by biological and cultural factors which contribute to the sex differences and to what extent will the continually changing status of women affect these so-called differences?

A number of workers have tried to discriminate between primary and secondary psychopaths (see, for example, Karpman, 1948). Much more recently, Blackburn has carried such work further; and he, too, suggests primary and secondary types. In addition, he has suggested that it is possible to identify four profile types for the psychopath. The first of these seems to be essentially similar to Karpman's primary type, to Cleckley's 'true' psychopath and to my classification of 'essential psychopathy' (see, for example, Blackburn, 1993: Chapter 3).

The need for differential diagnosis

Having made some attempt to delineate two major types of psychopathic disorder (the 'pseudo' and the 'essential'), it now seems important to examine the extent to which such disorder may be differentiated from ordinary criminal recidivism. Blair suggested that psychopathic disorder must be distinguished from:

1   Personality Disorders
2   Severe Psychoneurosis
3   Ordinary Adolescents
4   Hardened Criminals

(Blair, 1975: 56)

He also emphasised that in order to make an adequate assessment of the condition it was vital to obtain a detailed life history, since in almost all cases the true or essential psychopath has exhibited severe disturbance in all areas of behaviour from a *very early age*. Indeed, it is important to remember that the presence of long-standing disturbance is implicit in the criteria for the diagnosis of psychopathic disorder within the meaning of the Mental Health Act 1983 and in the clinical criteria (APA, 1994; WHO, 1992).

What, then, are some of the characteristics that distinguish true psychopaths from ordinary recidivists (Blair's 'Hardened Criminals')? Cleckley (1976) suggested that the following were important distinguishing features:

1 Ordinary recidivist criminals often seem to work to their own advantage through their offending; by this is meant that they seem to be more purposive. Psychopaths, on the other hand, appear so much more likely to be detected that their criminality has an almost irrational or 'insane' quality to it.

2 As already suggested, the criminal career of psychopaths seems to begin earlier; in addition it spreads into many areas of their social and personal behaviour. They appear to be more unmoved than ordinary recidivist offenders by overtures of help or by punishment and their criminal careers *seem more rapidly continuous*. Their words appear to bear no relationship to their feelings or activities.

3 Psychopaths' anti-social acts are often quite incomprehensible and they seem to indulge in them for quite obscure reasons. They also seem to be injuring themselves; in fact the greatest degree of harm they may often do to others is brought about largely through the concern of others for the psychopath and the psychopath's subsequent rejection of them. Reid (1978: 7) suggests that this quality represents the essential 'sadness' of their lives and the need to fill an emotional void. Thus, they would often leave a *characteristic chain of chaos in their wake*. I would regard this feature as being one of the most important points in trying to distinguish the true psychopath from the ordinary recidivist.

4 The male psychopath's sexual behaviour is not infrequently abnormal and seems to be indulged in at whim.

5 The ordinary recidivist criminal seems, generally speaking, to have a certain degree of loyalty to family and to fellow criminals. The psychopath almost always appears to have none and is essentially a 'loner'. Indeed, McCord describes the psychopath as 'the lonely stranger' (1982: 9; see also Smith, 1978).

6 Hare and Jutai (1983) have observed also that psychopaths commit a disproportionate number of crimes compared with other male criminals and Hare and McPherson have provided evidence that 'the crimes and behaviour of psychopaths are also more violent and aggressive than are those of other criminals' (1984: 35). The results of the latter's three separate retrospective studies (which involved about 500 male criminals) showed that psychopaths were much more likely to use violent and aggressive behaviour than were criminals in general. Hare and McPherson used very careful and explicit criteria for the diagnosis of psychopathy and the assessment procedures used in the studies were rated as both highly reliable and valid. It is also of interest to note that Hare and Jutai suggest that the aggressive psychopath may in fact engage in his or her aggressive activities for a longer period than has been supposed hitherto.

The criteria suggested above go some way to indicating the possibilities of framing a differential diagnosis. There will, of course, be areas of overlap and ambiguity. It should be noted, however, that Scott (1960), a highly respected authority in this field, once questioned the need to distinguish between psychopaths and recidivists and suggested that there was not a great deal to be gained by it.

SOME KEY CHARACTERISTICS

I shall now delineate some further characteristics of the psychopath in order to expand upon the more general picture painted above. Cleckley makes the very telling observation that

> a race of men congenitally without pain sense would not find it easy to estimate the effects of physical torture on others. A man who has never understood visual experience would lack appreciation of what is sustained when the ordinary person loses his eye.

(1976: 322)

He also states that the psychopath 'is invincibly ignorant of what life means to others' (p. 386). In order to emphasise some of the key characteristics, Cleckley's oft-quoted list of sixteen cardinal features is very useful:

1　Superficial charm and good intelligence.
2　Absence of delusions and other signs of irrational thinking.
3　Absence of 'nervousness' or psychoneurotic manifestations.
4　Unreliability.
5　Untruthfulness and insincerity.
6　Lack of remorse or shame.
7　Inadequately motivated anti-social behaviour.
8　Poor judgement and failure to learn by experience.
9　Pathological egocentricity and incapacity to love.
10　General poverty in major affective reactions.
11　Specific loss of insight.
12　Unresponsiveness in general interpersonal relations.
13　Fantastic and uninviting behaviour with drink and sometimes without.
14　Suicide rarely carried out.
15　Sex life impersonal, trivial and poorly integrated.
16　Failure to follow any life plan.

(Cleckley, 1964: 363)

Taken overall, these provide a very thorough framework for trying to distinguish the main characteristics of the pure or essential psychopath. Obviously not *all* sixteen characteristics will necessarily be present in every case, but for the diagnosis to be made the majority should be.

In this list of cardinal characteristics, and from the points and two quotations from Cleckley cited earlier, we may readily grasp the core features, namely *lack of real affect, an inability to relate feelings to the words with which they are expressed,* and *the chaos and destruction that the essential psychopath leaves behind.* The lack of affect and chaos has been well described by numerous authorities, but less attention has been given to the singular disparity between speech and feelings. In this connection, it has been well stated that the psychopath 'knows the words but not the music' (Johns and Quay, 1962: 217). More recently, this odd disparity has been given further confirmation by Hare and Connolly. They agree with Cleckley that the actual behaviour of psychopaths is often strikingly inconsistent with their verbalised thoughts, feelings and intentions. They suggest that this seems very different in quality from simple lying, dissimulation and hypocrisy. They agree also with Cleckley that 'the speech of psychopaths is in fact a mechanically correct artifact that masks a profound, deep-seated semantic disorder in which the formal, semantic, and affective components of language have somehow become dissociated from one another' (Hare and Connolly, 1987: 218–219). They postulate, on the basis of a variety of investigative procedures, that the cause of such behaviour is likely to be determined by differences in the functions of the two hemispheres of the brain (hemispheric asymmetry), one hypothesis being that in psychopaths the left hemisphere is not as specialised for linguistic processing as it is in normal individuals. The authors indicate that their conclusions must be regarded as tentative and confirmation must wait upon further research.

I am reminded of one good example from my own experience of this type of disparity. I once interviewed an offender-patient (who admittedly had been already labelled as a psychopath). He told me a highly complicated tale which was so obviously untrue from start to finish that his story had a quality of complete irrationality and a feeling akin to madness about it. This offender knew that the facts could have been checked with the minimum of difficulty and that they were so glaringly untrue that any individual of average intelligence would have known that they could not possibly deceive. In addition, the statements he was presenting as truth were clearly lies of such a grandiose nature that, again, this curious quality of madness came across even more forcefully. However, he was *not* regarded as clinically deluded in the sense that he might have been suffering from delusions of grandeur due to the type of psychotic illness described in Chapter 4. His lying was, in my view, the clearest possible example of that demonstrated by Cleckley's true or essential psychopath.

It was no doubt this disparity between speech and feelings that led Cleckley to formulate his interesting concept of *semantic disorder or dementia.* In developing this idea, Cleckley drew upon work that had been done by the neurologist Henry Head, in relation to a condition known as *semantic aphasia.* This concept of Cleckley's has received relatively little attention, perhaps because of its complexity; it is admittedly difficult to prove, though clearly it is deserving of further exploration. Crudely put, and at the risk of some distortion through compression, Cleckley suggests that just as damage to certain higher nerve centres in the brain may produce a physical inability to comprehend or produce language, so with the psychopath some form of neural damage (unspecified, but likely to be within that part of the brain dealing with the higher functions of speech and meaning) might produce this strange inability to gear in to the needs and wants of others. Cleckley indicates that the psychopath is able to present to the outside world a façade of normality, which in fact conceals a seriously disabled and often highly irresponsible individual.

This connection (or rather lack of it) between words and emotion already referred to, is of interest from another angle. In his book, *The Murdering Mind*, Abrahamsen (1973) illustrates how an unusually large proportion of murderers and others charged with repeated acts of serious personal violence seemed to share two common characteristics – serious errors in verbal usage and curious, but strangely consistent, spelling mistakes. Such mis-spellings he describes as *onomatopoiesis* – the making of a word or a name from a sound. Abrahamsen suggests that such people are not really anxious to communicate; their verbal communication is a way of merely exhibiting themselves. He goes on to suggest that such phenomena may offer diagnostic and predictive clues. Clearly, one cannot make too much use of such findings; they would require careful experimental validation and they are no more than peripherally linked with Cleckley's formulation. Nevertheless, they do provide food for further thought. Cleckley's concept of semantic aphasia is perhaps exemplified to some extent by what the psychopath Patrick Mackay had to say about the senseless and horrific crimes he committed. 'I feel terrible about what happened all the more because I do not know why or what made me do it. *I find it all a confusing matter*' (Clark and Penycate, 1976: 2; emphasis added).

One final important characteristic of psychopaths which is worth commenting upon is their lack of time sense. Harrington, an American lay author, collected information on the characteristics of psychopaths from a variety of expert sources. One of his expert witnesses pointed out that psychopaths

> never see their behaviour in the context of tomorrow . . . if I'm a psychopath and I have an appointment to meet you but – all at once, unexpectedly – I run into an old friend on the street I might spend my afternoon with him and simply not show up for our meeting . . .'
>
> (Harrington, 1972: 215)

We do not have to rely entirely upon clinical and mental health descriptions of the kind of disorder we are discussing. Its nature, early onset and manifestations are depicted clearly enough in the aged Duchess of York's reviling of her son Richard III in Act IV, Scene iv of Shakespeare's play of that name:

> Thou cams't on earth to make the earth my hell.
> A grievous burden was thy birth to me;
> Tetchy and wayward was thy infancy;

> Thy School days frightful, desp'rate, wild and furious;
> Thy prime of manhood daring, bold and venturous;
> Thy age confirmed, proud, subtle, sly and bloody,
> More mild but yet more harmful-kind in hatred,
> What comfortable hour cans't thou name
> That ever graced me with they company?

Here, we have the aged Duchess describing graphically some of the characteristics we regard as of importance in terms of both aetiology and presentation: an apparently difficult birth, long-standing anti-social conduct (a requirement for both the DSM IV (APA, 1994), the ICD-10 (WHO, 1992) and our own Mental Health Act 1983), becoming more marked in adulthood; all this accompanied by a veneer of charm and sophistication which only serves to act as a mask for the underlying themes of chaos and potential for destructiveness we have already identified. These latter qualities are well illustrated in Samuel Taylor Coleridge's comment about the character of Shakespeare's Caliban *c.* 1818: 'Caliban . . . is all earth, all condensed and gross in feelings and images; he has the dawnings of understanding without reason of the moral sense, and in him, as in some brute animals, his advance to the intellectual, without the moral sense, is marked by the appearance of vice' (quoted in RSC 'Programme Notes' for a performance of *The Tempest* at Stratford-upon-Avon on 21 August 1993). Such behaviour is not easy to change, as we shall now see.

PROBLEMS OF MANAGEMENT

There is little doubt, both from research findings and from clinical practice, that personality disorders in general, and psychopathy in particular, are very difficult conditions to treat or to ameliorate. For example, in child psychiatric practice it is a well-established fact that it is easier to treat anxiety states and phobic conditions in children than it is to treat behaviour disorders, though some such disorders, particularly those involving hyperactivity, seem to be amenable to behaviour modification techniques. As for the more serious cases, we have to admit that, in the present state of our knowledge and skills, these are most intractable. This is the more distressing since we know from careful research studies such as those carried out by Robins (1969) that the behaviour-disordered children of today not infrequently become the psychopaths of tomorrow. Such failure, in the light of my earlier remarks about our lack of accurate knowledge concerning explanations of psychopathy, is hardly surprising. It is, therefore, very tempting to write off all such offenders as untreatable.

One of the arguments often advanced for finding a new term for psychopathy is that it has become a word of abuse and a 'dustbin' category to which we have assigned all those patients, residents, inmates and offenders who seem unwilling to be helped, are unpredictable, unresponsive and who, in addition, may show aggressive behaviour to a severe degree. There is, of course, much truth in this, but it is only a partial explanation. It seems that whatever label we are going to use – be it psychopath, sociopath, psychopathic personality or severe personality disorder – we are *still* going to have to face problems of engagement, acceptance and communication.

Many people have drawn attention to the reluctance of professionals in the penal and mental health care services to deal with psychopaths (particularly the more aggressive). Admittedly the label we use *can* be used perjoratively and as a defence against involvement. One worker (a psychiatrist) has put this reluctance very well:

[C]ould it be after all these Freudian years, that psychiatrists have denied the hatred they feel for psychopaths and criminals, and thus have been unable to treat psychopaths adequately because their conceptual basis for treatment has been distorted by unconscious, denied feelings from the start?

(Maier, 1990: 766)

This implied need for self-inspection was also outlined in a contribution some years earlier by another psychiatrist, Treves-Brown:

As long as a doctor believes that psychopaths are mostly 'bad', his successful treatment rate will be dismal. Since it takes two to form a relationship, an outside observer could be forgiven for suspecting that a doctor who describes a patient as unable to form a relationship is simply justifying his own hostility to this patient.

(1977: 62)

Both these statements are by psychiatrists, but their lessons have application to other professionals who may have to deal with those adjudged to be exhibiting psychopathic disorder in one form or another. As can be seen, the basic difficulty lies in developing an especial awareness not only of the rejecting feelings that such clients arouse in us, but also of the way in which we can rationalise our negative responses by the use of the label. Somehow we have to rise above the rejecting behaviour of these clients, to 'hang on' to them, sometimes over many years, and hope that gradually there may be some modification of their attitudes; this is a theme to which I shall return shortly. There is little doubt that 'some workers intuitively obtain good results with certain psychopaths' (Scott, 1960: 1645); as Scott also went on to point out, 'it should be possible to find out how they do it' (p. 1645). This statement has been echoed more recently by Higgit and Fonagy. They state that 'Therapist commitment and enthusiasm appears to be of special significance and subjective aspects of the patient–therapist "fit" (complementarity) may be particularly important for this group of patients' (Higgit and Fonagy, 1993: 253).

Management may be highlighted as follows:

1 Those psychopathically disordered individuals whose behaviour is marked by serious episodes of aggression and violence should be carefully assessed and monitored for possible 'organic' causes. This is especially so if their persistent

violence seems to be unprovoked or minimally provoked by others and seems to be associated with the ingestion of even small amounts of alcohol and/or other drugs. It may be that they can be helped by *carefully monitored and controlled* amounts of medication. Stein (1993) has recently published an excellent and most detailed review of the extent and limitations of drug treatments in the management of personality disorders. I must make it clear that I am not an advocate of medicating people without the most scrupulous care and attention; I know of too many situations where medication may have been used unwisely to suggest anything to the contrary.

2   There appears to be some evidence to suggest that even some apparently intractable cases can be helped to behave more appropriately over time. It may be that in these cases (and particularly in those that also show some history of aggressive outbursts) their impulsivity tends to diminish with advancing years. Explorative, deeply psychoanalytic-type therapy does not seem likely to be particularly successful in such cases. Calm confrontation of their adverse behaviour (as it affects themselves and others) over prolonged periods may help to bring about change. Some workers advocate that this is best carried out in peer-group situations, but benefit can also accrue from one-to-one encounters. Whether the work is carried out on a group or individual basis, it is *essential* for workers not to feel *personally* affronted at being misled, lied to, evaded or made to feel helpless in the face of the chaos I referred to earlier. I am trying to get across something as deceptively simple as the possession of *patience* in dealing with such people. The late George Lyward, who was a gifted worker with maladjusted youths, some of whom were possibly psychopaths in embryo, once made the telling remark that 'patience is love that can wait'. It is this capacity to tolerate hate, hostility, manipulation and 'splitting' that is often so vital for any degree of success, however small.

3   When one examines the varieties of approaches that have been tried with psychopathically disordered individuals, it has always seemed to me that there are three key words that come to mind in trying to deal with them. These are *consistence*, *persistence* and *insistence*. Perhaps it is also wise to remember the words of the writer Zamyatin in his novel *We*: 'Man is like a novel; one doesn't know until the very last page how the thing will end' (quoted in Stone, 1993). A former President of the Royal College of Psychiatrists, in an address to that body on the future of psychiatry, had some comments that are relevant to my theme. He said that we should adopt

a willingness to embrace a truly eclectic approach, which rejoices in the complexity of the human mind and is aware of the equally valid contributions from genetics, biochemistry, pharmacology and psychology (both in its dynamic and behavioural mode) and from the social sciences.

(Rawnsley: 1984: 575)

Is the concept useful?

Finally, some brief comments about the usefulness of the concept as viewed by a variety of professionals.

A few years ago, some colleagues and I sought the opinions of three groups of forensic psychiatric professionals (psychiatrists, psychologists and probation officers) on two topics. First, was the concept of psychopathic disorder useful? Second, did they think psychopathic disorder was a treatable condition? Space does not permit a detailed presentation of our methodology and findings (these are described fully elsewhere: Tennent *et al.*, 1990, 1993). Despite a somewhat limited response rate to our questionnaires, we found our respondents considered that the concept of psychopathic disorder was a useful one. We also found that *psychiatrists'* opinions about psychopathic disorder have remained very constant. As to *treatability*, we again had to form our judgements on a limited response rate; however, our modest findings suggested that although few clear-cut views emerged as to the *best* treatment modalities, there were clearer indications as to those felt to be unhelpful. It would seem that there were higher expectations of treatment efficacy with 'symptoms' such as 'chronically anti-social', 'abnormally aggressive' and 'lacking control over impulses' and much lower expectations for symptoms such as 'inability to experience guilt', 'lack of remorse or shame' and 'pathological egocentricity'.

Support for our modest findings can be found in a recent and more extensive questionnaire survey of all forensic psychiatrists working in Regional Secure Units (RSUs), Special Hospitals and other forensic settings in England, Scotland and Wales (Cope, 1993). The questionnaire, submitted by the author on behalf of the Forensic Psychiatry Section of the Royal College of Psychiatrists, made use of case vignettes and included questions about current legislation, treatment and treatability, dangerousness, facilities and decision-making. (She achieved a response rate of 91 per cent.) The majority of the psychiatrists responding to her questionnaire were in favour of offering treatment to psychopaths; only about 10 per cent believed that psychopaths were untreatable. There was considerable support for setting up specialised units for treating such persons, especially in prisons and the Special Hospitals. Support for the foregoing may be found in work reported from Canada. In a recent review of a number of studies Hare *et al.* conclude that the studies

> provide considerable support for the validity of the psychopathic construct, its strong association with crime and violence and consequently, its importance to the criminal justice and correctional systems.

(1993: 175–176)

However, it is important to remember that Cope's sample consisted of forensic psychiatrists only; other (but admittedly small-scale) studies have not produced quite such positive results (Collins, 1991).

CONCLUSION

By way of conclusion we may return to the charges laid at Richard III's door by his elderly mother.[1] They graphically demonstrate some of the key characteristics of the individuals I have been discussing in this chapter. These include ambivalent parental feelings provoking in turn a cold, wayward response, resulting in long-standing behaviour difficulties, lovelessness, cunning, evasion and deceit, coupled with a superficial charm. All the 'hallmarks' appear to be there. Taken together they represent a tremendous challenge to those charged with the task of management. In addition, such a challenge presupposes the capacity to step outside narrow boundaries of learning and experience and to take on board findings from a wide range of disciplines. The words of Professor Rawnsley quoted earlier are highly relevant in this respect (see also Harding, 1992).

NOTES

1   It is of interest to note that in his account of his preparation for his portrayal of the part of Richard, the actor Anthony Sher placed great emphasis on Richard's relationship with his mother (see Sher, 1985, and correspondence between Sher and the present writer).

REFERENCES

Abrahamsen, D. (1973) *The Murdering Mind*, London: Harper (Colophon Books).
American Psychiatric Association (APA) (1994) *Diagnostic and Statistical Manual of Mental Disorders*, DSM IV, Washington, DC: APA.
Bavidge, N.M. (1989) *Mad or Bad*? Bristol: Classical Press.
Berrios, G.E. (1993) 'Personality Disorders: A Conceptual History', in P. Tyrer and G. Stein (eds), *Personality Disorder Reviewed*, London: Gaskell.
Blackburn, R. (1984) Unpublished lecture given as part of the commemoration of the opening of Park Lane Hospital, 4 October.
—— (1988) 'On Moral Judgements and Personality Disorder: The Myth of Psychopathic Personality Revisited', *British Journal of Psychiatry* 153: 505–512.
—— (1993) *The Psychology of Criminal Conduct: Theory, Research and Practice*, Chichester: Wiley.
Blair, D. (1975) 'The Medico-Legal Implications of the Terms "Psychopath", "Psychopathic" and "Psychopathic Disorder"', *Medicine, Science and the Law* 15: 51–61 and 110–123.
Chiswick, D. (1992) 'Compulsory Treatment of Patients with Psychopathic Disorder: An Abnormally Aggressive and Seriously Irresponsible Exercise?', *Criminal Behaviour and Mental Health* 2: 106–113.
Clark, T. and Penycate, J. (1976) *Psychopath: The Case of Patrick Mackay*, London: Routledge and Kegan Paul.
Cleckley, M. (1964) *The Mask of Sanity* (fourth edn), St Louis: C.V. Mosby.
—— (1976) *The Mask of Sanity* (fifth edn), St Louis: C.V. Mosby.
Coid, J. (1989) 'Psychopathic Disorders', *Current Opinion in Psychiatry* 2: 750–756.
—— (1992) 'DSM-III Diagnosis in Criminal Psychopaths: A Way Forward', *Criminal Behaviour and Mental Health* 2: 78–94.
—— (1993) 'Current Concepts and Classifications in Psychopathic Disorder', in P. Tyrer and G. Stein (eds), *Personality Disorder Reviewed*, London: Gaskell.

Collins, J. (1991) 'The Treatment of Psychopaths', *Journal of Forensic Psychiatry* 2: 103–110.

Cope, R. (1993) 'A Survey of Forensic Psychiatrists' Views on Psychopathic Disorder', *Journal of Forensic Psychiatry* 4: 214–235.

Davies, W. and Feldman, P. (1981) 'The Diagnosis of Psychopathy by Forensic Specialists', *British Journal of Psychiatry* 138: 329–331.

Dell, S. and Robertson, G. (1988) *Sentenced to Hospital: Offenders in Broadmoor*, Oxford: Oxford University Press.

Department of Health and Home Office (1994) *Report of the Department of Health and Home Office Working Group on Psychopathic Disorder* (Chairman, Dr John Reed, CB), London: Department of Health and Home Office.

Department of Health and Social Security (DHSS) and Home Office (1986) *Consultation Document: Offenders Suffering From Psychopathic Disorder*, London: DHSS and Home Office.

Department of Health and Social Security (DHSS), Home Office and Lord Chancellor's Department (1976) *A Review of the Mental Health Act, 1959*, London: HMSO.

Dolan, M. (1994) 'Psychopathy – A Neuro-biological Perspective', *British Journal of Psychiatry* 165: 151–159.

Feldman, M.P. (1977) *Criminal Behaviour: A Psychological Analysis*, London, Wiley.

Finlay-Jones, R. (1991) 'Psychopathic Disorder', *Current Opinion in Psychiatry* 4: 850–855.

Gough, H. (1956) 'A Sociological Study of Psychopathy', in A.M. Rose (ed.), *Mental Health and Mental Disorder*, London: Routledge and Kegan Paul.

Grounds, A.T. (1987) 'Detention of Psychopathic Disorder Patients in Special Hospitals: Critical Issues', *British Journal of Psychiatry* 151: 474–478.

Gunn, J. and Robertson, G. (1976) 'Psychopathic Personality: A Conceptual Problem', *Psychological Medicine* 6: 631–634.

Guze, S.B. (1976) *Criminality and Psychiatric Disorders*, Oxford: Oxford University Press.

Harding, T.W. (1992) 'Psychopathic Disorder: Time for a Decent Burial of a Bad Concept?', *Criminal Behaviour and Mental Health* 2: vi–ix.

Hare, R.D. (1980) 'A Research Scale for the Assessment of Psychopathy in Criminal Populations', *Personality and Individual Differences* 1: 111–117.

Hare, R.D. and Connolly, J.F. (1987) 'Perceptual Asymmetries and Information Processing in Psychopaths', in S.A. Mednick, T.E. Moffitt and S.A. Stack (eds), *The Causes of Crime: New Biological Approaches*, Cambridge: Cambridge University Press.

Hare, R.D. and Jutai, J.W. (1983) 'Criminal History of the Male Psychopath: Some Preliminary Data', in K.T. Van Dusen and S.A. Mednick (eds), *Prospective Studies of Crime and Delinquency*, Boston: Kluwer Nijhoff.

Hare, R.D. and McPherson, L.M. (1984) 'Violent and Criminal Behaviour by Criminal Psychopaths', *International Journal of Law and Psychiatry* 7: 33–50.

Hare, R.D. and Schalling, D. (1978) *Psychopathic Behaviour: Approaches to Research*, London: Wiley.

Hare, R.D., Hart, S.D. and Harpur, T.J. (1991) 'Factor Structure of the Psychopathy Checklist', *Journal of Consulting and Clinical Psychology* 56: 741-747.

Hare, R.D., Strachan, C.E. and Forth, A.E. (1993) 'Psychopathy and Crime: A Review', in K. Howells and C.R. Hollin (eds), *Clinical Approaches to The Mentally Disordered Offender*, Chichester: Wiley.

Harrington, A. (1972) *Psychopaths*, London: If Books.

Henderson, D. (1939) *Psychopathic States*, New York: Norton and Co.

Higgitt, A. and Fonagy, P. (1993) 'Psychotherapy in Borderline and Narcissistic Personality Disorders', in P. Tyrer and G. Stein (eds), *Personality Disorder Reviewed*, London: Gaskell.

Home Office and Department of Health and Social Security (DHSS) (1975) *Report of the Committee on Mentally Abnormal Offenders* (The Butler Committee), Cmnd 6244, London: HMSO.

Home Office and Ministry of Health (1957) *Royal Commission on the Law Relating to Mental Illness and Mental Deficiency* (1954–1957) (Chairman, Lord Percy), Cmnd 169, London: HMSO.

Johns, J.H. and Quay, H.C. (1962) 'The Effect of Social Reward on Verbal Conditioning in Psychopathic and Neurotic Military Offenders', *Journal of Consulting Psychology* 26: 217–220.

Karpman, B. (1948) 'Conscience in the Psychopath', *American Journal of Ortho-Psychiatry* 18: 455–491.

Koch, J.W. (1891) *Die Psychopathischen Minderwertigkeiten*, Ravensburg: Maier.

Lewis, G. and Appleby, L. (1988) 'Personality Disorders: The Patients Psychiatrists Dislike', *British Journal of Psychiatry* 153: 44–49.

McCord, W. (1982) *The Psychopath and Milieu Therapy: A Longitudinal Study*, New York: Academic Press.

Maier, G.J. (1990) 'Psychopathic Disorders: Beyond Counter-Transference', *Current Opinion in Psychiatry* 3: 766–769.

Mawson, A.R. and Mawson, C.D. (1977) 'Psychopathy and Arousal: A New Interpretation of the Psychophysiological Literature', *Biological Psychiatry* 12: 49–74.

Newson, E. (1992) 'Pathological Avoidance Syndrome: Its Relevance to Certain Psychopathic Adults', unpublished paper, Child Development Research Unit, Nottingham: Nottingham University.

Pinel, P.H. (1806) *A Treatise on Insanity*, New York: Hafner Publishing.

Prichard, J.C. (1835) *Treatise on Insanity*, London: Gilbert and Piper.

Prins, H. (1988) 'The Current Status of Personality Disorder', *Current Opinion in Psychiatry* 1: 184–187.

Rapoport, J. (1990) *The Boy Who Couldn't Stop Washing: The Experience and Treatment of Obsessive Compulsive Disorder*, London: Collins.

Rawnsley, K. (1984) 'Psychiatry in Jeopardy', *British Journal of Psychiatry* 145: 573–578.

Reid, W.H. (1978) 'The Sadness of the Psychopath', in W.H. Reid (ed.), *The Psychopath: A Comprehensive Study of Anti-Social Disorders and Behaviours*, New York: Brunner/Mazel.

Robertson, G. (1992) 'Objections to the Present System', *Criminal Behaviour and Mental Health* 2: 114–123.

Robins, L. (1969) *Deviant Children Grown Up: A Sociological and Psychiatric Study of Sociopathic Personality*, Baltimore: Williams and Wilkins.

Roth, M. (1990) 'Psychopathic (Sociopathic Personality)', in R. Bluglass and P. Bowden (eds), *Principles and Practice of Forensic Psychiatry*, London: Churchill Livingstone.

Rutter, M. (1987) 'Temperament, Personality and Personality Disorder', *British Journal of Psychiatry* 150: 443–458.

Schneider, K. (1958) *Psychopathic Personalities*, London: Cassell.

Scott, P.D. (1960) 'The Treatment of Psychopaths', *British Medical Journal* 2: 1641–1646.

Sher, A. (1985) *The Year of the King: An Actor's Diary and Sketchbook*, London: Chatto and Windus.

Slater, E.T.O. (1948) 'Psychopathic Personality as a Genetical Concept', *Journal of Mental Science* 94: 277–280.

Smith, R.J. (1978) *The Psychopath in Society*, New York: Academic Press.

Stein, G. (1993) 'Drug Treatment of Personality Disorders', in P. Tyrer and G. Stein (eds), *Personality Disorder Reviewed*, London: Gaskell.

Stone, M.H. (1993) 'Long-Term Outcomes in Personality Disorders', in P. Tyrer and G. Stein (eds), *Personality Disorder Reviewed*, London: Gaskell.

Tennent, G., Tennent, D., Prins, H. and Bedford, A. (1990) 'Psychopathic Disorder – A Useful Clinical Concept?, *Medicine, Science and the Law* 30: 39–44.
—— (1993) 'Is Psychopathic Disorder a Treatable Condition?', *Medicine, Science and the Law* 33: 63–66.
Trethowan, W. and Sims, A.C.P. (1983) *Psychiatry* (fifth edn), London: Baillière Tindall.
Treves-Brown, C. (1977) 'Who is the Psychopath?', *Medicine, Science and the Law* 17: 56–63.
Tyrer, P. (1989) 'Clinical Importance of Personality Disorder', *Current Opinion in Psychiatry* 2: 240–243.
—— (1990) 'Diagnosing Personality Disorders', *Current Opinion in Psychiatry* 3: 182–187.
Vetter, H. (1990) 'Dissociation, Psychopathy and the Serial Murderer', in S. Egger (ed.), *Serial Murder: An Elusive Phenomenon*, London: Praeger.
Wambaugh, J. (1989) *The Blooding*, London: Bantam Books.
Weller, M.P.I. (1986) 'Medical Concepts in Psychopathy and Violence', *Medicine, Science and the Law* 26: 131–143.
Widom, C.S. and Newman, J.P. (1985) 'Characteristics of Non-Institutionalised Psychopaths', in D.P. Farrington and J. Gunn (eds), *Aggression and Dangerousness*, Chichester: Wiley.
Wootton, B. (1959) *Social Science and Social Pathology*, London: Allen and Unwin.
World Health Organisation (WHO) (1992) *The ICD-10 Classification of Mental and Behavioural Disorders: Clinical Descriptions and Diagnostic Guidelines*, Geneva: WHO.

FURTHER READING

Note: Some older contributions to the literature are included as they still have considerable relevance.

Articles

Chiswick, C. (1987) 'Managing Psychopathic Offenders: A Problem That Will Not Go Away', *British Medical Journal* 295: 159–160.
Coid, J. (1991) 'Psychiatric Profiles of Difficult/Disruptive Prisoners', in K. Bottomley and W. Hay (eds), *Special Units for Difficult Prisoners*, Centre for Criminology and Criminal Justice, Hull: University of Hull.
—— (1993) 'An Affective Syndrome in Psychopaths with Borderline Personality Disorder?', *British Journal of Psychiatry* 162: 641–650.
Ferguson, B. and Tyrer, P. (1991) 'Personality Disorder: The Flamboyant Group', *Current Opinion in Psychiatry* 4: 200–204.
Gayford, J.J. and Jungalwalla, H.N.K. (1986) 'Personality Disorder According to the ICD 9 and DSM III and Their Value in Court Reporting', *Medicine, Science and the Law* 26: 113–124.
Lewis, W. (1974) 'Psychopathic Disorder: A Most Elusive Category', *Psychological Medicine* 4: 133–140. (A classic paper.)

Books

Craft, M. (ed.) (1966) *Psychopathic Disorders*, Oxford: Pergamon Press.
Dolan, B. and Coid, J. (1993) *Psychopathic and Anti-Social Personality Disorders*, London: Gaskell.

Doren, D. (1987) *Understanding and Treating the Psychopath*, Chichester: Wiley.

Hare, R.D. (1993) *Without Conscience: The Disturbing World of the Psychopaths Among Us*, London: Pocket Books (Simon and Schuster).

Hick, J. (1993) *Evil and the God of Love*, London: Macmillan.

Kernberg, O.F. (1984) *Severe Personality Disorders: Psychotherapeutic Strategies*, London: Yale University Press.

Lion, J.R. (ed.) (1974) *Personality Disorders: Diagnosis and Management*, Baltimore: Williams and Wilkins.

Masters, B. (1990) *Gary*, London: Jonathan Cape. (Biographical account by the well-known writer and novelist.)

Peck, M.S. (1983) *People of the Lie: The Hope for Healing Human Evil*, London: Rider.

Peterson, M.L. (ed.) (1992) *The Problem of Evil: Selected Readings*, Notre Dame, Indiana: University of Notre Dame Press.

Sturup, G. (1968) *Treating the Untreatable: Chronic Criminals at Herstedvester*, Baltimore: Johns Hopkins Press. (A classic account of institutional provision.)

Chapter 6

Violence and homicide

> No arts; no letters; no society; and, which is worst of all, continual fear and danger
> of violent death. And the life of man, solitary, poor, nasty, brutish and short.
>
> (Hobbes, *Leviathan*, Part 1, Chapter 4: 13)

Violence and homicide have been the subject of some limited discussion in earlier chapters. There is, therefore, a degree of overlap between those chapters and this one, for it is not possible to divide the material in this book up into neat compartments. It needs to be read as a 'whole'. Although, in this chapter, I am dealing almost exclusively with serious crimes of violence against persons, it is as well to remember that certain other crimes (such as burglary, aggravated burglary, sexual offences, malicious damage and arson) have violent undertones and overtones; any separation becomes somewhat artificial and is used for convenience and for purposes of clarity.

The chapter is divided into two sections: first, a limited general discussion of violence as a phenomenon, and its prevalence, with special reference to acts of criminal violence; second, a discussion of homicide, which in turn is divided into several sub-sections dealing with such matters as manslaughter, infanticide, other forms of child killing, children as killers and so-called 'serial' killing. The subject matter of this chapter is vast and can only be sketched briefly. Readers wishing to pursue the topic in more depth should consult the Further Reading listed at the end.

THE PHENOMENON OF VIOLENCE

The terms *aggression* and *violence* are often used synonymously. This is not strictly correct, since we can behave aggressively without necessarily being violent. Aggression is perhaps best regarded as denoting *assertive* behaviour, which may express itself physically or verbally. Aggression can be further divided into *manifest* aggression (physical aggression, verbal aggression) and *latent* aggression (aggressive fantasies, moods, etc.) The following further distinctions can be made: (1) aggression as evidenced in loss of control (as in some forms of crime and some psychiatric disorders); (2) planned aggression (sometimes known as instrumental aggression) or as goal-seeking; (3) structural or institutionalised aggression (as a means of imposing control and/or sanctions). Violence is frequently regarded as destructive aggression – that is, aggression harnessed for harmful purposes. Archer and Browne describe it as 'the exercise of physical force so as to injure or damage persons or property; otherwise to treat or use persons or property in a way that causes bodily injury and forcibly interferes with personal freedom' (1989: 3; see also Hollin, 1992: 147ff.; Blackburn, 1993: Chapter Nine).

In this chapter I am concerned mainly with those behaviours that are marked by force, threats and, in most instances, a degree of premeditation. The event or incident will usually have occurred over a short time-span, but not necessarily so. The debate as to whether aggression and a propensity for violence are all-pervasive, innate or acquired has continued over the centuries and is documented extensively. In the first edition of his book *Human Aggression* Storr stated

> that man is an aggressive creature will hardly be disputed. With the exception of certain rodents, no other vertebrate *habitually destroys members of his own species. No other animal takes positive pleasure in the exercise of cruelty upon another of his own kind* . . . there is no parallel in nature to our savage treatment of each other.
>
> (1975: 9; emphasis added)

In a revised and up-dated edition of this work he adds to this somewhat sombre propensity for violence, as follows:

> I think that *Homo Sapiens* has not altered very much in fundamental, physical or psychological characteristics since he first appeared upon the scene; and that the best we can hope for is some slight modification of his nastier traits of personality in the light of increased understanding. We cannot abolish man's potential for cruelty and destructiveness, but we may be partially able to control the circumstances which can lead to their overt expression.
>
> (1991: 141–142)

The way in which the circumstances that can lead to such destructive behaviour may be reduced or modified are considered in Chapter 9 below.

In view of the acknowledged universality of the capacity to behave violently, it is of interest to observe that its overt *expression* appears to be determined quite markedly by cultural conditions. In their studies of so-called 'primitive' societies, early anthropologists (such as Mead, Benedict, Murdock and others) demonstrated the great variety that can be shown to exist in the display of aggressive and violent behaviour (see Weller, 1985; Gunn, 1991; Tantam, 1993). Fromm has attempted to synthesise some of their early work and to apply it to more developed societies. He found that three different and clearly delineated forms of society could be discerned: *Life-Affirmative Societies*; *Non-destructive-Aggressive Societies*; *Destructive Societies*. In *Life-Affirmative Societies*, the main emphasis is upon the preservation and growth of life in all forms. 'There is a minimum of hostility, violence or cruelty among people, no harsh punishments, hardly any crime, and the institution of war is absent or plays an exceedingly small role' (Fromm, 1977: 229). In *Non-destructive-Aggressive Societies* 'aggressiveness and war, although not central, are normal occurrences, and . . . competition, hierarchy and individualism are present' (p. 230). *Destructive Societies* are 'characterised by much interpersonal violence, destructiveness, aggression and cruelty . . . pleasure in war, maliciousness and treachery' (p. 231). Fromm's view is admittedly very sweeping and some might consider it over-simple. Nevertheless, it may help us to understand the apparent overt differences in the phenomena of violence in various societies. It may also help us to understand what appears to be the ubiquitous phenomenon of violence in our own society, whether it be expressed in the home, the school or in some of those institutions established for the avowed purpose of the protection of the vulnerable (for example, establishments for the elderly and hospitals of one kind or another),[1] and in acts of terrorism and other international atrocities – both past and current.

Whatever view we may take about the causes of violence in society, the following points would find a degree of acceptance:

1 Violence when shown by non-human animals is usually purposive, self-protective and conforms to certain ritualised patterns (Lorenz, 1966).
2 In the human species, violence may be sanctioned by a community (Fromm, 1977).
3 It takes little to disinhibit violence in human societies. As Storr suggests, it seems likely that men and women have always had the potential for the commission of a great deal of violence, but that this is normally kept in check by society's sanctions. These sanctions can, however, change over time – witness the enormity of the atrocities against millions of people during the Nazi regime in the 1930s and 1940s.

An explanation of the manner in which apparently quite normal and law-abiding people can inflict wanton suffering on others has been provided by the psychologist Zimbardo in an interview with McDermott (1993). Zimbardo (1973) was the originator of the famous (or infamous, depending upon your ethical standpoint) Stanford Prison experiment, in which quite ordinary students were able to inflict suffering and deprivation upon their fellows – to such an extent that the experiment had to be stopped prematurely because of its effect upon those who were the detainees. Zimbardo suggests three key factors that may be at work in bringing about the capacity for quite normal human beings to behave inhumanely towards others. These consist of (a) de-individualisation (loss of personal identifiability and unique-ness); (b) dehumanisation (loss of a sense of personal value); and (c) present-time orientation (engaging in current actions without concern for future consequences or past commitments). As with Fromm's views, Zimbardo's also have a broad sweep to them but they have a certain credibility in the light of a great deal of theorising about the aetiology and manifestation of violent behaviour.

In this and other chapters we are most concerned with situations in which *individual internal* mechanisms of control have broken down (though the broader canvas should not be dismissed). Internal control appears to be mediated by various psychological defence mechanisms – such as denial, repression and projection. Some early psychoanalysts (notably the late Melanie Klein [1963] claimed, on the basis of not inconsiderable clinical data, that even small infants possess highly destructive and violent urges. These may come to the fore in the face of hunger and frustration (Segal, 1964; Williams, 1982). Such urges normally find appeasement, but, in the event of failure, serious distortions of personality may occur, as in the case of some of the psychopathically disordered persons described in Chapter 5.

Was it ever thus? A friend and colleague of mine has written:

> The world is steeped in the rhetoric of violence. The horror of international terrorism and the menacing of aggression acted out between factions and adherents of religious and political ideologies feed the media and in time may dull our senses. Perhaps it is no worse now than at any other period of man's history, but only seems so because modern communication has shrunk the world and the modern armoury has enormously increased the consequences of violence. Even if somehow we manage to distance ourselves from these horrors, however, they still provide a frightening backcloth to the violence and danger represented by some individuals in our society and expose the potential for devastating aggression in all of us.
>
> (Day, 1986: xii)

Literature abounds with references to the existence of violent behaviour through all periods of history. Edward Gibbon wrote of sixth-century Constantinople: 'It became dangerous to wear any gold buttons or girdles or to appear at a late hour in the streets of a peaceful capital' (quoted in Hankoff, 1993: 1–3). James Sharpe (1993), a University of York historian, suggests that mugging was as prevalent in London in the middle of the nineteenth century (in the form of 'garrotting') as it is alleged to be today. Pearson (1983) has shown that modern 'hooliganism' has its origins in pre-Victorian England and that serious crowd misbehaviour at professional football matches is as old as the game itself. In a search for causes, an article in *The Times* of 17 August 1898, suggested that climate might have a bearing:

> It is curious that simultaneously with reports of excessive heat should come the record of an unusual number of crimes of lawless violence ... Does the great heat fire the blood of the London rough or street arab, with an effect [comparable] to that of a southern climate upon the hot-blooded Italian or Provençal? Or, is the connection between heat and lawlessness not so much one of cause and effect as coincident circumstances – heat generating thirst, and thirst a too frequent consumption of fiery liquor unsuitable for a tropical climate?
>
> (quoted in Pearson, 1983: 75)

We should let the last word on this matter rest with that shrewd observer of human nature – Shakespeare:

> I would there were no age between ten and three and twenty, or that youth would sleep out the rest; for there is nothing in the between but getting wenches with child, wronging the ancientry, stealing, fighting.
>
> (*The Winter's Tale*, Act 3, Scene iii)

The current volume of criminal violence

It is important to bear in mind the caveat entered earlier in this chapter concerning the way in which crimes of violence are classified for legal and statistical purposes. Although such crimes understandably receive the most publicity and cause the most concern, it is important to state that, taken as a whole, they represent less than 5 per cent of offences recorded by the police – and the more serious of these, for example those that endanger life and armed robbery, constitute only about a third of one per cent of all recorded offences (Walmsley, 1986). However, there is no room for complacency, since the rates of robbery and wounding have increased by about a fifth since 1981, whilst recorded offences have almost doubled. Findings from the British Crime Survey summarised in 1992 suggest

> that reporting levels have risen, but not enough to account fully for the divergence in trends. One possibility is that the police are now giving higher priority to some types of violent crime, such as domestic violence, and street robbery; and where there are two options for classification (for instance between wounding and common assault, or between robbery and theft from the person) they may now choose the more serious.
>
> (Home Office, 1992a: 3; see also Davidoff and Dowds, 1989)

Confirmation for the above statement, insofar as it concerns domestic violence, is provided by Browne, who states that

> During the past decade, family violence and child abuse has been increasingly reported in our daily newspapers and news bulletins . . . this has forced us to recognize that violence within the family is a common phenomenon of modern society and there are common factors, for example, between wife abuse and child physical abuse.
>
> (1993: 149)

Some indication of the increase in the number of crimes of violence may be gleaned from Table 6.1.

Victims

Males are more likely than females to be the victims of more serious woundings and three times as likely to be the victims of less serious woundings. However, if

Table 6.1 Crimes of violence: offenders found guilty at all courts or cautioned, 1985–1990 (in thousands)

	1985	1986	1987	1988	1989	1990
Males:						
Violence against the person	50.9	47.2	53.4	59.1	62.3	60.6
Robbery	4.4	4.2	4.4	4.3	4.7	5.1
Females:						
Violence against the person[a]	5.6	5.3	5.8	7.1	7.9	8.6
Robbery	0.3	0.2	0.2	0.3	0.3	0.3

Source: Extracted from Home Office, 1992b: 118

Notes: [a] Note the steady increase in crimes of violence against the person committed by females, except for a slight decrease in 1986 and 1987.

These figures are clearly under-estimates of the *true* volume of serious violent crime. The British Crime Survey regularly estimates the volume of unrecorded crime. This estimate is based on interviews with a sample of some 10,000 people in order to determine the percentage who may have been the victim of crime in a given period. In a recent report it is suggested that recorded crime was only picking up about one in five offences of wounding and robbery actually being committed. (Mayhew *et al.*, 1989).

we treat sexual assaults as crimes of violence (as undoubtedly we should), then more than four times as many sexual assaults on women are recorded as compared with men (Walmsley, 1986). Despite a good deal of media insistence to the contrary, those most at risk of violence are young, males, single persons and those living in urban areas. However, as is well known, it is the elderly and a number of women who understandably express the greatest fear for their own safety (Gottfredson, 1984). It should also be emphasised that some rural areas are now witnessing an increasing number of incidents of violent crime. There is little doubt that alcohol and other drugs play an important but complex role in connection with all types of violent crime; however, this is a long way from saying, as the media so often do, that there is a direct causal connection (see, for example, Bowden, 1993).

The statistics quoted give no indication of the extent of physical and psychological trauma suffered by the victims of all types of assault. Their pattern and severity have been described in a number of important recent publications (see, for example, Shepherd *et al.*, 1990, and Shapland, 1990, who has usefully reviewed the range of victims). (Those occurring as a result of sexual attacks are considered in Chapter 8.) As part of what *appears* to be a general increase in violence, we should note that there has been serious under-reporting of various forms of violence and harassment in the workplace (Health Services Advisory Committee, DHSS, 1987).

A mixture of motives and crimes

The artificiality of legal classification and the range of motives involved in some of the selected crimes of violence referred to above is usefully demonstrated in the following case examples.

Example 1

A young man aged twenty-three was known by family and friends to be of uncertain temper. For some time, he had been courting a young woman he had met in a dance hall. She was something of a flirt, and evidently took some pleasure in taunting him from time to time. During one of these 'episodes' at his home, he warned her that unless she stopped he might harm her. Seeing that his warning had not the slightest effect, he picked up a cup and threw it at her, inflicting a nasty flesh wound to her forehead. He pleaded guilty to malicious wounding, was convicted and placed on probation. Although his temper always remained uncertain (if provoked), he did not repeat his offence during the probation period, nor, as far as is known, subsequently. Although the charge preferred was that of malicious wounding, the circumstances were not as serious as some other cases I have met.

Example 2

Three labourers of previous good character were committed for trial at the Crown Court charged with robbery with violence. The facts were that, following some altercation concerning the delivery of coal, they were charged with robbing the coal vendor. When the facts were outlined at Court, the judge took the view that these could not substantiate an indictment for robbery and ordered the charge to be reduced to common assault.

Although sexual offences are discussed in Chapter 8, the difficulty in determining the degree of violence purely from the legal description of, for example, indecent assault can be seen from the following illustration.

Example 3

A young unmarried man of twenty-four was convicted by the Crown Court of a series of indecent assaults on women. The facts were that, over a period of several weeks, he had gone out on his cycle at dusk and followed a number of young women along a lonely country lane. Coming up behind them, he attempted to pull them off their cycles, made various obscene suggestions to them, and attempted to put his hands up their skirts. He was of previous good character, but had suffered much deprivation in childhood and was of low intelligence. Because of these facts, the court placed him on probation, but the seriousness of his premeditated attacks could have well earned him a prison sentence.

Example 4

A man in his late forties was charged with the attempted murder of his wife by cutting her throat whilst she lay asleep. He was normally an extremely docile and placid individual, a carpenter by trade and a very good workman. At his trial it transpired that for some years his wife had carried on 'business' as a prostitute; despite all her husband's entreaties, she refused to give up her life-style. In a fit of despair and anger he attacked her. In view of the extenuating circumstances the judge passed a very light prison sentence and the man subsequently returned to live with his wife. The case might, of course, have ended more tragically; his wife might have died from her injuries. In other cases, only the fact that the assailant has been interrupted during his or her assault may limit the harm caused. In some, the intention might not be to kill or seriously injure, but factors unknown to the assailant may render the course of events tragic – such as the victim being infirm or having a thin skull.

Occasionally, the offence as charged may present in disguised fashion an underlying desire to perpetrate violence of a more personal kind. Charges of malicious damage (vandalism) sometimes fall into this category.

Example 5

Three boys of fourteen plus were charged with what amounted to an 'orgy' of malicious damage to a number of railway carriages parked in a siding. They had systematically broken a large number of carriage windows by hurling fire extinguishers through them, removed dozens of electric light bulbs, thrown them around the railway track, and urinated over the seats. Several thousands of pounds worth of damage had been caused. The history of each of these boys was revealing. The first lived with his elderly grandparents, who, though concerned, were not particularly affectionate. His parents were separated and he rarely saw them. He was decidedly a boy with a 'chip on his shoulder'. The second boy was illegitimate and came from a disordered home background where his mother and sisters engaged in prostitution. He felt himself to be the odd one out. The third boy, a cousin of the second, was spending a holiday with the family. He was the orphaned child of a distant relative, and spent much of his time in a large children's home. It is not unrealistic to speculate that, unconsciously at least, the offences they committed may have been a symbolic manifestation of the aggression they felt towards their families and other adults.

In other cases, the offender appears to have directed his or her violence from its original source to a more 'neutral' one. Scott (1977) cites the legendary Medea as an example, who, wishing to get back at her husband, killed her babies, saying 'that will stab thy heart'. He also quotes a clinical case which makes the point graphically:

> A man of 47 asked the female storekeeper at his place of work for an item; she failed to produce it and treated him with scant respect. He picked up a hammer and beat her about the head in a manner which nearly killed her [he was charged with inflicting grievous bodily harm] . . . When examined, he was not mentally ill, not depressed, not paranoid, and was distressed and perplexed by his behaviour. There was no previous crime of any sort. He was an excellent worker, employed beneath his capacity, but had never pressed for advancement. He was married to a dominant lady who nagged him and frequently expressed her dissatisfaction with his wages. He had not had a holiday away from home for 20 years. In the last few weeks he had had bronchitis, which kept him awake. He was tired and not feeling well, and he was taking a prescribed medication containing codeine. The storekeeper, he had hoped, would treat him with respect. She was an attractive and popular middle-aged woman whom he liked, but had never tried to make a relationship with. When she behaved like his wife he reacted in a way which *could* be interpreted as venting all his suppressed resentment of his wife upon her.
>
> (Scott, 1977: 133; emphasis added)

A somewhat similar case, from the point of view of the displacement of feelings, is drawn from my own experience.

Example 6

A youth of sixteen was charged with causing grievous bodily harm to his elderly employer. Apparently he had attacked him from behind, struck him violently over the head and stolen a sum of money which he had subsequently abandoned. Of previous good character and background, he was remanded for psychiatric examination. He was found to be a youth who experienced great difficulty in countenancing any degree of frustration. There was evidence that on the morning of the offence he had been 'got at' by various people in authority and his offence was seen, in part, as a result of poor tolerance of frustration. His mother, who was also interviewed as part of the psychiatric assessment, was felt to have a certain cold detachment about her and she, too, seemed to have problems in coping with frustration. The youth was committed to a local authority children's establishment and subsequently made reasonable progress.[2]

HOMICIDE[3]

The voice of thy brother's blood crieth
unto me from the ground.
(Genesis, 4:10)

And the Lord set a mark upon Cain.
(Genesis 4:15)

Homicide is at the extreme end of the spectrum of violent crime. Its primacy is indicated in the above quotations; as is well stated in Webster's *Duchess of Malfi*, 'Other sins only speak, murder shrieks out' (Act IV, Scene ii). Having stressed this point, it is useful to emphasise yet again that

the distinction between homicide and a lesser form of violence may simply be chance, the thickness of a victim's skull, the angle of a blow, the health of the victim, the efficiency and proximity of the medical services and so on.

(Gunn and Taylor, 1993: 511)

LEGAL ASPECTS

Homicide is the term used to describe all unlawful killings and covers a range of offences, including murder, manslaughter and infanticide.

Murder can be briefly described as the unlawful killing of another with malice. Bowden gives a definition, based on a précis of 'Archbold' (a standard legal text), as follows:

Subject to three exceptions, the crime of murder is committed when a person of sound mind and discretion unlawfully kills any reasonable creature in being and under the Queen's peace with intent to kill or cause grievous bodily harm, the death following within a year and a day.

(1990: 508)

Parts of this definition require some explanation. Killing the enemy in times of war is not murder; 'reasonable creature' means a life in being; it is not murder to kill a child in the womb; and the 'year and a day' statement 'refers to the fact that death must have been occasioned or expedited by the act or omission' (Bowden, 1990: 508).

The 'three exceptions' referred to above, where murder is reduced to man-slaughter, are if the accused:

(a) was provoked; or
(b) was acting in pursuance of a suicide pact; or
(c) suffered from diminished responsibility.

(a) and (c) were dealt with in Chapter 2 above in some detail.

Manslaughter is defined as unlawfully causing the death of another without malice aforethought. It includes voluntary manslaughter (which includes provo-cation, diminished responsibility, and 'killing in pursuance of a suicide pact') (Bowden, 1990: 508).

Involuntary manslaughter covers cases where the killing was not intended, but where there was an intention to commit an unlawful or dangerous act, gross negligence, or disregard for the lives and safety of others.

It is an offence to destroy the life of an unborn child (*child destruction*); that is to say unless the provisions of Section 1 of the Abortion Act 1967 are complied with.

The offence of causing death by dangerous (reckless) driving, which has gone through a number of classificatory revisions, replaced the prosecution of motorists for manslaughter.

Brief reference was made to the offence of *infanticide* in Chapter 2. Although there had been a number of statutes dealing with the killing of infant children by mothers from early times, current practice derives from twentieth-century statutes. (For a recent and thorough review of infanticide in England and Wales, see Marks and Kumar, 1993.) The specific offence of infanticide was introduced because of an increasing reluctance on the part of the judges to pass the death sentence in cases where mothers killed their infant children and the fact that, when they had, the Home Secretary reprieved all mothers so convicted. The Infanticide Act of 1922 referred to the killing of a 'newly born child'. The current legislation, the Infanticide Act 1938, changed this to specify a child of any age under twelve months. It also added a clause indicating that the effects of lactation consequent upon the birth could be considered. The relevant section of the Act (Section 1(1)) reads as follows:

> Where a woman by any wilful act or omission causes the death of her child being a child under the age of twelve months, but at the time of the act or omission the balance of her mind was disturbed by reason of her not having fully recovered from giving birth to the child or by reason of lactation consequent upon the birth of the child . . . she shall be guilty of the offence . . . of infanticide . . . and may for such offence be dealt with as if she had been guilty of the offence of manslaughter of the child.

Size of the problem

Browne (1993) has calculated that the homicide rate in Britain is 1.3 for every 100,000 citizens; in the USA the figure is about 10 individuals per 100,000.

Table 6.2 Number of persons indicted for homicide, 1985–1990

	1985	1986	1987	1988	1989	1990
Murder	498	546	566	553	520	330
Manslaughter	83	105	105	69	66	29
Infanticide	7	3	1	7	–	1
Total	588	654	672	629	586	360

Source: Home Office, 1992b: 91.

Notes: Although there are some variations between years, the figures remain fairly constant. The smaller total for the year 1990 is explained by a note appended to the full table which indicates that there were some 292 suspects for whom court proceedings were not completed at the time the data were ready for processing and publication. The figures for murder will fluctuate to some extent upon the numbers of convictions obtained for multiple murders as a result of terrorist activity or for so-called 'serial' killings. The numbers of women prosecuted for infanticide have always been small. A disturbing trend has been the increase in the numbers of racially motivated killings in Western Europe, most notably in Germany. Although there were a number of clearly identifiable incidents in Britain in 1993 in which racial influences were important, these figures were down in 1993 compared with other European Community countries – from twelve in 1992 to six in 1993 (Doyle, 1992).

The number of persons indicted for homicide for the years 1985–90 may be found in Table 6.2.

International comparisons

As Bowden suggests,

> any comparison . . . is rendered almost impossible; criminal justice systems emerge from a variety of social, political, religious and philosophical movements . . . even within countries there is no standardisation of criteria for case identification and analyses sometimes reveal more of the analyst than of that which is analysed.
>
> (1990: 513)

This author, basing his work upon some calculations reported by Heuni (1985), gives an 'intentional homicide rate per 100,000 population for eight countries, including the UK; These ranged from 1.2 in Norway to 7.1 in Denmark. The figure for the UK was 3.3' (Bowden, 1990: 513).

Clinical aspects

This heading will be interpreted broadly to provide some classification of homicidal behaviour in behavioural and clinical terms. There is naturally a degree of inevitable overlap between this description and those in earlier chapters.

Normal and abnormal homicide

To some people, any form of homicide must indicate a degree of abnormality. To the extent that life is held to be sacred, any measures which take it away by forceful or unlawful acts depart from those norms laid down by society. This is not to say that such acts may sometimes seem 'understandable' – which is not quite the same thing. For this reason, the law recognises gradations of responsibility for such crimes – as I showed in Chapter 2.

It is a truism that homicide is largely a domestic affair, and that the family is certainly not the 'safe haven' that some people have considered it to be. (See, for example, recent evidence on wife abuse – *Independent*, 18 January, 1994: 5.) This is evidenced not only by its primacy as a site for homicidal acts, but also by the wealth of evidence now accumulating of violence within the family – between partners, against children and against the elderly.

As already indicated in Chapter 4, certain forms of mental disorder and disturbance are not uncommonly associated with homicidal acts. Despite this, there have been very few large-scale or in-depth studies of abnormal homicides. However, one or two deserve special mention. The first (referred to in Chapter 4) was that carried out by West into some 150 cases of murder followed by suicide in London for the years 1946–62. Not altogether surprisingly, one of West's main conclusions was that depression in various forms was a very common precipitating factor (West, 1965; see also Coid, 1983). Another important study was that made by Mowat (1966). He examined a 'specialist' group of abnormal homicides, which included forty male and six female patients detained in Broadmoor Hospital. He found a high proportion of them suffered from delusional jealousy (see Chapter 4 of this volume). Mowat's findings are still of interest today because at the time they concentrated attention upon the distribution of delusions from a variety of causes and which have subsequently been investigated more comprehensively by workers such as Mullen and Martin (1994). Another significant study was that made by Brittain (1970). He had the distinction of being both a forensic psychiatrist and pathologist. He concerned himself with drawing up a picture of the so-called 'sadistic' murderer; his clinical profile continues to be regarded by most forensic psychiatrists as an accurate picture of such persons.

Hunter Gillies (1976) carried out a comprehensive study in the west of Scotland. His findings contradict some of those contained in earlier studies from 'south of the border'. He based his work on his psychiatric examination of 400 murder cases undertaken for the prosecution between the years 1953 and 1974 (367 males and 33 females); they had been accused of the murder of 307 victims. The salient features he found were maleness, youthfulness, the importance of alcohol, rarity of suicide, and a high percentage of psychiatrically 'normal' persons. Forty-seven per cent had histories of previous violence. Of the weapons used by the male accused, 56 per cent used sharp instruments, 37 per cent blunt; other methods used by both sexes included shooting and strangulation. Gillies found that most of the crimes in his sample appeared to be un-premeditated, apparently unintended and impulsive (for example, precipitated over trifles, often when the parties were 'in their cups').

Finally, mention must be made of a larger-scale study of mentally abnormal violent offenders carried out by Häfner and Böker (1982) in the former Federal Republic of Germany in the years 1955–64. They found many of the offences occurred within a family setting, but some 9 per cent were strangers. Half of the attacks were planned in advance (cf. this finding with those of Gillies); in only about a quarter of the cases was the crime impulsive. In about half the cases, a delusional relationship existed, but in about one-fifth there was no recognisable motive. In Häfner and Böker's group revenge constituted about one-third of the motives in the males; in some forty per cent of the females the desire was to release the victim from feared distress or illness. Häfner and Böker's study of violence and homicide amongst mentally abnormal offenders is one of the largest and most methodologically sophisticated of its kind. It is summarised in some detail by Bowden (1990).

Homicidal behaviour – summarised

Although some of the major studies provide conflicting results, it is possible, in somewhat simplistic fashion, to classify homicidal behaviour as follows:

1　'Simple', straightforward murders – for gain (as in some famous cases of spouse poisoning), or planned in order to get rid of an unwanted person or evidence (as, for example, a murder followed by arson in order to cover tracks – see Chapter 7). Other examples would be murder in the course of theft, to silence a victim or to kill apprehending officers or custodians. The foregoing over-simplified categorisation should be treated with a degree of caution, because even in these apparently 'straightforward' cases the motives may be 'mixed' and quite complex.

2　Homicide committed in association with recognisable mental illness (as described in Chapters 2 and 4). In an interesting contribution Cox (1990) has provided some illustrations of the motives provided by psychotic killers. For example, one patient said of killing his mother: 'I just went on killing her – it never occurred to me she'd die.' Parricide has been seen frequently as a crime committed by schizophrenics and sufferers from other psychotic illnesses. (See, for example, D'Orban and O'Connor, 1989, but for a somewhat contrary view see Clark, 1993.) For another, it was

　　essential that his victim was killed by multiple wounds caused by two swords, because 'he had to die a noble death'. In the patient's idiosyncratic construction of 'reality' the killing of the victim by two swords was more important than the forensic act of the death itself.

(Cox, 1991: 635)

Homicide can also be associated with mental retardation (as in the case of Straffen, the mentally subnormal killer, who escaped from a high security hospital and killed for a second time) and 'serial' homicide is associated with severe personality disorder (for example, Nilsen, Dahmer and others).

3 Homicide as a result of the ingestion of substances of abuse (alcohol, other drugs, solvents).

4 So-called 'mercy killings' and attempts at euthanasia.

5 Homicide by 'carers' committed as a result of certain rare personality disorders – such as Munchausen by Proxy – as alleged for example in the case of the nurse Beverley Allitt.

Some further clinical observations

Parents who kill their children

Such killings have been classified clinically in a variety of ways. Resnick (1990), as quoted by Bluglass (1990) describes two types: (1) neonaticide – the killing of a new-born child within the first few hours of life; and (2) filicide – the killing of a child who is more than one day old. Such killings will be carried out for a variety of reasons. For example, a young, lonely and immature mother may not be able to face the fact that she has had a child or the strains of child-rearing; in other cases, the behaviour may be driven by delusional ideas. In respect of filicide, Scott (1973) discerned five types of behaviour:

(a) the killing of an unwanted child by parents (most frequently the mother);
(b) aggression due to serious mental abnormality;
(c) behaviour due to the displacement of anger identified earlier in this chapter;
(d) cases in which the stimulus arises from the victim (as is sometimes found in the 'battered child' syndrome);
(e) for altruistic reasons – 'mercy killing'.

In a recent very comprehensive and detailed study the late Dr Patrick McGrath – former Medical Superintendent at Broadmoor Hospital – examined a fifty-year (1919–69) cohort of 280 female admissions to that hospital from England and Wales who had killed their children. McGrath distinguished maternal filicide from infanticide; he defined the former as 'the killing by a mother of her child over the age of one year'. He concluded from his survey

that the modal maternal filicide who was committed to Broadmoor was a white Anglo-Saxon Protestant, aged 31–5, married, suffering from an affective psychosis, altruistically motivated (there is only one 'baby-batterer' in the cohort) and not influenced by drink or drugs. She has a previous history of psychiatric referral. The modal victim was the youngest child, of either sex, healthy, the sole victim. The age of the victim was 2–5 years, ranging from

1–29 years. The offence was carried out by readily available domestic means (suffocation, strangulation, gassing, drowning).

(McGrath, 1992: 271)

McGrath states that there is broad agreement between his and other studies of mainly hospital populations.

Children as killers

> Even a child is known by his deeds.
> (Proverbs: 20:11)

The recent, sad case of the killing of little James Bulger by two ten-year-old boys has reawakened interest in the fairly rare phenomena of young children as killers. Gunn and Taylor comment that there are 'only two or three cases each year in Britain' (1993: 517). I take this to imply that some cases which are not reported in the press may be committed by children under the age of criminal responsibility (ten years) and thus not identified as homicide. Gunn and Taylor quote Wilson (1973) – a journalist – who identified and described some fifty-seven incidents of homicide involving children under the age of sixteen between the years 1743 and 1972. Forty-eight of the incidents involving seventy-five children (twelve girls and sixty-three boys) were British. Although Wilson described fifteen of the children as mentally abnormal, and several were of low intelligence, no cases of frank delusional insanity were recorded. Wilson's series of cases included older children (adolescents) and a recent report by another journalist – Richard Grant – has identified the alleged torturing and killing of a twelve-year-old girl by four teenage girls in the USA (*Independent Saturday Review*, 22 August 1992: 20–24).

The American child psychiatrist Lauretta Bender summarised her experiences with eight children under twelve years of age who had caused a death. In these cases her conclusions were overwhelmingly against premeditation – the death was always accidental and unexpected by the child.

> And the child had no concept of the irreversibility of death. The death occurred because the victim happened to be in the path of the activity initiated by the child and was unintentionally fatal. The child then responded with a severe depressive mourning reaction. His life pattern changed critically from that point. He tried by every means in fantasy and by acting out to deny the act and its consequences – the death of the victim and its irreversibility.
>
> (Bender, 1968: 40)

She found a considerable degree of social deprivation and family pathology. Follow-up revealed continuing deterioration and, for some, the need for mental hospital placement. In later work, in which she studied the homicides committed

by older children, she found that 'a constellation of factors was required for a boy
or girl to cause a death. There needed to be a disturbed, poorly controlled
impulsive child, a victim who acted as an irritant, an available lethal weapon, and
always a lack of protective supervision by some person who could stop the fatal
consequences' (p. 41). She went on to make the following important distinction
between pre-pubertal and adolescent killers:

> The psychodynamics of a prepuberty child who has caused a death is that he
> experiments in fantasy and by acting out to determine if irreparable death is
> possible. An adolescent makes an effort to deny both guilt and feelings of guilt
> for his part in the act that caused the death and to claim amnesia or other
> repressive defense. Both are usually misunderstood and dangerous.
>
> (p. 41)[4]

Her last words are important in connection with the interest aroused by the Bulger
tragedy. I have stated elsewhere (Prins, 1993) that as adults we find it very
difficult to comprehend that during the age of 'innocence' very young children
can engage in homicidal acts. As indicated earlier in this chapter, even very small
infants seem capable of murderous rage when frustrated. Experienced primary
school teachers are aware of the vigilance required to prevent mayhem in school
playgrounds. And a study of non-specialist literature reveals the capacity of
children to act murderously, as witnessed in Golding's *Lord of the Flies*. Perhaps,
in view of the above, we shall have to learn to confront the uncomfortable notion
that the killing of children by children may be more frequent than the easily
available records show and that only vigilance and active intervention prevent its
more frequent occurrence.

Multiple killing

> They come not single spies
> But in batallions.
> *(Hamlet*, Act IV, Scene iv)

Mass killing

The term 'multiple killing' is frequently used (or misused) to cover a number of
forms of killing in which numerous victims are killed. For present purposes I am
excluding genocide from consideration. Lunde and Sigal state that such 'killings
occur in the context of collective goals and activities (often political and
religious), and involve group more than individual pathology' (1990: 626).
Multiple killing includes *mass* killing; this latter term is best used to describe
those fortunately rare cases in which a single killer destroys a large number of
people in one sequence of events. One example is Charles Whitman, who, having
stabbed his mother and wife to death, shot forty-four people in Texas, killing
sixteen of them. Other examples are those of Richard Speck, who murdered eight

nurses in their hospital dormitory in Chicago in 1966, and James Huberty, who in 1984 shot twenty-one people in a McDonald's restaurant in California. In the UK in 1987, Michael Ryan shot sixteen people in Hungerford, Berkshire, in one day (for an account of this event, see Prins, 1990: 48–50). Ryan committed suicide before he could be apprehended – as Gunn and Taylor suggest, 'a not uncommon outcome' (1993: 520). Such evidence as we have available concerning the backgrounds of these 'amok-type' killers suggests that they are almost always male, suffer from a sense of being persecuted in some way (but not necessarily psychotically so) and above all are social isolates. There is some indication that they have occasionally given veiled hints to professionals and others as to their intended actions. Mass killing can also occur from time to time within a domestic situation, where one member of a family kills a number of other members – as alleged in the case of Jeremy Bamber in the UK. Some authorities identify another form of mass murder – 'spree killing', in which the perpetrators indulge in a series of apparently unplanned, motiveless killings, as, for example, in the activities of the infamous Bonnie and Clyde.

Serial killing

This term is usually reserved for the planned killing of a series of victims (usually more than three) over a period of time. The killer will usually make determined attempts to avoid detection. In the USA such offending is facilitated by differences in legal and police practices from state to state.

Contrary to popular belief, serial killing has a long history, although there has been a marked increase in such behaviour in recent times, especially in the USA. In the fifteenth century the infamous Marshal of France, Gilles de Rais (see also Chapter 8), tortured, sexually abused and killed several hundred children over a period of years. In fifteenth-century Scotland, Sawney Bean murdered numerous passers-by in order to steal their possessions; he then is said to have eaten parts of their bodies. In seventeenth-century France, Madame de Brinvilliers, over a prolonged period, murdered many of her extended family to secure their wealth. And, again in the same century in France, Catherine Montvoisin arranged, for payment, to eliminate hundreds of unwanted infants. (I am aware that these last two examples sit somewhat uneasily under the serial killer classification, and could perhaps he classified equally well under mass killings.) There are, of course, examples of female serial killers in more modern times. An elderly landlady in the USA is *alleged* to have murdered seven of her variously disabled boarding-house residents over a period of time (*Independent*, 11 February 1993: 9). There are also numerous examples of serial killings in nineteenth- and twentieth-century Europe. Haarman and Kurten in Germany were sadistic sexual serial killers, and the cases of Sutcliffe, Nilsen and Dahmer are also classic examples of serial killing (see Chapter 2).

Many attempts have been made to explain the motivation of the serial killer; most of these have been in terms of psychopathology. However Leyton, a

Canadian professor of anthropology, suggests that the phenomenon of the serial killer can be seen in socio-cultural terms. In his examination of serial killing from earliest times, he concludes that such activities are most likely to appear at times of serious social unrest and upheaval. He considers that the perpetrators are operating from more than individual psychopathological motives: their actions are a form of protest against the rise of an 'underclass' in each historical period up to the present day. His theory is an interesting one to set alongside those put forward by clinicians (those wishing to refer to his detailed exposition should consult Leyton, 1989: Chapter 9).

Some confirmation of the need to see serial killing in a socio-cultural context can be found in a significant recent paper by Soothill. Since very many serial killings are accompanied by sexual activity and/or defilement, Soothill suggests that such killings must be seen against a background of changing attitudes towards sexual activity. He suggests, for example, that in the UK rising concern about the prevalence of prostitution brought organised prostitution to public attention in the 1950s and the movement towards partial decriminalisation of homosexual activity was a focus of attention in the 1960s. Concerns about rape became prevalent in the 1970s and 1980s alongside concerns about child sexual abuse; and more recently concerns have emerged about HIV infection and AIDS and their moral implications. Soothill suggests that 'a focus on serial killings has similarities with other moral panics' (1993: 342). He suggests that serial killing in Britain is very limited, and that the

> current problem is probably over-stated . . . a serial killer industry is building up which gains much by a growth in fear of serial killers . . . the questions currently being asked are too narrow and there is a general failure to address the wider issues.
>
> (1993: 341)

Characteristics

In outlining some of the characteristics of serial killers, it is important to bear in mind the caveats entered by Leyton in Canada and Soothill in the UK. In the USA, Levin and Fox carried out a detailed survey of information concerning some forty-two 'multiple victim' killers, which included some that we would designate as serial killers. They stated that the serial killer

> is typically a white male in his late twenties or thirties . . . the specific motivation depends on the circumstances leading up to the crime . . . though the . . . killer often may appear cold and show no remorse, and even deny responsibility for his crime, serious mental illness or psychosis is rarely present.
>
> (1985: 47–48)

This picture is, of course, only partially true, since we know that some serial killers, such as Sutcliffe, suffer from serious mental *illness* and others, such as Nilsen, suffer from a serious *personality disorder*. Of ten cases of multiple killings studied in depth by Lunde and Sigal, eight would satisfy our criteria for serial-killing. The mean age for the group was thirty-three, 90 per cent were male and white, 30 per cent psychotic and 70 per cent sexually motivated, 70 per cent were heterosexual and 30 per cent homosexual. The authors caution their readers against drawing too many conclusions from such a small sample. However, some interesting findings do emerge, and these find confirmation in other studies (see, for example Liebman, 1989; Holmes and Holmes, 1992). White males predominated (for single-victim murders in the USA, black males predominate); their average age was higher than for other violent crimes; alcohol and other drugs were not involved; eight of the ten killers came from middle-class backgrounds; firearms were used less frequently than in other types of killings, strangulation being the preferred method in most cases. A significant characteristic of most serial killers is their apparent (but perhaps superficial) normality. In the USA Ted Bundy was a highly presentable student of law, Nilsen attracted little attention, other than being something of a loner, and Sutcliffe's bizarre behaviour appears to have been well hidden and his delusional ideas well encapsulated.

In a recent review article, written for 'lay' consumption, Andrae (1993) suggests that inborn predisposition to violence may play a part in some cases. In his view, the other central background theme is childhood trauma of some kind or another, whether this be overtly physical (as in the case of Albert de Salvo – the 'Boston Strangler') or expressed in more subtle forms, as in the case of Jeffrey Dahmer (see Masters, 1993). Andrae summarises some of these important characteristics:

> Abused, isolated and perhaps with a predisposition for anti-social self-gratification, potential serial killers start to create fantasies of an alternative world. Unlike the fantasies of many abused children, which evolve around care and acceptance, those of potential killers contain strong themes of domination and control. Classic warning signs of dangerous fantasies include fire-setting and cruelty towards animals. In both cases, the child feels a surge of power as he controls, forcibly, his environment or subject.
>
> (1993: 40)[5]

One might add that this theme of dominance and control seems to be a key characteristic in a large number of serial killers.[6]

Profiling

With the apparent rise in the number of serial killers, notably in the USA, there has developed an interest in building 'profiles' of such persons. Such profiles can assist police investigators in building up a picture of common psychological, social and environmental characteristics in cases where the killers may manage to elude detection over a prolonged period. Interest in profiling in this country developed sharply in the wake of the Sutcliffe case and involved setting up sophisticated computer-based retrieval systems (see, for example, Doney, 1990, for a description). Attempts to build profiles in both homicide and non-homicide cases are not new and all good detectives operate through their own 'computer base' (their brain) a means of forming pictures based upon their stored experience. Modern technology merely makes this more sophisticated and more readily available to others. In a very interesting paper Boon and Davies (1992) trace the history of profiling techniques in the USA. They credit its first major use to the work of a psychiatrist, Brussel, who accurately pinpointed the characteristics of a hard-to-catch bomber. In this country, work on profiling has been considerably advanced by the activities of Canter and his co-workers at Surrey University (Canter, 1989, 1994). Boon and Davies report that Canter and his colleagues

> have found five aspects of the criminal and his or her behaviour to be of help to investigators: residential location, criminal biography, personal characteristics, domestic and social characteristics, and occupational and educational history. Not all of these have been found to be of equal utility, with the researchers reporting that most help is derived from analysis of details relating to residential location and criminal offence history.

(1992: 4)

A crime writer who also has professional experience of criminal and forensic investigative techniques makes a poignant suggestion of what needs to be in the profiler's mind, whatever system he or she uses:

> If violent, aggressive behaviour dominates your thinking, your imagination, you're going to start acting out in ways that move you closer to the actual expression of these emotions. Violence fuels more violent thoughts and more violent thoughts fuel more violence. After a while, violence and killing are a natural part of your adult life and you see nothing wrong in it.

(Cornwell, 1992: 327)

CONCLUSION

I have tried to cover a great deal of material in this chapter, but there are a number of significant omissions. For example, I have not dealt with the physical abuse of children (except by passing reference), nor with the apparent increase in cases of serious physical abuse of the elderly. Violent death by assassination, genocide and terrorism are, again, only touched upon *en passant*. These, and other matters are covered in a number of works listed in the Further Reading section at the end of the chapter. Although the presentation has, for the most part, emphasised clinical aspects, it is of vital importance to try to understand all forms of violent behaviour within a context that includes race, culture, gender and political climate.

NOTES

1 Violence in institutions of various kinds is not considered here, for reasons of space, not because it is considered unimportant. Violent incidents in psychiatric establishments have been analysed in a range of papers (see, for example, Aiken, 1984; Coldwell and Naismith, 1989; Hodgkinson *et al.* 1985; Larkin *et al.* 1988; Shah, 1993). (The latter provides an extensive bibliography, and aspects of homicide between psychiatric in-patients are reviewed by Ferracuti *et al.*, 1993.) Violent incidents in ordinary hospitals have been studied by Gosnold (1978) and Davies (1978). Other aspects of violent confrontations are contained in numerous psychiatric hospital and prison inquiry reports. For some recent examples see: Department of Health (1992); Home Office (1991); SHSA (1993). The violent physical and sexual abuse of children in homes designed for their care have also been the subject of major inquiries. (For a recent example, see Leicestershire County Council, 1993.)

2 This and some of the other cases quoted in this chapter are derived, in part, from Prins (1960). A further interesting example of such displaced homicidal violence is that of Frederic Blanc, the killer of the English school-teacher Fiona Jones in France in 1990. Having quarrelled with his one-time girlfriend, who, he alleged, had been seeing other men, he became enraged at seeing Fiona looking so happy as she cycled through the French countryside. Having apparently failed in his first attempt to kill her, he returned to her body and finished her off with a knife. He claimed that his rage towards his girlfriend just welled up and overcame his hapless and innocent victim. In May 1993, some three years after the event, he was sentenced by a French court to fifteen years' imprisonment; the lightness of the sentence surprised many people. (Information derived from a *True Crimes* drama-documentary presented by Michael Winner on British television on 9 January 1994.)

3 *Homicide* is the generic legal and clinical term used to cover all forms of unlawful killing; *genocide* is the term used to refer to the deliberate extermination of a people or nation; *parricide* is the term for the killing of a near-relative or parent; *matricide* for the killing of one's mother; *patricide* for the killing of one's father; and *filicide* for the killing of one's child by a parent.

4 For a more detailed account, see Bender (1960).

5 I am indebted to a colleague Dr K. de Pauw, Consultant Psychiatrist at Doncaster Royal Infirmary, for bringing this paper to my attention.

6 However, this is not always the case. For example, a slightly different form of motivation may be found in Hindemith's opera *Cadillac*, based on a story by A.F.T. Hoffman. In the opera, a French goldsmith embarks upon a series of serial killings of his customers to retreive gold items he sold to them.

REFERENCES

Aiken, G.J.M. (1984) 'Assaults on Staff in a Locked Ward: Prediction and Consequences', *Medicine, Science and the Law* 24: 199-207.

Andrae, S. (1993) 'The Anatomy of a Serial Killer', *Observer Magazine* 12 December: 40–42.

Archer, J. and Browne, K.D. (1989) 'Concepts and Approaches to the Study of Aggression', in J. Archer and K.D. Browne (eds), *Human Aggression: Naturalistic Approaches*, London: Routledge.

Bender, L. (1960) 'Children and Adolescents Who Have Killed', *American Journal of Psychiatry* 116: 510–513.

—— (1968) 'Homicidal Aggression', *Federal Probation* XXXII: 35–41.

Blackburn, R. (1993) *The Psychology of Criminal Conduct: Theory, Research and Practice*, Chichester, Wiley.

Bluglass, R. (1990) 'Infanticide and Filicide', in R. Bluglass and P. Bowden (eds), *Principles and Practice of Forensic Psychiatry*, London: Churchill Livingstone.

Boon, J. and Davies, G. (1992) 'Fact and Fiction in Offender Profiling', *Newsletter of the Division of Legal and Criminological Psychology* 32: 3–9. Leicester, British Psychological Society.

Bowden, P. (1990) 'Homicide', in R. Bluglass and P. Bowden (eds), *Principles and Practice of Forensic Psychiatry*, London: Churchill Livingstone.

—— (1993) 'A Forensic Psychiatrist's View', in J. Russell, (ed.), *Alcohol and Crime*, London: Mental Health Foundation.

Brittain, R.P. (1970) 'The Sadistic Murderer', *Medicine, Science and the Law 10*: 198–207.

Browne, K.D. (1993) 'Violence in the Family and Its Links to Child Abuse', *Baillière's Clinical Paediatrics (Vol. 1)*.

Canter, D. (1989) 'Offender Profiles', *The Psychologist* 2: 12–16.

—— (1994) *Criminal Shadows: Inside the Mind of the Serial Killer*, London: Harper-Collins.

Clark, S.A. (1993) 'Matricide: The Schizophrenic Crime', *Medicine, Science and the Law* 35: 325–328.

Coid, J. (1983) 'The Epidemiology of Abnormal Homicide and Murder Followed by Suicide', *Psychological Medicine* 13: 855–860.

Coldwell, J.B. and Naismith, L.J. (1989) 'Violent Incidents on Special Care Wards in a Special Hospital', *Medicine, Science and the Law* 29: 116–123.

Cornwell, P. (1992) *All That Remains*, London: Little Brown and Co.

Cox, M. (1990) 'Psychopathology and Treatment of Psychotic Aggression', in R. Bluglass and P. Bowden (eds), *Principles and Practice of Forensic Psychiatry*, London: Churchill Livingstone.

Davidoff, L. and Dowds, L. (1989) *Recent Trends in Crimes of Violence against the Person in England and Wales*, Home Office Research Unit and Planning Unit, Bulletin, No. 27, London: HMSO.

Davies, J. (1978) 'Violence in the General Hospital: The Management of Violent or Potentially Violent Patients', *Journal of the Royal Society of Health* 4: 187–188.

Day, M. (1986) 'Foreword' to H. Prins, *Dangerous Behaviour, the Law and Mental Disorder*, London: Tavistock.

Department of Health (1992) *Report of the Committee of Inquiry into Complaints about Ashworth Hospital*, Vols 1 and 2. (Chairman, Sir Louis Blom-Cooper, QC), Cmnd 2028-I and II, London: HMSO.

Doney, R.H. (1990) 'The Aftermath of the Yorkshire Ripper: The Response of the United Kingdom Police', in S.A. Egger (ed.), *Serial Murder: An Elusive Phenomenon*, London: Praeger.

D'Orban, P.T. and O'Connor, A. (1989) 'Women Who Kill Their Parents', *British Journal of Psychiatry* 154: 27–33.

Doyle, L. (1994) 'Racism: West Europe's Mounting Death Toll', *Independent*, 13 January: 16.

Ferracuti, S., Palermo, G.B. and Manfredi, M. (1993) 'Homicide Between In-patients in a Mental Institution Ward', *International Journal of Offender Therapy and Comparative Criminology* 37: 331–337.

Fromm, E. (1977) *The Anatomy of Human Destructiveness*, Harmondsworth: Penguin.

Gillies, H. (1976) 'Murder in the West of Scotland', *British Journal of Psychiatry* 128: 105–127.

Gosnold, J.K. (1978) 'The Violent Patient in the Accident and Emergency Department', *Journal of the Royal Society of Health* 4: 189–191.

Gottfredson, M.R. (1984) *Victims of Crime: The Dimensions of Risk*, Home Office Research Unit Studies, Report No. 81, London: HMSO.

Gunn, J. (1991) 'Human Violence – A Biological Perspective', *Criminal Behaviour and Mental Health* 1: 34–54.

Gunn, J. and Taylor, P.J. (eds) (1993) *Forensic Psychiatry: Clinical, Legal and Ethical Issues*, London: Butterworth-Heinemann.

Häfner, H. and Böker, W. (1982) *Crimes of Violence by Mentally Abnormal Offenders: A Psychiatric and Epidemiological Study in the Federal German Republic*, Cambridge: Cambridge University Press.

Hankoff, L.D. (1993) 'Urban Violence in Historical Perspective', *International Journal of Offender Therapy and Comparative Criminology* 37: 1–3.

Health Services Advisory Committee (DHSS) (1987) *Violence to Staff in the Health Services*, London: HMSO.

Heuni, (1985) *Helsinki Institute for Crime Prevention and Control. No. 5: Criminal Justice Systems in Europe*, Helsinki.

Hodgkinson, P.E., McIvor, L. and Phillips, M. (1985) 'Patient Assaults on Staff in a Psychiatric Hospital: A Two-Year Retrospective Study', *Medicine, Science and the Law* 25: 288–294.

Hollin, C.R. (1992) *Criminal Behaviour: A Psychological Approach to Explanation and Behaviour*, London: Falmer Press.

Holmes, R.M. and Holmes, S.T. (1992) 'Understanding Mass Murder: A Starting Point', *Federal Probation* LVI: 53–61.

Home Office (1991) *Prison Disturbances, April 1990: Report of an Inquiry by the Rt Hon. Lord Justice Woolf (Parts I and II) and His Honour Judge Tumin (Part II)*, Cmnd 1456, London: HMSO.

—— (1992a) *Home Office Research and Statistics Department: Research Findings No. 2*, London: Home Office.

—— (1992b) *Criminal Statistics, England and Wales, 1990*. Cmnd 1935, London: HMSO.

Klein, M. (1963) *Our Adult World and Other Essays*, London: Heinemann.

Larkin, E., Murtagh, S. and Jones, S. (1988) 'A Preliminary Study of Violent Incidents in a Special Hospital (Rampton)', *British Journal of Psychiatry* 153: 226–231.

Leicestershire County Council (1993) *The Leicestershire Inquiry, 1992: Report of the Inquiry into Aspects of the Management of Children's Homes in Leicestershire between 1973 and 1986*, (Chairman, Andrew Kirkwood, QC), Leicester: Leicestershire County Council.

Levin, J. and Fox, J.A. (1985) *Mass Murder*, New York: Plenum Press.

Leyton, E. (1989) *Hunting Humans: The Rise of The Modern Multiple Murderer*, Harmondsworth: Penguin.

Liebman, F.H. (1989) 'Serial Murderers: Four Case Histories', *Federal Probation* LIII: 41–45.

Lorenz, K. (1966) *On Aggression*, London: Methuen.

Lunde, D. and Sigal, H. (1990) 'Multiple-Victim Killers', in R. Bluglass and P. Bowden (eds), *Principles and Practice of Forensic Psychiatry*, London: Churchill Livingstone.

McDermott, M. (1993) 'On Cruelty, Ethics and Experimentation: Profile of Philip G. Zimbardo', *The Psychologist* 6: 456–459.

McGrath, P.G. (1992) 'Maternal Filicide in Broadmoor Hospital, 1919–1969', *Journal of Forensic Psychiatry* 3: 271–297.

Marks, M.N. and Kumar, R. (1993) 'Infanticide in England and Wales', *Medicine, Science and the Law* 33: 329–339.

Masters, B. (1993) *The Shrine of Jeffrey Dahmer*, London: Hodder and Stoughton.

Mayhew, P., Elliott, D. and Dowds, L. (1989) *The 1988 British Crime Survey*, Home Office Research Study No. 111, London: HMSO.

Mowat, R.R. (1966) *Morbid Jealousy and Murder*, London: Tavistock.

Mullen, P.E. and Martin, J. (1994) 'Jealousy: A Community Study', *British Journal of Psychiatry* 164: 34–43.

Pearson, G. (1983) *Hooligan: A History of Respectable Fears*, London: Macmillan.

Prins, H. (1960) 'Social and Family Aspects of Violent and Aggressive Crime', *Criminal Law Review* October: 657–672.

—— (1990) *Bizarre Behaviours: Boundaries of Psychiatric Disorder*, London: Tavistock/Routledge.

—— (1993) 'Even a Child is Known by His Doings', *Probation Journal* 40: 188.

Resnick, P.J. (1969) 'Child Murder by Parents: A Psychiatric View of Filicide', *American Journal of Psychiatry* 126: 325–334.

Scott, P.D. (1973) 'Fatal Battered Baby Cases', *Medicine, Science and the Law* 13: 197–206.

—— (1977) 'Assessing Dangerousness in Criminals', *British Journal of Psychiatry* 131: 127–142.

Segal, H. (1964) *Introduction to the Work of Melanie Klein*, London: Heinemann.

Shah, A.K. (1993) 'An Increase in Violence among Psychiatric Patients: Real or Apparent?', *Medicine, Science and the Law* 33: 227–230.

Shapland, J. (1990) 'Victims of Violent Crime', in R. Bluglass and P. Bowden (eds), *Principles and Practice of Forensic Psychiatry*, London: Churchill Livingstone.

Sharpe, J. (1993) 'Hard Times Revive Law and Order Panic', *Independent*, 12 April: 2.

Shepherd, J.P., Shapland, M., Pearce, N. and Scully, C. (1990) 'Pattern, Severity and Aetiology of Injuries in Victims of Assault', *Journal of the Royal Society of Medicine* 83: 75–78.

Soothill, K. (1993) 'The Serial Killer Industry', *Journal of Forensic Psychiatry* 4: 341–354.

Special Hospitals Service Authority (SHSA) (1993) *Report of the Committee of Inquiry into the Death in Broadmoor Hospital of Orville Blackwood and a Review of the Deaths of Two Other Afro-Caribbean Patients: 'Big, Black and Dangerous?'* (Chairman, Professor Herschel Prins), London: SHSA.

Storr, A. (1975) *Human Aggression*, Harmondsworth: Penguin.

—— (1991) *Human Destructiveness: The Roots of Genocide and Human Cruelty (second edn)*, London: Routledge.

Tantam, D. 1993) 'The Nature of Aggression in Humans', in C. Thompson and P. Cowen (eds), *Violence: Basic and Clinical Science*, London: Butterworth-Heinemann and the Mental Health Foundation.

Walmsley, R. (1986) *Personal Violence*, Home Office Research Study No. 89, London: HMSO.

Weller, M.P.I. (1985) 'Crowds, Mobs and Riots', *Medicine, Science and the Law* 25: 295–303.

West, D.J. (1965) *Murder Followed by Suicide*, London: Macmillan.

Williams, A.H. (1982) 'Adolescents, Violence and Crime', *Journal of Adolescence* 5: 125–134.

Wilson, P. (1973) *Children Who Kill*, London: Michael Joseph.

Zimbardo, P.G. (1973) 'On the Ethics of Intervention in Human Psychological Research: With Special Reference to the Stanford Prison Experiment', *Cognition* 2: 243–256.

FURTHER READING

Violence – general

Groebel, J. and Hinde, R.A. (eds) (1989) *Aggression and War: Their Biological and Social Bases*, Cambridge: Cambridge University Press.

Howells, K. and Hollin, C.R. (eds) (1989) *Clinical Approaches to Violence*, Chichester: Wiley.

Roth, L.H. (ed.) (1987) *Clinical Treatment of the Violent Person*, London: Guilford Press.

Siann, G. (1985) *Accounting for Aggression: Perspectives on Aggression and Violence*, London: Allen and Unwin.

Thompson, C. and Cowen, P. (eds) (1993) *Violence: Basic and Clinical Science*, London: Butterworth-Heinemann in association with the Mental Health Foundation.

Toch, H. (1992) *Violent Men: An Inquiry into the Psychology of Violence*, (revised edn), Washington, DC: APA.

Family violence

Bentovim, A. (1990) 'Family Violence: Clinical Aspects', in R. Bluglass and P. Bowden (eds), *Principles and Practice of Forensic Psychiatry*, London: Churchill Livingstone. (Extensive coverage of clinical aspects.)

Greenland, C. (1990) 'Family Violence: A Review of the Literature', in R. Bluglass and P. Bowden (eds), *Principles and Practice of Forensic Psychiatry*, London: Churchill Livingstone. (A comprehensive review.)

Violence in institutions

Blumenreich, P.E. and Lewis, S. (eds) (1993) *Managing the Violent Patient: A Clinician's Guide*, New York: Brunner/Mazel.

Rice, M.E., Harris, G.T., Varney, G.W. and Quinsey, V.L. (1989) *Violence in Institutions: Understanding, Prevention and Control*, Toronto: Hogrefe and Huber Publishers.

Homicide: general

Capote, T. (1984) *In Cold Blood: A True Account of a Multiple Murder and Its Consequences*, London: Abacus.

Macdonald, J.M. (1961) *The Murderer and His Victim*, Springfield, Ill.: Charles C. Thomas.

Parker, T. (1990) *Life After Life: Interviews with Twelve Murderers*, London: Pan Books.

Reinhardt, J.M. (1962) *The Psychology of Strange Killers*, Springfield, Ill.: Charles C. Thomas.

Wilson, C. and Pitman, P. (1984) *Encyclopaedia of Murder*, London: Pan Books.

Biographical

Burn, G. (1984) '. . . Somebody's Husband, Somebody's Son . . .': The Story of Peter Sutcliffe*, London: Heinemann.

Jones, B. (1992) *Voices From an Evil God*, London: Blake. (About Peter Sutcliffe.)

Special aspects

Martingale, M. (1993) *Cannibal Killers: The Impossible Monsters*, London: Robert Hale. (Mainly concerning necrophilic killers.)

Radford, J. and Russell, D.E.H. (eds) (1992) *Femicide: The Politics of Woman Killing*, Milton Keynes: Open University Press. (Excellent account of gender issues.)

Ressler, R.K., Burgess, R.W. and Douglas, J.E. (1988) *Sexual Homicide: Patterns and Motives*, Oxford: Lexington/Macmillan.

Serial killing

Holmes, R.M. and De Burger, J. (1988) *Serial Murder*, London: Sage.
Norris, J. (1988) *Serial Killers: The Growing Menace*, London, Arrow Books.
Schreiber, F.R. (1984) *The Shoemaker: The Anatomy of A Psychotic*, Harmondsworth: Penguin.
Wilson, C. and Seaman, D. (1990) *The Serial Killers: A Study in the Psychology of Violence*, London: W.H. Allen.

Chapter 7

Fire-raising

A little fire is quickly trodden out,
Which being suffered rivers cannot quench.
(*Henry VI (Part 3)*, Act IV, Scene viii)

How great a matter a little fire doth kindleth.
(James 3:5)

In this chapter I deal with fire-raising against a brief contextual and historical background, discuss legal and statistical aspects and provide a classification of fire-raisers with implications for management. Those readers wishing for a more detailed treatment of the topic should consult my recent *Fire-Raising: Its Motivation and Management* (1994). A word of explanation is necessary concerning the choice of title for this chapter. The phenomenon of 'fire-raising' is also known in various parts of the world as arson (the *legal* term used), incendiarism, fire-setting (terms favoured in the USA and Canada), pyromania (a more restricted description once favoured in the nineteenth century and used to denote a specific form of insanity) and pathological fire-setting (a term used to indicate the involvement of abnormal mental states). I have chosen to use the term 'Fire-raising' as being general enough to encompass all these other terms and to embrace the various aspects of the phenomena to be discussed.

CONTEXTUAL AND HISTORICAL BACKGROUND

Fire: myth and symbol

The phenomenon of fire has always played a significant and many-faceted part in the history of humankind. Throughout this history it has been put to many uses: for example as an agent of succour, warmth and light, of healing and cleansing, but also of destruction. In addition, fire has held and continues to hold, a fascination every bit as powerful as that evoked by life and death. This universal fascination and its legacy has important implications for those who work in various capacities with individuals who use fire for destructive and unlawful purposes. As a phenomenon it is well documented. Bronowski reminds us that 'Fire has been known to early man for about 400,000 years. We think that implies that fire had already been discovered by Homo Erectus' (1976: 124).

The legends of the world are replete with references to fire and its fascination. Greek mythology contains the story of Prometheus, who having stolen fire from the Gods was condemned to the everlasting torment of having his liver torn out by vultures. Both Freud and Jung made use of this legend in connection with their attempts to understand fire as a phenomenon. In brief, they considered that Prometheus needed to outwit the Gods by stealing fire from them. It is said that, in so doing, he transported it in a hollow stick. This, they suggested, could be viewed at one and the same time as both a male and female symbol of sexuality. Implicit in this was said to be a degree of role and identity confusion – a characteristic sometimes found in those who indulge in fire-raising.

It has already been noted that Prometheus was punished for his crime in a particularly unpleasant fashion, demonstrating that the implied risks in handling potentially dangerous forces such as fire and sex were recognised since earliest times. In this context, Mary Douglas, the distinguished anthropologist, makes the following important point:

> Death, blood and coldness are confronted by their opposites, life, sex and fire. All six powers are dangerous. The three positive powers are dangerous unless separated from one another and are in danger from contact with death, blood or coldness.

> (1984: 138)

There are other Greek mythical references to fire. There is the legend of how Phaethon, son of the Sun God Helios and of the nymph Clymene, insisted on driving his father's chariot for a day. Being unskilled, he drove his chariot so close to the earth that he burned it. The God Zeus, concerned that this in-experienced youth might do further damage, directed a thunderbolt at the chariot, killing Phaethon. This and other myths, such as that of Icarus, merely add to the injunctions about the risks of leashing potentially dangerous forces such as fire (see, for example, Frazer, 1987; Hole, 1978).

In less mythical and more practical fashion it is interesting to note here that the Greeks also used fire for the destruction of the bodies of those who had taken their own lives. (They also cut off the hand by which the suicides had killed themselves and buried it separately). Roman culture had a goddess of the hearth named Vesta, who was worshipped in a temple tended by virgin priestesses. The link between fire and life eternal is well exemplified by the existence of the perpetual flames that burn at national war memorials to those fallen in battle. Indeed, there are few rituals in which fire has not played a significant part.

There are numerous references to fire, its uses and abuses, in the Bible; it also appears in liturgical practice. God revealed himself to Moses in the burning bush and the Book of Exodus recounts how fire guided the Israelites by night through the wilderness. Fire was also used as an indication of the presence of the Divine and as a symbol of direction to Moses when the Angel of the Lord appeared to him in the burning bush. Fire was of course also used for sacrificial purposes – sometimes to the point of human sacrifice, as in the case of Abraham and his son Isaac. It was also associated with notions of punishment. In the book of Deuteronomy we find the words 'The Lord thy God is a consuming fire, even a jealous God' (4:24) We also find reference to its use for purposes of revenge. Topp (1973) cites the illustration of the children of Judah putting Jerusalem to the sword and then firing it (Judges 1:8). Samson took revenge on his father-in-law by destroying his harvest by fire (Judges 15:6). The use of fire for purposes of revenge is an important factor in motivation – see later.

In the Christian era, fire is represented in somewhat different terms, markedly as a form of punishment for the souls of the damned and as a purifying force to be harnessed on behalf of those seeking the righteous life. However, it was its former purpose that no doubt provided the springboard for the use of fire for the burning of heretics and witches. One of the most notable people to have suffered in this way was the semi-legendary St Joan of Arc. History was also to record innumerable instances of clerics and others being burned at the stake. It would be erroneous to think that such barbaric activity was limited to Christian-Western culture, however. In the Hindu religion, its use in admittedly less overt punishing form, can be seen in the practice of *Suttee* – the highly symbolic self-immolation performed by widows on the funeral pyres of their husbands. Self-immolation is also seen in myth and legend, as for example in the manner in which Brünhilde dies on the massive funeral pyre in the final scene of Wagner's opera *Götterdämmerung*.

Fire as destructive power

The destructive capacity of fire is only too self-evident in contemporary society with almost daily reports of bombings, explosions and serious accidents involving deaths and maimings caused by fire. However, positive uses may be made of the capacities of explosive substances. For example, the Swedish scientist and explosives manufacturer Alfred Nobel put his vast fortune to the benefit of humankind by establishing the Nobel Peace Prize.

The deliberately destructive use of fire in its various forms is of course well documented in history. There are very early references to the use of mixtures of the chemicals potassium nitrate, charcoal and sulphur for making crude bombing devices. Macdonald (1977) notes that Leonardo da Vinci made sketches for the preparation of mortars. In the sixteenth century there are descriptions of various complicated 'noxious engines' that used explosive devices to cause horrifying injuries to those within range, and we are all familiar with the details of the Gunpowder Plot of 5 November 1605. In more recent years, it is sad to record that, in so-called civilised communities, more and more ingenious methods have been discovered by the technicians of terrorism to cause carnage and mayhem. It should be noted here that the *main thrust* of this chapter is about fire-raising specifically, not about bombing and terrorist activities – useful accounts of these may be found in Macdonald (1977).

Medical interest in the topic

Fire has, of course, a long history of medical usage, notably for purposes of cauterisation. Scott suggests that the Greek physician Hippocrates was well aware of the advantages of cauterisation when he stated that 'what medicine does not cure then the iron does . . . and what the iron does not cure fire exterminates' (1974: 6). He also quotes the early physician Paré who pointed out the disadvantages of such draconian treatment: 'Nature must regenerate a new flesh instead of that which hath been burnt, as also the bones remaines discovered and bare; and by this means from the most part there remaines an ulcer incurable' (ibid.). In the middle of the nineteenth century (and possibly earlier) medical men began to turn their attention and interest towards what were regarded as pathological forms of fire-raising. The term pyromania was probably first introduced at about this time by the French physician Marc.

Soon after this, German physicians were to develop this interest further. They suggested that these particular forms of fire-raising were most frequently found in sexually frustrated and rather slow-witted teenage country girls. Such statements would rightly be criticised today by those concerned about gender stereotyping. The German physicians also suggested that the condition was occasionally seen in older men, where it appeared to be associated with orgastic satisfaction. This association between fire and sexuality was, as we have already noted, developed later within the context of the myth of Prometheus, notably by Freud and later by Jung, who viewed it as a symbolic and archetypical outlet for sexual impulses. Currently, less extreme psychoanalytic interpretations of its complex basis prevail, but there are certainly some cases in which a specific association between fire and sexual problems appear to be of importance.

Following this brief context-setting review, we can now turn our attention to legal aspects and the current size of the problem.

THE LAW RELATING TO ARSON

The law relating to arson would appear to have a lengthy history. Geller states that

Ancient Roman legal texts recognized arson and defined penalties for this offence. In France, prior to the French Revolution, deliberate arson was punished by death – hanging for commoners and decapitation for nobles. Under some circumstances, arsonists were burned alive. . . . In Britain, during the reign of George II convicted arsonists . . . were banished from the country.
(1992: 283)

The legal definition of arson varies from one country to the next; no attempt is made to define it internationally. Other jurisdictions have comparable statutes and penalties. The word itself is derived from Anglo-French and old French and from mediaeval Latin – *ardere*; *ars* to burn (*Concise Oxford English Dictionary*). In England and Wales, prior to 1971, the offence of arson was dealt with under common law. Currently, it is dealt with under the provisions of the Criminal Damage Act, 1971. Similar provisions apply in Northern Ireland. In Scotland, it is dealt with as 'wilful fire-raising' and 'culpable and reckless fire-raising'. Section 1 of the Criminal Damage Act, 1971 states as follows (emphasis added):

(1) A person who without lawful excuse destroys or damages any property belonging to another intending to destroy or damage any such property or being reckless as to whether any such property would be destroyed or damaged shall be guilty of an offence.

(2) A person who without lawful excuse destroys or damages any property, whether belonging to himself or another –

    (a) intending to destroy or damage any property or being reckless as to whether any such property would be destroyed or damaged; and

    (b) intending by the destruction or damage to endanger the life of another or being reckless as to whether the life of another would be thereby endangered;

    shall be guilty of an offence.

(3) An offence committed under this section by destroying or damaging property by fire *shall be charged as arson*.

Under Section 4 of the Act, the offences of both arson and endangering life are punishable with maximum penalties of life imprisonment.

It is of interest to note that the Law Commission, in a report that led to the introduction of the Criminal Damage Act, 1971, mentioned that one of the reasons for treating damage by fire differently from other types of damage was that many arsonists were mentally unbalanced and in need of treatment. Accordingly, the retention of arson with the maximum life penalty would help to ensure that such defendants could receive restriction orders under the mental health legislation (R.D. Mackay, Professor of Law, De Montfort University, Leicester, letter to the author, 21 October 1992).

THE SIZE OF THE PROBLEM

> There are three kinds of lies;
> lies; damned lies, and statistics'.
> (Twain, *Autobiography*)

In recent years concern about the increase in the number of fires from various causes has been expressed by authorities throughout the world. In the UK, the Home Office had been concerned for a number of years about fires caused by vandalism and a working party was established to examine this problem; this reported in 1980. The working party stressed the difficulty of measuring the size of the problem accurately and, in particular, making comparisons between offences recorded as arson and those identified by the various fire service authorities as fires of 'malicious' ignition or doubtful origin (Home Office, 1980).

This problem remains, and for this reason a good deal of caution should be exercised in interpreting the figures quoted in this chapter. In a wide-ranging review of the topic, Woodward noted that the numbers of malicious fires in buildings had increased fourfold from 1956 to 1964 and that the position was getting steadily worse. He observed that

> world-wide it can be said that the cost of arson as a proportion of all costs of fire is at least fifteen per cent and can be as high as fifty per cent depending on the country . . . fire insurers throughout the world are having to devote between one quarter and a third of their total loss expenditure to pay for fire losses resulting from arson.

(1987: 55)

He also quotes evidence from the Gerling Institute of Cologne that there had been an '"alarming increase" in the number of deliberately started fires as reflected in the criminal statistics of all industrial countries' (ibid.). From the *Criminal Statistics, England and Wales* we can see a general rise in crimes of arson and criminal damage endangering life, though the numbers tend to fluctuate to some extent, notably decreases in 1984 and 1986 (see Table 7.1).

It should be noted that although arson and criminal damage are very serious crimes, they only constitute about 2 per cent of all offences against property as revealed in the *Criminal Statistics*. Figures from the Home Office Research and Statistics Department for the same period also show an accompanying steady increase in fires of uncertain origin or possible malicious ignition (Home Office, 1990). Similar trends are discernible in the rest of Europe and the North Americas (Woodward, 1987).

Table 7.1 Persons found guilty or cautioned for arson and criminal damage endangering life, 1982–1990

	1982	1984	1986	1988	1990
Arson	3,270	3,730	2,881	3,167	3,393
Criminal damage endangering life	45	64	74	93	85

Source: Home Office, 1992: 124

A recent phenomenon in the UK has been the increase in the number of cars destroyed by fire. They accounted for 31 per cent of all fires in road vehicles in 1988 (15,212) compared with 9 per cent in 1978 (2,439). There may be a number of reasons for this. First, it may be part of the general and disturbing trend in vandalism – a desire to take out one's sense of dissatisfaction and alienation on others better favoured by fortune. Second, it may be being used increasingly as a method of avoiding detection in taking a vehicle without the owner's consent (TWOC). (Fire will of course destroy fingerprints.) Third, it may be being used in the current recession as a means of avoiding hire-purchase payments on a vehicle, or of destroying it in the hope of reaping the financial reward of an unlawfully claimed insurance.

The cost of deliberate fire-raising is very considerable. For example, it has been calculated that in schools 80 per cent of the fires which cause more that £50,000 of damage are deliberate. Every week, forty schools are said to be seriously damaged by fire and one of these blazes may cost as much as £250,000. In 1986, according to the *Independent* (13 August 1987: 11), the cost of arson in schools was said to be in excess of £150 million. The article also refers to the traumatic impact on the children (particularly primary school children). One teacher is quoted as saying 'Some of the little ones were crying when they saw the remains of the building.' In the same article there is a description of how two teenage girls set fire to a school in Cheshire. They gave as their reason that they were harbouring a grudge because their teachers had failed to recognise sooner that they had been the victims of sexual abuse when younger. However, fire-raising in school is more often the work of teenage boys, mainly in the inner cities; their fire-raising is linked to other anti-social conduct. Vanity and vengeance may also play a part. A warped satisfaction might be derived from ransacking and then firing the building which may have provided the one real and possibly unhappy experience of authority in their lives. One of the main reasons that there are so few fatalities in deliberate fires in schools is that they usually occur at night. However, there have been some tragic incidents where young fire-raisers have been seriously injured as a result of their activities.

To return to the cost of fires, the Association of British Fire Insurers has indicated that a million pound fire claim is not an uncommon occurrence today. Twenty-six fires costing more than one million pounds took place in the period April–June 1990; and fire damage claims jumped to £239.3 million in the same quarter in 1989, an increase of 19 per cent. The organisation lists twenty-six fires in the UK where the costs to insurers were in excess of one million pounds; one being £16 million, one for £8 million and ten for £3 million and above (J.C. Munro, Secretary to the Crime Insurance Panel of the Association of British insurers, personal communication, 4 October 1990).

MOTIVES AND MANAGEMENT

Classification

It is a justified truism to state that the motives for fire-raising are extremely complex; in many cases they may defy elucidation and in some cases there may be more than one motive for the behaviour. Such behaviour has always been of interest to psychiatrists and in many cases their skills can bring light to bear on the problem. However, it is as well to remember that, as with other forms of delinquent conduct, there are dangers in stretching the psychiatric explanations of this behaviour too far (see, for example, Soothill, 1990). In setting out the following classification it is important to point out that it is necessary to distinguish between the *behavioural characteristics* of arsonists, various *types* of arsonists and their *motives*.

Faulk (1988: 91–97) has suggested two broad useful groupings. *Group I* consists of those cases in which the fire serves as a means to an end (such as revenge, fraud or a plea for help). *Group II* consists of those cases where the *fire itself* is the phenomenon of interest. Some years ago two psychiatrist colleagues and I studied a group of 113 imprisoned arsonists and suggested a possible classification (Prins *et al.*, 1985). Since that study I have modified the original classification somewhat as follows (Prins, 1994):[1]

(A) Arson committed for financial reward.
(B) Arson committed to cover up another crime.
(C) Arson committed for political purposes (terrorist and allied activities).
(D) Self-immolation as a political gesture (strictly speaking not arson but included here for completeness).
(E) Arson committed for mixed motives (for example, in a state of minor depression, as a cry for help or under the influence of alcohol).
(F) Arson due to the presence of mental disorder (for example, severe affective disorder, schizophrenic illnesses, organic mental disorder [dementia, brain tumour, disturbances of metabolism], mental impairment)
(G) Arson due to motives of revenge – against (i) an individual or individuals (specific); (ii) society or others, more generally.
(H) Arson committed as an attention-seeking act (but excluding the motives set out under (E) above, and arson committed as a means of deriving sexual satisfaction/excitement (for example, some forms of pyromania). This form of arson is described by some writers under the term 'pathological'; the literature has recently been extensively reviewed by Barnett and Spitzer (1994).
(I) Arson committed by young adults.
(J) Arson committed by children.

Rix (1994) has made a substantial recent contribution to the literature on the motivation of adult arsonists. He studied 153 arsonists who had been referred to him for pre-trial psychiatric reports. He broadened the categories of motives described by myself and others to fifteen: revenge; excitement; vandalism; cry for help/attention; rehousing; attempted suicide; carelessness; psychotic; financial; cover up; other manipulative; heroism; proxy; anti-depressant; political. Rix suggests that his motive of *rehousing* has not been identified previously. *Carelessness* included intoxication or where a fire had been claimed to have been started accidentally; *anti-depressant* referred to 2 per cent of cases in which the motive was allegedly to relieve depressed feelings; *proxy* referred to three cases in which the offender had acted on behalf of another who had borne a grudge. (See also Jackson, 1994.)

Some general characteristics and examples

> I stand as if a mine beneath my feet,
> Were ready to be blown up.
> (Webster, *Duchess of Malfi*, Act III, Scene ii)

Arsonists appear to be *mostly* young adult males and many of them have considerable relationship difficulties. A large proportion have problems with alcohol and many of them are not very intelligent. When women commit repeated acts of arson or have an accompanying history of mental disorder, they are more likely than their male counterparts to be given psychiatric disposal (Prins, 1994). Despite the cautionary note sounded earlier about the dangers of medicalising social problems, it is a good rule of thumb to ask for a psychiatric report in all cases of arson where the motivation seems unclear or where there is a background or current history of mental disturbance. Studies of arsonists indicate considerable evidence of unstable childhoods and serious psychological disturbance. However, despite what the media would sometimes have us believe, a direct sexual motivation for arson is rare, though many arsonists have problems in making satisfactory sexual relationships. Those who engage in arson for purposes of revenge are likely to be regarded as the most dangerous. Such persons are like the monster in Mary Shelley's *Frankenstein* who said 'I am malicious because I am miserable'. Many such arsonists have problems in dealing with their feelings of anger and frustration at real or (more often) imagined wrongs.

A few selected case illustrations will hopefully fill out on the rather sparse classification outlined above.

Arson committed for financial or other reward

In these cases the aim of the arsonist is to gain some financial or similar reward. The apparent increase in the burning of vehicles referred to earlier would fall into this category if, for example, the objective was to avoid hire-purchase payments or to seek some kind of compensation from an insurance company. However, the motives may not be so clear-cut, as some individuals who set fire for apparent gain in this fashion may, for example, also be suffering from a degree of depression due to overwhelming financial burdens.

Example 1

A woman set fire to her one-bedroomed flat, causing the destruction not only of her own home but of two neighbouring flats as well. As a result of the fires, an elderly neighbour, who lived two flats away, sustained injuries from which he died. In court it was alleged that the defendant had doubled her insurance on her home contents and set the fire in order to deal with increasing debts. It was also alleged that on the night before the fire she had removed some of her property to a relative's home. The judge told the defendant that although she did not intend to cause injury she knew there were elderly residents nearby and that the risk of injury would be high. She was sentenced to seven years' imprisonment (*Independent*, 16 June: 5, and 30 June 1992: 5).

Arson to conceal other crimes

Arson will sometimes be committed in order to conceal a variety of offences. These may range from theft to murder. Some fires will cause enormous damage, particularly if they are set to cover offences such as burglarious activities in large and well-stocked warehouses. Woodward (1987) cites two instances of this kind of fire-raising. In the first, a warehouse of a shipping company was destroyed by fire. The goods stored there included TV sets, car tyres and other goods that would catch fire quickly. From the forensic examination at the scene of the fire it was apparent that burglarious activity had taken place before the fire had been set. In the second case, a fire was set in a bonded warehouse containing video recorders amongst other items. The warehouse had been the object of repeated pilfering in the preceding months and it was considered that the fire had been set deliberately to divert attention away from these thefts.

Arson committed for political purposes

There are two main motives for arson committed by political activists. The first concerns the desire to destroy the property of those to whom they are opposed; the second is the publicity gained for the activists' cause. The alleged destruction of 'second homes' by Welsh activists would be illustrative of the first, and the work of the IRA and other paramilitary and fascist organisations might be illustrative of the second. A most disturbing trend in the last year has been numerous outbreaks of arson and similar attacks on so-called 'foreigners'. A graphic and sinister account of such activity has been described in the north-western German town of Möllen:

Two young girls and a woman, all of them Turkish, died from burns after their house . . . was fire-bombed. . . . Neighbours spoke of screaming and crying from inside the house where the three died, as it was rapidly consumed by flames. Nine people were seriously injured, including one child, both of whose legs were broken by jumping from an upper story window. An elderly physically handicapped next-door neighbour said 'I cannot get the sight of her body out of my mind. Little Yeliz was just a charred bundle when the firemen covered her up on the stretcher. The stairs must have been soaked with petrol for the whole thing just went up like a bonfire.' The Federal State Prosecutor said that the use of the words 'Heil Hitler' in an anonymous 'phone call indicates that the perpetrators wanted to help restore a Nazi dictatorship in Germany.

(*Independent*, 24 November 1992: 1 and 10)

Although the main motives are often seen to be political, there are also sometimes psychopathological elements, such as the feeling of power such activities may provide. To this extent, the motivation may be mixed as, for example, in the case of other offences such as serious sexual assault.

Cases of self-immolation

These cannot really be regarded as cases of arson, but an act of self-immolation may have serious consequences for the lives of others, as the following example shows.

Example 2

A young woman in the north of England tried to kill herself in her bedroom by dousing her body in petrol and then attempting to ignite it. This having failed, she subsequently tried to blow herself up (and the other residents of the house) by turning on the gas taps and striking matches. Fortunately, this attempt also failed. However, the legal ingredients of a charge of endangering life through arson were sustainable and the defendant was admitted compulsorily to a psychiatric hospital. At the time she was found to have been suffering from a serious depressive illness, but subsequently made a reasonably good recovery. This example also illustrates the problem of trying to 'pigeon hole' people, since the young woman's problem could have been classified under the heading of mental disorder.

We read not infrequently of 'outbreaks' of ritualised self-destruction – mainly for political reasons. A report in the *Independent* of 21 May 1991 (p. 2) describes the ritual suicide of Kim Ki Sol, who wrote 'There are many meanings to my act today' before 'setting himself alight and jumping in flames from the roof of a seven-storey building at Seoul's Sogang University.' In both North and South

Korea and elsewhere a disturbing increase in such behaviour has been noted. Cult self-immolation is not of course a new phenomenon, and reference has already been made to the ritual of *Suttee*. Barker describes a number of young members of a group known as Ananda Marga 'who immolated themselves' as a protest 'against the imprisonment in India of their leader'. Two of them said that their 'self-immolation is done after personal and independent decision. It is out of love for all human beings, for the poor, for the exploited, the suffering' (Barker, 1989: 54–55).

Topp (1973) has drawn attention to the extent to which self-destruction by fire seems to have shown a slow but steady increase in penal establishments in recent years. He has suggested that such individuals who choose an obviously very painful method of death are likely to be those who have some capacity for splitting off feelings from consciousness. Some may be epileptics in a disturbed state of consciousness.

However, in all such cases of self-immolation, we should remember that people probably vary enormously in their pain thresholds. Some would succumb very quickly to such an agonising method of self-destruction. One imagines that shock and asphyxiation would probably occur within a very short space of time so that the severe pain caused by the burning of vital tissues would not have to be endured for too long. Such may have been the fate of some of the early martyrs who chose to suffer death at the stake. Occasionally, such sufferers were 'granted the merciful privilege . . . of having a small bag of gunpowder hung around [the] neck in order to speed their demise and so reduce [their] suffering' (Abbott, 1991: 167).

Arson committed for mixed or unclear reasons

It is frequently very difficult to ascribe a single motive for an offence of arson; for more often than not the motives appear to be mixed. In the sample of 113 imprisoned arsonists referred to earlier, my colleagues and I found a number of cases in which it was difficult to attribute a *single specific* motive. We were forced to try to subdivide the group – in the following way. First, a small number of cases in which the offender appeared to be suffering from a mild (reactive) degree of depressive illness at the time of the crime. Such depression is some-times associated with anger directed at a spouse or partner, *so there may also be an element of revenge involved.* Second, cases in which the arson appeared to be a disguised plea for help. Third, one or two cases in which the arson appeared to have been precipitated by a sudden separation from a near relative or loved one or by a bereavement. Fourth, some cases in which alcohol seemed to play a part. As with other crimes, the ingestion of alcohol features quite frequently. The offender may state that he or she had been drinking very heavily at the time and cannot recall what happened. Such a lack of recall may be due, in rare cases, to genuine alcoholic amnesia, but is more likely to be due to a befuddled state caused by intoxication. It is possible that a fire may be set accidentally as a result of such a state. However, in my experience, such fires are comparatively rare.

The degree of mixed motivation that occurs is well illustrated in the following example.

Example 3

This involved a man in his mid-thirties who had a history of personality disorder, including past highly disturbed behaviour such as setting fire to the parental home on one occasion and making numerous 'false alarm' calls to the police and fire brigade. Following a period of compulsory hospitalisation by a court for one of his fire-raising episodes, he had been discharged to a mental health after-care facility. He did not get on at all well with the staff and considered they were 'picking' on him. During a depressive episode in which he had been drinking heavily, he set fire to the establishment, causing damage amounting to several thousand pounds.

Arson due to more serious mental disorder

The relationship between mental disorders and crime in general has been dealt with at length in Chapter 4, so its relationship to arson is only dealt with fairly briefly here.

Schizophreniform illness and arson

A number of arsonists, particularly those detained in the Special Hospitals or in secure units, suffer from a clearly diagnosable schizophrenic illness of one type or another. Some of them have set fire to dwellings or other premises as a result of their delusional and/or hallucinatory experiences. One such offender-patient told me: 'I set fire to it [the house] to get rid of the evil in it.' Others will allege that they have seen the image of God and heard Him directing them to set fires. Sometimes the association is not quite so clear-cut, as the following example demonstrates.

Example 4

A man in his late forties, who was already detained in an ordinary psychiatric hospital in the west country for an offence of arson, attempted to set fire to his room. A nurse spotted the small but growing blaze; it was put out, and the patient and others were not physically harmed. However, it was thought to be advisable to bring charges so that he could be held in more secure conditions. Accordingly, a hospital order was made in the Crown Court with added restrictions without limit of time. He had previous convictions for criminal damage and arson, on two occasions having been dealt with by means of hospital orders without restrictions. He had become ill as an adolescent and been diagnosed as suffering from schizophrenia and personality disorder. The latter had become more marked as time went by, as a result of the influence of his schizophrenic illness. He became increasingly subject to hallucinations and delusions, but it was difficult to determine the extent to which he acted directly as a result of these in his fire-raising activities. In hospital, though he remained ill and sometimes suffered from delusions and hallucinations, he had responded to medication. It was hoped that at some future date it would be possible to place him in less secure conditions. He was not thought to be basically an arsonist, but a person whose illness led him sometimes to light fires.

Occasionally, sufferers from a chronic schizophrenic illness may become vagrants. In their wanderings about the countryside they *may* set fire to a building or themselves as a result of their impaired mental state. However, Virkunnen (1974) makes the important point that they do not often choose dwellings for such activities but smaller objects such as telegraph poles or fences.

Severe affective disorder and arson

I have already shown in Example 3 how a mild degree of depressive disorder may contribute to an episode of fire-raising. I now consider the connection between more serious affective disorder and this behaviour. The following case illustrations also ended in death for the assailant.

Example 5

An inquest was told how a man in his forties doused his wife and two sons with petrol, then set fire to them believing that God had told him to do so. Fortunately his wife and two sons were saved by neighbours, but the man died from burns to most of his body. He is alleged to have said 'God told me to do this. He's been speaking to me for twenty years.' A psychiatrist told the inquest that the man had been suffering from a 'substantial depressive illness' and that he believed the 'family would be better off dead'. The coroner recorded a verdict that the man killed himself while the balance of his mind was disturbed. Had he survived, he would have probably been charged and, if successfully prosecuted, been made liable to a mental health disposal (*Independent*, 29 May 1992: 5).

Arson associated with 'organic' disorders

Very occasionally, arson may be committed by a person who is suffering from some form of 'organic' disorder (e.g. brain tumour, injury, epilepsy, dementia or metabolic disturbances). Epilepsy is not commonly associated with arson for example, but one should always be on the look-out for the case in which arson has been committed when the person concerned was not in a state of clear consciousness or when on-lookers were present. In their study of fifty arsonists detained in Grendon Underwood Psychiatric Prison, Hurley and Monahan (1969) found that 20 per cent had a history of head injury with loss of consciousness but without other neurological consequences.

Carpenter and King (1989) have described an interesting case in which a man temporarily developed a personality change, psychosis and epilepsy after having had brain surgery for a subarachnoid haemorrhage. While affected by these problems he set fire to his house and it was considered by the authors that his fire-raising was directly related to an epileptic seizure. He was charged, hospitalised informally, made a good recovery and remained symptom-free some three years later. The authors also make comment on the role of alcohol in such cases. The patient was not a heavy drinker but accepted advice not to drink at all because of its possible harmful effects on his condition. A further case prompted by the one just referred to has been described by Byrne and Walsh (1989). This concerned a woman who set fire to a shop – one of a series of fires set by her. She was originally given a diagnosis of personality disorder, but careful observation and re-assessment by the use of electro-encephalographic examination revealed gross abnormalities consistent with an epileptic focus in the temporal lobe of her brain. She was placed on a drug regime to deal with her newly diagnosed condition, has apparently remained symptom free and her fire-raising behaviour has ceased.

Arson and mental impairment

The use of the current legal description in the UK is meant to encompass those conditions also recognised under the terms mental deficiency, retardation, handi-cap, subnormality, learning disability. Not infrequently, a degree of mental impairment in offenders is also associated with personality disorder so the two conditions are considered together.

A history of mental impairment seems to occur quite frequently in those persons who have committed arson on more than one occasion. McKerracher and Dacre (1966) studied one such group of arsonists detained in Rampton (Special) Hospital (which at the time of their survey catered almost exclusively for dangerous mentally impaired [sub-normal] offender-patients). They considered that the arsonists were more emotionally unpredictable than other Rampton patients and displayed a wider range of psychiatric symptoms than did other residents. Very often, mentally impaired arsonists suffer from a variety of social and other handicaps as well. The following two examples illustrate some of these combined difficulties.

Example 6

This invovled a woman in her late twenties, formally diagnosed as mildly mentally subnormal (impaired) and personality disordered, who came from a highly disturbed background. Her parents had fought for years before finally divorcing. A number of her siblings had been before the courts on numerous occasions. Much of her behaviour was of the attention-seeking variety and over the years she had set fire to a number of establishments in which she had been detained. The offence for which she had received a sentence of life imprisonment (later made the subject of a 'transfer direction' to hospital) consisted of setting fire to bedding and furniture in a local hospital. Had it not been for the prompt intervention of the nurses a serious tragedy might have occurred involving the deaths of many patients and staff.

Example 7

A man in his late thirties, diagnosed as suffering from mental impairment and a degree of personality disorder, set fire to a store-room containing highly flammable materials. The fire spread quickly to a building next door where a number of people were working. The man had a long history of fire-raising activities and making hoax telephone calls to the police and fire services. He also suffered from concurrent physical disabilities – a severe speech impediment and a limp which greatly affected his self-esteem. His main interest in life was in raising fires and he was regarded as highly dangerous by the hospital authorities. When mental impairment is accompanied by severe physical disability or disfigurement it presents greater problems because the offender has to cope with two or more very real handicaps. In such cases, arson is often a way of drawing attention to oneself and one's plight.

Arson motivated by revenge

In considering the link between motives of revenge and arson it is important to reiterate the point that it is hazardous to try to place behaviours uncritically in discrete categories. For example, the vengeful arsonist may show clear signs of an identifiable mental illness, may be mentally and/or physically impaired, or may not be 'ill' at all in any formal psychiatric sense.

Thomas reminds us that arson was a common form of revenge in the seventeenth century

> for those who felt themselves injured by their neighbours, arson required no great physical strength or financial resources and could easily be concealed. It was an indiscriminate means of vengeance however, for a fire, once started, was likely to spread. As such, it perhaps appealed especially to those whose hatred for their neighbours was all-embracing.
>
> (1984: 634)

Thomas cites numerous cases of alleged witches threatening to or actually burning down the houses of neighbours or those they felt had wronged them.

Sometimes charges of arson and sorcery overlapped. Thomas cites the case of Anne Foster, who was convicted at Northampton in 1674 of bewitching the sheep of a rich grazier and of subsequently setting fire to his house and barns (p. 636). He also quotes a very graphic illustration of planned, vengeful and highly deliberate fire-raising in the case of Elizabeth Abbott. She announced that

> she had viewed the place where she resolved to do it, for she would get pitch and tar, and set fire in the Mayor's shop, or in some other shop where there was lint and tow, and would stand by it that she might be taken, and would own herself to have done it.
>
> (p. 635)

There are two points of special interest in this 'non-clinical' case. The first concerns the deliberation with which the perpetrator went about her business; this was no spur of the moment event. The second is the manner in which she made no attempt to conceal her activities. One may speculate whether this was due to bravado, a feeling of imperviousness to control by the authorities, or to a degree of mild hypomania. We have no way of knowing, but the motivation appears to be every bit as mixed as with a large number of contemporary cases. The motive of revenge may be directed towards a specific individual or individuals or it may be the expression of a more general vengeful feeling towards society. It is a motive that also seems to cut across many of the others already described. It may be said to be the commonest of all motives, but this is not always apparent on first inspection of the case. Very careful and persistent exploration may be required before it emerges.

Arson is not uncommon as a highly personal form of revenge against employers. Considerable damage may be caused to property by those who are seeking to redress some real or imagined wrong such as dismissal, or a reprimand, or the preferential treatment of others by management. Such employees may be very knowledgeable about the premises and how best to set the fire.

Other offenders and offender-patients direct their vengeful feelings towards intimates or those they feel should have reciprocated their own intimate intentions.

Example 8

A man aged about thirty had developed a passionate and quite unshakeable belief that a young woman was in love with him. His passions were not reciprocated; in fact they were actively resisted on several occasions. So obsessive were this man's amorous desires that they had a delusional quality. As a means of gaining attention to his plight and of getting back at the young woman concerned he placed an incendiary device in her home with the avowed intention of killing her and her family. Fortunately, a family member spotted the device and dealt with it before the fire took too great a hold. Many years after this event, the offender (detained in hospital on a hospital order without limit of time) still harboured vengeful feelings and seemed quite without insight into what he had done or compassion for his intended victims.

It is important to stress here that the vengeful arsonist is likely to harbour his or her destructive desires over a very long period.

Pyromania and sexually motivated arson

I now consider a group of arsonists who do not appear to be suffering to a significant degree from any of the mental illnesses described above or to be operating from clear motives of revenge. They appear to derive a pathological excitement and satisfaction from the involvement in setting the fire and in attending or busying themselves at the scene and calling out the fire brigade.

> The essential feature of Pyromania is the presence of multiple episodes of deliberate and purposeful fire-setting. . . . Individuals with this disorder experi-ence tension or affective arousal before setting a fire. There is a fascination with, interest in, curiosity about, or attraction to fire and its situational con-texts. . . . Individuals with this disorder experience pleasure, gratification, or a release of tension when setting the fire, witnessing its effects or participating in its aftermath. . . . The fire-setting is not done for monetary gain, as an expression of sociopolitical ideology, to conceal criminal activity, to express anger or vengeance, to improve one's living circumstances, or in response to a delusion or a hallucination. The fire-setting does not result from impaired judgement (e.g. in Dementia, Mental Retardation, or Substance Intoxication). The diagnosis is not made if the fire-setting is better accounted for by Conduct Disorder, a Manic Episode or Antisocial Personality Disorder.
>
> (APA, 1994: 614)

A fairly classic case of pyromania is illustrated in the following example.

Example 9

A woman in her late forties was initially praised as a heroine for her apparent efforts to rescue two children from a house fire. Later, she was to admit that she had started the blaze herself; she was jailed for life, having pleaded guilty to manslaughter and five counts of arson. Her history, as given in court, revealed that she had started fires on three previous occasions. She was described by prosecuting counsel as someone who had a compulsive fascin-ation for lighting fires, obtaining excitement by watching the arrival of the fire brigade. She also plagued the authorities with hoax phone calls. Described as not being very bright and by her own counsel as 'suffering from an illness, a sickness . . . in respect of which there appears to be no medical treatment . . . she is not evil in the normally accepted sense'. Commenting on this case and others, Dr Angus Campbell, an experienced forensic psychiatrist, suggested that many pyromaniacs suffered from serious personality disorder. 'This sort of behaviour often originates in one fire which gives the person a buzz and gets them hooked.' He describes how he once treated an auxiliary fireman 'who always dashed to the seat of the flames, naturally reaping accolades. Eventually, after fighting seven or eight fires, it was discovered that he was starting them himself' (*Independent*, 12 June 1992: 1 and 2).

Ever since Freud and his followers drew upon ancient myth to suggest a link between the sexual act and arson there have been numerous accounts in the psychoanalytic literature which have tended to support this view. However, such accounts are largely anecdotal and have tended to be repeated in learned journals over the years, thus giving a false credibility to a somewhat suspect concept. Some workers, for example Rice and Harris (1984), have been heavily critical of psychoanalytic theorising; and Foust (1979), somewhat more positively, has stressed the need for careful clinical evaluation of individual cases. One of the most sensible perspectives on the topic is provided by Fras:

Adult fire-setters (pyromaniacs) . . . represent a heterogenous group in terms of motivation and psychodynamics . . . they feel unbearable tension, which is released by setting the fire and watching it. Sexual excitement is sometimes described, but not necessarily so. Others derive need fulfilment through the process of extinguishing the flames, with its masculine symbolism. Both types of fire-setters may have histories of sexual humiliation and general feelings of inferiority, with fire restoring power and a kind of strong symbolic fulfilment, either by the act of setting the fire or extinguishing it, since both activities have enormous social effects as well.

(1983: 199)

Fras makes the point that such behaviour has strong similarities to sex offending. 'In its compulsive, stereotyped sequence of mounting pressure, pyromania resembles the sexual perversions, as it may parallel them in its imperviousness to treatment' (p. 199). The important place given by Fras to sexual problems finds some confirmation in Hurley and Monahan's (1969) study of imprisoned arsonists. They found that 54 per cent of the men had clear psychosexual difficulties and marital problems, and 60 per cent reported difficulties in social relationships with women.

Example 10

This involved a man in his mid-forties, detained in a psychiatric hospital, who suffered from both a degree of mental impairment and from psychopathic (personality) disorder. He had a long history of arson offences, some of them quite serious. He had always claimed to have obtained sexual arousal and occasional orgasm from watching the fires he set. But perhaps of equal significance was his additional predilection for the mutilation of the cadavers of both sexes. His case was indicative of gross psychopathology and illustrates the overlap between different categories of anti-social conduct, in this case the molestation of corpses.

Young adult vandalism and arson

The backgrounds and motivations of adolescent and young adult arsonists appear to be rather different from those characterising children who set fires. The latter form a separate group and are not considered in this book but are considered in some detail in my book *Fire-Raising: Its Motivation and Management* (1994: Chapter 6). The adolescents and younger adults we looked at in our prison sample seemed to have been motivated more specifically by boredom and to have engaged in the behaviour for 'kicks'. It is not unknown for bored young employees to set fire to their places of work. Cases have been reported in the hotel and catering industry. In some instances, there was also an accompanying element of getting back at a society that did not appear to care about them. Unlike child fire-raisers, their backgrounds seemed less socially and psychologically disturbed. It is also important to note that the arson offences committed by this age group are often closely associated with the ingestion of alcohol. The following example shows how some of these elements may be combined.

Example 11

A group of five unemployed older teenagers (ages ranging from sixteen to nineteen) had been to a disco where they had imbibed a fair amount of alcohol, though they were not drunk. They had waited for a considerable time for the last bus home only to find they had missed it. They had been whiling away their time at the bus stop indulging in a fair amount of horse-play. As they became more impatient, their horse-play escalated into more aggressive activity. They smashed the windows of a large outfitter's shop nearby, entered it, and began damaging the contents. In the course of this activity, one of them lit some waste paper while others looked on encouraging him. A fire soon took hold, engulfing the premises and rapidly destroying the shop and its contents.

Management

It will be obvious from the explanations, motives and examples outlined above, that no single form of management will be effective. But because fire-raising behaviour is so diverse, and because, as already suggested, motives may be obscure, it is very important that each case receives full analysis; this is particularly important when we come to consider the risk of re-offending. The classification I have outlined, for all its acknowledged deficiencies, should be of some help in enabling us to distinguish between those arsonists who engage in their offence for purely fraudulent motives; those who are politically motivated and those whose behaviour is vandalistic; those whose behaviour is motivated by clear evidence of mental disorder of one kind or another; and those whose motivation is more difficult to get to grips with: the vengeful, the so-called 'pyromaniacs' and the sexually motivated.

Predominantly non-mentally disordered arsonists

In these cases a full investigation of the social and personal circumstances of the individual concerned is valuable in order to rule out any significant psycho-pathological factors. As already indicated, an arsonist motivated by apparently fraudulent motives may be suffering from a degree of depression and this may be responsive to remedial measures even if a prison sentence is imposed. The same considerations apply to some politically motivated arsonists; it would be a mistake to believe that within their ranks there are not a small number who are suffering from a degree of mental disturbance, but not perhaps of a degree to fulfil a formal clinical psychiatric diagnosis. Apart from these considerations, politically motivated arsonists and those driven by a general urge to be destructive (the vandals) are best dealt with through general penal and other measures.

Mentally disordered arsonists

Those arsonists who engage in their activities because of serious psychiatric disturbance may well respond to treatment for their underlying illness. Medication, if taken regularly, may help to keep their most acute and intrusive hallucinations or delusions at bay. One of the problems that arises is the degree to which compliance with medication is continued by the patient once discharged to the community – a matter of much contemporary concern. The cases described by Carpenter and King (1989) and by Byrne and Walsh (1989) show that medication for an organic condition such as epilepsy or some form of hormonal imbalance may also be most helpful; indeed, as their cases show, it may change not only the outcome but also the diagnosis. Medication may also be helpful for some mentally impaired arsonists whose behaviour is aggressively impulsive. It is here that effective social and psychiatric supervision is essential. One of the most critical problems is that of accommodation (and this applies to all convicted of what we might perhaps describe as 'pathological arson'). Hostels are understandably very reluctant to take known arsonists, not only for reasons of safety and the protection of other residents, but also because insurance cover may be difficult to obtain or maintain. It is sad, but perhaps understandable, that some workers will endeavour to hide the fact that a client or patient has a history of arson (if their most recent offence is for something else) in order to gain a residential place. Serious thought needs to be given to the provision of special facilities enhanced by regular and intensive psychiatric and psychological support. At present such provision is extremely rare (but see, for example, Gower, 1992).

It would be a mistake to believe that formal psychotherapy of varying degrees of intensity has no place in the management of psychotic or psychopathic arsonists detained in hospital. Cox has carried out much interesting long-term group work with psychotic offender-patients (including arsonists) detained in Broadmoor Hospital. Such work requires considerable skills and imagination if one is to become tuned in to what such offender-patients are trying to communicate. Cox says:

> An arsonist may be able to relive his experience of setting fire to the house of his ex-'flame', who had jilted him, in the presence of therapist A (a non-arsonist); whereas therapist B (also a non-arsonist) 'would not understand.'

He asks:

> What does this mean? It implies that there must be empathic understanding between therapist A, which is not present with therapist B. There will be other occasions when therapist B will be able to receive what the patient says, whereas therapist A will not.
>
> (Cox, 1978: 140)

Elsewhere, Cox demonstrates the helpful elements that are present within a group psychotherapeutic setting:

> This means that a disclosure from one patient is frequently followed almost immediately by similar disclosures from other patients, 'I was waiting for you to start so that I could join in' . . . 'Funny, I was just going to say that.' In actual fact, the patient who was '*just* going to say that' was a reticent arsonist, terrified of making personal disclosures. But when, after eighteen months in another group, another patient admitted that he was an arsonist, the certainty of not being the odd man out allowed him to say something that he had 'just' been going to say!
>
> (Cox, 1979: 320)

Describing a further case, Cox suggests that

> His arson was no substitute sexual activity, but rather a way of getting his family, highly respectable and respected in the local Cornish village, into the headlines of the local paper, by ensuring that the reporters knew of his activity: 'Fancy one of them doing that. They were always such a good family.'
>
> (1979: 332)

One of the advantages of such an approach with a range of offender-patients suffering from varied psychiatric conditions is that it reinforces the importance of carefully examining the *individual* case. Elsewhere Cox says:

The arsonist may be diagnosed as subnormal, neurotic, psychotic, or psychopathic. The act may be of profound symbolic importance to the patient or almost incidental. It may be of overt sexual significance, and the patient will claim that he had his best orgasm as he watched the flames leaping up, or that his greatest moment of sexual excitement was when he was helping the fire service unsuccessfully to put out the fire which he had started. . . . On other occasions the act may be symbolically associated with love or hate. ('My best flame, you set me on fire, burning anger . . .'). The arsonist may show psychotic concrete thinking so that self-immolation occurred when Charles Wesley's hymn, 'Kindle a flame of sacred love on the mean altar of my heart' was taken literally.

(1979: 334)

Cox goes on to stress a point made earlier that 'the almost limitless range of clinical presentations means there is no neat unitary hypothesis which can underlie the behaviour of all patients convicted of arson . . .' (1979: 344).

Vengeful and other arsonists

As will readily be seen, the sub-classifications made here are somewhat artificial and readers should bear in mind Cox's injunction above. If we accept the fact that a number of vengeful arsonists and pyromaniacs may commit their offences because they are confused about their identities and feel wronged or misunderstood, any attempts to help them to explore such alleged wrongs may be useful. Attempts can then be made to find ways in which they may achieve more satisfaction from their life's experiences. Since we know that many of them are socially inept, and that they set fires in order to draw attention to themselves, techniques aimed at improving their self-regard, self-image and social competence should help to minimise the risk of future offending. This might best be achieved by specific social skills training such as the development of legitimate forms of social assertiveness, since we know from the work of Jackson *et al.* and others that a number of arsonists have problems in asserting themselves in an acceptable manner. They suggest that 'factors which militate against alternative behaviours to arson may be equally as important to a thorough analysis of his pathological behaviour, as those factors which directly promote the use of fire' (Jackson *et al.*, 1987: 151). The serious 'assertion deficits' in arsonists have also been noted by Rice and Harris (1984).

The need for a multi-disciplinary and multi-causal approach is demonstrated very ably in a recent paper by Clare *et al.* (1992). The authors adopted a cognitive-behavioural approach to the management of a twenty-three-year-old man suffering from psychopathic disorder. He had been previously convicted of two charges of arson and spent four and a half years in a Special Hospital. At the time of the study he was resident in a specialist psychiatric facility catering for patients with learning disabilities and severe behavioural problems. Most patients in the unit stayed for about eighteen months. The patient was subjected to a very careful multi-disciplinary assessment. Sadly, he had been born with a harelip and a cleft palate. These had been badly repaired, leaving him speech-impaired. In addition, he suffered from a mild degree of mental impairment. He was unhappy about his appearance but had declined offers of surgery in the past. In his early teens he had begun to make hoax telephone calls to the fire brigade and followed this activity by two acts of arson. On the first occasion he had been placed under a supervision order; on the second he was made the subject of a hospital order with restrictions under the Mental Health Act. His therapists formulated a multi-faceted approach that would aim to enhance his social skills, improve his educational standard and offer a programme of desensitisation to impulses to engage in fire-raising conduct. (This was carried out by graded exposure over several months to holding matches.) He also agreed to undergo facial surgery and to accept plans for later operations to improve his speech. However, he was still considered to be vulnerable to engagement in fire-raising behaviour. Because of this, controlled situations were devised in which he was subjected to the arousal of negative feelings and stress. Over a long period of time he was taught coping mechanisms to deal with these. Eventually he was able to use these independently of his therapist's interventions. These were said to be especially useful in situations in which he felt put down or unwanted. He was able subsequently to undertake a part-time job (despite some lapses in attendance) and to develop a relationship with a girlfriend. During his stay in the facility no instances of hoax calls or fire-raising behaviour were said to have occurred, despite some acknowledged temptation to do so on the patient's part. At the time of last follow-up (some four years later) he was in full-time work, had formed a new, and apparently mutually happy, relationship with a young woman, had been conditionally discharged from his restriction order and was living in the open community. No further instances of fire-raising behaviour had been reported, though on two occasions, when under stress, he had felt tempted to offend in this way. The authors concluded that 'his recent success in forming an intimate relationship and in gaining paid employment, both of which will alleviate his social isolation, provide some cause for optimism that he will not engage in fire-setting again' (Clare *et al.*, 1992: 266).

CONCLUSION

Several important points emerge from this seminal piece of work, and can form the basis of my concluding remarks. First is the importance of careful assessment, if necessary, over a prolonged period. Second is the need to adopt a multi-causal approach to the problem presented by such offenders. This is likely to involve the willing collaboration of a range of professionals from a variety of disciplines. Third, such management is a time-consuming business, it requires patience and tenacity. Fourth, because of this, it is labour-intensive and costly. However, such expense needs to be set against the costs for all concerned in both human and economic terms of further instances of fire-raising.

NOTE

1   It is obvious that a number of these classifications will overlap. Despite this, they help to create some kind of order in what has always been (and still is) a confusing area.

REFERENCES

Abbot, G. (1991) *Lords of the Scaffold: A History of the Executioner*, London: Robert Hale.
American Psychiatric Association (1994) *Diagnostic and Statistical Manual of Mental Disorders*, DSM IV, Washington, DC: APA.
Barker, E. (1989) *New Religious Movements: A Practical Introduction*, London: HMSO.
Barnett, W. and Spitzer, M. (1994) 'Pathological Fire-Setting: 1951–1991 – A Review', *Medicine, Science and the Law* 34: 4–20.
Bronowski, J. (1976) *The Ascent of Man*, London, BBC.
Byrne, A. and Walsh, J.B. (1989) Letter, 'The Epileptic Arsonists', *British Journal of Psychiatry* 155: 268.
Carpenter, P.K. and King, A.L. (1989) 'Epilepsy and Arson', *British Journal of Psychiatry* 154: 554–556.
Clare, I.C.H., Murphy, D., Cox, D. and Chaplin, E.H. (1992) 'Assessment and Treatment of Fire-Setting: A Single Case Investigation Using a Cognitive-Behavioural Model', *Criminal Behaviour and Mental Health* 2: 253–268.
Cox, M. (1978) *Structuring the Therapeutic Process: Compromise with Chaos – The Therapist's Response to the Individual and the Group*, Oxford: Pergamon.
—— (1979) 'Dynamic Psychotherapy with Sex Offenders', in I. Rosen (ed.), *Sexual Deviation* (second edn), Oxford: Oxford University Press.
Douglas, M. (1984) *Purity and Danger: An Analysis of the Concepts of Pollution and Taboo*, London: Ark Books.
Faulk, M. (1988) *Basic Forensic Psychiatry*, Oxford: Blackwell Scientific Publications.
Foust, L.J. (1979) 'The Legal Significance of Clinical Formulations of Fire-Setting', *International Journal of Law and Psychiatry* 2: 371–387.
Fras, I. (1983) 'Fire-Setting (Pyromania) and Its Relationship to Sexuality', in L.B. Schlesinger and E. Revitch (eds), *Sexual Dynamics of Anti-Social Behaviour*, Springfield, Ill.: Charles C. Thomas.
Frazer, Sir J.G. (1987) *The Golden Bough: A Study in Magic and Religion* (abridged edn), London: Macmillan.
Geller, J.L. (1992) 'Pathological Fire-Setting in Adults', *International Journal of Law and Psychiatry* 15: 283–302.
Gower, G. (1992) *Arson: An Issue for Hostel Managers*, Chester: Cheshire Probation Service.
Hole, C. (1978) *A Dictionary of British Folk Customs*, London: Paladin.
Home Office (1980) *Report of a Working Party on Fires Caused by Vandalism*, London: Home Office.
Home Office (1990) *Home Office Research and Statistics Department: Fire Statistics, 1988, United Kingdom*, London: Home Office.
—— (1992) *Criminal Statistics, England and Wales, 1990*, Cmnd 1935, London: HMSO.
Hurley, W. and Monahan, T.M. (1969) 'Arson: The Criminal and the Crime', *British Journal of Criminology* 9: 4–21.
Jackson, H.F. (1994) 'Assessment of Fire-Setters', in M. McMurran and J. Hodge (eds), *The Assessment of Criminal Behaviour of Clients in Secure Settings*, London: Jessica Kingsley.

Jackson, H.F., Hope, S. and Glass, C. (1987) 'Why Are Arsonists Not Violent Offenders?', *International Journal of Offender Therapy and Comparative Criminology* 31: 143–151.

Macdonald, J.M. (1977) *Bombers and Firesetters*, Springfield, Ill.: Charles C. Thomas.

McKerracher, D.W. and Dacre, A.J.I. (1966) 'A Study of Arsonists in a Special Security Hospital', *British Journal of Psychiatry* 112: 1151–1154.

Prins, H. (1994) *Fire-Raising: Its Motivation and Management*, London: Routledge.

Prins, H., Tennent, G. and Trick, K. (1985) 'Motives for Arson (Fire-Setting)', *Medicine, Science and the Law* 25: 275–278.

Rice, M.E. and Harris, G.T. (1984) 'Mentally Disordered Fire-Setters: Psychodynamic versus Empirical Approaches', *International Journal of Law and Psychiatry* 7: 19–34.

Rix, K.B. (1994) 'A Psychiatric Study of Adult Arsonists', *Medicine, Science and the Law* 34: 21–34.

Scott, D. (1974) *Fire and Fire-Raisers*, London: Duckworth.

Soothill, K. (1990) 'Arson', in R. Bluglass and P. Bowden (eds), *Principles and Practice of Forensic Psychiatry*, London: Churchill Livingstone.

Thomas, K. (1984) *Religion and the Decline of Magic: Studies in Popular Beliefs in Sixteenth- and Seventeenth-Century England*, Harmondsworth: Penguin.

Topp, D.O. (1973) 'Fire as a Symbol and as a Weapon of Death', *Medicine, Science and the Law* 13: 79–86.

Virkunnen, M. (1974) 'On Arson Committed by Schizophrenics', *Acta Psychiatrica Scandinavica* 50: 152–154.

Woodward, C.D. (1987) 'Arson: The Major Fire Problem of the 1980s', *Journal of the Society of Fellows, The Chartered Insurance Institute, Pt.I.* 2: 55–68.

FURTHER READING

Arson Prevention Bureau (1993) *Arson Up-Date 1/93: Arson in Schools*, London: APB.

Barker, A. (1994) *Arson: A Review of the Psychiatric Literature*, Oxford: Oxford University Press.

Canter, D. (ed.) (1980) *Fires and Human Behaviour*, Chichester: John Wiley.

Cooke, R.A. and Ide, R.H. (1985) *Principles of Fire Investigation*, Leicester: Institution of Fire Engineers.

Prins, H. (1994) *Fire-Raising: Its Motivation and Management*, London: Routledge.

Wooden, W.S. and Berkey, M.L. (1984) *Children and Arson: America's Middle-Class Nightmare*, London: Plenum Press.

Chapter 8

Sexual behaviour and misbehaviour

> You shall not lie with a man as with a woman; that is an abomination. You shall not have sexual intercourse with any beast . . . nor shall a woman submit herself to intercourse with a beast; that is a violation of nature.
>
> (Leviticus 18: 23–24)

Some explanation is required for the title of this chapter. I chose it with some care since I wanted to make the point that the sexual misbehaviours deemed by the law to be offences must be seen in the context of attitudes towards sexuality in general; and that not all sexual 'misbehaviours' come within (or should come within) the purview of the criminal law. This latter point is particularly relevant at the present time, since, as I draft this chapter, there is heated debate as to the appropriate age of consent for homosexual behaviour between males. Most groups of professionals involved consider that what is good for young women is good for young men. They have put forward quite powerful arguments for rationalisation, and these are based largely on sound medical and physiological evidence.[1] Against such views are the voices of those whose beliefs are more motivated by the kind of fears and injunctions about sexuality that have been with us since the dawn of humankind, as evidenced in part by the quotation at the beginning of this chapter. Indeed, all the great religions of the world indicate varying degrees of proscription against sexual activity. These divergences of views are powerful and important and must have a profound bearing upon the attitudes of those who work with individuals whose sexual behaviours are deemed to have infringed the criminal law.

The chapter is divided into the following sections. First, I provide a brief context-setting background. The second and third sections are concerned with two classifications of sexual offences (clinical and legal). In the fourth section I comment briefly on the size of the problem. The major section which follows is devoted to a discussion of some of the more serious sexual offences and brief comment is made on some rarer sexual misbehaviours that sometimes come within the purview of the law.

BACKGROUND AND CONTEXT

Sexual behaviour depends for its expression upon a number of factors: biological (hormonal influences), social, familial and environmental. In the human species, although hormonal and other influences have always been considered to be important, there are some who consider that this importance is increasing. (MacCulloch and Waddington, 1981; Goodman, 1983). However, others have recently expressed caution in placing too much emphasis upon such factors (Abracen *et al.* 1991; Baron, 1993). The truth is likely to lie somewhere between these opposing points of view. (A useful social-psychological perspective embracing some of these divergencies has recently been provided by Breakwell, 1994.) A former student and colleague of mine has aptly stated that

> Sexual behaviour in humans does not necessarily conform to any single pattern. People differ in the type as well as the frequency of preferred sexual activity. The attitudes that different cultures have towards types of sexual behaviour differ as do the attitudes of the same society over a period of time. . . . Sexual preference is varied, not only with regard to the physical or other attributes of the partner one chooses, but also the type of sexual activity engaged in.
>
> (Kaul, 1993: 207; see also Prins, 1991)

These variations are reflected in the criminal law and the manner in which it penalises some behaviours and not others. As we shall see, not all sexual deviations constitute criminal behaviour, so that 'all sexual deviations are not sexual offences and certainly all sexual offences are not sexual deviations' (Kaul, 1993: 207).

There are a number of other points to be made by way of introduction. First, from what has already been said, it is clear that sexual behaviour is an emotive topic. Attitudes towards the physical expression of sexuality – *even amongst some professionals* – are still sometimes based upon a degree of ignorance and anxiety. Although there is a great deal more talk about, and open portrayal of, sexual activity than in the past, it is by no means certain that such public acknowledgement has done all that much to remove anxieties and inhibitions. Recent concerns about HIV infection and AIDS have revived fears and taboos about sexual activity – and are certainly reminiscent of those that used to be prevalent in discussions of sexually transmitted diseases such as syphilis and gonorrhoea. Such taboos probably also have their origins in a fact that is perhaps not remembered as often as it should be – namely that the sexual (and procreative organs) are also those used for, or associated with, the elimination of bodily wastes – hence the importance attached by Freud and his followers to this anatomical conjunction.

Second, we should note that sexual *attractiveness* is often at the heart (either implicitly or explicitly) of much media advertising. The promotion of sexual prowess and attractiveness as highly desirable attributes may, in fact, only serve to make people more concerned about their sexual *performance* than about sexual expression as part of caring adult relationships – be they hetero- or homosexual.

Third, changes in our attitudes to women, in what is still a highly male-dominated society, are of great importance. With a degree of ignorance and prejudice we continue to place women in a very ambiguous position. In his memoirs, Hadrian provided a timely recognition of this many centuries ago:

> The condition of women is fixed by strange customs: they are at one and the same time subjected and protected, too much despised and too much respected. In the chaos of contradictory usage, the practices of society are superimposed upon the facts of nature, but it is not easy to distinguish the two.
>
> (Hadrian, 1955: 105)

Fourth, we should note some changes in our references to sexual behaviours and misbehaviours. We no longer use needless euphemisms for certain forms of sexual activity. In my youth, buggery (anal sex) was never referred to as such; instead a certain well-known Sunday newspaper, which carried detailed accounts of sex offence trials, always referred to such activities as 'serious or un-natural offences'. In similar terms, oral sex activity (fellatio and cunnilingus) was never referred to publicly; now it is commonplace, both in court reports and in publicity about HIV infection and AIDS. Such practices are now much more openly acknowledged in the light of more liberated views about the legitimacy of a variety of forms of sexual expression (see Ferris, 1993). However, the law still seems capricious in this matter. This was evidenced recently by the well-known 'Operation Spanner' case in which a group of adult sexual sado-masochists were prosecuted, convicted and sentenced to imprisonment for engaging in mutually consenting private activity in which various injuries were inflicted on their genitalia. Their pleas that their activities as adult consenting males were in private (and that no serious injuries were caused) were rejected both at trial and upon appeal. The law continues to hold that when such behaviour occurs among several people it is to that extent public, and, more importantly, that the law should protect people in certain circumstances from their own consenting activities. Such propositions are not really tenable with any great degree of certainty in today's more liberal climate. The defendants' cases are likely to be argued before the European Court of Human Rights. (For a short but informative discussion of sado-masochistic practices, see Storr, 1990.) The matter of consent in relation to sexual activity is, as has already been pointed out, a current topic of concern. Maybe what we require are not so much laws that deal with consent, but more rational laws that deal with the protection of those judged to be either minors or vulnerable in other ways (Brongersma, 1988). Fifth, any discussion of sexual deviation (and particularly that also judged to be criminal) must take into account the notion that sexual feelings and expression are not as dichotomous as some people imagine; we all have physical and emotional elements of the opposite sex within us – some more than others. In this respect, it is important to be sure that when we talk about overt sexuality we try to be clear about physically endowed sex and what might be called gender sex (what we feel about our own sexuality) (see Wolff, 1977; Hamilton and Walker, 1975). Bancroft states:

We tend to take our gender for granted: 'Of course you are male if you have a penis.' Usually we can afford to do so, but the processes leading to the ascription of gender identity are so complex it is little wonder they occasionally go wrong.

(1989: 153)

Bancroft also suggests that

gender can be manifested in at least seven different ways:

(1) Chromosomes;
(2) Gonads;
(3) Hormones;
(4) Internal sexual organs;
(5) External genitalia and secondary sexual characteristics;
(6) The gender assigned at birth ('it's a boy');
(7) Gender identity ('I am a girl').

(ibid.; see also Bancroft, 1991)

The complex web of factors that to go determine sexual offending behaviour has been well reviewed by Lanyon (1991).

Having made the above points, should we question to what extent we can make any useful distinctions between so-called 'normality' and deviation in relation to sexual behaviour? I think the answer has to be a carefully qualified 'yes'. This is because, as we have already seen, any distinctions will have to be culture-bound; they may change over time and can therefore only be seen as broad generalisations. They will also be dependent upon different aesthetic preferences. Perhaps I can best put it this way. Non-criminal sexual behaviour encompasses those forms of sexual activity between two adults (and the age of adulthood may vary over historical time) which are acceptable to both parties, do not involve coercion, exploitation or degradation, and do not affront the notions of public decency prevailing at the time.

Finally, it is important to avoid the kind of stereotyping of the sex offender common amongst the general public. Rarely does he conform to the graphic caricature deliberately provided by Cohan and Boucher as 'brutal and depraved, immoral and oversexed, a social isolate who spends his time haunting dirty movies, a godless, brainless fellow, a dirty old man, crippled or disfigured, dope addicted and incurable' (1972: 56). But, as Crawford suggests in the paper that contains this quotation, neither is he likely to be 'a well-adjusted family man, happily married with a satisfactory sex life, who has a responsible and enjoyable job, leads an active social life and rapes women' (1979: 151; see also Cowburn, 1990).

I now turn to the next two sections of this chapter – a clinical and a legal classification. It is important to remember that there is no universal agreement about clinical classification (see, for example, Grubin and Kennedy, 1989; Briggs, 1994) and, as already indicated in this chapter, and elsewhere in this book, conceptions of what should be regarded as moral and what should be regarded as unlawful change over time.

CLINICAL CLASSIFICATION

The following is a classification which derives from several sources (see, for example, Scott, 1964; Prins, 1991).

1 Sexual activity not requiring a human partner – for example, the use of animals (bestiality, zoophilia, zooerasty) or objects (fetishism).
2 Sexual activity not requiring a *willing* partner – for example, rape (hetero- and homosexual), voyeurism ('Peeping Tom' activities), exhibitionism (indecent exposure), necrophilia. These categories link very closely with those in (3) below.
3 Sexual activity under *unusual* conditions – and here, matters of consent may be all important and continue to occupy a grey area. Some examples are: sexual activity with the elderly (gerontophilia [see Kaul and Duffy, 1991]); sexual activity with children of both sexes (paedophilia); consanguinous sexual activity (incest); sexual activity requiring excessive punishment or suffering (sado-masochistic activities); non-self-induced sexual asphyxia (eroticised hanging), which sometimes results in death.
4 Certain other sexually motivated activities which may present in *masked* form. For example, some types of stealing (underclothes or similar garments from clothes-lines); some forms of fire-raising (see Chapter 7); sexual gratification from the sight of, or contact with, bodily secretions; blood (vampirism), excrement (coprophilia), or urine (urolagnia).

It will be obvious that many of these activities will overlap and that the para-philias (to give them their generic title) cover a very wide range of behaviours. Perkins (1991), in a recent review of classification, suggests the following:

1 *Compensatory* – as a result of social/sexual relationship problems.
2 *Displaced aggression* – motivated by anger or hatred. Here the concentration is upon degrading or defiling the victim and the use of more force than is necessary to overpower the victim. Particular victims may be sought out, for example, prostitutes.
3 *Sadistic* – use of more violence than is necessary, as in (2), but it is also cold and deliberate. Sexual gratification is derived from the infliction of pain and from the fear shown by the victim.
4 *Impulsive/opportunistic* – such offenders have histories of various forms of anti-social behaviour. Obtaining sex by force is just another aspect of this life-style.

LEGAL CLASSIFICATION [2]

There are areas of overlap and the choice of offences to be included is, to some extent, idiosyncratic: rape and attempts; indecent assault (on females and males);

buggery and attempts (on males and females); unlawful sexual intercourse with females under age; procuration for sexual purposes; abduction; indecency with children; gross indecency; indecent exposure; bestiality; soliciting for prostitution; importuning; trading in, or possession of, obscene publications; use of children for pornographic purposes (for example, in order to make films, videos, or to take still photographs); making obscene phone calls; interference with a cadaver; homicide committed for purposes of sexual gratification; conspiracy to corrupt public morals. To this list we would add some less obvious 'sexual' crimes where an apparently non-sexual offence may be sexually motivated. Examples would be some forms of larceny (stealing women's underclothing from clothes-lines); 'proving' offences, such as taking motor-cycles without the owners' consent; certain forms of burglarious activity (where the goods stolen may have sexual connotations, for example shoes belonging to the female occupier of the premises), or where the behaviour of the burglar appears unusual (for example, slashing bed-sheets with a knife).

It is worth noting that, contrary to general assumption, the more serious sexual offences are almost always punished by immediate imprisonment. This is particularly noticeable in rape cases (see Lloyd and Walmsley, 1989). Where sentences for sexual offences have been regarded as too lenient, the Court of Appeal has not been reluctant to increase them.

Finally, it is important to observe that the legal classification of sexual offences (see below) does not necessarily describe the severity or importance of the offence to the victim. For example, an indecent assault may be as severe to the victim as an attempted rape; and the decision to charge for one or other offence may be fairly arbitrary. As we shall see shortly, the offence of indecent exposure (often regarded quite lightly by some males) can have a marked and traumatic effect upon some victims.

THE SIZE OF THE PROBLEM

Sexual offences constitute a very small proportion of all crimes, something in the order of 2 per cent of all recorded offences and about 1.75 per cent of all persons found guilty of indictable offences. There is also a considerable discrepancy between the numbers of sexual offences *known to the police* and the number actually *dealt with or prosecuted*. Reasons for this are not hard to find. Victims (and witnesses) may be reluctant to come forward, and corroboration may thus prove problematic. In addition, consenting parties may be reluctant to admit to having engaged in unlawful sexual activity (see earlier discussion). It may, therefore, be difficult to prove that an offence has occurred. In addition, many more sexual offences are committed *than are ever reported to the police*. There may be reluctance to admit involvement or fear of blackmail. In some cases (rape, for example) the victim may not wish to suffer the embarrassment and trauma of medical and police inquiries, followed by a public court appearance which could involve rigorous examination of both fact and reputation. Parents and other guardians of sexually assaulted children may wish to spare them a similar experience, though the increasing use of video-taped interviews may go some way to alleviate this problem. There is also evidence to suggest that many males who have been subjected to serious sexual assault (such as buggery) are very reluctant to report the offence because of the sense of defilement and humiliation they feel, much like their female counterparts (Mezey and King, 1987, 1989). The number of offenders found guilty at all courts or cautioned for more serious sexual offences, for the years 1985–90, is shown in Table 8.1.

Table 8.1 Offenders found guilty at all courts or cautioned for the more serious sexual offences, 1985–1990

	1985	1986	1987	1988	1989	1990
Buggery	281	301	332	412	335	336
Indecent assault on a male	770	656	685	736	713	831
Indecency between males	826	831	1,106	1,496	1,718	1,298
Rape	450	415	453	540	613	561
Indecent assault on a female	3,316	3,127	3,529	3,961	4,119	3,990
Unlawful sexual intercourse with a girl under 13	168	162	175	214	179	182
Unlawful sexual intercourse with a girl under 16	1,550	1,426	1,479	1,555	1,384	1,288
Incest	149	211	244	245	200	181
Procuration	509	347	378	479	520	444
Abduction	23	29	23	26	30	26
Gross indecency with a child	328	291	332	334	297	370

Note: There are some annual fluctuations, but the figures show a steady increase for most offences.
Source: Home Office 1992a: 122

Most sexual offences are committed by males; a review of the *Criminal Statistics* for the years 1975–84 made by O'Connor (1987) indicated that only 0.95 per cent of all sex offences were committed by women. O'Connor made a detailed study of nineteen women convicted of indecency and sixty-two convicted of other sexual offences. He found a high incidence of mental illness, mental handicap and alcohol problems. Two of the group were convicted of indecent exposure under local public order statutes. A sizeable proportion were convicted of gross indecency and sexual assaults on children, or aiding and abetting such assaults. There are indications that an increasing number of women are becoming involved in sexually abusive acts towards children (see, for example, Hunt, 1990; Banning, 1989).

SEXUAL OFFENCES

Having considered briefly the size of the problem I now propose to examine certain sexual offences in more detail. There are obvious difficulties in singling out specific categories: an offender not infrequently commits more than one type of sexual offence and some of the categories will overlap. For example, rape may end in homicide, either because the killing was planned as part of, or sequel to, the rape, or the victim may have died as a result of the attack. Death may also have resulted in the assailant's wish to silence the victim to avoid subsequent identification. It is therefore important to remember that *every case is different* and great care should be taken before reaching any generalised conclusions. Despite this caveat, it seems helpful to divide the categories of sexual offences in a fairly crude way. I deal first with *indecent exposure*; second, with *sexual offences against children and young persons and incest*. I include incest with more general sexual offences against children and young persons because incestuous behaviour (particularly with young victims) may be regarded as a highly specific form of serious sexual assault. Third, I deal with *rape*, and finally with certain aspects of *sexual homicide and other more rare offences, such as necrophilia and bestiality*.

Indecent exposure

> And up to the windowe dide he hastily,
> And out his ers he putteth prively
> Over the buttok, to the haunche-bon.
> (Chaucer, *The Miller's Tale*)

Indecent exposure is the commonest of all the sexual offences, though the number of prosecutions is but a minute proportion of its actual incidence. In 1990, 966 males were found guilty of the offence; 24 aged between 14 and 17; 132 aged between 17 and 21; and 810, 21 and over (Home Office, 1992b: 24).

Custodial penalties are rarely imposed and most offenders have been dealt with in the past by fines or probation. As we shall see, it is exclusively a male offence, though doubtless the very small number of women who expose themselves are occasionally prosecuted for breach of the peace or a similar public decency offence. Throughout history, the display and emphasis of the male genitalia and surrounding areas have been commonly recorded in art, history and literature – as, for example, in the quotation at the head of this section. In more modern times, we have seen instances of both male and female 'streaking' and the exhibiting of naked posteriors by young males in cars ('mooning'), though these behaviours do not constitute indecent exposure as currently defined in law. It would appear that the latter did not begin to concern itself specifically with indecent exposure until the Victorian era, though Rooth (1975) managed to find some court cases occurring in earlier times; the most notable of these would seem to be that of Sir Charles Sedley, who exposed himself and urinated over a crowd at Covent Garden (see also Gayford, 1981; Snaith and Bennett, 1990). Currently, the offence is dealt with under the terms of the Vagrancy Act 1824. Section 4 of the Act states that it is an offence 'for a person to wilfully, openly, lewdly and obscenely, expose his person with intent to insult any female'. The offence is punishable by a maximum sentence of three months' imprisonment or a fine of £400. On second conviction it is possible for the offender to be committed to the Crown Court as 'an incorrigible rogue and vagabond' – where a maximum sentence of twelve months may be imposed. Later enactments and High Court rulings have defined 'his person' to mean penis, and the act may be subject to prosecution even if it occurs on private property. Other means of dealing with indecent exposure are the Town Police Clauses Act of 1847 and various bylaws. It is also possible for an act of indecent exposure to be deemed to be an outrage on public decency at common law. The common law would seem to cover acts of exposure by females, so, as Snaith and Bennett (1990: 675) suggest, whatever the good Lady Godiva's motives may have been she could have been liable to prosecution! As already indicated, the offence of indecent exposure by males is not often reported. In surveys carried out in England by Gittleson *et al.* (1978) and by Cox and McMahon in the USA (1978), over 80 per cent of the victims did not report the matter to the police.

Clinical considerations

Most victims are adult females or children of either sex. (I am excluding acts of exposure in the course of male soliciting.) Sometimes the exposer will merely expose himself, usually with a flaccid penis and at some distance from the victim(s). This seems to be the commonest form; the behaviour is compulsive and highly recidivistic. For this reason, the number of instances actually prosecuted in court in respect of an individual offender may merely be the tip of the iceberg. Although the experience can be very traumatic for the victim, such exposers do not normally go on to commit more serious sexual crimes. (For one such account of the unpleasantness of the experience see Lindsey, 1994.) However, if the exposure is to adult women accompanied by threats or gestures of an aggressive kind, and takes place with an erect penis and the exposer masturbates, then the chances are that such behaviour may be a prelude to more serious sexual offending at a later date (see Bluglass, 1980 and Sugarman *et al.* (1994)). Masters, in his book about the serial killer Jeffrey Dahmer, suggests that had the latter's repeated acts of indecent exposure been spotted and dealt with early enough, his progression to more serious sexual offending might have been halted:

> He did not consider the feelings or susceptibilities of the people who were made props in this experiment; to him they were already as objects.
>
> (Masters, 1993: 70–71)

Masters also makes the interesting point that Dahmer engaged in *frotteurism* (the pressing of one's groin or genital area against a stranger in a public place, such as a crowded train or bus). Like indecent exposure, it represents, as he says, 'a wish for sensuality without involvement' (ibid.).

Various attempts have been made to classify the behaviour and personality types of indecent exposers – with varying degrees of success (see, for example, MacDonald, 1973; Rooth, 1975; and Snaith and Bennett, 1990). Readers may find the following rough classification helpful:

1 The inhibited (and possibly latently homosexual) young man who struggles against his impulses to expose himself. He usually exposes with a flaccid penis and feels anxious about his behaviour. When such behaviour occurs in adolescence against a family background of prudery or reticence in discussing sexual matters, sex education and counselling will be helpful. This kind of behaviour might be regarded as a form of love-making at a safe distance.

2 Situational exposure. Here, the exposure may take place against a background of marital or similar stress. Counselling is also likely to be helpful in these cases.

3 The less inhibited type – described earlier – who exposes with an erect penis and may masturbate at the same time. Intervention in such cases may prevent progression to more serious sex offending. For this reason it is very important for the professionals involved to ascertain the circumstances of the exposure in as much *detail* as possible.

4 Exposure that occurs in a setting of clear mental illness, such as depression, hypomania, schizophrenia or dementia. Medical intervention will, of course, be necessary in such cases.

5 Exposure committed by the mentally impaired. In these cases, the exposure is most likely to be due to lack of social skills and against a background of a mounting need for sexual expression. Counselling in such cases can also be helpful. It is a mistake to assume that even quite severely mentally impaired people cannot be helped by counselling, provided it is tailored to their particular levels of need and understanding.

6 Cases in which the exposure is facilitated by substance abuse, such as alcohol, reactive depression or loneliness. Such exposers may persist with their behaviour. (For a sensitive biographical account see Parker, 1970.)

7 A group who may be regarded as true exhibitionists; these individuals practise exposure as the sole means of obtaining sexual release (MacClay, 1952).

8 The 'neurotic' exhibitionist. Pollock (1960) has described a case in which a man's indecent exposing came to light quite by chance while he was serving a prison sentence for an entirely different offence. The man had fought for years to combat his compulsive tendency, which seemed to Pollock to have its origins in a complex and fraught relationship with his mother.

The classification given above provides clues to aetiology. Additional explanations include a need to assert a wavering or undeveloped masculinity. In some cases, such as those in group (3) above, there may be a need to assert power over, or to insult or shock, women; the exposure may be a suppressed desire to commit rape. It is also important to remember that indecent exposure may not always be an exclusively erotic act. Treatment has already been touched upon. Counselling of various kinds will be the treatment of choice; this may take the form of simple sex education and the development of social skills (in how to approach women comfortably). In some cases, behavioural forms of treatment such as teaching self-control, on either an individual or a group basis, have been said to have some degree of success (Snaith and Bennett, 1990). As with all sex offenders, the communication of genuine interest and warmth on the part of the therapist and a degree of 'unshockability' are more important than the particular school of thought or mode of practice espoused. In addition, sex offenders require to be worked with over long periods of time (Kaul, 1993).

Sexual assaults on children

Child molestation and paedophilia

In this first sub-section, I am concerned with sexual assaults on children by persons outside the family. Child sex abuse committed by parents is the subject of the sub-section which follows. The latter is a major topic in its own right and readers are also referred to some of the specialist literature cited under Further Reading. It is fair to state that a number of the characteristics shown by those who molest children outside the family situation are very similar to those who do so within it however. For example, men who commit incest with their young children have a number of characteristics in common with those who sexually assault children outside the family.

Sex offences against children have been widely prevalent throughout history. Molesters of children have spanned the entire age and social spectrum – from the notorious fifteenth-century Marshal of France, Gilles de Rais, to the most lowly itinerant. It seems highly likely that sexual assaults on children (within and outside the family) have been, and are, much more common than most of us have supposed. It has been suggested that Freud probably needed to revise his original theory about the origins of sexual neurosis in females (namely that such patients had *actually* been the subject of sexual assaults by close family members) because, in the climate in which he lived, he could not face the professional opprobrium, preferring to describe the events as being of hysterical origin (Masson, 1985). But he was also aware of the dangers of patients reinterpreting the past events in a sinister light – *nachträglicht*. For example, they might be encouraged by their therapists to recall events that had not in fact taken place – false memories; a topic of much current debate.

Non-platonic love of children is as old as civilisation itself and there are those who assert that there should be more opportunity afforded to individuals who wish to form sexual relationships with children. (For some controversial comments on this aspect, see Brongersma, 1988.) However, most thinking people are well aware that such relationships may become warped, self-indulgent and destructive. Sadly, those often placed in positions of trust (parents, family friends, teachers, clergy, social workers, nurses and doctors) abuse it. Some have themselves been the victims of seduction in their own childhood.

Despite asseverations to the contrary, there is good evidence to suggest that the physical and emotional trauma that may be caused as a result of sudden, unexpected and coercive sexual relationships with children is considerable (see for example, Paul, 1990; Glasser, 1990; Mullen, 1990; Dare, 1993; Beitchman *et al.*, 1992). The most significant determinants of trauma would appear to be (a) the victim's previous and current social and psychological environment; (b) the anxiety caused by being forced to keep a 'guilty' secret (particularly in incest cases); (c) the opportunities (or lack of them) for off-loading this guilt; (d) the nature of the pre-existing or current relationship with the assailant and avenues of 'escape' from it, if any; (e) reactions of those having the care of the victim; these reactions are probably as important in determining later guilt or trauma as any of the foregoing factors. In recent years, increasing attention has been paid by professionals and researchers to the need to try to assess more specifically the effects of early childhood sexual abuse upon later development (for recent examples, see Jehu, 1988; Finkelhor *et al.*, 1989; Sparr, 1989).

It is very unwise to attempt mutually exclusive classifications, but it is usually recognised that there are differences between *homosexual* and *heterosexual* paedophiles, though such individuals may assault victims of both sexes. Bluglass (1982) suggests that *homosexual* paedophiles are more likely to have had past involvement with children, to prefer them as sexual partners and show deviant patterns of sexual arousal. *Heterosexual* paedophiles are more likely to be situationally motivated, to prefer adult women, and to seek a child because of social and environmental stresses. A further crude form of classification is to divide paedophiles into (a) young and (b) adult offenders. Young offenders may be divided into two rough sub-categories: (i) bisexual (as distinct from homosexual) inadequate adolescents who bribe young children to engage in deviant sexual practices; (ii) rather more dangerous adolescent offenders who have a history of being sexually abused themselves and who have shown sexually inappropriate behaviour from an early age (see Bagley, 1992). The latter may go on to become highly sexually deviant adults (Longo and Groth, 1983). Adult offenders may be divided roughly into the following sub-categories. (i) Middle-aged heterosexual paedophiles, socially isolated and incompetent, seeking the company of small girls for comfort. (ii) Senile or pre-senile homosexual paedophiles, whose sexual preferences are by no means dulled by age, even though their sexual capacity may be. *It is extremely unwise to think that as these people become older they necessarily become potentially less dangerous.* They may, in fact, become more easily frustrated and feel less in command (powerful). Any feeling that their young victims (or would-be victims) are humiliating or rebuffing them may serve as a reminder of their waning powers. In frustration they may resort to violent means to achieve their ends. (iii) Paedophiles of impaired intelligence. Social ineptitude and lack of 'moral' sense may contribute to their offending. (iv) A group described as multi-anti-social. These men are lacking in general social conformity and have mixed patterns of offending. (v) Exclusively homosexual paedophiles (sometimes referred to as pederasts). Such offenders can exert a powerful and coercive influence over their victims, often see themselves as the 'protectors' of disadvantaged youth and are highly resistant to treatment attempts. More generally, it is very important to distinguish between those who use force as a means of gaining co-operation in the act and those offenders for whom the infliction of pain and terror is an end in itself (Crawford, 1982).

A fairly recent refined classification has been provided by Knight *et al.* (1989). They postulate six types of sex offence behaviour against children – as follows:

- *Type 1: Interpersonal* – the offender has shown interest in the child in a way in which he feels the relationship has some mutually satisfying elements. Sexual contacts are of a very limited kind.
- *Type 2: Narcissistic* – the interest in the child is more self-centred and the primary aim is to achieve a degree of sexual gratification.
- *Type 3: Exploitative, non-sadistic* – no more aggression is used than necessary to secure the victim's compliance. In other words, the inducement of fear is not for sexual gratification.
- *Type 4: Muted-sadistic behaviour* – behaviour that shows the use of sadistic fantasies or their behavioural evidence, such as non-aggressive insertion of foreign objects into the victim, or acts of buggery.
- *Type 5: Non-sadistic-aggressive* – the behaviour is motivated by anger, but not eroticised anger, or the injury to the victim is caused by an accident during the sexual encounter.
- *Type 6: Sadistic* – the key characteristic in such cases is sexual arousal on the part of the offender as a result of placing the victim in pain or fear.

There will, of course, be areas of overlap between the above categories, but they do appear to provide a useful framework that could help to determine the most effective management.

Management

Although it is a recurring truism that every case will be different, it seems possible to make some observations about management which have general applicability. In my view, the first and perhaps most important point to make is that one should not talk of 'curing' sexual offenders. This is because most available evidence supports the view that sexual preferences are laid down very early in life and are hard to change. The problem is exacerbated because we have, as yet, only a hazy picture of the respective contributions made by morphology, genetics and wider familial and environmental influences. It is more realistic to talk about management or attitude change, whether this be brought about by intensive individual or group psychotherapy of different schools, by powerful behavioural techniques of one kind or another that aim to produce gradual change in sexual orientation, or by limited and careful use of chemotherapeutic methods (as to the latter, see, for example, Clarke, 1989). Whichever technique is used, it is best to avoid thinking of 'cure' and to concentrate upon helping sex offenders make more satisfactory adjustments to their behaviour and its consequences (see Cook *et al.*, 1991; Adshead and Mezey, 1993). No *single* method of management is likely to be successful; it is best to espouse a multi-method approach (for example, chemotherapy is more successful when allied to counselling). It is best not to think globally about sexual offence behaviour but to try to break the behaviour down into manageable segments and typologies. But perhaps of most importance is the need to remember that all persistent sex offenders (and some less persistent ones) are *highly reluctant to admit to their role in sexual offending and will persistently use evasion and denial* (see Wiest, 1981; Murphy, 1990; McGrath, 1991).

This phenomenon of denial is a most important one in dealing with such offenders. Mezey *et al.* (1991) suggest that there are six aspects of denial: (a) denial of the act itself; (b) denial of the child as a person; (c) denial of the child as a victim; (d) denial of adult responsibility; (e) denial of consequences for the child; and (f) denial of consequences for the offender (see also McGrath, 1991; Jackson and Thomas-Peter, 1994). Denial may, of course, hold a very prominent place in the mind of the sexual offender sentenced to imprisonment; fear of reprisal from fellow inmates will be uppermost in mind. Although attempts have been made to introduce special 'treatment' centres in a small number of selected prisons, their success has yet to be assessed (see Clark, 1993; Briggs, 1994).

One method that has been used to supplement an offender's own account of his sexual preferences and practices is that of phallometric assessment. This involves the measurement of erectile tumescence by a guage attached to the penis. The offender is then shown a variety of arousing situations by means of videos or audio tapes and the degree to which he continues to be aroused when aversive stimuli are introduced or suggested can thus be measured. Such testing is by no means fool-proof, since it has been shown that offenders can 'fake' their responses. However, such measures may prove useful as adjuncts to reliance upon self-reports and the observations of professionals such as nurses. (For brief reviews of the 'state of the art', see Quinsey, 1988; Launay, 1994.)

Incest

> No man shall approach a blood relation for intercourse.
>
> (Leviticus, 18: 6)

Incest is the sexual crime that probably provokes the most emotive reaction. In general, taboos have existed against its practice from time immemorial, although history reveals some notable exceptions (for example, in the cultures of ancient Egypt, Greece and Japan). Mythology and literature are replete with allusions to incestuous conduct or to incestuous themes.[3] There are, of course, many reasons for the strict prohibitions against incestuous behaviour. First, there are the religious injunctions, more particularly in the Old Testament (as above). Second, there appears to be a deeply held and primitive horror of consanguinous sexual relationships between parents and their offspring. Third, there is the Freudian belief (stemming from Darwin's theory of the primal horde) that suggests that in primitive societies the incest taboo was erected to preserve the power of the paternal tyrant in order that he might prevent the younger males from banding together to deprive him of his sexual rights over the females. Fourth, taboos are said to be strong because of the serious role confusion that can occur when close kin have sexual relationships. Finally, there is evidence that incestuous relationships may produce a higher incidence of genetic weakness than those found in normal sexual unions (Cooper and Cormier, 1990). However, it seems more likely it is the *combination* of poor ante-natal care, poor nurturing, environment *and* the incestuous relationships that occur in socially disordered families that produces these results rather than genetic transmission alone.

Incest did not become a specific criminal offence until 1908, and the present law is now incorporated into the Sexual Offences Act 1956 and the Criminal Law Act 1977.[4] Simply put, the law states that a man who has sexual intercourse with a woman he *knows* to be his granddaughter, daughter, sister or mother is guilty of incest, as is a woman of or above the age of sixteen who, with consent, permits her grandfather, father, brother or son to have sexual intercourse with her. It is also an offence to incite a girl under the age of sixteen to have incestuous sexual intercourse. Incest is punishable with a maximum sentence of imprisonment for seven years; in the case of the offence being committed against a girl under thirteen, it is punishable with imprisonment for life. Although a number of cases come to the attention of the police (see Table 8.1), comparatively few are prosecuted. Generally, a veil of extreme secrecy is preserved within the family. Not infrequently, the case may only come to light because of pregnancy, because of an attempt at blackmail, through the investigation of some non-related offence behaviour, or as a result of a confession by one of the parties.

The most outstanding characteristic in the background of a large proportion of incestuous families is that of social and emotional disorder. Lukianowicz (1972), in his classic study, found a 4 per cent incidence of incest amongst an unselected group of psychiatric patients in Northern Ireland. Hall Williams (1974) found a high incidence of mental impairment and previous criminal convictions, and Virkunnen (1974) found alcohol to be heavily associated with the offence. Most frequently the victim is likely to be the man's own child or children (Maisch, 1973; Hall Williams, 1974). Gibbens *et al.* (1978) made a comparative study of *sibling* and *parent–child* incest cases. Sixty-one per cent of the fathers were first offenders, and 12 per cent had subsequent convictions; some 13 per cent of these fathers had prior sexual offences. Seventy-two per cent of the parent incest cases were over forty at the time of the offence and 90 per cent of them sent to prison. Of the sibling offenders, 60 per cent were aged twenty or less; 54 per cent of them had previous findings of guilt or convictions, but few were for sexual offences. However, over the next twelve years, they continued to be heavily convicted: 49 per cent for property offences and 14 per cent for violence. In indicating possible reasons for these different profiles, the authors make three suggestions. First, incest behaviour may come to light more readily where the family is already under surveillance by social workers. Second, sibling incest may well be more common in large, overcrowded families where a high rate of ordinary criminal behaviour is common. Third, their sample may have comprised a group of young recidivists who continued offending wholly or partly because of sexual mal-adjustment which was not always revealed in *convictions* for sexual offences. (See also earlier discussion of 'masked' sexual offences.)

It is not hard to see that family composition and life-style are likely to be significant in creating conditions for the occurrence of incestuous behaviour. These conditions may be classified broadly as follows:

1 Incest occurring in large, overcrowded families, where the participants almost slip into an incestuous pattern of behaviour (see also Batten, 1983).
2 Very rarely, incestuous relations develop because of intellectual impairment or psychotic illness in either or both of the parties.
3 Cases where the wife is either absent through death or separation and where the daughter(s) may take over the wife's role. It may also occur in cases where the wife is still physically present but where she has abrogated her sexual role. In such cases she is sometimes not only quite aware of what is occurring but also prepared to collude in the practice.
4 Cases in which the father is a dominant individual who uses threats or violence to get his way in the full knowledge that such behaviour is wrong. Such men may also engage in alcohol abuse.
5 Occasional instances where the parties do not know that they are in a consanguinous relationship. For example, a brother and sister who have been separated from each other very early in life may meet much later and unknowingly enter into a sexual relationship.[5]

6   Cases of 'object fixation incest'. Bagley (1969) suggests that incest may occur in those instances where the dominant partner was sexually fixated on an earlier object of sexual gratification, a child or an adolescent with whom he had his first sexual experience when he was a child himself.

Management considerations

In work with incest cases, it is important to have come to terms with one's own incest anxieties and fears. The courts, on the whole, deal severely with adult males convicted of incest with their children. Sometimes, one wonders whether more harm than good is done by the additional stress created for the family by sentencing the father to a very long term in prison. However, the welfare of the children has to be protected, particularly in those cases where multiple incestuous relationships have occurred. These days, precautions are now taken by both the probation service and the local authority social services departments in all cases where children have been, or are likely to be, the subject of injury or attack from whatever cause. In view of this, some have argued for the removal of the crime of incest from the statute book because it would still be possible to take the necessary prosecutory and precautionary steps under existing sex offence legislation. In this way, the special abhorrence with which the offence is viewed might be diminished to some extent. It could then be seen for what it really is, an offence connected with adverse family attitudes and living conditions, calling for social and other intervention rather than punitive wrath borne of irrational feelings.

In addition, the global use of the term incest means that we link together all its variants and treat them all alike. In order to offer more effective treatment we need to discriminate more carefully. The courts are now being encouraged to take a more flexible approach to sentencing and to take into account some of these varying conditions. In the case of a man who had been awarded an eighteen month suspended prison sentence, the Court of Appeal (Criminal Division) refused leave to the Attorney-General to *increase* the sentence on the grounds that it was too lenient (Criminal Justice Act 1988, Section 36), and substituted a three-year probation order with conditions as to residence and counselling instead (see *Independent* Law Report, 17 November 1989: 19; and general guidelines given in Attorney-General's Reference No.1 of 1989 – *Independent* Law Report, 1 August 1989: 20). Perhaps the law should only intervene heavily in cases under (4) above? In other instances, arrangements would have to be made for the withdrawal of the offending party from the family (perhaps by means of a probation order with a requirement of residence) while the complexities of the situation were clarified. The local authorities have adequate powers already for the supervision of younger members of the family and to effect their removal should the situation escalate. The overall aim of treatment should be to restore family functioning rather than to disrupt it further by the imposition of inflexible and punitive sanctions.

Because of the close family ties involved, these cases are likely to be more difficult to resolve than other cases of child molestation. Decisions as to whether children or the offending parent should be removed cause great anguish to the professionals involved and they are often in a 'no win' situation. In families where there is *not* widespread family disorganisation and other anti-social behaviour, it may be possible to proceed on lines that are less draconian than long-term removal of the parent or residential care for the children. Dr Eileen Vizard has rightly suggested that for many child abusers prison is counter-productive and may in fact exacerbate the problems. She and her colleagues are reported as having successfully reassured some members of the judiciary that

> At one end of the sex-abuse scale there is the extremely dangerous, grossly disordered offender who needs to be locked up. At the other end, there is intra-familial abuse, usually chronic, but where the danger is much more circumscribed. This 'non-dangerous' category which may account for 75 per cent of all cases, can be treated in the community.
>
> (quoted in Davies, 1989)

In other cases, where the parents' behaviour (sometimes involving both parties) has been blatantly coercive and where several children have been involved, long-term removal by way of imprisonment may be the only option. In any event, it seems that society will find it necessary to register its firm disapproval of close consanguinous sexual activity for some time to come.

Rape

Rape of females

> He in a few minutes ravished this fair creature,
> or at least would have ravished her, if she had
> not, by a timely compliance, prevented him.
> (Fielding, *Jonathan Wild*, Book III, Chapter 7)

Sadly, some women do not manage to avoid the assaultative and predatory attentions of the male described above. The quotation also encapsulates some of the difficulties and ambiguities surrounding consent and compliance that some-times make the prosecution of rape problematic. Recent court cases have, happily, tended to support the view that when a woman says 'no' she means it; however, this has not always been the case.

Reference to Table 8.1 indicates not only that rape constitutes a fairly sizeable proportion of prosecuted sexual offences, but also that its frequency seems to have increased consistently. Over the years there has also been evidence to suggest that the circumstances in which rape has been carried out has been becoming 'nastier' (Lloyd and Walmsley, 1989).[6] As already indicated, the statistical classification of an offence may give no real indication as to its severity; thus there are many gradations of rape and of indecent assault, from fairly minor attempts at rape to serious indecent assaults that only just fall short of it. Stereotypes of the rapist abound, and the act of rape, like incest, has its place in myth and legend. Mistaken interpretations of anthropology and history have encouraged men in their chauvinistic belief that manhood and virility can only be demonstrated by taking a woman against her will; a point made by Marina Warner in her second Reith Lecture ('The Making of the Male', BBC Radio 4, 2 February 1994). Such misinterpretations lead to the belief that a woman may 'enjoy' the act of rape but fail to recognise the horror and distress experienced by rape victims. Much of the more recent literature on rape victimology helps to present the picture in its true light (see Newburn, 1993; Soothill 1991). However, it is the view of some that a few women may unwittingly make themselves vulnerable by for example, hitch-hiking alone, leaving doors and windows open at night, or by wearing provocative clothes. Those familiar with court proceedings will have observed how the allegedly provocatively dressed schoolgirl may impress quite differently when clad in school gym-slip in court. Unwise though the behaviour of some victims may be, this cannot condone the conduct of the offender. Carried to their logical conclusion, such arguments would suggest that we *deserve* to lose our cars if we leave them unlocked or have our houses burgled if we leave doors unfastened.

It is not surprising that much rape has, until recently, been under-reported. A woman may be understandably reluctant to go through the ordeal of a searching medical examination and a public exploration of the circumstances of the alleged assault. Some women are also reluctant to report the offence to their partners or other family members. They may suffer much torment and guilt as a result. The physical sequelae, apart from any vaginal, anal or other injury that may have been caused, are very important. The victim may also have become pregnant, have contracted venereal disease, HIV infection or AIDS; all this just compounds their distress. Many women feel so defiled by the experience that they go to extreme lengths to cleanse themselves, for example by repeatedly scrubbing their genitalia with strong disinfectants. Gradually we have begun to recognise the importance of the emotional state of the victim and the need for post-rape counselling. The development of rape crisis centres has been useful, but *all* who come into contact with rape victims and their families require help to develop knowledge and skills in this area (Sparr, 1989).

Legal aspects

It is only in recent years that the ingredients of the offence of rape have been fully defined by statute. Until then, rape was a crime at common law, the only statutory reference to it being in Section 1 of the Sexual Offences Act 1956. It is worth noting here that, until recently, it was not a criminal offence for a man to rape his wife. Changes in the law owe much to the work of feminists who viewed the legal approach to the crime of rape as one example of discrimination by men against women (see Scully, 1991). In 1975, in the case of *DPP* v. *Morgan* (1 All ER 8), the Law Lords ruled that belief in a woman's consent, *even if unreasonable*, must exonerate the accused. This ruling resulted in the setting up of a government committee of inquiry into the law of rape. The Committee did not disagree with the Law Lords' decision, but made certain recommendations concerning the preservation of the anonymity of the parties in court proceedings and evidence as to the victim's previous sexual history. They also recommended joint representation of the sexes on juries in rape cases. Most of the Committee's recommendations were incorporated into the Sexual Offences (Amendment) Act 1976. *The law now holds that a man commits rape if (a) he has unlawful sexual intercourse with a woman who at the time of the intercourse does not consent to it; and (b) at that time knows that she does not consent to the intercourse or is reckless as to whether she consents to it.* Concerning consent, the law now states that if at a trial for a rape offence the jury has to consider whether a man believed that a woman was consenting to sexual intercourse, the presence or absence of reasonable grounds for such a belief is a matter to which the jury should have regard, in conjunction with other relevant matters, in considering whether he so believed. As a result of this more adequate statement of the ingredients of the offence, some clarification of the issues concerning consent, and the preservation of anonymity, it appears that rather more women are prepared to risk court proceedings. However, as has already been pointed out, there is still considerable reluctance to do so on other grounds.

Characteristics of rape and rapists

A number of studies have been made of what might loosely be described as the epidemiology of rape. One of the earliest of these was by Amir (1971) and it is still probably one of the most comprehensive. Amir found that, contrary to common belief, about a third of the victims had been in previous contact with their assailants. Alcohol was an important factor in two thirds of his cases (see also McMurran and Bellfield, 1993). In 75 per cent of cases, the rape had been planned and 50 per cent of the victims had failed to resist their attackers. Amir also found a high proportion of multiple rape cases (43 per cent). Recent studies in the UK have shown that a sizeable proportion of rapists are re-convicted *a long time after their first conviction* (Soothill *et al.*, 1976; Soothill and Gibbens, 1978; Gibbens *et al.*, 1981). Howells and Wright (1978) found that some rapists scored significantly higher than controls on scales measuring sexual maladjustment and loss of control. Additionally, Wright (1980) found evidence that serious physical assault often accompanied the rape. This, he considers, puts the lie to the oft-repeated assertion that women either enjoy the experience or acquiesce in it too readily. He says 'it becomes apparent that to the woman involved, the attack might justifiably be seen as a *life-threatening* situation' (Wright, 1980: 112).

Classification

The arbitrary nature of attempts at classification must again be acknowledged, as must be the degree of overlap between groups. Gibbens *et al.* (1977) discerned three groups: paedophilic rapists; aggressive rapists; and isolated rape offences. Hall Williams (1977) divided serious sexual offenders into the following four groups: the extensively aggressive; a mixed aggressive group; serious sexual offences used as a means of resolving personal problems or reactions to stress; essentially paedophilic types. In attempting any classification, problems arise because we are sometimes describing the offence by the nature of the behaviour displayed (for example, aggressive or over-inhibited), sometimes by the choice of victim (for example, children), and sometimes by the presence of other features, such as mental disorder. If we disregard for a moment those rapes that arise out of allegedly mistaken consent, we find that a key characteristic under-lying, or associated with, most rapes is anger or aggression. In most cases, rape is best regarded as a crime of extreme personal *violence* rather than an offence aimed at achieving sexual satisfaction *per se*. For this reason, a classification proposed by Groth and Hobson (1983) seems helpful. Their typology suggests three clear-cut, but overlapping, classes of rape:

1 *Anger rape* – motivated by feeling 'put down' or by retribution for perceived wrongs.
2 *Power rape* – engaged in as a means of denying deep feelings of inadequacy and insecurity.
3 *Sadistic rape* – victims are usually complete strangers; they may be subjected to torture, bondage and highly deviant sexual practices.

It will be obvious that even this attempt at classification is not entirely satis-factory and that it will overlap with some of the classifications suggested earlier. These problems have been identified very usefully in recent contributions by Grubin and Kennedy (1991), Canter and Heritage (1990) and Leonard (1993).

Taking all these cautions into account, I give below a more detailed classi-fication of those who commit rape on women:

1 The sexually virile young man, out for what he can get, whose exploitative hedonism is not counterbalanced by finer scruples or concern – the oppor-tunistic rapist.
2 The more inhibited, shy young man, who is trying to overcome his feelings of sexual inferiority. He may misinterpret the responses of his victim and not register that 'no' means 'no'. Some such rapists may be latently homosexual and their behaviour may be seen as a defence against their homosexuality. (See also the classification of indecent exposers.)
3 The sexually violent and aggressive. Such offenders have records of other forms of violence, alcohol often plays a large part in narcotising inhibition and they may hold the mistaken belief that it improves their performance; the reverse is of course the case.

4 A group who are potentially highly dangerous, in that they need to gain reassurance by a show of force. In West *et al.*'s (1978) study of incarcerated rapists who were undergoing group psychotherapy, one of the main features that emerged was that these men suffered severe feelings of inferiority concerning their masculinity. Confirmation for this finding may be found in later work by Perkins (1991). This group includes those who set out to defile and denigrate their victims, forcing them to participate in acts of both vaginal and anal intercourse and in oral sex. Many of these men appear to be women-haters and one or two may eventually commit sadistic sexual murder (see later).

5 A sub-group of (4) above. These men, also potentially highly dangerous, have psychopathic tendencies, seem to have insatiable sexual appetites and may need the resistance of their victims to arouse their potency. Such offenders may obtain sexual pleasure from their sadistic activities (true sadists).

6 Rapists who are found to be suffering from a definable form of mental disorder such as psychosis or mental impairment. Such cases are comparatively rare and the grossly psychotic or mentally impaired rapist is likely to be detained in a Special Hospital.

7 A predominantly young group who rape in groups or packs ('gang-bangs'). They are likely to have previous convictions for violence and sex offences. They may engage in deviant sexual practices with their victims and subject them to other forms of defilement, such as urinating on them. Some of them may belong to gangs such as 'Hell's Angels'. Unlike some of the other typologies presented above, they are not, in the main, characterised by gross personal pathology (Wright and West, 1981).

Management

Much of what has been said earlier about other forms of sexual offending can be applied to rape of females. The formulation of some kind of typology based upon an in-depth assessment will afford clues as to the most appropriate form of management. Some type of brief counselling or training in sexual and social skills may be of help with the first two groups. Those in group (3) may respond to measures aimed at improving their life-styles and in helping them with their drinking problems. Those in groups (4) and (5) are much harder to manage and may need long-term incarceration in order that psychotherapeutic treatment programmes may take effect. Some success with programmes designed to develop social competence and to modify deviant sexual preferences by various means has been reported, but long-term results are not readily available (Marshall and Barbaree, 1984). The use of hormonal and allied treatments has already been referred to in the discussion of paedophilia. Those in group (7) may outgrow their unpleasant proclivities, but they need to be removed from circulation for a time, for the protection of a society, for purposes of retribution and deterrence, and to allow their consciences to develop. No *single* form of management is likely to be effective. It is highly dangerous to espouse with messianic enthusiasm any one theory or treatment model. A multi-disciplinary approach, based upon a full assessment of the personal and situational factors in the rapist's life is essential.

Male rape

Far less attention has been paid to cases of rape of males. In the *Criminal Statistics* these are covered as acts of buggery or attempted buggery. Such acts are sometimes committed with great force and the person concerned (perhaps a minor) may suffer severe emotional trauma and fear as well as serious internal injury. Moreover, the reluctance to talk about the attack, or to report it, is, if anything, greater than it is among women. We have few documented accounts of the male victims of rape but Mezey and King (1987, 1989) have made a very useful contribution to this field. Their work suggests that the sequelae are just as severe as they are for women. For accounts of the rape of males in institutions, see the items listed under *Further Reading*.

Bestiality (zoophilia, zooerasty)

Bestiality is 'a form of buggery which consists in the use of animals as sexual objects' (Bluglass, 1990: 729). The law defines it as being 'a felony for a person to commit buggery with another person *or with any animal*' (Sexual Offences Act 1956, Section 12(1)). The number of prosecutions hardly reflects the incidence of the phenomenon. Its occurrence is most likely in rural areas. Most commonly, the cases that come to light involve those suffering from mental impairment, psychopathic disorder and those heavily influenced by drink or drugs. Variants of the practice include the incitement by a male of an animal to have intercourse with a female. In the cases where this occurs, a distinction is made between bestiality – to describe the offence of buggery when committed with an animal – and sodomy, when committed with a human being. There is a body of opinion which argues for the abolition of the offence in its present form and that prosecutions could best be brought under the legislation that deals with cruelty to animals (Howard League for Penal Reform, 1985).

Sexual murder

> I will kill thee,
> And love thee after.
> (*Othello*, Act V, Scene ii)

If we exclude the *crime passionelle* and murder committed as a result of sexual jealousy, sexual murder is, fortunately, a rare event (Quinsey, 1990). As indicated earlier, it is sometimes very difficult to determine whether a killing has occurred as a result of the pursuit of sadistic pleasure, as a means of keeping the victim quiet (unable to give evidence), or as a result of an *unintentional* act of violence that has become lethal during some form of sexual activity. For example, it is possible for manual strangulation to occur during some forms of anal intercourse and incidents have been described in which death has occurred in the course of fellatio due to aspiration of ejaculate or from impaction of the penis in the hypopharynx. West (1987) suggests that certain groups of individuals may be especially vulnerable to sexual murders: prostitutes and promiscuous male homosexuals; and children, because of their physical vulnerability. Some years ago, Gibson and Klein (1969) estimated that there were between ten and twelve sex-related murders in any one year, out of a total of something like 500 or more murders known to the police. In a later study, West (1987) calculated that some 8 per cent of homicides could be classified in this way.

The motivation for sexual murder may be very complex. Hyatt Williams (1964) has emphasised the manner in which different facets of the sexual murderer's personality may seem to be out of touch with each other. He suggests that kindness and compassion can co-exist with a high degree of cruelty and savage destructiveness; there is a capacity to 'split off' the activity from other aspects of a so-called normal life (as, for example, in the cases of Nilsen and Christie described earlier in this book). (See also Revitch and Schlesinger, 1981: esp. Chapter 9.) In a landmark paper, Brittain (1970) provided a graphic composite picture of the sadistic sexual murderer. He brought a unique combination of skills to bear upon the topic for he was a forensic pathologist as well as a psychiatrist. It is important to emphasise that Brittain suggested a *composite* picture and that we would not expect to find all the many features he describes in any one case. I merely select a few of them for purposes of illustration.

He says such killers are often withdrawn, introverted, over-controlled, timid and prudish, for example taking offence at 'dirty jokes'. The killer is likely to be over thirty and come from any occupational status, but an unusual number seem to have been employed as butchers or as workers in abattoirs. They often seem to be remarkably ambivalent towards their mothers and their personality profiles appear to show a mass of contradictions with many unresolved psychological conflicts. Their mothers tend to be gentle, over-indulgent, but not particularly maternal. Fathers are notably either absent or, if present, rigidly strict. Such offenders tend to have a keen interest in depictions of torture, atrocities, Nazi activities and regalia, the occult and the more bizarre type of horror film. They frequently keep such materials locked away in a room or a shed. They show an irrational pre-occupation with the size of their genitalia, which they regard as excessively small; and their sex lives are poor or non-existent. In the course of the offence, the offender may insert articles such as a torch, milk bottle or poker with great force into the victim's vagina or rectum. Their murders, usually carefully planned, are ferocious and bizarre in their execution. Sexual intercourse may not necessarily accompany the murder and they may masturbate beside the corpse. It has been suggested that 'the brutal and murderous assaults actually are a substitute for the sexual act' (Schlesinger and Revitch, 1983: 214). The prognosis for such offenders is not good and some of them seem to welcome the control afforded by incarceration because they are troubled by their sadistic impulses and activities. However, those in charge of them and who share the responsibility for making recommendations about future dangerousness have to guard against being misled by *appearances* of good behaviour and apparently sincere protestations of reform (see Chapter 9 of this volume). Revitch has wisely said that 'many of these cases have a tendency to repeat aggression . . . even after years of imprisonment' (1980: 10).

Necrophilia

> Defaced, deflowered and now to death devote!
> (Milton, *Paradise Lost*, Book 9)

The sexual molestation of corpses appears to be an uncommon event, though, as with bestiality, the number of prosecutions for such behaviour is probably far less than its true incidence. Legally, it is not specifically prescribed under English law, though it might constitute an offence of outraging public decency, or, in theory at least, an act of malicious damage. Such behaviour has been known for centuries, as have the precautions taken to preclude it (see Prins, 1990: 84–87 for a detailed discussion, and Hucker, 1990). There are also accounts in the literature of certain brothels catering for such interests; prostitutes dressing as corpses for those with such predilections. The phenomenon is defined in a variety of ways. Some take it to cover *any* interference with a corpse, others limit it to sexual molestation, and yet others subsume it under the general heading of vampiristic activity (Prins, 1990). In a case reported in 1987, a man received four years' imprisonment for mutilating corpses. When his house was searched, police found photographs of a man's severed genitalia. He admitted mutilating three bodies and told the police he had nursed a phantasy for a long time about cutting off male genitalia (*Guardian*, 27 March 1985: 5). It is not surprising that necrophilic activity appears to be an uncommon phenomenon. By its very nature, its perpetration is likely to be highly secret and there is no victim to complain. Those who commit such offences are likely to be grossly disordered personalities, though not necessarily mentally ill. It has been suggested that some occupations such as those of mortuary attendant, undertaker or grave-digger may lend themselves to those motivated toward necrophilic activities. The literature on the topic is fairly sparse, but for reviews see Smith and Dimock (1983), Prins (1990) and Hucker (1990).

CONCLUSION

> Few love to hear the sins they love to act.
> (*Pericles*, Act I, Scene i)

The range of behaviours that constitute sexual offending is vast and complex. It is necessary to reiterate the need for professionals to try to overcome their misconceptions and prejudices so that we may 'hear' what such offenders are saying as non-judgementally as possible. This is very important because the behaviour of some sex offenders is not only bizarre but may well fill us with revulsion. However, demonstrations of dispassionate compassion should not blind us to the manner in which such offenders or offender-patients may engage in various forms of denial of their behaviour. On the credit side, some sex offenders (and sometimes those convicted of the more serious crimes) are distressed and disturbed by their behaviour and by its effects upon others, and wish to change. Although there is an undoubted need for the development of sensible typologies, there is also a need to avoid stereotyping and to maintain an open mind. To achieve this, a multi-method and multi-disciplinary approach is likely to be the most effective. Sexual offending appears in many guises, and sometimes the most disguised forms may be the most ominous prognostically. It is premature to talk about 'cure'; management of the offender and work towards helping him deal with his impulses in a more acceptable way, and the provision of viable alternative forms of behaviour, are the most we can hope to achieve.[7] Whichever approach we adopt, our own 'blind-spots' may be the biggest hindrances. Sir Denis Hill, who was a member of the Aarvold Committee of Inquiry into the case of Graham Young (see Chapter 9), once wrote, 'Personal and emotional maturity . . . means freedom from personal neurotic nostalgia with one's own past' (1978: 105). We should try to obtain such freedom for ourselves and those we seek to help refrain from sexual offending.

NOTES

1   Such groups have included the British Medical Association, child care agencies such as Barnardos, the National Association of Probation Officers, and a research group sponsored by the Medical Research Council. Other non-specialist groups who have argued for a uniform age of consent have included the 'agony aunts' of various newspapers and figures drawn from public life (the 'good, the great and the wise'). See, for example, reports in the *Independent* of 17, 24, 29 January and 1 February 1994.

2   In the original edition of this book (and elsewhere) I included the offence of bigamy in this list. Reflection now leads me to consider that this is best regarded as an offence against family life rather than a sexual offence.

3   For example, incestuous themes appear in *Hamlet*, *The Duchess of Malfi*, *Wuthering Heights*, Poe's *Fall of the House of Usher* and, more recently, Murdoch's *A Severed Head*.

4   For a brief history of the manner in which incest became a statutory offence see Bluglass (1979). There is some debate as to the legal position of siblings or half-siblings who, having been separated, perhaps since birth, meet up, fall in love and marry. Since the relevant section of the Act states that 'knowing' is an important ingredient of the offence, lack of knowledge would seem to rule out prosecution. However, the trauma involved in subsequent discovery of the parties' true relationship is likely to be considerable (see Cohen 1994). It is also important to note that the degrees of proscribed consanguinous relationships vary from country to country.

5 See note 4 *supra*.
6 The authors describe three trends: first, a slight increase in the proportion of offences involving the threat or use of violence; second, an increase in sexual practices in addition to the rape (for example, anal intercourse); third, an increase in the length of time that victims were under the coercion of the offenders. (See also Lloyd, 1991.)
7 This would seem to be the ethos of such organisations as the Faithful Foundation, set up following the closure of the Gracewell Clinic in Birmingham. The Foundation is probably the only body in the UK that not only provides 'treatment' for a range of sex offenders and victims, but is also engaged in training staff from various agencies to deal with such offenders.

REFERENCES

Abracen, J., O'Carroll, L. and Ladha, N. (1991) 'Neurophysiological Dysfunction in Sex Offenders', *Journal of Forensic Psychiatry* 2: 167–177.

Adshead, G. and Mezey, G. (1993) 'Ethical Issues in the Psychotherapeutic Treatment of Paedophiles: Which Side Are You On?', *Journal of Forensic Psychiatry* 4: 361–368.

Amir, M. (1971) *Patterns in Forcible Rape*, Chicago: Chicago University Press.

Bagley, C. (1969) 'The Varieties of Incest', *New Society* 21 August: 280–282.

—— (1992) 'Characteristics of 60 Children and Adolescents with a History of Sexual Assault against Others: Evidence from a Comparative Study', *Journal of Forensic Psychiatry* 3: 299–309.

Bancroft, J. (1989) *Human Sexuality and Its Problems* (second edn), London: Churchill Livingstone.

—— (1991) 'The Sexuality of Sexual Offending: The Social Dimension', *Criminal Behaviour and Mental Health* 1: 181–192.

Banning, A. (1989) 'Mother–Son Incest: Confronting a Prejudice', *Child Abuse and Neglect* 3: 363–570.

Baron, M. (1993) 'Genetic Linkage and Male Homosexual Orientation: Reasons to be Cautious', *British Medical Journal* 307: 337–338.

Batten, D.A. (1983) 'Incest – A Review of the Literature', *Medicine, Science and the Law* 23: 245–253.

Beitchman, J.H., Zucker, K.J., Hood, J.H., Costa, D.A. *et al.* (1991) 'A Review of the Long-Term Effects of Child Sexual Abuse', *Child Abuse and Neglect* 16: 101–118.

Bluglass, R. (1979) 'Incest', *British Journal of Hospital Medicine* August: 152–157.

—— (1980) 'Indecent Exposure in the West Midlands', in D.J. West (ed.), *Sexual Offenders in the Criminal Justice System*, Cambridge: Institute of Criminology.

—— (1982) 'Assessing Dangerousness in Sex Offenders', in J.R. Hamilton and H. Freeman (eds), *Dangerousness: Psychiatric Assessment and Management*, London: Gaskell.

—— (1990) 'Bestiality', in R. Bluglass and P. Bowden (eds), *Principles and Practice of Forensic Psychiatry*, London: Churchill Livingstone.

Breakwell, G. (1994) 'The Echo of Power: A Framework for Social Psychological Research', *The Psychologist* 7: 65–72.

Briggs (1994) 'Assessment of Sexual Offenders', in M. McMurran and J. Hodge (eds), *The Assessment of Criminal Behaviours of Clients in Secure Settings*, London: Jessica Kingsley.

Brittain, R.P. (1970) 'The Sadistic Murderer', *Medicine, Science and the Law* 10: 198–208.

Brongersma, E. (1988) 'A Defence of Sexual Liberty for All Age Groups', *Howard Journal* 27: 32–43.

Canter, D. and Heritage, R. (1990) 'A Multivariate Model of Sexual Offence Behaviour; Developments in Offender Profiling', *Journal of Forensic Psychiatry* 1: 185–212.

Clarke, D.J. (1989) 'Antilibidnal Drugs and Mental Retardation: A Review', *Medicine, Science and the Law* 29: 136–146.

Clark, N.K. (1993) 'Sexual Offenders: An Overview', in N.K. Clark and G.M. Stephenson (eds), *Sexual Offenders: Context, Assessment and Treatment*, Division of Criminal and Legal Psychology, Monograph No.19, Leicester: British Psychological Society.

Cohen, D.J. (1994) 'Love That Dare Not Speak Its Surname', *Independent*, 26 January: 21.

Cohen, M.L. and Boucher, R.J. (1972) 'Misunderstandings About Sex Criminals', *Sexual Behaviour* 2: 56–62.

Cook, D.A.G., Fox, C.A., Weaver, C.M. and Rooth, F.G. (1991) 'The Berkeley Group: Ten Years' Experience of a Group for Non-Violent Sex Offenders', *British Journal of Psychiatry* 158: 238–243.

Cooper, I. and Coromier, B. (1990) 'Incest', in R. Bluglass and P. Bowden (eds), *Principles and Practice of Forensic Psychiatry*, London: Churchill Livingstone.

Cowburn, M. (1990) 'Assumptions about Sex Offenders', *Probation Journal* 37: 4–9.

Cox, D.J. and McMahon, B. (1978) 'Incidents of Male Exhibitionism in the United States of America as Reported by Victimised Female College Students', *International Journal of Law and Psychiatry* 1: 453–457.

Crawford, D. (1979) 'Modification of Deviant Sexual Behaviour: The Need for A Comprehensive Approach', *British Journal of Medical Psychology* 52: 151–156.

—— (1982) 'Problems for Assessment and Treatment of Sexual Offenders in Closed Institutions', in D.A. Black (ed.), *Symposium, Broadmoor Psychology Department's 21st Birthday*, Issues in Criminological and Legal Psychology No. 2, Leicester: British Psychological Society.

Dare, C. (1993) 'Denial and Childhood Sexual Abuse', *Journal of Forensic Psychiatry* 4: 1–4.

Davies, P.W. (1989) 'Prisoners of Perversion', *Independent*, 17 November: 11.

Ferris, P. (1993) *Sex and the British: A 20th Century History*, London: Michael Joseph.

Finklehor, D., Hotaling, G.T., Lewis, I.A. and Smith, C. (1989) 'Sexual Abuse and Its Relationship to Later Sexual Satisfaction': Marital Status Religion and Attitudes', *Journal of Interpersonal Violence* 4: 379–399.

Gayford, J.J. (1981) 'Indecent Exposure – A Review of the Literature', *Medicine, Science and the Law* 21: 233–242.

Gibbens, T.C.N., Way, C. and Soothill, K.L. (1977) 'Behavioural Types of Rape', *British Journal of Psychiatry* 130: 32–42.

—— (1978) 'Sibling and Parent-Child Incest Offenders', *British Journal of Criminology* 18: 40–52.

Gibbens, E., Soothill, K.L. and Way, C. (1981) 'Sex Offences against Young Girls: A Long-Term Record Study, *Psychological Medicine* 11: 351–357.

Gibson E. and Klein, S. (1969) *Murder, 1957–1968*, Home Office Research Studies No.3. London: HMSO.

Gittleson, N.L., Eacott, S.E. and Mehta, B.M. (1978) 'Victims of Indecent Exposure', *British Journal of Psychiatry* 132: 61–66.

Glasser, M. (1990) 'Paedophilia', in R. Bluglass and P. Bowden (eds), *Principles and Practice of Forensic Psychiatry*, London: Churchill Livingstone.

Goodman, R.E. (1983) 'Biology and Sexuality: Inborn Determinants of Human Sexual Response', *British Journal of Psychiatry*, 143: 216–220.

Groth, A.N. and Hobson, W.F. (1983) 'The Dynamics of Sexual Assault', in L.B. Schlesinger and E. Revitch (eds), *Sexual Dynamics of Anti-Social Behaviour*, Springfield, Ill.: Charles C. Thomas.

Grubin, D.H. and Kennedy, H.G. (1991) 'The Classification of Sexual Offenders', *Criminal Behaviour and Mental Health* 1: 123–129.

Hadrian (1955) *Memoirs of Hadrian*, ed. M. Yourcenar, London: Secker and Warburg (Readers' Union).

Hall Williams, J.E. (1974) 'The Neglect of Incest: A Criminologist's View', *Medicine, Science and the Law* 14: 64–67.

—— (1977) 'Serious Heterosexual Attack', *Medicine, Science and the Law* 17: 140–146.

Hamilton, W. and Walker, D.M. (1975) 'Gender: Quaesto Quid Juris?', *Medicine, Science and the Law* 15: 79–93.

Hill, D. (1978) 'The Qualities of a Good Psychiatrist', *British Journal of Psychiatry* 133: 97–105.

Home Office (1992a) *Criminal Statistics, England and Wales, 1990*, Cmnd 1935. London: HMSO.

—— (1992b) *Criminal Statistics: England and Wales: Supplementary Tables (Vol. 4)*, London: Home Office.

Howard League for Penal Reform (1985) *Unlawful Sex*, London: Waterlow.

Howells, K. and Wright, R. (1978) 'The Sexual Attitudes of Aggressive Sexual Offenders', *British Journal of Criminology* 8: 170–174.

Hucker, S. (1990) 'Necrophilia and Other Unusual Philias', in R. Bluglass and P. Bowden (eds), *Principles and Practice of Forensic Psychiatry*, London: Churchill Livingstone.

Hunt, L. (1990) 'Surely a Woman Couldn't be Guilty of Such an Act?', *Independent*, 23 May: 20.

Hyatt Williams, A. (1964) 'The Psychopathology and the Treatment of Sexual Murderers', in I. Rosen (ed.), *The Pathology and Treatment of Sexual Deviation*, London: Oxford University Press.

Jackson, C. and Thomas-Peter, B.A. (1994) 'Denial in Sex Offenders: Workers' Preferences', *Criminal Behaviour and Mental Health* 4: 21–32.

Jehu, D. (1988) *Beyond Sexual Abuse: Therapy with Women Who Were Childhood Victims*, Chichester: Wiley.

Kaul, A. (1993) 'Sex Offenders – Cure or Management?', *Medicine, Science and the Law* 31: 207–212.

Kaul, A. and Duffy, S. (1991) 'Gerontophilia – a Case Report', *Medicine, Science and the Law* 31: 110–114.

Knight, R.A., Carter, D.L. and Prentky, R.A.. (1989) 'A System for the Classification of Child Molesters: Reliability and Application', *Journal of Interpersonal Violence* 4: 3–23.

Lanyon, R.I. (1991) 'Theories of Sex Offending', in C.R. Hollin and C. Howells (eds), *Clinical Approaches to Sex Offenders and Their Victims*, Chichester: Wiley.

Launay, G. (1994) 'The Phallometric Assessment of Sex Offenders: Some Professional and Research Issues', *Criminal Behaviour and Mental Health* 4: 48–70.

Leonard, R.A. (1993) 'The Family Backgrounds of Serial Rapists', in N.K. Clark and G.M. Stephenson (eds), *Sexual Offenders: Context, Assessment and Treatment*, Division of Criminal and Legal Psychology, Monograph No.19, Leicester: British Psychological Society.

Lindsey (1994) 'What the Man on the Train Did to Me', *Independent*, 4 February: 18.

Lloyd, C. (1991) 'Changes in the Pattern and Nature of Sex Offences', *Criminal Behaviour and Mental Health* 1: 115–122.

Lloyd, C. and Walmsley, R. (1989) *Changes in Rape Offences and Sentencing*, Home Office Research and Planning Unit, London: HMSO.

Longo, R.E. and Groth, A.N. (1983) 'Juvenile Sexual Offenders in the Histories of Adult Rapists and Child Molesters', *International Journal of Offender Therapy and Comparative Criminology* 27: 150–155.

Lukianowicz, N. (1972) 'Incest (I) Paternal Incest (II) Other Types of Incest', *British Journal of Psychiatry* 120: 301–313.

MacClay, D.T. (1952) 'The Diagnosis and Treatment of Compensatory Types of Indecent Exposure', *British Journal of Delinquency* III: 34–45.

MacCulloch, M.J. and Waddington, J.L. (1981) 'Neuroendocrine Mechanisms and the Aetiology of Male and Female Homosexuality', *British Journal of Psychiatry* 139: 341–345.

MacDonald, J.M. (1973) *Indecent Exposure*, Springfield, Ill.: Charles C. Thomas.

McGrath, R.J. (1991) 'Sex Offender Risk Assessment and Disposition Planning: A Review of Empirical and Clinical Findings', *International Journal of Offender Therapy and Comparative Criminology* 35: 329–350.

McMurran, M. and Bellfield, M. (1993) 'Sex Related Alcohol Experiences in Rapists', *Criminal Behaviour and Mental Health* 3: 76–84.

Maish, H. (1973) *Incest*, London: André Deutsch.

Marshall, W. and Barbaree, H.E. (1984) 'A Behavioural View of Rape', *International Journal of Law and Psychiatry* 7: 51–77.

Masson, J. (1985) *The Assault on Truth: Freud's Suppression of the Seduction Theory*, Harmondsworth: Penguin.

Masters, B. (1993) *The Shrine of Jeffrey Dahmer*, London: Hodder and Stoughton.

Mezey, G. and King, (1987) 'Male Victims of Sexual Assault', *Medicine, Science and the Law* 27: 122–124.

—— (1989) 'The Effects of Sexual Assault on Men: A Survey of 22 Victims', *Psychological Medicine* 19: 205–209.

Mezey, G., King, Vizzard, E., Hawkes, C. and Austin, R. (1991) 'A Community Treatment Programme for Convicted Child Sex Offenders: A Preliminary Report', *Journal of Forensic Psychiatry* 2: 11–25.

Mullen, P. (1990) 'The Long-Term Influence of Sexual Assault on the Mental Health of Victims', *Journal of Forensic Psychiatry* 1: 14–34.

Murphy, W.D. (1990) 'Assessment and Modification of Cognitive Distortions in Sex Offenders', in W.L. Marshall, D.R. Laws and H.E. Barbaree (eds), *Handbook of Sexual Assault: Issues, Theories and the Treatment of the Offender*, London: Plenum Press.

Newburn, T. (1993) 'The Long-Term Impact of Criminal Victimization', Home Office Statistical Department, *Research Bulletin No. 33*: 30–34. London: Home Office Research and Planning Unit, Home Office.

O'Connor, A.A. (1987) 'Female Sex Offenders', *British Journal of Psychiatry* 150: 615–620.

Parker, T. (1970) *The Twisting Lane: Some Sex Offenders*, London: Panther Books.

Paul, D. (1990) 'Pitfalls That May be Encountered During an Examination for Signs of Sexual Abuse', *Medicine, Science and the Law* 30: 3–11.

Perkins, D. (1991) 'Clinical Work with Sex Offenders in Secure Settings', in C.R. Hollin and K. Howells (eds), *Clinical Approaches to Sex Offenders and Their Victims*, Chichester: Wiley.

Pollock, C.B.R. (1960) 'A Case of Neurotic Exhibitionism', *British Journal of Criminology* 1: 37–49.

Prins, H. (1990) *Bizarre Behaviours: Boundaries of Psychiatric Disorder*, London: Tavistock/Routledge.

—— (1991) 'Some Aspects of Sex Offending: Causes and Cures?', *Medicine, Science and the Law* 31: 330–337.

Quinsey, V. (1988) 'Sexual Deviancy', *Current Opinion in Psychiatry* 1: 688–690.

—— (1990) 'Sexual Violence', in R. Bluglass and P. Bowden (eds), *Principles and Practice of Forensic Psychiatry*, London: Churchill Livingstone.

Revitch, E. (1980) 'Gynocide and Unprovoked Attacks on Women', *Corrective and Social Psychiatry* 26: 6–11.

Revitch, E. and Schlesinger, L.B. (1981) *Psychopathology of Homicide*, Springfield, Ill.: Charles C. Thomas.

Rooth, F.G. (1975) 'Indecent Exposure and Exhibitionism', in T. Silverstone and B. Barraclough (eds), *Contemporary Psychiatry*, Ashford: Headley Brothers.

Schlesinger, L.B. and Revitch, E. (1983) 'Sexual Dynamics in Homicide and Assault', in L.B. Schlesinger and E. Revitch (eds), *Sexual Dynamics of Anti-Social Behaviour*, Springfield, Ill.: Charles C. Thomas.

Scott, P.D. (1964) 'Definition, Classification, Prognosis and Treatment', in I. Rosen (ed.), *The Pathology and Treatment of Sexual Deviation*, London: Oxford University Press.

Scully, D. (1991) *Understanding Sexual Abuse: A Study of Convicted Rapists*, London: HarperCollins.

Smith, S. and Dimock, J. (1983) 'Necrophilia and Anti-Social Acts', in L.B. Schlesinger and E. Revitch (eds), *Sexual Dynamics of Anti-Social Behaviour*, Springfield, Ill.: Charles C. Thomas.

Snaith, P. and Bennett, G. (1990) 'Exhibitionism, Indecent Exposure, Voyeurism and Frottage', in R. Bluglass and P. Bowden (eds), *Principles and Practice of Forensic Psychiatry*, London: Churchill Livingstone.

Soothill, K. (1991) 'The Changing Face of Rape', *British Journal of Criminology* 31: 383–392.

Soothill, K. and Gibbens, T.C.N. (1978) 'Recidivism of Sexual Offenders: A Reappraisal', *British Journal of Criminology* 18: 267–276.

Soothill, K., Jack, A. and Gibbens, T.C.N. (1976) 'Rape: A 22-Year Cohort Study', *Medicine, Science and the Law* 16: 62–69.

Sparr, L.F. (1989) 'Victims and Survivors', *Current Opinion in Psychiatry* 2: 757–763.

Storr, A. (1990) 'Sadomasochism', in R. Bluglass and P. Bowden (eds), *Principles and Practice of Forensic Psychiatry*, London: Churchill Livingstone.

Sugarman, P., Dumughn, C., Saad, K., Hinder, S. and Bluglass, R. (1994) 'Dangerousness in Exhibitionists', *Journal of Forensic Psychiatry* 5: 287–296.

Virkunnen, M. (1974) 'Incest Offences and Alcoholism', *Medicine, Science and the Law* 14: 124–128.

West, D.J. (1987) *Sexual Crimes and Confrontations: A Study of Victims and Offenders*, Aldershot: Gower.

West, D.J., Roy, C. and Nichols, F.L. (1978) *Understanding Sexual Attacks*, London: Heinemann.

Wiest, J. (1981) 'Treatment of Violent Offenders', *Clinical Social Work Journal* 9: 271–281.

Wolff, C. (1977) *Bisexuality – A Study*, London: Quarter Books.

Wright, R. (1980) 'Rape and Physical Violence', in D.J. West (ed.), *Sex Offenders in the Criminal Justice System*, Cambridge: Institute of Criminology.

Wright, R. and West, D.J. (1981) 'Rape – A Comparison of Group Offences and Lone Assaults', *Medicine, Science and the Law* 22: 25–30.

FURTHER READING

Paedophilia

Portman Clinic/Institute for the Study and Treatment of Delinquency (1989) *Understanding the Paedophile*, London.

Child sexual abuse

CIBA Foundation (1984) *Child Sexual Abuse within the Family*, London: Tavistock.
Walker, M. (1993) *Surviving Secrets*, Buckingham: Open University Press.

Incest

Meiselman, K.C. (1978) *Incest: A Psychological Study of Causes and Effects with Treatment Recommendations*, London: Josey-Bass.
Morris, M. (1982) *If I Should Die Before I Wake*, London: Souvenir Press.
Renvoize, J. (1982) *Incest: A Family Pattern*, London: Routledge.

Rape – on females

Toner, B.B. (1977) *The Facts of Rape*, London: Arrow Books.

Rape – on males

Lockwood, D. (1980) *Prison Sexual Violence*, London: Elsevier.
Priestley, P. (1980) *Community of Scapegoats: The Segregation of Sex Offenders and Informers in Prisons*, Oxford: Pergamon Press.
Sccaco, A.M. (ed.) (1982) *Male Rape: A Casebook of Sexual Aggressions*, New York: AMS Press.

Male prostitution

West, D.J. (1992) *Male Prostitution: Gay Sex Services in London*, London: Duckworth.

Media presentation of sex offenders

Soothill, K. and Walby, S. (1991) *Sex Crime in the News*, London: Routledge.

General

Cook, M. and Wilson, G. (eds) (1979) *Love and Attraction*, Oxford: Pergamon Press.
Ettore, E.M. (1980) *Lesbians, Women and Society*, London: Routledge.
Kraft-Ebing, R. von (1978) *Psychopathia Sexualis*, New York: Stein and Day (first Published in German, 1892).
Laws, D.R. (ed.) (1989) *Relapse Prevention with Sex Offenders*, New York: Guilford Press.
Lewin, J., Beary, M., Toman, E., Skinner, G. and Sproul-Boulton, R. (1994) 'A Community Service for Sex Offenders', *Journal of Forensic Psychiatry* 5: 297–310.
Marmor, J. (ed.) (1980) *Homosexual Behaviour: A Modern Reappraisal*, New York: Basic Books.
Prison Reform Trust (1992) *Beyond Containment: The Penal Response to Sex Offending*, London.
Yaffe, M. and Nelson, E.C. (1982) *The Influence of Pornography on Behaviour*, London: Academic Press.

Chapter 9

Will they do it again?

Nemo repente fuit turpissimus.
(No-one ever becomes thoroughly bad in one step.)
(Juvenal, *Satires* ii: 83)

These violent delights have violent ends.
(*Romeo and Juliet*, Act 2, Scene vi)

Dangerousness is a dangerous concept.
(Shaw, 1973: 269)

In previous chapters I have dealt with offenders and offender-patients, the majority of whom have committed serious offences against persons or property. This chapter is concerned mainly with some practical steps that can be taken to limit the risk of such offenders committing acts of further mayhem whilst living in the community under supervision. There are, of course, instances where an individual who has no previous history of serious offences against persons or property suddenly embarks upon such behaviour. Sometimes, with hindsight, we can see that the warning signs may have been missed. Although this chapter is concerned mainly with the commission of *criminal* offences, it is worthwhile remembering that there are instances in which actions may fall short of the criminal (but have an equally lethal potential), for example the case of the wife or partner being held hostage in her own home by a husband or partner who has disobeyed civil court injunctions to leave her alone. The thrust of this chapter is thrown into sharper relief by the requirements of the Criminal Justice Act 1991 to have regard to the assessment of risk in sentencing (notably in cases relating to violence and sex) and by current central government concerns about the need to have adequate supervision for a very small group of psychiatrically ill persons who may commit violent acts because of their illness (see for example, Boyd, 1994; Department of Health, 1994; Royal College of Psychiatrists, 1991; MacCulloch *et al.* 1993).

This chapter is divided into the following sections: first, some comments upon dangerousness as a concept; second, dangerousness and the law; third, prediction; fourth, the value of hindsight; and, finally, general issues of management.

DANGEROUSNESS AS A CONCEPT

Dangerousness means different things to different people. If asked to rank a group of people in order of their dangerousness, we should probably find ourselves in some difficulty, thus emphasising the third quotation at the head of this chapter, that dangerousness is, indeed, a dangerous concept. Of the following, who, for example, is the more dangerous? The bank robber, the bigoted patriot or blinkered politician (who is always convinced he or she is right), the over-zealous chief officer of police, the persistent paedophile, the person who peddles dangerous drugs to children for profit, the person who drives, knowing him- or herself to be unfit through drink or other drugs, the swimmer who uses the public baths knowingly suffering from a highly contagious and dangerous disease, the person who knows he or she is HIV positive or suffering from AIDS who continues to have unprotected intercourse with a variety of partners, the consortium that disposes of toxic waste without proper safeguards? All of the foregoing present potential hazards of some kind; it is this capacity to create a potential hazard to the safety of others that is our central concern (see also Prins, 1990, 1991; Baker, 1992, 1993). Moreover, the words 'danger' and 'dangerousness' have little meaning on their own. It is only when contextualised that they can be useful, but any interpretation must inevitably be somewhat subjective. The Butler Committee went to a great deal of trouble to try to define dangerousness and received a number of definitions. They stated that

> In our discussions we were not entirely satisfied with any of these definitions, and, for our part have come to equate dangerousness with a propensity to cause serious physical injury or lasting psychological harm. Physical violence is, we think, what the public are most worried about, but the psychological damage which may be suffered by some victims . . . is not to be underrated.
>
> (Home Office and DHSS, 1975: 59)

It is important to recognise that not all mentally disordered offenders are dangerous and that not all dangerous offenders are mentally disordered. Tennent (1975) suggests that there are three types of relationship that can exist between dangerous behaviour and mental disorder. First, dangerous behaviour can occur as a result of mental illness. In such cases successful treatment of the illness may be expected to change the behaviour. Second, dangerous behaviour may occur in those with mental illness, but in some cases the successful treatment of the illness may not affect the dangerous behaviour. Third, dangerous behaviour may be found in individuals without any evidence of mental disorder. Tennent adds that 'In practice, these categories, especially the first two, merge into one another' (1975: 311).

LEGAL ASPECTS

In the UK, at the present time, there are no statutes that attempt to define dangerous individuals specifically, though the law does recognise offences such as reckless (dangerous) driving, having vehicles in a dangerous condition and being in possession of, or distributing, dangerous drugs. In recent years there has been an increase in the use of the life sentence for cases not involving homicide. This has been justified in various appeal court decisions, on the grounds that by such means offenders considered to be dangerous, but not necessarily mentally disordered within the meaning of the current mental health legislation, can be incarcerated until such time as the authorities consider, on the basis of expert advice, that they may be safely released (see also Baker, 1993). So far as those formally judged to be mentally disordered are concerned, current mental health legislation recognises their potential dangerousness. Thus Sections 2 and 3 of the Mental Health Act, 1983 make provision, *inter alia*, for the compulsory detention of an individual with a view to 'the protection of other persons'. In addition, Section 41 of the Act makes provision for a restriction order to protect the public from 'serious harm' (see Chapter 3). More specifically, the proclivities of some offender-patients are recognised in the setting up and maintenance of the three Special Hospitals in England and Wales for those patients who exhibit 'dangerous, violent or criminal propensities' (National Health Service Act 1977, Section 4). It is not difficult to conclude from the foregoing brief summary that there are likely to be considerable difficulties in determining legal definitions of dangerousness in relation to both offenders and non-offenders alike. In addition, it will be readily apparent that ethical issues will be of paramount importance. (For discussion of some of these, see Prins, 1990.[1])

PREDICTION: CAN DANGEROUS BEHAVIOUR BE PREDICTED?

If we mean by prediction the capacity to be right every time, the short answer is *no*. If we have more modest goals, should we ask if there are measures, based upon past experience, that could be taken to attempt a possible reduction in dangerous conduct, then the answer is *yes*. Some of these practical measures will be discussed shortly. Pollock and Webster put the issues very clearly:

> From a scientific perspective [the] question is impossible to answer since it is based on an unscientific assumption about dangerousness, namely that it is a stable and consistent quality existing within the individual.
>
> (1990: 493)

They suggest that translating the question into more appropriate terms would require the following question:

> What are the psychological, social and biological factors bearing on the defendant's . . . behaviour and what are the implications for future [behaviour] and the potential for change?
>
> (ibid.)

Many workers suggest that 'statistical studies of the prediction of dangerousness . . . indicate a high rate of error, usually in the direction of over-prediction' (Greenland, 1980: 99). However, Greenland also reminds us that 'much less attention is paid to the havoc caused by the "false positives". These are the patients who kill or maim people after being considered safe for discharge'. Mental health professionals, and psychiatrists in particular, have been criticised by some observers for making apparently unrealistic claims to expertise in the assessment of dangerousness (for reviews, see Poythress, 1988; Clark *et al.*, 1993; Steadman *et al.*, 1993).

Greenland suggests that a number of these criticisms are ill-founded. He bases this assertion largely on the grounds that psychiatrists are no worse than other professionals in making such predictions, and that when charged with predicting dangerousness in *mentally ill* offenders they have a considerable degree of expertise to offer. Greenland's more optimistic views have been offset to some extent by the results of a large-scale study carried out in six countries by Montandon and Harding (1984). They found that the level of agreement between assessors of dangerousness was generally low, the level of 60 per cent being reached for only four cases out of sixteen. Moreover, psychiatrists did not reach a higher degree of agreement on the ratings of dangerousness than non-psychiatrists. Sadly, there are no statistical or actuarial measures available that offer the prediction of dangerousness in either so-called normal or mentally disordered offenders with any degree of certainty. Despite the fact that considerable research has been carried out into the prediction of anti-social behaviour generally, this has merely tended to suggest that although actuarial techniques can discriminate between high-risk and low-risk groups, there will always be a residual majority in the middle-risk groups whose re-offending rates are too near 50–50 to be much use prognostically. (See Prins, 1986; Chapter 4 for more detailed discussion of this topic.)

It is not unreasonable to ask, in the light of the above comments, are we left with any indicators of the probability of future dangerous behaviour? To answer this question we have to turn to clinical and allied experience and the degree to which we can learn from this, even if, sadly, from time to time, we have to be wise after the event. We start our discussion with one or two case examples by way of illustration.

WITH THE BENEFIT OF HINDSIGHT

Example 1

The initial series of incidents in this example occurred over thirty years ago. In July 1962 the late Graham Young – then just under fifteen years of age – was made the subject of a fifteen-year hospital order with restrictions under the 1959 Mental Health Act. He had been convicted of three charges of causing grievous bodily harm to his sister, father and a school friend by means of poison. Three important points were made (amongst others) in the psychiatric evidence given at his trial, and which pointed to his likely future dangerousness: first, his long-standing interest in, and obsession with, poisons (dating back to quite early childhood); second, his apparent lack of remorse; third, the calculated nature of his activities. Despite whatever reservations there were about this young man's capacity to refrain from committing further serious personal harm to others (and there were some), he was discharged conditionally from hospital in February 1971 – some nine years after his original detention and placed under probation and psychiatric supervision.

It has been suggested that in the period leading up to his eventual release Young made two interesting but (fortunately) unsuccessful applications for employment. One is said to have been to a forensic science laboratory and the other to a pharmaceutical training school! It is not altogether clear whether the Special Hospital authorities were fully aware of these applications; most likely they were not (see Holden, 1974, for further details). It is of more immediate interest that Young found employment quite quickly with a firm of optical and photographic equipment manufacturers in Bovingdon, Herts. With hindsight, one might wish to ponder the wisdom of allowing him to obtain that particular employment given his previous history. Accommodation was found for him in lodgings. By April 1971 (only two months after his release) a number of his workmates were taken seriously ill and two of them subsequently died. It appears that even after these occurrences it took a considerable time before any suspicion was directed towards him. That suspicion arose at all was largely (and fortunately) due to the perspicacity of his employer and the firm's factory doctor. Eventually, in July 1972, he appeared in court once again and was found guilty on two counts of murder and two counts of attempted murder; he was sentenced to life imprisonment. Having pleaded not guilty (on the facts) to murder, a mental health disposal was not available to him. (See Prins, 1976: Chapter 4 and Holden, 1974, for more detailed accounts of this case.)

This *cause célèbre* led to three important events. First, the regulations governing the public availability of poisons were tightened up. (Young had in fact obtained the poison from a pharmacy and *not* through his workplace.) Second, the appointment of the Aarvold Committee (Home Office and DHSS, 1973) to look into the arrangements for the discharge and supervision of restricted patients and the subsequent establishment of the Aarvold Board (now known as the Home Secretary's Advisory Board, see Egglestone, 1990). Third, the setting up of the Butler Committee to inquire more generally into the question of the law and practice concerning mentally abnormal offenders (Home Office and DHSS, 1975).

Example 2

This is the case of a man named Simcox. His first marriage ended in divorce, but not before he had assaulted his wife and mother-in-law. His second marriage ended more violently. He was convicted of murdering his wife with a knife wound to the throat. He was sentenced to death and reprieved. Ten years later, he was released from prison on licence. In 1961, he married for the *third* time and was soon in court again for carrying an offensive weapon. The judge made a probation order with a condition that he never saw his wife again. In less than two weeks, he had breached that order, killed his sister-in-law and wounded another of his wife's relatives. At his second trial for murder, evidence was given that he had a paranoid personality. Blom-Cooper, in his analysis of this case, suggests that a paranoid personality is not developed overnight, nor is it a temporary condition. It is suggested that Simcox telegraphed his future homicidal plans by informing people that he intended to kill himself and his wife, and by prowling around his wife's house with a dangerous weapon, ten days before the killing (Blom-Cooper, 1965).

Example 3

This concerns the case of Terence John Iliffe and is referred to by the Butler Committee (Home Office and DHSS, 1975: 58). Iliffe was conditionally discharged from hospital because the assessments made at the time gave no reason to believe that he would present any general risk to the public. However, it was appreciated that 'if Iliffe were to re-marry there might be a specific risk to his wife'. Those responsible for his supervision recognised that if he indicated any such intention his 'prospective wife must be fully informed of his background'. What was not foreseen, however, was that he might marry *without the knowledge* of his supervising officer. When this marriage was discovered, attempts were made to inform the wife, 'but tragically, to no avail'. He was sentenced to life imprisonment for her murder on 9 April 1974. As the Butler Committee stated: 'Clearly, where specific risks are involved, the assessment of the likely effectiveness of subsequent control in the particular circumstances must be a major consideration (Home Office and DHSS, 1975: 58).

The following are more recent examples:

Example 4

Christopher Clunis, a paranoid schizophrenic, stabbed to death a random victim at Finsbury Park London Underground railway station. At his trial his history revealed that he had demonstrated violent intentions and actions in the past, and that despite repeated requests for his detention under mental health legislation, this had not taken place. In part, this was due to the stricter criteria now applied for the compulsory detention of such patients and to lack of adequate communication and community care. (See reports in *Independent*, 19 July 1994: 6 and 8; 23 July 1994: 23. For more detailed accounts, see North East Thames and South East Thames Regional Health Authorities, 1994; Coid, 1994; and Prins, 1994.)

Example 5

This concerns Sharon Dalson, aged twenty-four, who killed her two children. She had a history of severe schizophrenia, which led her to respond to voices telling her to kill them. She had a prior conviction for assault and affray and had been made the subject of a hospital order. In this case, the final tragic outcome could not have been predicted, but the social services department was criticised for allegedly not taking formal care proceedings in respect of the children despite the knowledge that they were at risk from their mother (*Independent*, 4 January 1994: 4).

Example 6

My final illustration concerns the case of Daniel Mudd (Wiltshire County Council, 1988). Mudd had been released on conditional discharge from a special hospital where he had been originally detained for a non-homicide offence. During the period of supervision he killed a female resident in a mental after-care hostel and was subsequently sentenced to life imprisonment. A committee of inquiry was set up and their findings revealed what appeared to be some serious errors of judgement and practice. These are summarised below:

1 Too little attention was paid to the nature of Mudd's previous offences, behaviour and convictions prior to hospitalisation; these had included making indecent phone calls, assault with intent to commit actual bodily harm, and indecent assault on an adult female.
2 Too little attention appeared to have been paid to the views of the doctors who examined him at his trial; they had said that he was potentially very dangerous and, because of the nature of his particular personality disorder, might well kill someone at some future date.
3 Although this young man had been in the care of the local authority concerned with his current supervision for many years, no attempt appeared to have been made to collate the data in the numerous files about him that were available.

In addition, no-one had thought it sensible to consult the social worker who had known and supervised him as a youngster. It was also alleged that her attempts to keep in contact with him when he was sent to hospital had not been met with any interest by the hospital authorities.

4   Mudd had very serious drinking problems during the period of supervision. These were never properly identified or placed into the context of his past behaviour and attitudes. There were said to have been occasions when he was so affected by drink that he could not get up to go to work.

5   This lack of identification continued even when he was picked up on several occasions by the police for being drunk and when he had assaulted a man whilst under the influence of drink. He had also been discharged prematurely from a training scheme because of alleged sexual advances to a woman.

6   His supervising social worker left and no attempt appeared to have been made to prepare the client for his departure. It was alleged he was left unsupervised for a month.

7   The committee found that throughout the period of supervision, the client's version of events had been accepted at face value and without challenge. The records available (which were in any case difficult to interpret) showed no indications of any critical analysis of events and attitudes. Supervision by senior management had not been effective. The social workers seemed to have adopted a preconceived notion that here was someone who needed to be 'rescued' from an adverse experience (that is, being in a Special Hospital) and that this preconception had blinded them to the realities of the case. Finally, it was suggested that the supervisors took too much upon themselves and did not liaise sufficiently well with the relevant department of the Home Office (C.3 Division). They also failed to provide that department with adequate information about the progress of the case.

The above case examples have a number of elements in common concerning the importance of warning signs and other indicators of vulnerability. I now examine some of these.

1   The first concerns the need to have *full* details of the original (index) offence or offences, the circumstances surrounding them and what various professionals thought at the time, especially their views about the offender's apparent motivation and attitudes. (These aspects do not appear to have been considered sufficiently carefully in the cases of Young and Mudd.) As already indicated elsewhere in this book, the mere statutory description of an offence may give insufficient information as to its severity. Two short illustrations make the point.

Example 7

This concerned the case of a man serving a short sentence of imprisonment for an indecent assault on a boy of fifteen. Detailed examination of the police accounts of the attack demonstrated that the boy's attacker used both considerable force and fear to overpower the boy during the assault.

Example 8

A man convicted of rape had subjected his victim to both vaginal and anal penetration. Not only had she been tied up whilst the assault took place, but in addition her attacker had used a leather belt to induce unconsciousness, only releasing this 'garotte' in order to bring his victim round sufficiently for a further assault to take place. The formal legal charge of rape afforded no immediate indication of the real nature of the man's behaviour; this was only revealed when the full police reports and witness statements were examined. It is often very important to have sight of such statements and in some cases the 'scene of crime' reports and photographs may also be of considerable value. They may serve to remind the worker of the seriousness of the offence and may also prove useful in confronting attempts at denial by the offender during the course of therapeutic work. For example, the act of killing involves a great deal of very real unpleasantness which may diminish over time. One is mindful of the firm resolution of Lady Macbeth, when she criticises her husband for his infirmity of purpose in not being able to return to the bed-chamber to incriminate the grooms with the slain King Duncan's blood. Much later in the play, when events overtake her, and she begins to disintegrate mentally, she utters those significant words: 'yet who would have thought the old man to have had so much blood in him?' (Act V, Scene i). And, in murder, it is not just blood, but other bodily fluids and matter that may be discharged before or at the point of death.

2 As indicated in Chapter 8 above on sexual offences, it is as well to remember that some apparently 'minor' sexual offences may be ominous prognosticators of future serious harm (see, for example the discussion of indecent exposure). In addition, certain other offences may not appear, on first inspection, to have ominous prognostications of life-threatening potential. It is only when the full details are examined that this may become apparent. Burglary is a good example. As Morneau and Rockwell (1980) indicate, the burglar who merely makes off with portable items and/or cash needs to be distinguished from the burglar who only steals the shoes belonging to the female occupant of the house, or from the burglar who pulls back bedclothes and slashes the sheets with a knife. Masters, in his book about Jeffrey Dahmer, recounts how he had drugged various youthful members of the 'bath-club' he frequented; it was not until one of them became so ill as to require hospitalisation that the management recognised the bizarre nature of Dahmer's activities and rescinded his membership. They did *not*, however, inform the police. Masters suggests that such behaviour should have provided an 'obvious clue to a necrophilic character . . . the comatose state

being at one remove from the dead state' (1993: 74). Elsewhere, Masters notes how insufficient attention was paid to the details and nature of some of Dahmer's earlier sexual escapades and to the lack of follow-up which might have revealed his escalating problems with alcohol (p. 104). With hindsight, one may ask whether sufficient regard was paid at their trials to the circumstances of Young's and Mudd's previous offence patterns, and the prognostications given by the professionals who gave evidence. Example 8 above emphasises the importance of knowing the exact details of an offence. For, although rape is a dreadful offence under any circumstances, we need perhaps to distinguish between the 'one-off' rape situation in which a woman's person and rights are gravely abused and the rape that occurs in circumstances of sadistic activity and/or highly deviant sexual practices.

One worker emphasises the need for this kind of distinction very well:

> The patient may be generally categorized as a rapist, or a child molester, or a murderer. What kind of rape, what kind of 'molestation', what kind of murder, is often brushed over. The therapist may have felt like a voyeur, or may have been repelled and sickened by violence and have found ways of avoiding it. But very early [on] the question must be, 'What did you do? . . . and how, and with what, and to whom?' By this is meant a step-by-step, possibly even a blow-by-blow description of the violent act, and all the circumstances surrounding it. Who was the victim? Why this victim and not another? What was the offender's frame of mind, from the beginning of the day? How long had he or she been thinking or fantasizing about the crime . . . what preparations had been made, *what exactly did the offender do*?
>
> (Weist, 1981: 273; emphasis added)

Serious sex offenders may frequently present *themselves* as victims. The same author quotes the example of the paedophile in group treatment who had persistently described himself as alone, unhappy, sinking into heavy drinking and

> 'then there were those local children who were so bright and friendly and sweet and . . . I acted on impulse, because children can be so seductive', etc. On persistent questioning by the therapist and others in the group, it emerged that what he described was not the case. He was asked specifically 'who were the children . . . how did you meet them . . . when was the first time you talked with them . . . what did you talk about . . . when was the next time you saw them?' As he responded to these questions, it emerged that there had been a period of gentle, active seduction on his part lasting several months. The alcohol problem was relevant, but not as a primary factor – it served more as an alibi for his behaviour.[2]
>
> (1981: 274)

It should be obvious by now that only a full account of the offence will help us to make useful prognostic distinctions. The painstaking collation of facts and the checking of information from a variety of sources are essential. Scott suggests that

It is patience, thoroughness and persistence in this process [data collection], rather than any diagnostic brilliance that produces results. In this sense, the telephone, the written request for past records and the checking of information against other informants, are the important diagnostic devices. Having collected the facts under the headings (1) the offence; (2) past behaviour; (3) personal data; (4) social circumstances, it is useful to scan them from a number of different directions with a view to answering certain key questions relating to dangerousness.

(1977: 129)

Freud once said, 'I learned to follow the unforgotten advice of my master Charcot; to look at the same things again and again, until they themselves began to speak' (1914: 22). This need for careful history-taking was of course recognised in biblical times. For example, Jesus caused very careful inquiry to be made when he asked the father of the boy thought to be possessed for full details of the history of his alleged state of possession (Mark 9: 20–27). And, in more recent times, Umberto Eco has stated: 'No piece of information is superior to any other. Power lies in having them all on file and then finding the connections' (1989: 225). There is a further telling statement to this effect in the Report of the Allitt Inquiry.

We were struck throughout our Inquiry by the way in which fragments of medical evidence, which, if assembled, would have pointed to Allitt as the malevolent cause of the unexpected collapses of children, lay neglected or were missed altogether. Taken in isolation, these fragments of medical evidence were not all very significant nor was failure to recognise some of them very culpable. But collectively they would have amounted to an unmistakable portrait of malevolence. The principle failure of those concerned lay in not collecting together those pieces of evidence.

(Trent Regional Health Authority, 1994: 131)

3 An offender's or an offender-patient's performance in an institution may not be a reliable indicator of future behaviour unless it is viewed in relation to his or her whole history and life-style. For an example, an individual may win high praise for her brilliant performance on an Open University course. A careful study of all her activities and the attention she has received for them in the institution may reveal that there may have been rather less concern with her *motives* and *feelings* about her original offence and her future behaviour. It is easy to be seduced by intellectual achievement and lulled thereby into a false sense of security. One may speculate that during Graham Young's period in Broadmoor, although there was (rightly) concentration upon his education needs, perhaps not enough attention was paid to his emotions and continuing preoccupations with poisons and killings. Similarly, the man with a long history of achieving his goals in life by violent means may win praise for his involvement in body-building classes whilst in prison. A more questioning (and some may think more cynical) view might be that he was keeping himself fit for further

mayhem upon discharge. It is important to underline the point that we have to be very cautious in such cases and need to operate with a considerable degree of suspiciousness. In my view the quality of supervision and its intrusiveness in these cases is of a different order from that required where the risk of further serious harm is not so likely. Those exercising supervision are under an obligation to make this aspect of the relationship very clear to the offender (or offender-patient) from the beginning.

4 The question of intrusive intervention is worth taking a little further. In the case of Graham Young, it is highly relevant to note that when the police gained entry to his lodgings they found gruesome and explicit pictorial evidence of his continuing preoccupation with poisons (Holden, 1974: 107). Had those responsible for his supervision insisted upon regular access to his accommodation they might have obtained valuable clues at an earlier stage as to his sinister preoccupations. The crime novelist P.D. James has a very compelling observation in this respect: '[P]eople's living space, and the personal possessions with which they surround themselves [are] inevitably fascinating . . ., an affirmation of identity, intriguing both in themselves and as a betrayal of character, interests, obsessions' (1987: 241). The detective in Ackroyd's novel *Hawksmoor* says:

> You can tell a great deal about the killer from the kind of death he inflicts; an eager person will kill in a hurried manner, a tentative person will do it more slowly . . . you must remember, too, the sequence of actions which follow the murder; most killers are stunned by their action. They sweat; sometimes they become very hungry or thirsty; many of them lose control of their bowels at the moment of death, just as their victims do . . . murderers will try to recall the sequence of events; they will remember exactly what they did just before and just after . . . but they can never remember the actual moment of killing. The murderer always forgets that, and that is why he will always leave a clue.
>
> (1985: 159)

It is helpful to remember that some offenders and offender-patients are frequently preoccupied by fantasies of what they have done and what they may wish to do to future victims – a form of wishful rehearsal (MacCulloch *et al.*, 1983). In some cases these are carefully concealed and take a good deal of eliciting. In others, questioning may produce quite easily evidence of a rich and ongoing fantasy life. From time to time, such offenders will commit their fantasies to writing or depict them through drawings (as did Young). The recently reported case of Colin Hatch (a parolee from a prison sentence), who choked to death a boy of seven, is revealing from this point of view. It was alleged at his trial that Hatch (who had previous convictions for sexual offences against young boys) had written down detailed sexual fantasies of his intentions. Following his arrest, it was alleged that descriptions of some of these were found secreted in a wardrobe. 'They described in detail a fantasy where he tempted a 10-year-old girl to his room, stripped, raped, strangled and finally dumped her body in two bin liners.' Counsel for the prosecution said 'His writings include references to deliberate killing . . . in the fantasy story lack of consent is part of the story, that's part of the excitement. Killing and disposing of the body was part of the plan' (*Independent*, 18 January 1994: 2; 20 January 1994: 3). As already indicated, offenders and offender- patients may go to great lengths to conceal such fantasies. Others, when asked, will readily admit to them and provide concrete evidence of their existence by revealing material which helps to facilitate such fantasy (for example, pictures, writings, photographs, tapes; see also Prins, 1975). It is important to be on the look-out for such material and to ask direct questions about its existence. (See Briggs, 1994, for a helpful discussion of the assessment of fantasies in forensic-psychiatric settings.) All this material is useful grist to the assessor's prognostic mill. However, it should be stressed that such material, its importance and its relevance, needs to be judged against other less subjective evidence.

5 It is also clear from the cases quoted that the offenders still had what Cox (1979: 310) called 'unfinished business' to complete. It is very difficult to ensure that there is no longer a need for substitute or surrogate victims. For example, it would be incorrect to conclude that an offender convicted and sentenced for matricide had resolve his or her problems through the killing. Cases come to mind where, following discharge, relationships have been formed with persons who closely resembled the original victim. One must always be on the look-out for such occurrences. The 'unfinished business' may, of course, still involve the original victim. The individual suffering from irrational jealousy (as described in Chapter 4) may have tried unsuccessfully to kill his partner. At some point, he may apply for, or be eligible for, release into the community. We know that this is an intractable disorder and the offender may try to kill or cause serious injury again. We may ask ourselves what advice or help we can offer to the potential victim in the face of her assailant's unshakeable belief in her infidelity. Some observers (perhaps somewhat cynically) have suggested that the 'treatment' is largely geographical: that is, advise the potential victim to move as far away as possible and change her name. This may sound unduly pessimistic, but the irrational and persistent nature of this disorder is well documented. In these and similar cases the supervisor has to have a keen awareness not only of any changes in the offender's social environment, but, more importantly, of any changes in his or her relationships with significant others as well.

6 I have already made reference to the manner in which our poisoner obtained a form of employment which, with hindsight, appeared to be fraught with potential hazards. Do employments ever give clues to the possible commission of further harm? Sometimes, as with the case of fantasy, they may help us, provided that they are considered alongside other factors. It is worthy of comment (and one would not wish to put it higher than this) that employment as a butcher and in abattoirs has sometimes been found in the histories of those convicted of particularly bizarre or sadistic murders (Brittain, 1970). It is of interest that Dennis Nilsen probably developed the skills needed to dismember some of his victims as a result of his employment as a cook and butcher in the Army Catering Corps. As

we saw in Chapter 8, those with necrophilic tendencies may seek work as mortuary attendants and Scott (1977) has observed that children given to sadistic behaviour sometimes showed an unusual interest in sick and damaged animals.

GENERAL MANAGEMENT ISSUES

All who work in this field have to come to terms with a process that I can best describe as 'ambivalent investment'. The process has three elements. First, the worker (of whatever discipline) has to come to terms with his or her feelings of revulsion and horror about some of the crimes these offenders have committed (see also Wiest, 1981). It is all too easy for professionals to make a somewhat superficial acknowledgement of such feelings without really working through them and coming to grips with them. It is only through systematic reflection and self-monitoring of the kind advocated by Casement in his thoughtful books *On Learning from the Patient* (1985) and *Further Learning from the Patient* (1990) that we can be reasonably sure of our possible blind spots within the offender–worker relationship. Second, having tried hard to achieve this, the worker then has to face the fact that he or she carries a great burden of responsibility for the welfare of both offender and the community – an area fraught with ethical dilemmas. Third, the worker in his or her counselling role has an investment in seeing that things are going well. This is because most people enter the counselling and caring professions from a desire to offer a service of care and restoration to people with a variety of needs. This may lead to a degree of unrealistic optimism about the progress of the case and the need for strict supervision.

For all the aforementioned reasons there is, therefore, an overall 'investment' in things going well from the outset because of the initial hurdles that have been overcome. Professionals may not wish to hear the 'bad news' – that things are perhaps not going quite so well. They may ignore the half-spoken messages from both offender and partner or family. They may block off attempts by all parties to give them the 'bad news' because they do not wish to hear it; thus, opportunities for therapeutic confrontations may be missed and the need to unburden frightening thoughts and fantasies may go unheeded. (We should be mindful of the statement by the nineteenth-century physician William Osler, who once said in a lecture, 'listen to the patient, he is telling you the diagnosis'.) It is erroneous to think, therefore, that denial is the sole prerogative of clients or patients.

One way in which to try to avoid the pitfalls just described is to keep good and regular records, and, more importantly, *to consult them at frequent intervals*. We all suffer from the arrogant assumption that we can easily recall our ongoing counselling in adequate detail. This is not the case – as one soon discovers if one looks back on a series of interviews undertaken, say, over a six-month period. The missed opportunities and the gaps in the accounts will emerge all too clearly. In addition, in recent years, a trend towards short-term counselling has been developing. This has probably militated against positive attitudes towards the desirability of long-term work with difficult and highly vulnerable people. To paraphrase: the price that supervisors pay for ensuring the liberty of the subject to live safely in the community is that of 'eternal vigilance'. Supervisors must therefore be willing to ask unimaginable, unthinkable and unaskable questions if they are to engage effectively in this area of work.[3]

The 'unimaginable', the 'unthinkable' and the 'unaskable'

Reference is now made to some specific points which I hope will illustrate the need to ask the 'unimaginable', the 'unthinkable' and the 'unaskable'.

1 Have past precipitants and stresses in the offender or offender-patient's background been removed? If still present, are they amenable to further work and has the supervisor the courage to deal with them? Some apposite words upon this theme were spoken by HRH Prince Charles in an address on the occasion of the one hundred and fiftieth anniversary celebrations of the Royal College of Psychiatrists in 1991 (emphasis added):

> In our contemporary society there is every incentive to believe that suffering can be banished, avoided, or at worst postponed. Psychiatrists have to confront the evidence to the contrary every day. Just being with a patient who is frightened *or frightening* must be incredibly difficult and takes immense courage and dedication; the human contact can awaken shadows in the doctor's own psyche, testing that inner strength which has the most profound influence on the patient.

Although he was addressing psychiatrists, his words have relevance for all professionals who engage in this difficult area of work.

2 What is the person's current capacity for dealing with provocation? In Chapter 7, I pointed out that displaced aggression is a very worrying phenomenon and that serious violence may be displaced from a highly provoking source to one that may be scarcely provoking at all. Some of our most worrying cases are those in which serious violence has been caused to the innocent stranger. We have to continually ask ourselves: has the original source of that violence been fully explored, localised or neutralised?

3 Can we obtain any clues concerning the offender's self-image? As we have seen, this is of vital importance if we are considering prognosis in relation to serious sex offending such as rape. In other cases we need to ask: how vulnerable and 'fragile' does this person still seem to be? Were the original circumstances the last straw in a series of stressful events, or does the individual see everybody around him or her as hostile as in the case of the 'true' (as distinct from the wrongly labelled) psychopath. Does he or she treat others as objects upon which to indulge his or her deviant desires? The serial killers Christie, Nilsen and Dahmer, in their different ways, appeared to show certain of these qualities and a capacity to create what some have called a 'false self' in order to perpetrate their killings (see Holmes and de Burger, 1988).

4 Can we be satisfied that the behaviour was person specific? Was the behaviour directed towards a particular individual, for a specific purpose, or was

it a means of getting back at society in general as with some arsonists? Such people feel 'despised and rejected of men' (Isaiah 53: 3). Is this offender-patient the kind of person who still feels threatened or persecuted? Is this a personality attribute developed in relation to some past experience or the result of ongoing mental illness which may yet be amenable to further modification or alleviation with the use of carefully monitored medication? And what are the chances of the offender-patient continuing to take such medication if released into the community, and how adequate are the resources for attempting to ensure it? It is worth noting that some individuals may harbour feelings of rage for long periods before they explode with catastrophic results. Some forms of 'amok-like' behaviour (as in the Hungerford disaster) would fall into this category. Often, only very subtle clues may be given and it requires great skill to discern them.

5 Has the offender or offender-patient come to terms in part, if not *in toto*, with what he or she did? Has he or she shown some capacity for self-examination? To what extent does he or she continue to use the mechanism of denial? Mezey *et al.* (1991) suggest six aspects of denial that should be considered in paedophilic offences.

(a) Denial of the act itself. Such denial will include denial by offender-patients to the police, prosecutors, the courts and those charged subsequently with managing them. By this means they set their own limits on what they felt was admissable, playing down their own involvement.
(b) Denial of the child as a person. They see the child as an *object only* – thus denying the child's personal integrity. For example, they tend to speak of the child as a 'victim', and are not able (at least initially) to use the child's name.
(c) Denial of the child as a victim. They tend to see *themselves* as victims and the child as an instigator or willing participant, denying that there might be any unwillingness on the part of the child. (One can discern here a similar mechanism operating in the manner in which rapists refuse to accept that 'no' means 'no'.) They cannot accept the fact that they are in a position of power and acknowledge a child's fear.
(d) Denial of adult responsibility. They indulge in such ploys as blaming the mother, spouse or partner. In some cases, their own past histories of abuse enable them to engage in such denial more easily.
(e) Denial of consequences for the child, that is, tending to minimise effects of abuse on the child.
(f) Following 'treatment' (in the work described by Mezey and her colleagues, this consisted of attendance in a group as a condition of a probation order) they felt that after its conclusion they could start again. They had paid their price and were reluctant to admit their continuing interest in children. One member of the group said 'a future without children simply wasn't a future worth living' (Mezey *et al.*, 1991: 18).

Do these offender-patients now appear to have great insight into their condition? This is a highly problematic area to assess with any degree of certainty. It is often our task to help such people face feelings and experiences that hitherto have been intolerable. We can only do this if we 'open' ourselves to their troubled and terrifying worlds. It *may* be an ominous sign if an offender-patient talks about his or her offence in an *apparently* guilt-free and callous manner. As counsellors we tend, for the reasons stated earlier, to hope for protestations of guilt and/or remorse and we may be disquieted when these are not forthcoming in full measure.

Wiest (1981) has suggested that offenders or offender-patients tend to go through five stages in working through their guilt and remorse for what they have done (but not always in the sequence that follows). The first is *confession*: 'I take responsibility, and that's an end of it.' If I own up, 'all will be forgiven'. The second is *acceptance* of punishment: the offender accepts what has happened to him or her (for example, being institutionalised for a long period) and this is seen as a kind of reciprocity that makes everything OK. The third phase is *denial* (which can of course operate at any time): the offender may say in so many words, 'it's all over, I can't undo it, life must go on.' The fourth is the *grieving* stage; grief for themselves and/or the victim. Significant questions asked by offenders of themselves during this stage may be 'Who am I? What kind of person am I?' The possibility of a suicide attempt may be very real (see also Fraser, 1988).

The fifth stage is that of *remorse*, which, as the poet Emily Dickinson said with such meaning, 'is memory awake'. This needs to be handled and assessed with care for one may be misled. A child molester may dwell obsessively upon how the children's lives have been ruined – 'they will never be normal themselves when they grow up – they will never recover from the experience'. These feelings *may*, of course, be genuine, but the preoccupation may indicate an ongoing molestation in the offender's imagination (see earlier discussion of the role of fantasy). Some offenders can, of course, be afforded the chance to say they are sorry in a very practical way to their victims – as evidenced in many current reparation schemes. Not so the murderer. As Wiest suggests, to whom can the murderer apologise and make his or her peace? It is, therefore, not perhaps altogether surprising that some such offenders turn to religion of a strongly evangelical and charismatic type and others to a solitary preoccupation with the Bible. It is difficult to assess the 'genuineness' of this kind of 'conversion'.

We should remember also that after the commission of a particularly horren-dous crime a number of mechanisms may operate. Not all of them are at a conscious level. In some cases, the act may have been so horrendous to its perpetrator that it may literally have been blotted out of consciousness; he or she may even have experienced an amnesic episode or a fugue state. What indivi-duals actually did after committing the crime may be of considerable prognostic importance. Did they just wander off or did they realise what they had done and summon help immediately? Or did they, having cut up the body into little pieces, or subjected it to some other form of mutilation, go off for a fish and chip supper and thence to bed to a good night's sleep? In other instances, the offender may claim he or she was under the influence of alcohol and/or other drugs at the material time. This may have less importance in law than in terms of future behaviour since the ingestion of drugs and alcohol are usually regarded as exacerbating rather than mitigating factors, though there are some rare exceptions. Rix has proposed that we should make a distinction between alcohol intoxication and drunkenness. He proposes that

> (1) the term 'alcohol intoxication' should refer to a state in which alcohol is present in the body; (2) its diagnosis should be based on toxicological evidence for the presence of alcohol in body fluids or tissues; and (3) the term 'drunkenness' should be used to describe behaviour displayed by people who have consumed, believe that they have consumed or want others to believe that they have consumed, alcohol.

(1989: 100)

Hospitals and prisons are obviously not the best places for measuring the capacity for coping with the future likely effects of such substances. A series of graded experiences are required so that such tendencies may be carefully monitored under conditions of increasing freedom from constraints. This is somewhat easier to achieve in a hospital situation than in the penal system. For example, offender patients in Special Hospitals and secure units may be taken on outside 'trips', exposed to a small amount of alcohol and such exposure monitored by escorting staff. In similar fashion, the continuing interests of the persistent paedophile may be discerned by watchful staff if his attention and interest seem concentrated solely upon the children he sees on the beach. Some offenders may be highly reluctant to acknowledge that they have actually committed the crime for fear of the distress such an acknowledgement would cause to family and/or friends. At one Mental Health Review Tribunal hearing I recall vividly the acute distress caused to a patient's mother when she heard the full details of her son's sex offences for the first time. Until that point she had apparently been almost wholly unaware of their true nature. The late Dr McGrath (sometime Physician Superintendent at Broadmoor Hospital) quotes the case of a paedophilic, sadistic killer who consistently denied his guilt in order to spare hurt to his 'gentle devoted parents who could not believe his guilt'. When they died, he willingly admitted his guilt, and in due course was released (McGrath, 1989; Hombridge, 1994).

The worker's feelings

So far most of the concentration in this chapter has been upon the feelings of the offender or offender-patient. Less has been said about the fears, attributes and skills that the worker brings to this difficult task. This is partly because few of us are prepared to admit that some of the people described in this book may frighten us. Often, we cannot put the reason for this very clearly into words. Some say 'they have a hunch'; others will say 'it's something in their eyes'. This may *sound* absurd; indeed, I was once taken to task by a good friend and colleague for explaining dangerous behaviour *post hoc* and for suggesting that hunches should be relied upon

(Webb, 1976). But, as professionals working in this demanding field, we do, from time to time, have to rely upon our 'hunches'. Our task is to try to make them more *informed* hunches by learning from one case to the next and by sharing problems with other workers and advisers and participating in continuing education (see Chapter 10). There is certainly little doubt that the manner in which some offenders and offender-patients present themselves can fill us with an intangible disquiet and even apprehension. I am reminded of the second witch in *Macbeth* when she says, 'By the pricking of my thumbs, something wicked this way comes' (Act IV, Scene i). Can we be any more precise about what it is we are afraid of? We are all afraid of physical violence.[4] However, it is useful to remember that some dangerous or potentially dangerous people not only wish to be controlled but are, in addition, afraid of their own dangerous impulses. With such individuals it may be helpful to bring this out into the open. A phrase such as 'I know that you are fearful of losing control, but I'm going to try to help you' may be quite useful. Cox (1974) has suggested in this context that some offenders and offender-patients may be frightened to talk about their feelings and fantasies because they feel the therapist or counsellor is too frightened to listen to them (see also Scott, 1973). It is, therefore, essential that counsellors make some attempt to overcome these fears, though the process is a very demanding one. Are we afraid that we may *unwittingly* provoke a violent assault or are we afraid that somehow we may be overcome by the dangerous individual's violent fantasy system?

Sarbin (1967) suggests a helpful formulation in this context. He says that there are three ways (amongst others) of meeting a crisis: the autistic, the social and explosive violence. One can withdraw and do without, or one copes on a realistic basis of new adjustment, or one goes like 'a bull in a china shop' for a simple solution. Scott uses the case of a non-commissioned officer to illustrate Sarbin's formulation. This man had suffered long conflict with his wife. He went through a period of very heavy drinking (autistic) and tried to obtain a divorce (social). He then got himself posted to Ireland and volunteered for dangerous duty (the commencement of the violent solution, but against himself). He subsequently deserted his post, hoping to be dismissed from the service (a variety of suicide) and finally shot his wife with a high velocity rifle in their kitchen (the final violent solution) (Scott, 1977: 139–140).

A last useful illustration of the importance of understanding an apparently irrational and unpredictable outburst would be a serious assault or homicide committed in circumstances that amounted to what has been described as homosexual panic. The so-called 'normal' person who violently attacks another because of an alleged homosexual overture may well need to have his own actions better understood in terms of his own possible repressed homosexuality than solely as the reactions of an outraged victim responding to an unwelcome overture. Certainly, some killings that *appear* to have a sexual setting need to be understood in this way.

CONCLUSION

The emphasis in this chapter has been upon practical concerns; to this end it cannot be stressed too often that a most careful review of the offender or offender-patient's total experience and the impressions of him or her *gained by a variety of observers* are of crucial importance. Frequently we may have of course to act on 'hunches'. However, we must aspire to make these 'hunches' better informed and articulated. To do this, we have to pay careful attention to the following points: first, the multi-factorial and multi-disciplinary nature of our task; second, the need for adequate and full communication between disciplines; third, the need for a disciplined and painstaking approach; fourth, a recognition of and a coming to terms with a high level of surveillance in this particular type of work; and fifth (and perhaps the most difficult) the need to develop a capacity within ourselves to understand our own anxieties and blind-spots. Some of these points are the subject of discussion in the next chapter.

NOTES

1   In addition, see Walker (1983). It is worth noting that in the USA and in Canada the courts have held in some circumstances that professionals may well have a duty of care to warn third parties of possible dangers to themselves. See *Tarasoff* v. *Regents of the University of California*, 529P 2d 553 Superior Ct Alameda Co. 1974. A comparable decision appears to have been reached in the Canadian case of *Wellesley Hospital* v. *Lawson*, 1976, DLR (3d) 688 (SCC). See also Mackay (1990) and Sluder and Del Carmen (1990). It has also been held in the UK that the duty of confidence owed by a doctor instructed by a patient detained in a Special Hospital does not extend so far as to bar disclosure of the doctor's report on the patient if, in the doctor's opinion, the public interest requires such disclosure to ensure that the authorities were fully informed about him (*W.* v. *Egdell and others* [1989], *Independent* Law Report, 10 November: 11). (See also *Medicine, Science and the Law* 30, 1990: 180.)

2   It is worth noting how we tend to use euphemisms to categorise people or behaviours we find hard to explain or accept. Thus, the term 'lifer' is used to describe a very wide range of prisoners whose crimes are infinitely varied and form part of a spectrum from the very 'understandable' to the inexplicably bizarre and revolting. The use of such terms also tends to depersonalise patients and clients and may prevent workers from coming to terms with their own behaviour.

3   Professor Nigel Walker places considerable stress on the monitoring (surveillance) function of the supervisor, seeing the need for control as well as for support of a welfare nature: 'The relationship between a professional carer and someone who has been given into his charge by law, and for the protection of others, is not a voluntary relationship, and so does not carry the same moral obligations or constraints. The compulsory patient's or ex-patient's interests should not over-ride the interests of others' (1991: 757). See Taylor (1989) for an account of the forensic-psychiatrist's dilemmas in this area.

4   In this chapter I am not dealing with violence by clients or patients towards professionals. This is best treated as a separate topic and there is now a growing literature in this field – see under Further Reading. (For a short account, see Prins, 1986: 127–129.)

REFERENCES

Ackroyd, P. (1985) *Hawksmoor*, London: Sphere Books (Abacus).

Baker, E. (1992) 'Dangerousness: the Neglected Gaoler: Disorder and Risk under the Mental Health Act, 1983', *Journal of Forensic Psychiatry* 3: 31–52.

—— (1993) 'Dangerousness, Rights and Criminal Justice', *The Modern Law Review* 56: 528–547.

Blom-Cooper, L. (1965) 'Preventable Homicide', *Howard Journal of Penology* XI: 297–308.

Boyd, W.D. (1994) *A Preliminary Report on Homicide. Steering Committee of the Confidential Inquiry into Homicides by Mentally Ill People*. Unit Office, PO Box 1515: London, SW1X 8PL.

Briggs, D.I. (1994) 'Assessment of Sexual Offenders', in M. McMurran and J. Hodges (eds), *The Assessment of Criminal Behaviours of Clients in Secure Settings*, London: Jessica Kingsley.

Brittain, R.P. (1970) 'The Sadistic Murderer', *Medicine, Science and the Law* 10: 198–208.

Casement, P. (1985) *On Learning from the Patient*, London: Tavistock.

—— (1990) *Further Learning from the Patient: The Analytic Space and Process*, London: Tavistock/Routledge.

Clark, D.A. Fisher, M.J. and McDougall, C. (1993) 'A New Methodology for Assessing the Level of Risk in Incarcerated Offenders', *British Journal of Criminology* 33: 436–448.

Coid, J. (1994) 'The Christopher Clunis Inquiry', *Psychiatric Bulletin* 18: 449–452.

Cox, M. (1974) 'The Psychotherapists' Anxiety: Liability or Asset? (With Special Reference to Offender/Patients)', *British Journal of Criminology* 14: 1–17.

—— (1979) 'Dynamic Psychotherapy with Sex Offenders', in I. Rosen (ed.), *Sexual Deviation* (second edn), Oxford: Oxford University Press.

Department of Health (1994) *Draft Guidance on the Discharge of Mentally Disordered People from Hospital and Their Continuing Care in the Community*, 12 January, London: Department of Health.

Eco, U. (1989) *Foucault's Pendulum*, London: Secker and Warburg.

Egglestone, F. (1990) 'The Advisory Board on Restricted Patients', in R. Bluglass and P. Bowden (eds), *Principles and Practice of Forensic Psychiatry*, London: Churchill Livingstone.

Fraser, K.A. (1988) 'Bereavement in Those Who Have Killed', *Medicine, Science and the Law* 28: 127–130.

Freud, S. (1914) *On the History of the Psychoanalytic Movement* (standard edn), Vol. 14, London: Hogarth Press and the Institute of Psycho-analysis.

Greenland, C. (1980) 'Psychiatry and the Prediction of Dangerousness', *Journal of Psychiatric Treatment and Evaluation* 2: 97–103.

Hambridge, J.A. (1994) 'Treating Mentally Abnormal Killers in a Regional Secure Unit: Some Suggested Guidelines', *Medicine, Science and the Law* 34: 237–242.

Holden, A. (1974) *The St Albans Poisoner: The Life and Crimes of Graham Young*, London: Hodder and Stoughton.

Holmes, R.M. and de Burger, J. (1988) *Serial Murder*, London: Sage.

Home Office and Department of Health and Social Security (DHSS) (1973) *Report on the Review of Procedures for the Discharge and Supervision of Psychiatric Patients Subject to Special Restrictions* (Aarvold Report), Cmnd 5191, London: HMSO.

—— (1975) *Report of the Committee on Mentally Abnormal Offenders* (The Butler Committee), Cmnd 6244. London: HMSO.

James, P.D. (1987) *A Taste for Death*, London: Sphere Books.

MacCulloch, M., Snowden, P.R., Wood, P.J.W. and Mills, H.E. (1983) 'Sadistic Phantasy, Sadistic Behaviour and Offending', *British Journal of Psychiatry* 143: 20–29.

MacCulloch, M., Bailey, J., Jones, C. and Hunter, C. (1993) 'Nineteen Male Serious Offenders Who Were Discharged from a Special Hospital: II. Illustrated Clinical Issues', *Journal of Forensic Psychiatry* 4: 451–467.

McGrath, P. (1989) Book Review: S. Dell and G. Robertson, *Sentenced to Hospital: Offenders in Broadmoor*, Oxford: Oxford University Press, 1988, *British Journal of Psychiatry* 154: 427.

Mackay, R.D. (1990) 'Dangerous Patients: Third Party Safety and Psychiatrists' Duties: Walking the Tarasoff Tightrope', *Medicine, Science and the Law* 30: 52–56.

Masters, B. (1993) *The Shrine of Jeffrey Dahmer*, London: Hodder and Stoughton.

Mezey, G., Vizzard, E., Hawkes, C. and Austin, R. (1991) 'A Community Treatment Programme for Convicted Child Sex Offenders – A Preliminary Report', *Journal of Forensic Psychiatry* 2: 11–25.

Montandon, G. and Harding, T. (1984) 'The Reliability of Dangerousness Assessments: A Decision-Making Exercise', *British Journal of Psychiatry* 144: 149–155.

Morneau, R.H. and Rockwell, B.S. (1980) *Sex, Motivation, and the Criminal Offender*, Springfield, Ill.: Charles C. Thomas.

North East Thames and South East Thames Regional Health Authorities (1994) *The Report of the Inquiry into the Care and Treatment of Christopher Clunis. Presented to the Chairman of North East Thames and South East Thames Regional Health Authorities* (Chairman, J.H. Ritchie, QC), February, London: HMSO.

Pollock, N. and Webster, C. (1990) 'The Clinical Assessment of Dangerousness', in R. Bluglass and P. Bowden (eds) *Principles and Practice of Forensic Psychiatry*, London: Churchill Livingstone.

Poythress, N. (1988) 'Violence and Dangerousness', *Current Opinion in Psychiatry* 1: 682–687.

Prins, H. (1975) 'A Danger to Themselves and to Others: Social Workers and Potentially Dangerous Clients', *British Journal of Social Work* 5: 297–309.

—— (1986) *Dangerous Behaviour, the Law and Mental Disorder*, London: Tavistock.

—— (1990) 'Dangerousness: A Review', in R. Bluglass and P. Bowden (eds), *Principles and Practice of Forensic Psychiatry*, London: Churchill Livingstone.

—— (1991) 'Dangerous People or Dangerous Situations? – Some Further Thoughts', *Medicine, Science and the Law* 31: 25–37.

Prins, H. (1994) 'Editorial: All Tragedy is the Failure of Communication (John Wilson) – The Sad Saga of Christopher Clunis', *Medicine, Science and the Law* 34: 277–278.

Rix, K.J.B. (1989) '"Alcohol Intoxication" or "Drunkenness": Is There a Difference?', *Medicine, Science and the Law* 29: 100–106.

Royal College of Psychiatrists (1991) *Good Medical Practice in the After-Care of Potentially Violent or Vulnerable Patients Discharged from In-Patient Psychiatric Treatment*, London: RCP.

Sarbin, T.R. (1967) 'The Dangerous Individual: An Outcome of Social Identity Transformations', *British Journal of Criminology* 7: 285–295.

Scott, P.D. (1973) 'Violence in Prisoners and Patients', in *Medical Care of Prisoners and Detainees*, CICA Foundation: Symposium 16 (New Series), Excerpta Medica. Amsterdam: Elsevier.

—— (1977) 'Assessing Dangerousness in Criminals', *British Journal of Psychiatry* 131: 127–142.

Shaw, S.H. (1973) 'The Dangerousness of Dangerousness', *Medicine, Science and the Law* 13: 269–271.

Sluder, R.D. and Del Carmen, R.V. (1990) 'Are Probation and Parole Officers Liable for Injuries Caused by Probationers and Parolees?' *Federal Probation* LIV: 3–12.

Steadman, H.J., Monahan, J., Robbins, P.C., Applebaum, P., Grisso, T. *et al.* (1993) 'From Dangerousness to Risk Assessment: Implications for Appropriate Research Strategies', in S. Hodgins (ed.), *Mental Disorder and Crime*, London: Sage.

Taylor, P.J. (1989) 'The Patient and the Community: Priorities for Protection', *Irish Journal of Psychological Medicine* 6: 128–134.

Tennent, T.G. (1975) 'The Dangerous Offender', in B. Barraclough and T. Silverstone (eds), *Contemporary Psychiatry*, Ashford: Headley Brothers.

Trent Regional Health Authority (1994) *The Allitt Inquiry: Independent Inquiry Relating to Deaths and Injuries on the Children's Ward at Grantham and Kesteven Hospital During the Period February to April, 1991.* (Chairman, Sir Cecil Clothier), London: HMSO.

Walker, N. (1983) 'Protecting People', in J.W. Hinton (ed.), *Dangerousness: Problems of Assessment and Management*, London: Allen and Unwin.

—— (1991) 'Dangerous Mistakes', *British Journal of Psychiatry* 158: 752–757.

Webb, D. (1976) 'Wise After the Event: Some Comments on "A Danger to Themselves and to Others"', *British Journal of Social Work* 6: 91–96.

Wiest, J. (1981) 'Treatment of Violent Offenders', *Clinical Social Work Journal* 9: 271–281.

Wiltshire County Council (1988) *Report of a Departmental Enquiry into the Discharge of Responsibilities by Wiltshire Social Services in Relation to Daniel Mudd from His Release from Broadmoor in May, 1983 until His Arrest in December 1986 for the Murder of Ruth Perrett*, Trowbridge: County Hall.

FURTHER READING

Supervision of dangerous offenders and offender-patients

Home Office (1987a) *HM Inspectorate of Probation: Issues for Senior Management in the Supervision of Dangerous and High Risk Offenders*. London: Home Office.

Home Office and Department of Health and Social Security (DHSS) (1987b) *Mental Health Act, 1983: Supervision and After-Care of Conditionally Discharged Restricted Patients: Notes for the Guidance of Social Supervisors*, London: Home Office and DHSS.

—— (1987c) *Mental Health Act, 1983: Supervision and After-Care of Conditionally Discharged Restricted Patients: Notes for the Guidance of Supervising Psychiatrists*. London: Home Office and DHSS.

—— (1987d) *Mental Health Act, 1983: Supervision and After-Care of Conditionally Discharged Restricted Patients: Notes for the Guidance of Hospitals Preparing for the Conditional Discharge of Restricted Patients*. London: Home Office and DHSS.

Miller, R.D. (1993) 'The Criminalisation of the Mentally Ill: Does Dangerousness Take Precedence over Need for Treatment?', *Criminal Behaviour and Mental Health* 3: 241–250.

Monahan, J. (1993) 'Limiting Therapist Exposure to Tarasoff Liability: Guidelines for Risk Containment', *American Psychologist* 48: 242–250.

Monahan, J. and Steadman, H. (eds) (1994) *Violence and Mental Disorder: Developments in Risk Assessment*, Chicago: University of Chicago Press.

Mullen, P. (1993) 'Care and Containment in Forensic Psychiatry', *Criminal Behaviour and Mental Health* 3: 212–225.

Shaw, R. (1991) 'Supervising the Dangerous Offender: Communication the Vital, But Often Missing Factor', *NASPO News* 10: 3–12.

Dealing with violence by clients/patients

Breakwell, G.M. (1989) *Facing Physical Violence*, London and Leicester: Routledge, in collaboration with the British Psychological Society.

Department of Health (1994) *Draft Guidance on the Discharge of Mentally Disordered People from Hospital and Their Continuing Care in the Community*, 12 January, London: Department of Health.

Kaplan, S.G. and Wheeler, E.G. (1983) 'Survival Skills for working with Potentially Violent Clients', *Social Casework* June: 339–346.

Owen, J. (1992) 'Death Threats to Psychiatrists', *Psychiatric Bulletin* 16: 142–144.

Chapter 10

Training: enhancing understanding

Books will speak plain when counsellors blanch.
(Bacon, 'Of Counsel', *Essays*)

A good book is the precious life-blood of a master spirit
Embalmed and Treasured up on purpose to a life beyond life.
(Milton, 'Areopagitica')

In this penultimate chapter I have two purposes: first, to suggest ways in which we may enhance our understanding of the difficult and demanding people described in earlier chapters; second, to outline the basic content of short workshops that have proved useful to a variety of penal and other professionals over the past fifteen years. In outlining these, I must pay tribute here to the large number of participants and co-workers who have assisted me and advanced my own (often faltering) understanding of this difficult field. Such understanding will obviously be enhanced by careful reading of the 'technical' literature, by discussion with colleagues, from supervision by senior staff and, of course, by the lessons learnt from our clients and patients over the years. It will have become obvious to my readers that a number of disciplines make up the 'technical' literature, and one requires more than a nodding acquaintance with the subject matter of psychology, psychiatry, anthropology, history, forensic science and the law. However, it is my strong belief that these excellent sources can be supplemented usefully by a study of literature, metaphor, myth and legend and it is these sources (notably literature) that form the substance of the first part of this chapter.[1] A famous American judge – Judge Learned Hand – once said:

> I venture to believe that it is as important to a judge called upon to pass [a view] on a question of constitutional law, to have a bowing acquaintance with Thucydides, Gibbon and Carlyle, with Homer, Dante, Shakespeare and Milton, with Machiavelli, Montaigne and Rabelais, with Plato, Bacon, Hume and Kant as with books that have been written specifically on the subject.
>
> (quoted in Lee, 1988: 177)

Two further short quotations will help to set the scene. The first is a statement by Salman Rushdie in an unpublished lecture (sadly, given on his behalf by another):

> Literature is the one place in any society, where, within the secrecy of our own heads, we can hear voices talking about everything in every possible way.

Rushdie seems to be suggesting that literature can sometimes help us to face and deal imaginatively with those difficult bits of reality with which, unaided, we cannot easily cope. The second quotation was written some seventy years earlier by the ill-fated Edith Thompson, in the condemned cell, for a crime she probably did not commit: 'We live and die in the books we read' (quoted in Weiss, 1988: 7).

AMBIGUITY AND UNCERTAINTY

Those who work with highly deviant and disturbed individuals – particularly those whose behaviour has been adjudged to be unpredictable and potentially dangerous – have to tolerate a considerable degree of uncertainty and ambiguity in their work. This is never easy for, as the Chief Rabbi of the UK, Dr Jonathan Sacks, said in his Reith Lectures in 1990, 'man is a meaning seeking animal' (1991: 9). He searches for meaning in all kinds of behaviours, particularly those deemed to be abnormal, baffling and frequently bizarre. Just as nature is said by scientists to abhor a vacuum, so do men and women seek relief from ambiguity and uncertainty. The problems inherent in this are well depicted by the late J.B. Priestley in his book *Over the Long High Wall* (1972):

> Both the fanatical believers and the fixed attitude people are loud in their scorn of what they call 'woolly minds' . . . it is the woolly mind that combines scepticism of everything with credulity about everything. Being woolly it has no hard edges because it bends, it does not break . . . the woolly mind realises that we live in an unimaginable, gigantic, complicated, mysterious universe. To try to stuff the vast bewildering creation into a few neat pigeon-holes is absurd. We don't know enough, and to pretend we do is mere intellectual conceit . . . the best we can do is to keep looking out for clues, for anything that will light us a step or two into the dark . . . the woolly mind can be silly at times, but even so, it finds out more and enjoys more than the rat-trap intelligence. Second-rate scientists are never woolly minded, whereas great scientists let their minds go woolly between experiments.
>
> (quoted in Casement, 1990: 14–15)

LISTENING AND OBSERVING

Those involved in what I shall call generically the counselling professions, pride themselves on being good listeners and observers. However, we all know from experience that this not always the case and golden opportunities for therapeutic intervention and confrontation are sometimes missed. An American educationalist, writing of the contribution that literature can make to criminology, has suggested that the great playwrights such as

Shakespeare, Sophocles, or Dostoevsky . . . were as dauntless as Columbus, ranging fearlessly over the geography of interior life. Though often melancholy, the insights of artists are alert to subtleties of thought and emotion and represent the harvests of the candid eye.

(Kelly, 1991: 45)

It takes a bold professional to expose, for public gaze, his or her missed perceptions and opportunities for therapeutic engagement. Casement, whose work I referred to in the last chapter, has done this with much courage. In a description of his analysis of a patient's dream-life, he points out to the patient what appears to be the latter's preoccupation with his need to protect his penis from some expected hurt or threat. The patient says 'I'm afraid of it being broken off'. The patient's *own* description and implied interpretation of what psychoanalysts would term 'castration anxiety' was, in fact, more compelling and graphic than that of the therapist for, as Casement suggests with hindsight, the patient was not just describing a penis, but an excited penis: 'it cannot be broken off unless it is erect' (1990: 18). One does not have to be a committed Freudian or an adherent of psychoanalytic thinking to see the diagnostic and prognostic importance of such an illustration. It demonstrates the need to engage in encounters with clients or patients with a degree of what Cox (1990) illuminatingly describes as 'hovering attentiveness'.

This need to listen attentively is urged upon us by all modern teachers of psychotherapeutic techniques, but its claim for urgent attention is not new. In the Old Testament, Job reminds us of the need to *really* listen when he rebukes his companions for their apparent lack of emotional engagement and succour: 'listen to me, but do listen, and let that be the comfort you offer me. Bear with me while I have my say' (Job 21: 2–3).

I referred earlier to the need for the 'candid eye'. One sometimes wonders whether it is always as effective as it should be in observing outward appearances as indicators of inner turmoil. St Augustine once said: 'My words were uttered in no ordinary manner; my forehead, cheeks, eyes, colour, tone of voice, cried out more clearly than the words I spake' (quoted in Cox and Theilgaard, 1987: 152). In Shakespeare's *The Winter's Tale* the thought-provoking words may be found: 'there was speech in their dumbness, language in their very gesture' (Act V, scene ii). A further good example is to be found in *Richard II*. Richard, having imposed life-long banishment upon Henry Bolingbroke, rescinds it in part, imposing it for a finite period. For he has recognised the grief it has caused Bolingbroke's father (Richard's uncle, the ageing John of Gaunt); he says to Gaunt: 'Uncle, even in the glasses of thine eyes / I see thy grieved heart' (Act I, Scene iii). There is a similar and finely observed piece of behaviour in one of Shakespeare's less well-known plays, *Troilus and Cressida*. Ulysses says of Cressida, who is being somewhat intransigent, 'There's language in her eye, her cheek, her lip. / Nay, her foot speaks; her wanton spirits look out / At every joint and motive of her body' (Act IV, Scene v). And, in the second part of *Henry IV*, we find the line, 'Thou tremblest; and the whiteness in thy cheek / Is apter than thy tongue to tell thy errand' (Act I, Scene i). Of course, the converse of what has just been suggested may also be true. Ben Johnson, in *Discoveries*, has a character say, 'Speak that I may *see* thee' (emphasis added); and does not Lear say 'Look with thine ears' (Act IV, Scene v)? Finally, we can note the wise guidance of Marcus Aurelius Antoninus, who once said 'Remember this, that there is a proper value and proportion to be observed in the performance of every act' (*Meditations* IV: 10 and 32).

Specific forensic implications

I now turn to more specific psychological and forensic-psychiatric allusions. Workers in these fields are frequently concerned with the prevention of vulnerability caused by psychotic beliefs – not only in the over-riding interests of the public at large, but in those of the offender or offender-patient. A graphic reminder of the need to reduce this dual vulnerability is to be found in some words spoken by Shakespeare's King John. Reflecting upon, and perhaps regretting, what he has ordered to be done to the young Prince Arthur, the King says 'How oft the sight of means to do ill deeds makes deeds ill done' (Act IV, Scene ii). Workers are often faced with having to recognise and deal with such vulnerability and take steps to reduce it. This is often an uncomfortable experience, but they need to be mindful of Northumberland's words in the second part of *Henry IV* when he says 'But I must go and meet with danger there, / Or it will seek me in another place' (Act II, Scene iii). At a much later point in historical time, Edmund Burke made the equally compelling observation that 'Dangers by being despised grow great' (speech on the Petition of the Unitarians, 1792). On a more humorous note, the dangers of not recognising vulnerability are caricatured cleverly in Evelyn Waugh's *Decline and Fall* (1937); here, the progressive prison governor Sir Wilfrid Lucas-Dockery provides a psychotic and deluded carpenter, serving a life sentence for decapitation, with a saw with which the deluded man promptly cuts off the prison chaplain's head!

Forensic workers are often faced with the problem of having to make statements and predictions based upon what offenders or offender-patients say about what they have done or not done many years earlier. It is often extremely difficult to get 'inside their heads', as it were, in order to try to determine what their *true* feelings may have been at the time of their crime. Denial, facilitated perhaps by the passage of time, may well have obscured what they really felt and believed. A comment by Job is pertinent: 'When I stop to think I am filled with horror and my whole body is convulsed' (21: 6); and in *Julius Caesar* Brutus says 'Between the acting of a dreadful thing / And the first motion, all the interim is / Like a phantasma or a hideous dream' (Act II, Scene i). Even more dramatically, in *Hamlet*, Horatio reminds us of the need to 'hear of carnal, bloody and un-natural deeds'. The need to blot out recollection is cogently expressed in Donna Tartt's recent novel *The Secret History* (1992). One of her characters says 'some things are too terrible to grasp at once. Other things – naked, sputtering indelible in their horror – are too terrible to really ever grasp at all. It is only later in solitude, in memory, that the realisation dawns'. The primacy of homicide in the catalogue of crime is well attested to in many sources. As Ben Jonson says in *Bartholomew Fair*, 'It is the very womb and bed of enormity' (Act I, Scene vi). In the Book of Genesis, the Lord says to Cain:

What have you done? Hark! Your brother's blood that has been shed is crying out to me from the ground. Now you are accursed, and banished from the ground which has opened its mouth wide to receive your brother's blood which you have shed.

(4: 10–12)

And, in his adjuration to Noah, the Lord says: 'He that sheds the blood of a man, for that man his blood shall be shed, for in the image of God has God made man' (Genesis 9: 6).

Guilt for the commission of homicide is depicted in all its horror in a single but remarkably chilling line in Webster's *Duchess of Malfi*. Having had their sister strangled, Ferdinand, the Duchess's twin brother, says, 'Cover her face, mine eyes dazzle: she died young' (Act IV, Scene ii). (The first three words were, of course, used by P.D. James as the title of one of her highly successful works of detection.) And what of the torment suffered, but so often concealed, by some who have murdered? In another of Webster's plays *The White Devil*, there is the evocative line 'my soul like to a ship in a black storm is driven I know not whither' (Act V, Scene vi). Macbeth is chided by his wife for his infirmity of intent, 'infirm of purpose, give me the daggers'. Macbeth's conflicting feelings about his activities seem to be echoed by a much later writer, the poet George Crabbe, when he says 'I've dreaded all the guilty dread and done what they would fear to do' ('Frenzy'). Here are two other examples of violent death. The first concerns death by strangulation. The Earl of Warwick is describing Gloucester's death in the second part of *Henry VI*.

But see, his face is black and full of blood;
His eye-balls further out than when he lived,
Staring full ghastly like a strangled man;
His hair uprear'd, his nostrils stretched with struggling,
His hands abroad displayed, as one that grasped
And tugg'd for life, and was by strength subdued.
Look, on the sheets, his hair, you see is sticking;
His well proportioned beard made rough and rugged,
Like to the summer's corn by tempest lodged,
It cannot be but he was murd'red here;
The least of all these signs were probable.

(Act III, Scene ii)

The second is of death by poisoning. In his description of it, Hamlet's father says that its effect:

> Holds such an enmity with blood of man
> That swift as quicksilver it courses through
> The natural gates and alleys of the body;
> And with a sudden vigour it doth posset
> And curd, like eager droppings into milk,
> The thin and wholesome blood. So did it mine.
>
> (Act I, Scene v)

A modern fictional detective stresses the need to absorb the full details of such serious offences and the offender's situation. Inspector Wexford in *Kissing the Gunner's Daughter*

> sat looking at the scene-of-crime photographs . . . the kind of pictures no-one but himself would ever see, the results of *real* violence, real crime. Those great dark splashes and stains were real blood. Was he privileged to see them or unfortunate?
>
> (Rendell, 1992: 148)

As we have seen, one of the most challenging phenomena in working with the highly deviant and disturbed is the manner in which those who can commit the most sickening of crimes can appear to be so thoroughly ordinary and inoffensive, as is illustrated by some of those who commit sadistic sexual murder. Such jarring incompatibilities are brilliantly demonstrated in analogous fashion in Marlowe's historical tragedy *Edward II*. In Act V, Scene v, Edward is in prison, having been reduced to a state of disorientation through being moved from one dungeon to the next over a prolonged period. He is in a state of what would today be described as sensory deprivation. It has been resolved to murder him; the barely hidden theme behind the murder is the revenge to be taken by those of so-called normal sexual orientation for the King's homosexuality, and in particular his favouritism for his beloved Piers de Gaveston. (It is important to remember that Marlowe wrote his play during a time of considerable repressive activity against homosexuals and against a background of recent legislation that gave legal sanction for this.) Lightborn, the hired assassin (who seems, on hindsight, to have qualities of gratuitous cruelty amounting to the psychopathic), tells his assistants, 'I shall need your help; / See that in the next room I have a fire, / And give me a spit, and let it be red hot. . . . / A table and a feather-bed'. Later, he seems to take a sadistic delight in toying with the enfeebled King, 'ne'er was there any / So finely handled as this King shall be'. 'O speak no more, my lord: this breaks my heart. / Lie on this bed and rest yourself awhile.' Edward seems to realise that his time has come and appears to recognise the significance of the instruments assembled to bring about his death. He says 'O spare me – or despatch me in a trice'. Lightborn says to his assistants, 'So; lay the table down and stamp on it – / But not too hard, lest that you bruise his body'. There follows the horrendous anal assault with the red hot spit. History records that Edward took a long time to die in agony. A further, and much more recent, dimension has been given to Marlowe's interpretation of the event by the modern writer Peter Whelan in his play *The School of Night* – first performed by the Royal Shakespeare Company at The Swan, Stratford, on 4 November 1992 (Whelan, 1992). Musing on his likely fate, Marlowe says of the Queen,

> Her only concern is whether I be killed for sodomy, atheism or treason . . . and which dreadful deaths to devise. Perhaps for sodomy, the one they used on Edward the Second that I was not allowed to put in the play. Held down while a cow's horn was inserted in his anus and a red hot iron pushed through to his bowels. No, that was a secret killing arranged so that when the horn was taken out there was no mark visible on the body. They wouldn't want that! What use is an invisible injury to the State . . .?

> (Act II, Scene iv)

Not infrequently, forensic-psychiatric professionals and their colleagues have to deal with those whose behaviour is either caused by, or closely allied to, frank mental illness. Delusional jealousy, the 'Othello Syndrome', in its various guises, has been described in Chapter 4. Depression, often in severe form, features in the lives and activities of many offenders and offender-patients. As we have seen, it may, of course, involve the taking of life, as in the case of severely depressed parents who kill or attempt to kill their children and then kill or attempt to kill themselves. It is not at all easy to enter the psychic world of the severely depressed individual and empathise with the bleak agony that this condition creates. Many writers have tried to capture its quality. Burton, in *The Anatomy of Melancholy*, considered that 'if there is a hell upon earth, it is to be found in a melancholy heart'. The poet John Clare (who spent long periods in asylums), in one of his more lucid and productive periods, evoked the condition magnificently. 'Yet nothing starts the apathy I feel, my soul is apathy, a ruin vast. Time cannot clear the ruined mass away, the summer looks to me as winter's frost.' He also described in graphic terms the familiar picture of a fading body image. 'Wilt thou go with me, when the path has lost its way . . . when stones will turn to flooding streams . . . where life will fade like visioned dreams and mountains darken into caves . . . wilt thou go with me, through this sad non-identity?' And again, on the same theme, 'Life is to me a dream that never wakes. Night finds me on this lengthening road alone. Love is to me a thought that ever aches, a frost-bound thought that freezes life to stone' (Clare, 1973: xxv). More modern writers have also evoked the mood of true melancholia very ably. Ruth Rendell, writing as Barbara Vine, describes it in *Gallowglass*, as follows:

> People talk about being depressed when they really mean they're feeling low, pissed off, under the weather. They don't know what depression is. Real depression is something else. It's when you haven't got anything, when

everything goes – wants, needs, will, caring, hope, desire. . . . It's when you can't make decisions any more, any sort of decision, like, shall I get up out of this bed and go to the bathroom or not? Or, shall I pick up this cup of tea and drink some or shall I just go on staring at it? It's when you don't want anything and can't do anything and don't want the opposite of not wanting anything, whatever that is, and haven't got anger or fear any more or even panic. And that's not the end of it. You get deeper in. You get to the place where you can't see colours or hear people speaking to you and inside your head is something that washes around when you move. It's water in there, a sink of it, dirty water with oil floating on top in those rainbow rings. That's the only colour that you can see, the rainbow circles of the oil on the dirty water slurping round inside your head.

(1990: 14)

The finer shades of frank insanity and its relationship to powerful sexual impulses are well delineated in Middleton and Rowley's comic-tragedy *The Changeling*. In this play, the two plots (sub- and main) – often seen as operating on two distinct levels – provide fascinating insights into the relationship between madness and imbecility at both the subtle and more obvious levels. In Act V, Scene iii, Beatrice, recognising the depth of both her madness and her adulterous folly, makes this poignant statement to her father: 'O come not near me, sir; / I shall defile you. / I am that of your blood was taken from you / For your better health. Look no more upon't . . .'

Madness, in its various forms, has been depicted by an enormous number of writers: for example, Gogol in *Diary of a Madman*, Sayers on a catatonic schizophrenic state in *The Comforts of Madness* (1988), and Waugh's description of a drug-induced psychotic episode in *The Ordeal of Gilbert Pinfold* (1962). A more recent writer, Patrick McGrath, also manages to capture the powerful evocations of both severe and borderline psychosis (see, for example, his novels *Spider*, 1992, and *Dr Haggard's Disease*, (1993). He acknowledges that these skilful and often haunting depictions owe much to his early upbringing at Broadmoor Hospital, where his late father was its distinguished Medical Superintendent for twenty-five years. Two other contributions to the literature are worth mentioning. The first is by the late Professor Derek Russell Davis, entitled *Scenes of Madness: A Psychiatrist at the Theatre*, (1992). In this volume, Davis uses some of the world's great literature, in particular Shakespeare and Ibsen, to illustrate clinical psychopathology. The second, edited by Murray Cox, is entitled *Shakespeare Comes to Broadmoor* (1992). This is a moving account of the impact of the performance of some of Shakespeare's tragedies upon the acting and directing staff of the Royal Shakespeare Company, the hospital residents and their carers.[2]

Music also has its uses in the search for empathic evocation of mood in mental illness. Depressed feelings and their accompanying apathy are depicted beautifully in the first section of the fourth movement of Tchaikovsky's Symphony no.

6 (the 'Pathétique'). More contemporary evocations may be found in the blues music of the deep American South of the mid-nineteenth and mid-twentieth centuries. In sharp contrast, the mood of the hypomanic individual is, for me, well captured in the opening bars of Handel's 'Arrival of the Queen of Sheba'. The sheer terror that must be felt by some people knowing that they are becoming ill and out of control finds fine evocation in the 'Dies Irae' in Verdi's *Requiem*. The feeling of health restored as illness abates or remits is depicted in the opening triumphant bars of Handel's *Zadok the Priest* and in the introduction to Mendelssohn's *Elijah*.

At its best, literature demonstrates the powerful and persuasive function of metaphor – a phenomenon of inestimable value in promoting understanding of baffling and worrying deeds and misdeeds. The tyrant Tamburlaine in Marlowe's play showed surprising sensitivity on this matter when he said:

If all the pens that ever poets held, had fed the feeling of their masters' thoughts,
and every sweetness that inspired their hearts,
their minds, and muses on admired themes
. . . wherein as in a mirror we perceive the highest reaches of a human wit . . .
(Act V, Scene ii)

One of the most compelling examples of its use may be found in what is probably Shakespeare's greatest play – *Hamlet*. Dr Murray Cox, in his programme article for the Adrian Noble production of the play at Stratford on 20 March 1993, suggests that in the play 'it is as we move from mortuary to myth that we find the more firmly woven fabric of context and content through which *Hamlet* envelops us'. Cox sees the theme of defective ceremony 'as being central to the play . . . The theme of the dead not letting go of the living is . . . one of the constant thematic threads in *Hamlet*.' (The powerful presence of dead souls is, of course, pervasive in a number of Ibsen's plays – a notable illustration being found in *Ghosts*.) In Act III, Scene ii, Hamlet, perplexed, ambivalent, hostile, yet indecisive, demonstrates the depth of his confused and turbulent feelings towards his mother and others when he says, 'Now could I drink hot blood, / And do such bitter business as the day / Would quake to look on'. Bearing in mind his fraught condition, these are powerful words indeed – conjuring up powerful imagery of a potential for future mayhem – especially if we also remember Claudius' later words: 'How dangerous is it that this man goes loose!' (Act IV, Scene ii). Hamlet's words are not of course intended to convey that he is about to behave like Count Dracula! However, as already indicated, they are important in relation to his *possible* future behaviour for does he not, in the same scene, make plans to see his mother? 'Soft, now to my mother . . . / Let me be cruel, not unnatural. / I will speak daggers to her, but use none' (Act III, Scene ii).[3] One may think this a poignant statement of hostility, but not one *necessarily* pressaging future mayhem *until* one reviews with the benefit of hindsight the events in the very next scene. For in the course of confronting his mother, Hamlet stabs and kills the unfortunate Polonius, who is hidden behind the arras. Was this a sad coincidence brought about as a result of Hamlet's psychic turmoil and stress and/or a piece of displaced aggression (see Chapter 9)? If Prince Hamlet had already been under supervision on a form of licence or hospital conditional discharge for some prior serious violent crime, would his utterances have been regarded as serious enough to warrant consideration of an approach to the Home Office for his recall to prison or hospital?[4] One would not wish to take such literary analogies too far, but they serve the purpose of posing and heightening our awareness of the dilemmas caused when people under supervision utter threats of murder or other serious mayhem. Leyton, in his book on serial killers, puts this difficult issue into perspective when he states:

> If we insist upon the right to understand the dark forces that propel a person into launching a war upon the innocent, we must also assume responsibility of recognising the unholiness of his acts and the tragedies he perpetuates. A cultural system which does otherwise, as does our own, is guilty of much more than misplaced tenderness; it must be charged with encouraging the repetition of such acts.
>
> (1989: 33–34)

The main thrust of this part of the chapter has been that, in addition to clinical and technical sources, there are others which can be called upon to enhance our empathic understanding of seriously disturbed and deviant individuals. Put another way, there is need for a *combination* of technical and artistic approaches. Kelly, whom I quoted earlier, summarises the position very well when he says:

> Though the style of presentation differs, the logic of analysis and the intuitive understanding of interpretation fill the works of the artist *and* the scientist. Scientists create hypotheses, test them, and draw conclusions; writers create plots and develop characters. In *both* styles of work, inspiration and imagination are the driving forces.
>
> (1991: 56; emphasis added)

I would contend that the words forensic-psychiatric or allied professional can be substituted without any major loss of meaning or purpose.

DESIGN FOR A SHORT COURSE

During the past fifteen years I have run a large number of two-day workshops, mainly for members of the probation service, on 'Dangerous and High-Risk Offenders'. Membership of such courses usually consists of experienced career-grade officers, but from time to time senior management have also attended, as have workers in other disciplines, such as psychiatrists and the police. The workshops originated out of longer events organised under the auspices of the Northern Office of the Regional Staff Development Organisation for the Probation Service. On these workshops, officers came for an initial four-day residential period, returned to their areas for about three months and worked on a case they had identified for such a purpose during the first part of the course. They then returned for the third (and residential) phase of the workshop – again lasting three to four days. Financial constraints and organisational changes led to the demise of these events; to fill the gap, I was asked by various probation areas to offer short, mainly two-day, workshops instead.[5] The content of these shorter workshops has inevitably involved a degree of compression and consequent loss of the more detailed inputs and experiential work that was possible on the longer version. However, they seem to have met with a degree of success and it may be of interest to readers to have a description of the content and organisation of such an event in case they wish to mount them for themselves.[6] Much of the content of this book has formed the background to my teaching on them.

Background material

Officers are selected by their own authorities and I have no say in their selection. I usually ask that membership be confined to a maximum of fifteen to twenty persons in order to facilitate discussion. Participants should preferably have had at least two years' experience and have supervised or been otherwise involved in a high-risk case of the kind described in this book.

In the preliminary material that is sent to participants there is a request that they bring 'in their heads' a relevant case, part of a case, or a situation that has caused them particular concern. They are also sent some short preliminary reading material concerning the assessment of risk. Other written material is made available at the workshop to supplement the lecture-discussion, much of it consisting of highly summarised accounts of some of the material covered in this book. (The handout material also includes relevant official circulars and local notes of guidance on practical aspects of supervision.) Participants are also informed that although a good deal of the workshop consists of formal inputs from myself, they will be encouraged to interrupt and ask questions. Over the years, I have found this the most useful approach. There is nothing worse than having to sit through a forty-five-minute presentation with a burning question or comment and then find that it has lost its impact (or even faded from memory) when 'question-time' is reached! I try to work towards an 'ideal' mixture of 'background information' and the use of the participants' own (often very considerable) experiences. The two-day events have the following general format.

DAY ONE[7]

Arrival

Introduction: Enhancing Understanding   ('And What if Hamlet Had Been
                                                  on Licence?': a much abbreviated
                                                  version of the first part of this
                                                  chapter)

Mental Abnormality and Violent Crime (I)

Coffee
Mental Abnormality and Violent Crime (II)
Lunch
Management of Dangerous Behaviour (I)
Tea
Management of Dangerous Behaviour (II)   (Small group exercise)[8]

Four Case Examples

1   'J' is on conditional discharge, having served ten years in hospital for the homicide of his wife. He had secreted her body and it was some months before it was discovered. At the time of his arrest he was seeing another woman regularly. A year after his release he informs you that he has been seeing another woman regularly and hopes to marry her eventually.

State what action you would take and give your reasons.

2   'D' was released on parole from prison about six months ago. He still has three months of his parole to serve. He has obtained a one-bedroom flat and, on a visit to your office, tells you that the sixteen-year-old son of a friend has moved in with him after a row between the boy and his parents. 'D' has a long record of convictions for buggery. His last conviction concerned buggery against a seventeen-year-old youth.

State what action you would take and give your reasons.

3   'A' is a sixty-year-old man on life licence. He killed a child during a sexual assault. He has been on licence for nearly two years and has, so far, given no cause for concern. You have just been informed that he has been seen loitering by the bus stop outside the local primary school.

State what action do you take and give your reasons.

4   'C' is under your supervision on conditional discharge from hospital having spent fifteen years there as a result of three offences of arson. He had previously served a four-year prison sentence for a similar offence. On each occasion he is said to have been drinking heavily. You suspect that 'C' has started drinking and, on checking with his landlady, you discover that he has returned home on a number of occasions under the influence of drink; she suspects he is gradually increasing his intake of alcohol.

State what action you would take and give your reasons.

DAY TWO

Arrival
Management of Dangerous Behaviour (III)   (Film or video presentation and
                                                     discussion)
Coffee

Case Discussions (I)[9]
Lunch
Case Discussions (II)
Tea
Plenary Session for 'Unfinished Business'

It is important to emphasise that the outline programme given above is not intended to be an 'ideal', but merely to serve as an example of what *might* be undertaken over a two-day period. Some areas have special needs (for example, a large number of penal or hospital establishments in their area, or a concentration of life licensees or conditionally discharged offender-patients); these variations will, to some extent, determine the focus of a particular workshop. The workshops' aims are to provide some factual information (both clinical and administrative) and to deal with participants' anxieties and thus hopefully promote more effective and comfortable working with this particular group of people. An important common element in all of them has been the encouragement of the need for good inter-professional communication and co-operation. In this respect Wilson and Wilson (1985), writing about the relationships between community psychiatry and general practice, provide some graphic illustrations of the manner in which defensive ploys may be engaged in so as to maintain autonomy and status. They suggest that, in order to overcome such defensive manoeuvres, one must take account of some of the unconscious motivations that may stand in the way of progress. Although they are writing about medical practice, their views have relevance for the participants in the workshops I have described. I make no attempt to promote a deep understanding of unconscious resistances at such events, but I do endeavour to encourage participants to see where their 'blind-spots' about their own behaviour and that of other professional colleagues may hinder effective collaborative work.

CONCLUSION

In this chapter I have sought to demonstrate that there are a number of ways of enhancing our understanding of those offenders and offender-patients who arouse fear, bewilderment and sometimes revulsion in us. Not the least of these is the ability to call upon literature of many kinds and upon other 'arts' that may provoke and promote our empathic imagination. Such manner of enhancement has always played a significant part in the workshops described in the second section of this chapter. It would be a pity to see the two sections of the chapter as separate entities; they should be viewed as a whole.

NOTES

1   The choice of materials for presentation is somewhat idiosyncratic. Myth, legend and folklore all have their part to play. For some discussion of the importance of under-

standing these phenomena as a background to clinical endeavour with highly deviant and disturbed people, see Prins (1990: esp. Chapter 5).

2 I owe much to the work and writings of Dr Murray Cox in making use of analogy and metaphor in literature, particularly his work with Alice Theilgaard (Cox and Theilgaard, 1987).

3 I am grateful to Murray Cox for drawing my attention to this aspect of Hamlet's behaviour. For elaboration see his Preface to my book *Bizarre Behaviours* (Prins, 1990: ix).

4 I am grateful to Mr Ken Ward, Senior Probation Officer, Devon Probation Service, for first suggesting this hypothetical consideration at a workshop on 'Dangerous and High-Risk Offenders'. Though the suggestion was made in somewhat light-hearted vein, its potential usefulness as an illustration of powerful metaphor was not lost upon me and the workshop members.

5 I would like to register my sincere thanks to all those staff who have helped me with these events over the years and of course participants who have much enriched my understanding. (Further details of the original RSDO courses may be found in Annex E to Home Office Circular [Provision for Mentally Disturbed Disordered Offenders] 66/90 [MNP/90/1/55/8 dated 3 September 1990.)

6 It is possible, but not altogether satisfactory, to compress the material further into a one-day event, and I have done this from time to time with very experienced staff from probation, social services, nursing and psychology. The National Association for the Care and Resettlement of Offenders has recently produced a helpful training pack on working with mentally disordered offenders. Though aimed more specifically at local authority social workers and probation officers, it has applicability to a wider range of staff involved in managing mentally disordered offenders (NACRO, 1994).

7 Times omitted. These vary according to need. Ideally no formal input session should last longer than forty-five minutes without a short break.

8 The small group exercises are designed to encourage participants to begin to examine some hypothetical illustrations of some of the ethical and professional dilemmas involved in the work. Each small group is given a different short case vignette and asked to decide upon the appropriate action to be taken. This takes about twenty minutes. They then report back their 'case' and findings to the larger group for discussion. Ideally, each small group should consist of five people at most.

9 The arrangements for these are flexible. Normally, there is no shortage of case examples from participants, and these also serve as reference points for further discussion of some of the material raised in the earlier plenary sessions.

REFERENCES

Casement, P. (1990) *Further Learning From the Patient: The Analytic Space and Process*, London: Tavistock/Routledge.

Clare, J. (1973) *Selected Poems of John Clare*, ed. J. Reeves, London: Heinemann.

Cox, M. (1990) 'Psychopathology and Treatment of Psychotic Aggression', in R. Bluglass and P. Bowden (eds), *Principles and Practice of Forensic Psychiatry*, London: Churchill Livingstone.

—— (ed.) (1992) *Shakespeare Comes to Broadmoor: The Performance of Tragedy in a Secure Hospital*, London: Jessica Kingsley.

Cox, M. and Theilgaard, A. (1987) *Mutative Metaphors in Psychotherapy: The Aeolian Mode*, London: Tavistock.

Davis, D.R. (1992) *Scenes of Madness: A Psychiatrist at the Theatre*, London: Routledge.

Kelly, R.J. (1991) 'Mapping the Domains of Crime: The Contributions of Literary Works to Criminology', *International Journal of Offender Therapy and Comparative Criminology* 35: 45–61.

Lee, S. (1988) *Judging Judges*, London: Faber and Faber.

Leyton, E. (1989) *Hunting Humans: The Rise of the Modern Multiple Murderer*, Harmondsworth: Penguin.

McGrath, P. (1992) *Spider*, Harmondsworth: Penguin.

—— (1993) *Dr Haggard's Disease*, Harmondsworth: Penguin.

National Association for the Care and Resettlement of Offenders (NACRO) (1994) *Working with Mentally Disordered Offenders: A Training Pack for Social Services Staff and Others*, London: NACRO.

Priestley, J.B. (1972) *Over the Long High Wall*, London: Heinemann.

Prins, H. (1990) *Bizarre Behaviours: Boundaries of Psychiatric Disorder*, London: Routledge/Tavistock.

Rendell, R. (1992) *Kissing the Gunner's Daughter*, London: Arrow Books.

Sacks, J. (1991) *The Persistence of Faith: Religion, Morality and Society in a Secular Age*, London: Weidenfeld and Nicolson.

Sayer, P. (1988) *The Comforts of Madness*, London: Constable.

Tartt, D. (1992) *The Secret History*, Harmondsworth: Penguin.

Vine, B. [Ruth Rendell] (1990) *Gallowglass*, London: Viking.

Waugh, E. (1937) *Decline and Fall*, Harmondsworth: Penguin.

—— (1962) *The Ordeal of Gilbert Pinfold*, Harmondsworth: Penguin.

Weiss, R. (1988) *Criminal Justice: The True Story of Edith Thompson*, Harmondsworth: Penguin.

Whelan, P. (1992) *The School of Night*, London: Warner Chappell Plays.

Wilson, S. and Wilson, K. (1985) 'Close Encounters in General Practice: Experiences of a Psychotherapy Liaison Team', *British Journal of Psychiatry* 146: 277–281.

FURTHER READING

Cox, M. and Theilgaard, A. (1994) *Shakespeare as Prompter*, London: Jessica Kingsley.

Kail, A.C. (1986) *The Medical Mind of Shakespeare*, Balgowlah, New South Wales: Williams and WIlkins.

Nichol, C. (1992) *The Reckoning: The Murder of Christopher Marlowe*, London: Picador. (A fascinating study which combines detailed examination of the writer's life and death with an eye for forensic issues.)

Chapter 11

Concluding comments

> Attempt the end and never stand to doubt:
> Nothing's so hard but search will find it out.
> (Herrick, 'Seek and Find', *Hesperides*)

I had two somewhat contradictory aims in producing this book. I wished to keep to a format similar to that used in the first edition but, in the light of time and experience, to produce a revised work with a rather more restricted focus in order to encapsulate new thinking and approaches. It is not easy to achieve the best of all possible worlds. Only those familiar with the first version will know to what extent I have succeeded. It is now some eighteen years since the first work was conceived and fifteen years since its publication. In Chapter 1 I referred to a number of changes that have occurred since that time, not the least of these being the arrival of specialist texts in forensic psychiatry, and the arrival on the scene of two major forensic-psychiatric journals – the *Journal of Forensic Psychiatry* and *Criminal Behaviour and Mental Health* – to which we now must add the arrival of a new forensic psychology journal, *Psychology, Crime and Law*.

Despite all these changes, it is tempting to ask to what extent many of them have produced the results desired by those who produced them. For example, the Mental Health Act 1983 made quite substantial changes to aspects of mental health law and practice – some of them to the advantage of the individuals described in this book. However, powerful and generally laudable concerns with issues of civil liberties have brought with them certain iatrogenic consequences. These include an increasing difficulty in securing compulsory admission to hospital when the very real need for it is described by relatives and relatives' organisations. The 1983 Act is also more complex than its predecessor, particularly in relation to discharge procedures. These and some allied issues have resulted in a large number of applications for judicial review and subsequent fresh interpretations of the law. The last decade has seen a considerable increase in concerns about patients' rights, particularly those detained in Special Hospitals. It is not altogether clear that the body set up under the 1983 Act to secure these rights – the Mental Health Act Commission – has always been able to achieve its aims. For example, the malpractices revealed by the Ashworth Inquiry (Department of Health, 1992) occurred during a period when members of the Commission were pursuing an active and diligent policy of regular visits to that institution with the avowed aim of investigating patients' complaints.

It is not easy to bring about change in closed and highly secure institutions, as my colleagues and I found in the reluctance of the Special Hospitals Service Authority to accept one or two of the more important recommendations in our report into the death of Orville Blackwood at Broadmoor Hospital (SHSA, 1993). At the time of writing, the future of the Special Hospitals is uncertain. Even if, as some hope, they become smaller, we should not assume too readily that 'small' will necessarily be 'beautiful'.

There is still much concern that too many mentally disordered individuals are located in prisons, be they on remand or sentenced. In the current political climate it seems likely that the prison population will certainly not diminish, and, indeed, it may well rise. Such growth is likely to see the proportion of mentally disturbed inmates rise also. The debate over those elusive individuals – the psychopathically disordered – continues; their future, in terms both of law and clinical practice, remains uncertain.

Many issues of race remain to be addressed. For whatever reasons (under-standable and otherwise) black people (notably Afro-Caribbeans) are over-represented in certain mental health categories, in hospitals and penal institutions. They also tend to be seen as more dangerous than they really are (SHSA, 1993). Much work still needs to be done in this area. The special needs of women are just beginning to be addressed and there remains a degree of confusion about their place as 'offenders, deviants or patients'.

Changes in the National Health Service, particularly funding arrangements, have left a considerable state of confusion. Despite government protestations to the contrary, the people who form the subject matter of this book continue to be badly served. However, it is only fair to add that there are times when funding and lack of facilities are used as excuses when it is professional attitudes and entrenched positions that are more likely to be the stumbling blocks.

The foregoing comments read rather like a tale of woe and readers might well ask whether there are any breaks in the clouds. There are a few. For example, the multi-disciplinary conferences organised by the Mental Health Foundation in conjunction with the fifteen Regional Health Authorities for England and Wales during the past two years seem to have had a measure of success. They have demonstrated that there exists not only much good-will and a desire to exchange views but, perhaps more importantly, a keen desire to continue such exchanges at local level in order to develop better working practices. The crossing of professional boundaries has been shown to be important and the implications of true inter-disciplinary work have begun to be addressed. This is also evident in some of the work being carried out by organisations such as NACRO through its Mental Health Advisory Committee, which currently I have the privilege of chairing.

In this book I have aimed to provide information of practical value but which is also theoretically well grounded. In addition, I have attempted to demonstrate that difficult and disturbing people present a stimulating challenge which can best be met in the light of such knowledge and by a commitment to share the burdens with, and learn from, others – from whatever source this sharing and learning may come.

REFERENCES

Department of Health (1992) *Report of the Committee of Inquiry into Complaints About Ashworth Hospital*, Vols 1 and 2 (Chairman, Sir Louis Blom-Cooper, QC), Cmnd 20280I and -II, London: HMSO.

Special Hospitals Service Authority (SHSA) (1993) *Report of the Committee of Inquiry into the Death in Broadmoor Hospital of Orville Blackwood and a Review of the Death of Two Other Afro-Caribbean Patients: 'Big, Black and Dangerous?'* (Chairman Professor H. Prins), London: SHSA.

FURTHER READING

Criminal Behaviour and Mental Health, Vol. 3, No. 4 (1993). Special Issue on 'Institutions and Mental Health in the Context of Dangerous and Criminal Behaviour'). (In effect, a wide-ranging review of current provision at national and international levels.)

Richardson, G. (1993) *Law, Process and Custody: Prisoners and Patients*, London: Weidenfeld and Nicholson. (Notably Part III.)

Name index

Subject index